FURTHER ANGLICAN LITURGIES
1968-1975

FURTHER ANGLICAN LITURGIES

1968-1975

EDITED BY

COLIN O. BUCHANAN

Director of Studies, St. John's College, Nottingham
Member of the Church of England Liturgical Commission

GROVE BOOKS

BRAMCOTE   NOTTINGHAM

1975

Grove Books, Bramcote, Nottingham NG9 3DS

*Introductions, selection, arrangement
and annotation*
Copyright Colin O. Buchanan 1975

PRINTED IN GREAT BRITAIN

First Impression May 1975

ISBN 0 901710 66 0

PREFACE

THIS volume stands third in a line of liturgical reference books. In 1962 the Oxford University Press published B. J. Wigan's collection, *The Liturgy in English* (**LiE**), which included in English all the Anglican eucharistic texts from 1549 to 1960 which he had been able to obtain.[1] A second edition was published in 1964,[2] and is still in print at the time of writing. In 1968 this was followed by the present writer's *Modern Anglican Liturgies* 1958-68 (**MAL**) from the same Press. **MAL** supplemented **LiE** in several ways, not only by adding new texts, but also by giving a brief background history to the production of *all* texts in both books (with the exception of the Church of England's own texts of 1549-1662, which are very fully covered in many other writings).

The seven and a half years which have elapsed between the compilation of **MAL** and the work on this volume have seen a further spate of new eucharistic liturgies, which are duly collected here. An introduction is again provided for each text, but instead of going back over the whole of the respective Province's liturgical history, the account simply runs from 1968 to 1975. Thus this volume supplements **LiE** and **MAL**, and with them gives a conspectus, with texts, of the whole of Anglican eucharistic liturgy since 1549.[3]

In **MAL** the African Provinces came first in the order of sections through the book. However, in the seven and a half years the pendulum of liturgical influence has swung back to the Church of England, and so here the United Kingdom and Eire again head the list. There have been some suggestions that a collection such as this should also include liturgies from the Philippine Independent Church, the Reformed Episcopal Church of Spain, the Old Catholic Churches etc. This point may be made all the more surely when it is noted that there are here liturgies from the Churches of North and South India, as well as from Anglican Churches and Provinces. Texts from these united Churches

[1] He had missed the Madagascar rite (which he acknowledged), and the Scottish rite of 1912 and the Hong Kong rites of 1938 and 1957 (which he did not). See **MAL** pp.102-10, 146, 268-9, 271-8. It was perhaps a minor blemish that *The Order of the Communion* of 1548 was not included. Since then this has been reprinted as an appendix to G. J. Cuming *A History of Anglican Liturgy* (Macmillan 1969), which must be recommended as a background to the whole period covered by **LiE** and almost all that covered by **MAL**.

[2] This added no texts but corrected the 1962 translation of **Kor**.

[3] The texts in this book indicate in part how **MAL** has been used. Thus PECUSA has made use of **NZ**, the Anglican Church of Ceylon has drawn upon **EAUL**, and the diocese of Kuching has employed parts of **LfA**. The American *Prayer Book Studies 21* specifically cites **MAL** as a main source-book.

are included for the sake of convenience and completeness, and not in any sense to hint at their being properly classified as 'Anglican'. The demarcation adopted is justifiable as being that of the Anglican Consultative Council, which at Dublin in July 1973 gave those united Churches which include ex-Anglicans an entrenched position on the Council, and, equally, by conscious decision omitted those other episcopal Churches which may be in communion with Anglican Churches, but have not quite the same historical relationship with the Anglican Communion.[1] That is not to say that there is not a case for a collection of liturgies from such Churches (and indeed the writer would be glad to take up the project). It is only to say that this is not it, and does not anticipate it.

The list of contributors reflects the march of the years. Two of the essayists of **MAL** are now Bishops—Colin Bazley of Chile, and Donald Robinson of Paramatta in the Sydney Diocese. Two more have become members of their Provincial Liturgical Commissions since contributing to **MAL**—John Mears of Wales and Roger Bowen of Tanzania. Four others have had to nominate successors, and do not appear in this volume. Two more had so little to report that they do not reappear for that reason—one of these being Joyce Bennett of Hong Kong, who in 1971 carved herself some sort of a niche in Anglican history by being one of the first two deaconesses ordained to the presbyterate in the Anglican Communion. The team is then strengthened by the addition of two new notable contributors, worthy of special mention here. Tom Garrett, until 1974 Bishop in Tirunelveli in the Church of South India, was one of the original compilers of the South Indian Liturgy in the years 1948-50, and is the author of *Worship in the Church of South India* (Lutterworth 1958) and *Christian Worship* (Oxford 1963). He was also influential in the 1960s in the production of the Nigerian Union Liturgy (**NUL**) of 1965, which followed **CSI** closely and was published in **MAL**.[2] He then returned to South India and became a Bishop, and was there in time to serve on the Committee revising and modernizing the liturgy. With him there appears Richard Rutt, M.B.E., till 1974 Bishop of Taejon in Korea. Bishop Rutt is an expert on Koreanology, and has provided invaluable information for the editors of both **LiE** and **MAL**. As a new rite has been written in Korea (**Kor1**), it seemed very appropriate that so eminent a member of the Committee

---

[1] *Partners in Mission* (S.P.C.K. London 1973) pp.63-6.
[2] **MAL** failed to note his article on **NUL** in *Studia Liturgica* Vol. V, No. 3 (1966), and the omission is thus here made good.

should contribute the introduction to it. There was an overtly evangelical character to the list of contributors to **MAL**—if this is still generally true, yet the presence in the list of these two distinguished Bishops (one 'high' and one 'low') gives a variety and breadth to the whole team.[1]

There were some further difficulties in selecting the texts for this volume. With the benefit of hindsight it has been possible to omit as of little importance the 1970 Iran text, the 1971 further recension of **Aus1** in Australia, and the 1971 (North) Chile rite. These have all been in official use, but were all quickly superseded by somewhat more enduring rites of the same families, and are therefore only presented here by brief description. Other rites, such as those from Scotland and Mauritius, give printed form to uses already canonically permitted,[2] and again are merely described. A harder decision was needed in relation to Wales, and here the 'study' rite which has been publicly circulated has been included in the book (**WalR**[3]), though its status is precarious. A definitive rite for Wales is only now at early stages of preparation.

These notes will suggest the need for a critical judgment to be exercised on the significance of the publication here of each particular text. The editor wrote in **MAL** 'In this quantity of new rites it is timely to utter a warning which will help the situation to be interpreted in a balanced way. Anglicans are not spread equally among the Churches and Provinces with new rites. Nor are they equally enthusiastic for new rites in every place that has them'.[4] These words are still appropriate, and if it is not possible, as it was in late 1967, to go on to say 'it is probable that . . . 1662 is still far and away the most frequently celebrated Anglican rite on the world's surface', yet it is possible to warn that several rites here are very *in*frequently celebrated compared with others or indeed compared with 1662 itself.

The editor has been involved in covering somewhat similar ground fairly frequently during the latter part of the period since **MAL**. There is a limit to the number of different ways one can view similar material and thus chapters 1 and 2 inevitably reflect these other writings, whilst they also rely upon them for important further background information. It is also true that chapter 1 reflects the editor's Englishness, though the very facts of the last seven years necessitate a strong emphasis upon England in any case.

---

[1] Bishop Robinson of the Church of North India gave such help for chapter 17 that he virtually became a contributor also.

[2] See pp.77-8 and 291.

[3] See pp.82-8.

[4] **MAL** p.7.

Many other persons, apart from the contributors mentioned above, have given assistance of various sorts, and they are listed in the acknowledgments following. However, special thanks are due to a former student of St. John's College, Nottingham, Lionel Simpkins, now ministering in the Leicester diocese. Whilst awaiting a Michaelmas ordination in 1973, he prepared over half the texts (and almost all the Proper Prefaces of Appendix C) for publication, editing them into a standard form, and working on the 'Common Form' texts and variants contained within them. Without his help, publication might well have taken up to 12 months longer to complete. A debt is also due to the editor's secretary, Miss Pat Morris, for constant help in the latter stages.

Mention must also be made of the good offices of the Society for the Promotion of Christian Knowledge. It was originally intended that they should be the publishers of this volume, and it was only at a late stage in preparation that inflationary costs made it necessary for them to withdraw. But without the work put in by Mr. Robin Brookes, their senior editor, it is doubtful whether the volume could have been published when it is, and without some financial underwriting by the S.P.C.K. it is arguable that it would never have appeared at all. Equally, it is a venture of some magnitude for Grove Books, the editor's own publishing firm, for although the Grove Booklets on Ministry and Worship indicate the publisher's specialist interest in liturgy, yet up till now such booklets have been the limit of his publishing ambitions.

There may remain a certain inconsistency of presentation. Contributors have not been reduced to a single style, length or emphasis, though they have at times suffered severe editing. As with **MAL**, it is too much to hope that the book will avoid all minor errors of fact or slightly subjective judgments. Notification of these will be gratefully received.[1] As before also, whilst the contributors would acknowledge the satisfaction many of them have felt in assisting at the birth of new liturgies, they would all disavow any suggestion of being engrossed in them. If new texts will serve the building up of God's kingdom, even in small ways, they will have been worth having. But it is their role to *serve*.

Colin Buchanan

13 February 1975

[1] Appendix G, on p.420 below, lists such minor errors as it has been possible to trace in the previous two volumes, in order to keep the record straight.

THE CONTRIBUTORS

The Rt. Rev. COLIN F. BAZLEY: Assistant Bishop for Cautin and Malleco in the Diocese of Chile, Bolivia and Peru. Member of Synod Executive Committee and of the Liturgical Group working in the Southern Region of Chile. [Contributor to **MAL**]

The Rev. J. ROGER BOWEN: Till 1974 Tutor at St. Philip's Theological College, Kongwa, Tanzania. Since 1974 Chairman and co-ordinator of the Swahili Text Books Committee of the Association of East African Theological Institutions. Member of the Theological and Liturgical Committee of the Church of the Province of Tanzania. [Author *A Guide to Romans* (S.P.C.K. 1975) (T.E.F. Study Guide). Contributor to **MAL**]

The Rev. JOHN BURGESS: Till 1974 Rector of Marlborough, Salisbury, Church of the Province of Central Africa. Since 1974 Vicar of St. Andrew's, Nottingham (England). [Contributor to **MAL**]

The Rev. BRIAN R. CARRELL: General Secretary of New Zealand Church Missionary Society. Member of New Zealand Provincial Commission on Prayer Book Revision. [Author *Guide to the Liturgy*. Contributor to **MAL**]

The Rt. Rev. THOMAS S. GARRETT: Till 1974 Bishop in Tirunelveli, Church of South India. Since 1975 Rector of Hallaton, Market Harborough, and Assistant Bishop of Leicester (England). Member of the C.S.I. Liturgy Committee till 1974. [Author *Worship in the Church of South India* (Lutterworth 1958), *Christian Worship* (Oxford 1963)]

The Rev. F. CHARLES JAMESON: Rector of Easkey, Co. Sligo, Church of Ireland. Member of the Liturgical Committee of the Church of Ireland. [Contributor to **MAL**]

The Rev. DAVID K. MAYBURY: Till 1975 Rector of St. James' Church, Leith. Since 1975 Rector of Jedburgh, Episcopal Church of Scotland.

The Rev. JOHN C. MEARS: Vicar of St. Mark's Church, Gabalfa, Cardiff, Church in Wales. Member of the Church in Wales Standing Liturgical Commission. [Contributor to **MAL**]

The Rt. Rev. DONALD W. B. ROBINSON: Bishop in Paramatta, Diocese of Sydney, Church of England in Australia. Member of the Liturgical Commission of the General Synod of the Church of England in Australia. [Contributor to **MAL**]

The Rev. PETER R. RODGERS: Till 1974 Assistant Minister of St. John's Episcopal Church, Williamstown, Massachusetts, Protestant Episcopal Church of the United States of America. Since 1974 doing research at Oxford (England). [Composer of Folk Hymn Tunes for Christian Worship]

The Rt. Rev. C. RICHARD RUTT: Till 1974 Bishop of Taejon, Anglican Church in Korea. Since 1974 Suffragan Bishop of St. Germans, Diocese of Truro (England). Chairman of the Liturgical Advisory Committee of the Anglican Church in Korea till 1974. [Author of works on Koreanology]

The Rev. REGINALD N. SAVARY: Rector of Kirkton with Granton and Saintsbury, Diocese of London, Anglican Church of Canada. [Author of articles on Christian missions in Japan, and joint compiler of the Japanese translation of the Canadian Prayer Book]

The Rev. WARWICK J. SEYMOUR: Till 1975 Rector of St. John's Church, Fort Beaufort, Cape. Since 1975 Rector of Holy Trinity Church, Port Elizabeth, Cape, Church of the Province of South Africa. Member of the Liturgical Committee of the Church of the Province of South Africa.

ACKNOWLEDGEMENTS

THE editor and contributors wish to acknowledge the following help which they have received:

(i) Permission to make use of copyright material has been kindly granted by the following bodies:

The Church Hymnal Corporation, New York (**Amer1, Amer2, Amer3, Amer1-3**)

The Liturgical Commission of the General Synod of the Church of England in Australia (**Aus1A, Aus3, Aus4**)

The Primate of the Episcopal Church of Brazil (**BrazR**)

The Doctrine and Worship Committee of the Anglican Church of Canada (**Can1**)

The Synod Executive Committee of the Diocese of Chile, Bolivia and Peru (**ChilR**)

The Indian Society for the Promotion of Christian Knowledge (**CNI**)

The Secretariat of the Synod of the Church of South India, and the Christian Literature Society, Madras, and the Oxford University Press, London (**CSIR**)

The Registrars of the Provinces of Canterbury and York (**Eng3, Eng1-2A**)

The Diocesan Council of Iran (**IranR**)

The Standing Committee of the General Synod of the Church of Ireland (**Ire1**)

The Liturgical Advisory Committee of the National Synod of the Anglican Church in Korea (**Kor1**)

The Bishop of Kuching (**Kuch**)

The Archbishop of Melanesia (**Mel**)

The Bishop of Papua New Guinea (**NG**)

The Provincial Secretary of the Church of the Province of New Zealand (**NZR**)

The Publications Department of the Church of the Province of South Africa (**SAfr1, SAfr2**)

The Chairman of the Synod of the Church of the Province of Tanzania (**Tan**)

The Standing Liturgical Commission of the Church in Wales (**WalR**)

The Diocesan Authorities of the Dioceses of Kootenay and Qu'Appelle in the Anglican Church of Canada (two eucharistic prayers).

The International Consultation on English Texts (ICET texts)

The Society for the Promotion of Christian Knowledge (quotations from *Modern Liturgical Texts, The Time is Now, Partners in Mission,* etc.).

(ii) Further informal help has been given in the years since 1968 by the following persons to whom grateful thanks are due:

The Most Revs. E. E. Curtis (Archbishop of the Indian Ocean), A. R. Kratz (Primate of Brazil) and J. Luum (Archbishop of Uganda)

The Rt. Revs. L. W. Brown (Bishop of St. Edmundsbury and Ipswich), L. H. S. Chhoa (Bishop of Sabah), C. H. W. De Soysa (Bishop of Colombo), D. M. Goto (Bishop of Tokyo), D. Hand (Bishop of Papua New Guinea), M. Y. Mori (Bishop of Kyoto), G. E. D. Pytches (Bishop of Chile, Bolivia and Peru), F. Reus-Froylan (Bishop of Puerto Rico) , C. J. G. Robinson, B. Tenong-Gong (Bishop of Kuching), W. G. Young (Bishop of Sialkot)

The Ven. R. C. D. Jasper

The Rev. Canons A. G. Baker, E. M. B. Green, C. Guilbert

The Revs. P. R. Akehurst, K. B. Anderson, J. Arnold, S. T. Arpee, J. M. Ball, R. T. Beckwith, Joyce M. Bennett, F. D. Chaplin, C. G. Chapman, J. O. Hewlett, S. M. Houghton, M. J. Lloyd, B. J. McDonald-Milne, W. F. Marriott, J. Meadowcroft, P. C. Moore, A. D. Rogers, L. F. Simpkins, J. E. Spencer, H. Todt, R. A. Ward, J. D. Wilkinson.

The late Rev. M. Olagundoye

Messrs. D. J. Barnes, R. J. Brookes, B. Garcia, S. Robertson

Miss M. D. Fraser, Mrs. Elspeth Grant, Miss P. A. Morris

CONTENTS

(Where no contributor is named, the section is by the editor)

Contents xv

ABBREVIATIONS AND
TYPOGRAPHICAL RULES

LITURGICAL texts are represented throughout the book by a code in bold type as shown in the list below. The actual texts are to be found printed out in one of the three volumes, *The Liturgy in English* (**LiE**), *Modern Anglican Liturgies* 1958-68 (**MAL**) and this present volume *Further Anglican Liturgies* 1968-75 (**FAL**). In each case the volume in which the text is to be found is shown in the right-hand column. The Church of England texts contained in the various Prayer Books of 1549, 1552 etc. are in this volume called '1549', '1552' etc. without the use of bold type. The context usually prevents confusion, and where this is not so a fuller description has been used.

Afr	The South African Liturgy (1929)	LiE
Amer	The American Liturgy (1929)	LiE
AmerR	The American Experimental Liturgy (1967)	MAL
Amer1	The American Experimental Liturgy (1970/3) 'The First Service'	FAL
Amer2	The American Experimental Liturgy (1970/3) 'The Second Service'	FAL
Amer3	The American Experimental Liturgy (1970/3) 'The Order of Celebration'	FAL
Amer1-3	Liturgical Material common to **Amer1**, **Amer2**, and **Amer3**, and appended to them all (1970/3)	FAL
Aus1	The Australia 1662 Recension (1966)	MAL
Aus1A	The Australian 1662 Recension modernized (1972)	FAL
Aus2	The Australian 'A Modern Liturgy' (1966)	MAL
Aus3	The Australian Experimental Liturgy (1969)	FAL
Aus4	The Australian Experimental Liturgy (1973)	FAL
Bom	The Bombay Liturgy (1922)	LiE
BomR	The Revised Form of the Bombay Liturgy (1948)	LiE
Braz	The Brazil Experimental Liturgy (1967)	MAL
BrazR	The Brazil Experimental Liturgy (1972)	FAL
Can	The Canadian 1662 Recension (1918)	LiE
CanR	The Canadian Liturgy (1959)	LiE
Can1	The Canadian Alternative Liturgy (1974)	FAL
Cey	The Ceylon Liturgy (1938)	LiE
Chil	The (South) Chilean Experimental Liturgy (1967)	MAL
ChilR	The Chilean Liturgy (1972)	FAL
CNI	The North India Liturgy (1973/4)	FAL
CSI	The South India Liturgy (2nd edition 1954) (*also* Proper Prefaces, 3rd edition 1963)	LiE MAL
CSIR	The Modern English South India Liturgy (1972)	FAL
EAUL	The United Liturgy of East Africa (1966)	MAL
Eng1	The English *Series* 1 Liturgy (1966)	MAL
Eng1-2A	The English '*Series* 1 *and Series* 2 *Revised*' Liturgy (1975)	FAL
Eng2	The English *Series* 2 Liturgy (1967)	MAL
Eng3	The English *Series* 3 Liturgy (1973)	FAL

HK1	The Hong Kong and Macao Liturgy (1957)	MAL
HK2	The Hong Kong and Macao Experimental Bilingual Liturgy (1965)	MAL
Ind[1]	The Indian 1662 Recension (1960)	LiE
IndR	The Indian Liturgy (1960)	LiE
IndS	Propers contained in the Supplement to the C.I.P.B.C. Prayer Book (1966)	MAL
Iran	The Iran Experimental Liturgy (1967)	MAL
IranR	The Iran Experimental Liturgy (1971)	FAL
Ire	The Irish Liturgy (1926)	LiE
IreR	The Irish Experimental Liturgy (1967)	MAL
Ire1	The Irish Experimental Liturgy (1972)	FAL
Jap	The Japanese Liturgy (1959)	LiE
Kor	The Korean Liturgy (1939)	LiE
Kor1	The Korean Experimental Liturgy (1973)	FAL
Kuch	The Kuching Experimental Liturgy (1973)	FAL
LfA	*A Liturgy for Africa* (1964)	MAL
Mad	The Madagascar Liturgy (1945)	MAL
Mel	The Melanesian Liturgy (1972)	FAL
MLT	The modernization of **Eng2** in *Modern Liturgical Texts* (1968)	—
NG	The Papua New Guinea Liturgy (1970)	FAL
NUL	The United Liturgy for Nigeria (1965)	MAL
Nyas[2]	The Nyasaland Liturgy (?1929)	LiE
NZ	The New Zealand Experimental Liturgy (1966)	MAL
NZR	The New Zealand Experimental Liturgy (1970)	FAL
Rhod[2]	The Northern Rhodesia Liturgy (?1925)	LiE
SAfr1	The South African Experimental Liturgy (1969)	FAL
SAfr2	The South African Experimental Liturgy (1975)	FAL
Scot	The Scottish Liturgy (1929)	LiE
ScotE	The Scottish 1662 Recension (1929)	LiE
ScotR	The Scottish Experimental Liturgy (1966)	MAL
ScotRR	The 1970 form of **ScotR**	—
ScotS	Propers authorized to supplement those in **Scot** and **ScotE** (1966)	MAL
Tan	The Tanzanian Liturgy (1973/4)	FAL
Wal	The Welsh Experimental Liturgy (1966)	MAL
WalR	The Welsh Modern English Study Liturgy (1972)	FAL
WInd	The West Indies Liturgy (1959)	LiE
Zan	The Swahili Mass (Zanzibar Diocese) (1919)	LiE

[1] The code 'IndE' was used in the writing of **MAL**, inconsistently with the coding set out in this section in both **LiE** and **MAL**, to indicate the Indian 1662 Recension, i.e. **Ind**. This is listed as under corrigenda to **MAL** in Appendix G to this volume (p.421).

[2] These titles are retained here for the sake of uniformity with **LiE**, in which the texts appear, and for no other reason. The countries and dioceses concerned have changed their names, and both the texts lapsed from use soon after (see chapter 12 below). The countries are now called Malawi and Zambia respectively. It should also be noted that the dates here ascribed to the texts are guesswork based on bare inference. No dates appeared for them in **LiE**.

The liturgical texts have been laid out to conform as nearly as possible to their originals, subject to the need for standard type-sizes, and some uniformity of appearance. Disciplinary rubrics have usually been omitted, and notes standing before or after services have sometimes been reported in brief rather than reprinted in full. Numbers have been inserted in the margins to give easy reference to particular sections of text, and editorial footnotes below a section refer to the whole section thus demarcated by the numbering. In many cases the numbering is reprinted from the original, and this is indicated at the beginning of the text as set out here. Where alternatives are set out in parallel in the original, this layout is retained, and where congregational parts are laid out in lines in the original (for easy corporate participation) this arrangement has also been retained. Anything that appears to be commentary rather than text has been excluded, and appendixes have often been digested also.

'ICET' ('International Consultation on English Texts') and 'CF' ('Common Forms') denote the two categories of 'Common Forms' set out once and for all in Appendix A. Very occasionally the code '**MAL** CF' is used to refer to forms in Appendix A to **MAL**. Variants from the Common Forms (ICET or CF) are printed as an *apparatus* wherever they occur.

Italic type is used for rubrics.

Roman type is used for the text of liturgies where the minister alone is directed to say or sing it.

Bold type is used for the text of liturgies where it is either to be said or sung by the minister and people together, or by the people alone, or by the individual recipient at the administration. This type is used where doubts exist, whether the doubt arises from an ambiguous rubric, or from the laying out in lines, or from both. Rubrical directions from the original (e.g. *People: . . .*) are retained even where a distinctive type as used here makes the original rubric appear redundant.

Asterisks * and square brackets [ ] are used as in the originals, and in fact almost always indicate optional items.

Double square brackets ⟦ ⟧ enclose editorial comment, whether in the text or in footnotes. Other footnotes are reprinted from the original.

SMALL CAPITAL TYPE is also used for editorial comment, usually only of one word. OM means that a particular word or phrase is omitted, OMIT that a whole section is omitted.

All other punctuation and presentation reflects what is found in the originals. Where, through different printings, there are uncertainties as to what the original form is, every attempt has been made to recover the form authorized. Very occasionally a misprint in the original has been corrected.

PART I
ANGLICAN EUCHARISTIC LITURGY
1968-1975

CHAPTER 1

ANGLICAN EUCHARISTIC LITURGY
1968-1975

Introduction

THIS volume contains twenty-four eucharistic liturgies produced, and in most cases authorized, in Anglican (and ex-Anglican) Churches in the years 1968-75. This compares with a similar number in the decade 1958-68[1], and a somewhat smaller number for the whole four hundred years prior to that. At the same time, it is clear that the rites are not all independent productions, but they are linked by a whole series of informal bonds: a common language in many cases, a common structure in the Anglican Consultative Council and that Council's Secretary General, a commonly agreed set of principles (converging with those of other denominations), the sheer availability of earlier rites to the compilers of later ones, the interchange of personnel from one area to another, and the force of 'families' of rites which interplay with each other. At the same time the Church of Rome has produced new eucharistic prayers which have been studied everywhere, and in some places the rites of other denominations also have been of influence. The twenty-four rites thus exhibit a combination of centrifugal and centripetal forces. Their number stands witness to the number of autonomous bodies in the Anglican Communion, whilst their common features set limits to any possible inference of liturgical fragmentation in the Communion. The rites are of course often only available in booklets, and only in their own areas. In a few cases they are only available in a vernacular tongue. Thus it is the task of a collection such as this to bring together in standard form these scattered compilations. The actual time of publication of the volume is determined largely by the fact that, as with **MAL** before it, it looks as though the rites are largely settled for a year or two ahead, and so the book can be safely put together without being greatly out of date before publication day.

[1] In fact **MAL** contained 16 new rites emanating from the years 1964-7, but the decade as a whole also included **CanR, Jap, WInd** (all dating from 1959) and **IndR** (of 1960). These four latter rites are all in **LiE.**

Some Historical Factors

(i) *The Pan-Anglican Framework*

In 1968 **MAL** was taken through the press in time to be published during the period of the Lambeth Conference meeting in London in August of that year. **MAL** itself, however, was an unofficial production, and there can be added in addition three other more official publications of that year which related in one way or another to eucharistic liturgy.[1] These were:

(a) *Lambeth Conference* 1968: *Preparatory Information.* In this book a chapter entitled 'Liturgical Revision in the Anglican Communion since 1958' was contributed by R. M. C. Jeffery. Insofar as this chapter was concerned with *eucharistic* liturgy, the present writer and Mr. Jeffery had already exchanged all their information so that **MAL** and this chapter reflected each other.

(b) *Modern Liturgical Texts* by the Church of England Liturgical Commission. This contained the first texts from the Church of England Commission to address God as 'you'. In particular it included a complete rendering of **Eng2** (of 1967) into this 'you' form.[2] The rite thus set out was never authorized anywhere, but its contents proved to be seminal in various ways which are traced out later in this chapter. This was published during the Lambeth Conference.

(c) *The Daily Office* by the Joint Liturgical Group.[3] This in retrospect has had a delaying effect at one point—the production of modern collects. Although the suggestions for a daily office were not directly related to the eucharist, yet because the language of the office was still in 'thou' form, the collects listed out for each week were traditional collects, shuffled and arranged with some reference to the 'themes' of each Sunday in the Joint Liturgical Group's

---

[1] All of them were published by S.P.C.K. London in 1968.

[2] This rendering was the work of one man, Canon G. J. Cuming. It can be reconstructed in its ante-communion and penitential section from **SAfr1** (on pp.203-6 below), which reproduces them *verbatim*. Its canon is to be found in the pull-out table in Appendix F, and its Agnus Dei (again Canon Cuming's work) has become the official ICET one—see ICET 8 on p.396 below. For the place of this rite, known as **MLT** hereafter, in the Church of England itself, see p.39 below.

[3] This interdenominational group covers England, Scotland and Wales, and now includes Roman Catholics as well as non-episcopalians. This is a change from the position mentioned in **MAL** p.117. See also C. O. Buchanan *Recent Liturgical Revision in the Church of England* (Grove Books, Bramcote 1973) pp.11-12.

earlier proposals *The Calendar and Lectionary*.[1] When the Church of England Liturgical Commission took up the Sunday proposals, in *The Calendar and Lessons*,[2] then it associated the collects from *The Daily Office* with the Sunday lectionary. This was acknowledged as a stopgap measure, but it did prolong the life of 'thou' form collects, and delay the quest for 'you' form ones.[3]

After the 1968 Lambeth Conference a Liturgical Consultation was held in London on 27 and 28 August 1968, and attended by thirty delegates, mostly bishops. Insofar as this Consultation affected the eucharist the following points were raised:

(a) There was discussion of the liturgical English in *Modern Liturgical Texts*.

(b) There was a welcome for the simplifying of the Calendar recommended by the Joint Liturgical Group, except in respect of the nine Sundays before Christmas.

(c) There was a detailed discussion of the structure of the eucharist, and the Consultation asked Dr. Leslie Brown and Canon Jasper to revise the existing Pan-Anglican Document on the structure of the eucharist.[4] In particular the structure was to provide for the combination of daily office and eucharist—a recommendation arising from earlier discussion of *The Daily Office* at the Consultation.

(d) There was some puzzlement about the best procedure for supplementary consecration. The mood had swung strongly against the repetition of the words of institution, but had not settled on a clear alternative. A further study of this problem was requested.

---

[1] This is mentioned in **MAL** p.121. It differed from *The Calendar and Lessons* in assuming a fixed Easter, and making no provision for the sanctorale. In this it was followed by *The Daily Office*. It was edited by R. C. D. Jasper, and published by O.U.P. in 1967.

[2] S.P.C.K. London 1969. The lessons in this became the basis of the lectionary in **Eng3**, but the collects have not gained any authorization.

[3] Thus modern collects from the Church of England Liturgical Commission were not published till 10 April 1975, and will not be authorized till 1976 at the earliest. These are in a report *Collects to accompany the Series 3 Lectionary* (S.P.C.K.), and are largely modernizations of those in the 1969 report. Sets were produced to accompany **NZR** and **Amer2** which were both authorized in 1970, but the first ones to relate to this particular calendar and lectionary were the South African ones of 1972—see p.200 below. A Church of Ireland set also now exists.

[4] The previous Document is printed with a full introduction in **MAL** chapter 3, pp.22-32.

From these four points varying actions have resulted. The discussion and introduction of modern English is further reported below. The Calendar questions were not handled in the Church of England until 1974,[1] but the whole Joint Liturgical Group pattern (including the nine Sundays before Christmas) was accepted by the South African Liturgical Committee, and is found with **SAfr1** (1969) and **SAfr2** (1975).

The new structure Document was duly produced and first circularized in late 1969, and is reproduced as an appendix to this chapter. It was reprinted in *Prayer Book Studies* 21[2] in 1970, and again in *Partners in Mission*[3] in 1973. Like its predecessor, it does not seem to have been greatly valued in many Provinces and it was never even discussed on the Church of England Liturgical Commission. It is mentioned in the chapters below from Ireland,[4] Canada,[5] and the United States.[6] Further discussion of its contents occurs during this chapter.

Supplementary consecration was committed ultimately to the Church of England Commission for a report. This proved an intractable task and no such report has in fact been sent round the Anglican Communion. An explanation of this failure follows below as a second appendix to this chapter.

The next stage in Pan-Anglican handling of liturgy came with the setting up of the Anglican Consultative Council on the request of the 1968 Lambeth Conference. The A.C.C. first met at Limuru in 1971, and did not then discuss liturgy. In its report the A.C.C. records the following resolution

'26 *Liaison between Liturgical Commissions*

'Having received a request from the Liturgical Commission of the Church of England in Australia for the setting up of a Consultative Liturgical Committee, the Council recommends that the Secretary General:

(a) provide liaison between the Liturgical Commissions in the various Provinces of the Anglican Communion;

---

[1] The General Synod of the Church of England first debated it in February 1974, when, paradoxically, of the new features it was this very pre-Christmas season of nine Sundays which escaped defeat. The other provisions were referred for reconsideration.

[2] This is the American Standing Liturgical Commission's report on the eucharist (published by the Church Hymnal Corporation, New York 1970). See pp.123ff below

[3] S.P.C.K. London 1973, pp.70-73.

[4] See p.91.

[5] See p.110.

[6] See pp.123 and 128.

(b) arrange for a report on liturgical matters to be made to the Anglican Consultative Council in 1973.'[1]

It will be clear that the first of these two recommendations falls far short of the recorded request from the Australian Liturgical Commission, and in effect leaves the Anglican Secretary General's responsibilities exactly as they were before. Certainly they have not been noticeably differently exercised since 1971. The second recommendation duly led to a report, as shown below.

The A.C.C. next met in Dublin in July 1973. The report requested at Limuru was duly produced and circulated prior to the meeting, having been put together by Canon R. C. D. Jasper. The report is entitled 'Liturgy 1968-73'[2], and it includes both the Pan-Anglican Document and separate reports from each Church or Province of the Anglican Communion, arranged in alphabetical order. The reports range much further than a study of eucharistic rites alone can do, and include details about revision of daily offices, initiation rites, occasional services, and calendar and lectionary matters. But eucharistic rites draw generous attention, and thus at intervals the present volume has to cite, develop or amend points stated or raised in the relevant section of *Partners in Mission*.

However, *Partners in Mission* refers to liturgical developments in two other places, which must here be juxtaposed:

'While expressing the feeling that a central liturgical commission is impracticable at the present time, the Council recommends continuing collaboration among the various Liturgical Commissions. It questions whether the problems connected with the provision of liturgies in acceptable modern English have been satisfactorily solved, and notes the difficulties involved in the translation, adaptation, and development of modern liturgies in other languages. It suggests that expert help should be given to member Churches which face these problems. It recognizes that within a common eucharistic structure the present tendency is towards variety and transience.'[3]

'We are critical of the liturgies being produced by different Churches of the Anglican Communion as being mainly rearrangements of 1662 and Series 2 of the Church of England. We hope that consideration might be given to the possible inclusion of elements of worship

[1] *The Time is Now* (S.P.C.K. London 1971) p.38.
[2] It is set out in *Partners in Mission* (S.P.C.K. London 1973), the report of the Dublin meeting of the A.C.C., on pp.70-86.
[3] *Partners in Mission* p.35.

from the traditional religion of the country where the Church carries on its mission.'[1]

The former of these two extracts comes from the section on 'Order and Organization in the Anglican Communion' and the latter from the section on 'Mission and Evangelism'. Both are adopted by the Council as reports of the full Council, and the Secretary-General, in his introduction to the whole report, stated 'there has been no attempt . . . to make them [the reports] inhumanly consistent at every point'.[2] He might well have had these very passages about liturgy in mind—for the Council seems to have committed itself to two principles which are almost as inconsistent with each other as can be imagined. One or other will provide a charter for *any* steps in liturgical revision which a Province may care to undertake.

The official pan-Anglican scene is completed by a note that during the period under review agreements on eucharistic doctrine have been registered by international teams representing Anglicans and Roman Catholics in one instance, and Anglicans and Lutherans in the other.[3] The latter of these is of relevance to the present volume in relation to the Province of Tanzania, where the new provincial rite (**Tan**) has been developed from the previous **EAUL**,[4] in the compilation of which Lutherans were involved.[5] The former agreement is probably of greater significance, and it was cited during the handling of **Eng3** in the Church of England General Synod in 1972—and this rite in turn, as will emerge below, is already of greater worldwide significance than was recognizable even at the time of the Dublin A.C.C. meeting. In particular, the section of the Anglican-Roman Catholic agreement which deals with the sacrifice of Christ and eucharistic sacrifice is strong with liturgical implications, whilst it was a later treatment of the role of the Spirit in sacramental efficacy which provided a basis for one specific amendment to the **Eng3** text.[6]

(ii) *The growth of modern liturgical English*

Whilst it is impossible to define modern English solely in terms of addressing God as 'you', it is easy to take this as *symptomatic* of a

[1] *Partners in Mission* p.48.
[2] *Ibid.* p.ix.
[3] The text of both of these is set out in *Modern Eucharistic Agreement* (S.P.C.K. London 1973).
[4] See **MAL** pp.70-89.
[5] For further reference to the importance of Anglican-Lutheran agreements in relation to Tanzania, see pp.234 and 238 below.
[6] See pp.19 and 44 below.

movement into a modern language. In point of fact there are other factors which are of greater significance—e.g. sentence structure, the use of adjectives and adverbs, the use of latinisms, and the choice of active or passive verbs. It is possible to have a modern 'feel' to prayers which retain the 'thou' form of address to God. The second post-communion prayer of **Eng2** was a good instance of this.[1] But if the step from 'thou' to 'you' is taken, it is almost impossible not to take other steps at the same time. 'Dost' and 'wast' are the first victims, but the consequences usually run much further. Therefore, with the caveats noted, it is helpful here to trace out the growth of 'you' form liturgy round the Anglican Communion—and the evidence is that the English-speaking Anglican world has crossed a watershed in the very period under review.

In **MAL** three rites alone appeared in 'you' form: **Aus2, Chil** and **NZ. Chil** may be discounted, as it was a translation from the Spanish which was only to be found in **MAL** itself. The other two rites were the pioneers, and they were ahead of the trends represented otherwise in **MAL.** It was still possible in that volume, for instance, to reproduce the 1662 'Common Forms' and Proper Prefaces (which had been used by Wigan in **LiE**), and find them serviceable for the great preponderance of the rites of the 1960's. To take a few instances from 1967 itself, **AmerR, Eng2** and **IreR** were all written in 'thou' form, and were only just coming into use in the last two months before **MAL** went to press. And the 'you' form rites of Australia and New Zealand were also ahead of large sections of their own respective Churches. Indeed in Australia the General Synod deleted the 'you' form Lord's Prayer,[2] and in New Zealand the first questionnaires received very equivocal answers from the over-34s.[3]

The next 'you' form production, the first in the period not covered by **MAL,** was **MLT** in 1968. This was of course not for authorization and use in the Church of England, but was only a study document. Nevertheless it took root the next year in South Africa in **SAfr1**,[4] though this

---

[1] Almighty God,
we offer thee our souls and bodies,
to be a living sacrifice,
through Jesus Christ our Lord.
Send us out into the world
in the power of thy Spirit,
to live and work
to thy praise and glory. Amen.
[2] See **MAL** p.320, and note the 'thou' form in the text—p.324.
[3] See **MAL** p.327.
[4] See pp.197-8 below.

rite went to the Roman Catholic texts for modern English forms of the Creeds, Gloria in Excelsis and Lord's Prayer. The **MLT** text has in places, particularly in the intercession, also had its effects on the rite of Kuching (**Kuch**), and a similar process of updating was used in Papua New Guinea (**NG**).

Whilst the Church of England Liturgical Commission was working on *Modern Liturgical Texts,* there was forming an international body, the International Consultation on English Texts (ICET). This arose from the post-Vatican II Roman Catholic body, the International Committee on English in the Liturgy.[1] Its Advisory Committee started meeting with representatives of the other Churches from English-speaking countries, and this meeting was then formed into the semi-official 'Consultation'. The chairmen are the Rev. Harold Winstone, an English Roman Catholic, and Canon Ronald Jasper, the chairman of the Church of England Liturgical Commission. Denominations represented have included Roman Catholic, Anglican, Presbyterian, Lutheran, Methodist, United Reformed (i.e. the English union of Presbyterians and Congregationalists), and Baptist Churches. In addition some members of ICET have been specifically representing or relating to ecumenical bodies such as the Consultation on Church Union in America or the Joint Liturgical Groups in England and Australia. Whilst distance has often prevented full participation from South Africa and Australasia, there has been a good cross-section at each of the more or less annual[2] meetings since 1969.

ICET from the outset took in hand the translation work required for common forms in English of traditional liturgical material, such as the Lord's Prayer and the Creeds. The various Liturgical Commissions corresponded with it, and the relevant parts of *Modern Liturgical Texts* in time formed part of such correspondence, and were heavily laid under contribution in the draft texts issued in early 1969.[3] Further comment on these drafts was then received, and in early 1970 ICET

---

[1] The Vatican Constitution on the Sacred Liturgy had laid down that territorial authorities should where possible consult with 'neighbouring' authorities of the same language and culture. In the early years of the use of the vernacular in the Roman Catholic Church (i.e. from Advent 1964) there was little coherence between the English-speaking areas, but from 1967 this International Committee gradually produced norms. Some were used in **SAfr1** in 1969, and these are shown in the *apparatus* to the ICET forms in Appendix A.

[2] It met each year from 1969 to 1974, except in 1973.

[3] The texts concerned were included in **Aus3** in 1969, and can be reconstructed from the *apparatus* to the ICET forms in Appendix A. One of the most daring points in these drafts was the use of 'glorify' in the second line of the Lord's Prayer.

published its texts, mostly in definitive form, in a booklet *Prayers we have in Common*.[1]

The ICET texts provide a completely new set of 'Common Forms' for eucharistic liturgy, but they are not specifically Anglican ones. They are not above criticism,[2] but are intended to provide prayers and other material in which all English-speaking Christians can easily unite across the world and across the denominations.

From mid-1970 onwards these ICET texts were generally incorporated in new Anglican rites. In 1970 itself they were found in **NZR** and **Amer2** (and in **Amer1-3**, the cognate material added to all three new American rites). In 1971 they appeared in **Eng3** as first published before it went to Synod, and also in **CSIR**. In 1972 they passed into **Aus1A, Ire1** and **WalR**.[3] In 1973 they were incorporated in **Aus4, CNI** and **SAfr2** also. They are now common liturgical currency. However, in England they ran into serious trouble. An attempt to restore 'I' in the Creed failed ultimately in Synod, but the second and ninth lines of the Lord's Prayer were amended. In the course of revision ICET met again in London in May 1972 and issued a statement that 'hallowed' was an acceptable alternative to 'holy' in the second line, and that 'temptation' and 'the time of trial' were acceptable alternatives to 'the test' in the ninth.[4] The English text has been adopted in North India, whilst the Church of Ireland and the diocese of Kuching have reverted to 'temptation'. In 1974 ICET produced new variants (including 'hallowed'), and called them 'final'. These texts were dubbed into **Can1** at proof stage.

[1] Geoffrey Chapman, London, and Fortress Press, Philadelphia, 1970. This booklet was published in a blue cover, and a second edition in a yellow cover was published in 1971. Most texts relating to eucharistic liturgy were already definitive in 1970, but a few alterations to other texts were made in 1971. The 1971 texts are standard in Appendix A below, but an *apparatus* to each text shows both the previous forms, and also the 1974 texts where these differ again. It is the 1971 texts which appear in most uses of ICET material. (The 1972 meeting allowed the **Eng3** variants as possible alternatives in the Lord's Prayer, but attempted nothing definitive).

[2] Quite apart from points noted below, the Gloria in Excelsis shows great freedom in translation (though not as much as the Agnus Dei, lifted entire from **MLT**) and the Nicene Creed (in its 1970-71 form) committed the Churches to the unhelpful 'One in Being with the Father'. It was perhaps too much to expect anything daring in relation to the 'epiousion' and 'daily bread' (the point where the **Aus2** text came unstuck in General Synod in Australia). The 1970 Salutation, lifted also from *Modern Liturgical Texts* (pp.31-32), has been outdated by bolder redrafting in **Eng3**, at least in its role of introducing the Sursum Corda, and by a more timid draft in ICET 1971 (cf. p.396).

[3] **WalR** is only a study text, as the change to modern English was apparently thought too breathtaking for the Church in Wales to accept at that point.

[4] The allowing of alternatives by ICET ran contrary to its original purpose of providing single texts for all to use, and *could* be represented as self-defeating.

This mainstream liturgical use has left the pre-ICET texts looking slightly odd. However, **Aus3** and **SAfr1** have already been superseded, and **NG** (like the later, non-ICET, **Mel**) was designed for ease of translation into vernacular tongues.[1] Indeed the ICET texts have set a problem for translators—a problem which is reflected in this volume where a Swahili Gloria in Excelsis is reproduced in English as the ICET form—which is not really close to a Swahili which is in fact unchanged since **MAL** represented it in **EAUL** as identical to 1662 in English. The policy in this volume with **BrazR**, **ChilR**, **Kor1** and **Tan** has been to translate into a 'you' form with ICET texts throughout. But that does not mean that vernacular liturgical language has itself been updated since 1967. It almost invariably has not.

Finally in this section, the last remaining 'thou' form texts should be noted. In 1970 came **Amer1**, which was comparable in principle to **ScotR** in **MAL**—a restructuring of a traditional rite without much change of language. In 1970 and 1971 there were revisions of **Iran**, now represented by **IranR** (1971). But this itself is being superseded in English-speaking congregations by **Eng3**. The combination of **Eng1** and **Eng2** (**Eng1-2A**) has appeared last.[2] In Mauritius the informally accepted 'Interim Rite' has now been accorded official status in a bilingual edition. But that is all. 'Thou' form liturgy in practical terms found its last new expression in **Eng2**—and **Eng2** itself conveniently closed **MAL**. Thus the present volume represents a new era in liturgical English.[3]

(iii) *The Influence of the Church of England rites* (**Eng2, Eng3**)

Within the **MAL** rites, a clear 'family' of rites was discernible springing from **CSI**, Lambeth 1958 and **LfA**. **Eng2** was authorized only weeks before **MAL** went to press, and virtually no international influence of it could then be traced.[4] However, in 1975 with seven years' hindsight it is clear that first **Eng2** and then **Eng3** have become very powerful

---

[1] See also p.353 below, where the probability that **NG** will include the ICET texts is mentioned.

[2] This hardly includes anything new—only an editing down of the old. See pp.46-8 below.

[3] The editor has tried to work out the significance of this in the presentation of the contents. One instance is the pull-out chart of Proper Prefaces in Appendix C, where all the 'you' form texts known to the Anglican Communion are collected on one sheet of paper, where they can all be seen at once.

[4] An early ripple from **Eng2** (prior to its authorization) is noted on **MAL** p.162, and its first trial use overseas is reported on **MAL** p.305.

factors in the Anglican Communion, and indeed in united Churches as well.[1] The 'family' has displaced the **CSI-LfA** 'family' in influence.

The characteristics of **Eng2-Eng3** which indicate that they are a separate 'family' are as follows:

(i) The intercessions are a complete break from the previously prevalent litanies, and have a now well-known format.

(ii) In the eucharistic prayer the preface has a long, but not invariable, recitation of the 'mighty acts' of God 'through Christ'. The post-Sanctus 'link' with the narrative of institution is minimal, but a Western-type 'petition for consecration' is retained. The anamnesis is very restrained in its interpretation of what 'we do' in remembrance of our Lord. There is no epiclesis of the Spirit on the elements. Although there is a return to a traditional pattern of eucharistic prayer, it is with an economy of words (**Eng2** has been said to have the shortest ever of such prayers). Self-oblation is excluded from the latter part of the prayer, and comes after communion.[2]

(iii) The Lord's Prayer comes after the Fraction as a last devotional approach to reception.

(iv) Certain characteristic forms of prayer recur—such as the second post-communion one.[3]

(v) For the rest the main features of **CSI-LfA** are found, and the tendency is certainly for the two families to flow together.

The independence of this family is attested not only by its distinctive features (which are not so hard and fast as to admit of no resemblance to other rites), but also by the known fact, in the present writer's experience, that other families were ignored in the original drafting of **Eng2**, which appeared therefore as a new rite.[4]

The various chapters which follow indicate that **Eng2** has over the recent years been used at the very least in Scotland, Canada, Central Africa, Tanzania, Iran (and elsewhere in the Jerusalem Archbishopric), Singapore, and Australia. Its intercessions have been specifically

---

[1] For a fuller account of the background and influence of this 'family' of rites see the present writer's chapter 'Series 3 in the Context of the Anglican Communion' in *The Eucharist To-Day : Studies on Series* 3 edited by R. C. D. Jasper (S.P.C.K. London 1974).

[2] This is less controversial than in the past. Self-oblation in the canon has been omitted from some of the new American prayers, and excised from **Eng1-2A**.

[3] i.e. the prayer set out in footnote 1 on p.9 above.

[4] cf. *The Eucharist To-Day : Studies on Series* 3, pp.14-20.

included, or allowed for inclusion in previously existing rites, in Scotland, America, Iran, Ceylon, Kuching and North India. Through **MLT** its text at large has passed into **SAfr1**, and thus into **SAfr2**. It is found again in **NG**. Its features are reflected in the new Pan-Anglican Document. And it has increased its influence further through the spawning of **Eng3**.

Eng3 is in direct descent from **Eng2**, with the language modernized. Nevertheless there are developments. There are many more Propers for high seasons, as shown in Appendix D below. There is a restructuring of the intercessions, though still within the same category. There is a new place and text for the Decalogue and the Lord's Summary of the Law. There is a rewritten confession, and first post-communion prayer. There is a removal of options from the sacramental part of the service. The eucharistic prayer is enriched at several points, and congregational acclamations are added. In particular the anamnesis refers to 'his perfect sacrifice made once for all upon the cross'— language reminiscent of the Epistle to the Hebrews (and 1662) but completely missing from **Eng2**.

And **Eng3** is also well launched on the international scene. It is found in use in the same countries as **Eng2**, mentioned above. And its text is reproduced in **SAfr2** (where one option allows the use of the **Eng3** eucharistic prayer *verbatim*) and in **CNI** (where a text which started near to **CSIR** has been strongly influenced by features of **Eng3**). It has provided much of **Ire1**, apart from the eucharistic prayer, and in its original 1971 form was imaginatively adapted by the Australian Liturgical Commission in the compilation of **Aus4**.[1] It even had its Proper Prefaces lifted and put into Spanish by the Liturgical Committee in Chile.[2] All this was remarkable in its first year after authorization,[3] and suggests a stature which is *not* due merely to its coming from 'the mother church' (for there was no recent precedent for such an influence

---

[1] A point of obvious dependence is the anamnesis (cf. the respective columns in Appendix F). **Aus4** has a sentence with a single verb which terminates upon the 'perfect sacrifice made once for all upon the cross'. This was criticized in England, as creating an unfortunate split between the death and resurrection of our Lord, though paradoxically it is well paralleled in the new Roman Catholic eucharistic prayers. **Eng3** was duly changed to its final, rather clumsy, form. In addition **Aus4** uses the verb 'celebrate' with 'redemption' as its object. This pattern of words also came under attack in England, but survived. It is well defended by D. L. Frost in *The Language of Series* 3 (Grove Books, 1973) p.26, and by P. Bradshaw in an essay entitled 'Celebration' in *The Eucharist To-Day: Studies on Series 3*, pp.130-41.

[2] See Appendix C.

[3] Since then it has been translated almost entire into Persian, (see p.252 below).

by rites in England, and there *was* precedent for a non-English 'family'
—viz. that of **CSI** and **LfA**—to be influential). Rather it must be reckoned to have some self-evident merits.

(iv) *Other 'Families' of Rites*

Other 'families' also make their contribution, albeit a lesser one, to this
collection.

The **CSI-LfA** strand is to be found continuing in **NZR** (1970),
IranR (1971), **CSIR** (1971), **Tan** (1973/4).[1] Some influence is still to be
traced in **CNI** (1973/4), and its impact on **Eng3** (e.g. as with the acclamations) should not be overlooked. Curiously, the anamnesis from **LfA**
seems to have been adopted in **Kuch** (1973). On the other hand **LfA**
itself has proved unable to establish itself, and is ignored in most parts
of Africa. Some brief mention is found here in the contribution from
Central Africa, and in that alone.

The older 1549-Scottish-American 'family' reaches on with the three
American rites of 1970—the last of these being no more than a set
of rubrics—and with **BrazR**. At this point the 'family' influence fades
into insignificance. In Scotland itself no new rite has emerged. In
different ways **Kor1**, **Mel** and **WalR** ought perhaps also to be treated
as offsprings of the same 'family'.

The 1552-1662 strand has one and a half representatives here—
Aus1A and **Eng1-2A**. But this does not mean that 1662 has ceased to
be used. It may no longer be true to say, as **MAL** did, that '1662 is still
far and away the most frequently celebrated Anglican rite on the
world's surface'.[2] But it has by no means disappeared—and the result
of modernizing its language in Australia is well worth investigating. It
remains an all-weather, unchallenged, datum point in the liturgical
life of many parts of Africa also, and there are very many who use it at
least sometimes in England and Ireland. It has run out beyond the
Anglican Communion into unexpected places.[3] Whilst it may at last
bow to competitors, its strengths cannot be doubted by those who have
lived long with it.[4]

---

[1] See the table in Appendix E.

[2] **MAL** p.7.

[3] E.g. Bishop Colin Bazley, who contributes the chapter on Chile here,
states that in Chile the Pentecostalists cling to 1662 (which they obtained via
American Methodism), whilst the Anglicans are only just reaching a stage where
they may do without it . . .

[4] It was an amazing feature of the famous Parliamentary debate in England
on 4 December 1974 (see p.38 below), that its strengths were if anything
overstated by many members of the House of Commons who rarely go to
Church!

There remain two families which do not conform to the above groupings—those of Australia and Chile. Both were noted as displaying independent characteristics in the second chapter of **MAL**, and the succeeding rites from both areas have confirmed the trend.[1] In Australia the separate thanksgivings for the bread and the cup were in 1969 phased into a single prayer in **Aus3,** forming two paragraphs prior to the narrative of institution. In **Aus4** the tradition of independence is maintained by the division of the narrative of institution itself into two, each part following its related thanksgiving paragraph. In Chile the criticism that the 1967 rite (**Chil**) had no thanksgiving has led to a rite (**ChilR**) which has a very rich thanksgiving—but also has a 'consecration' which is a totally separate item.

Some Liturgical Principles

(i) *The Structure of the Service*

At most important points the structural questions were already settled by the year 1967, and there is little more to add. The basic pattern of ministry of the word, prayers, and sacramental liturgy with four-action 'shape' is almost universal. The sermon follows the gospel everywhere, though it may still come after the creed, at least as an option, in **Aus4**. One curious oddity of structure appears in **BrazR**, where the intercession precedes the ministry of the word, and another in **ChilR**, where the sacramental section is composed of thanksgiving-penitence-consecration. In America provision is made for the penitential section to come at every celebration, unlike the 1967 provision in **AmerR** which allowed for it only five times in the year. In addition, it may now be used after the intercession, instead of in the 1967 position between the creed and the intercession.

But the most obvious structural difference between rites remains the position of the penitential section itself. In the **CSI-LfA** family it comes at the beginning, and this is also found in **BrazR** and in **Aus3**, and it remains a possible option in **Aus4**. In **SAfr1** and **SAfr2**, despite their dependence on **Eng2** and **Eng3**, the penitential section is very deliberately moved to the beginning, whilst in **CNI**, despite its origins in **CSIR**, the **Eng3** position is followed for the penitential section. There is an understandable tendency for rites which may be led by a catechist

---

[1] The two areas are not comparable except in one point—they are the two areas where evangelicals have had a leading (or, in Chile, exclusive) role in the drafting of the liturgies. This has led to a direct approach to scripture with less obvious deference to Dix or strong pre-reformation traditions. See also pp.20-2 below.

or reader and used without the sacrament to have the penitence at the beginning so that it may be a regular part of the worship. But in Australia, New Zealand and Wales it is obviously preferred in this position (as it was in 1966) for reasons different from this. The pan-Anglican Document of 1965 set out this structure exclusively, and the 1969 one only just allows the English position. It is noticeable too that the Decalogue and the Lord's Summary are being joined with the penitential section (in whichever place it comes)[1] to avoid the 1662-**Eng2** suggestion that there are in fact *two* penitential sections in a service.

The Peace is now a more regular feature of the rites—perhaps epitomized by its non-existence in the 1965 pan-Anglican Document, and its modest appearance in the 1969 one. The Lord's Prayer is slowly moving to the position adopted first in **Eng2**—after the breaking of the bread and prior to reception. This had been copied by **Wal** in 1966 (following the draft order in England), but in **MAL** was not found in any rites apart from **Eng2** and **Wal**. It has now spread to **Ire1** and **CNI**, though further rites of the **CSI-LfA** family (such as **NZR** and **CSIR**) keep the 'Western' position at the end of the canon. Some rites in the **Eng2-Eng3** family have actually moved the Lord's Prayer to the end of the canon, e.g. **SAfr1**, **SAfr2**, **Kuch** and **NG**. Australia, which in **Aus2** and **Aus3** pioneered the use of the Lord's Prayer at the end of the intercessions, has in **Aus4** made Cranmer's post-communion position an optional alternative to this. **IranR** is an instance of a rite now trying the Australian position. **Eng1-2A**, which on the whole is trying to bring the **Eng2** structure to bear upon **Eng1** (as well as **Eng2**) material, still allows the 'western' position as an alternative.

(ii) *The Eucharistic Prayer*

The most obvious point about the eucharistic prayer is that right across the front there has been a further move away from a 'moment of consecration'. Manual Acts during the narrative of institution are now a comparative rarity, the two most obvious remaining instances being the American rites and **Ire1**. Even the skeletal **Amer3** requires in its rubrics *'In the course of the prayer, he takes the bread and cup into*

---

[1] They are found with it at the beginning in **Aus3** (and less certainly in **Aus4**), in **IranR** and in **NZR**; and after the intercessions with it in **Eng3** and **Ire1** (both with the English 'improved' version of the Decalogue [see p.59-69]) as also (with the Lord's Summary only) in **CNI**. The *'two* penitential sections' recur in **Amer1** and **Amer2**.

his hands, or places his hand upon them',[1] but the situation, though out of line with other trends, ought to be interpreted in the light of the traditional American use of an epiclesis following the narrative in the Eastern position. In eucharistic prayers containing this epiclesis, it would be hard to interpret the narrative of institution as the 'moment of consecration' anyway. **IreR** in 1967 was the last new rite to have five manual acts in the narrative,[2] now **Ire1** of 1972 is one of the last to have two.[3] **Eng3** has abolished them, and the **CSI-LfA** family had long before. It thus becomes even easier to see the whole prayer as consecratory. This in turn lays greater emphasis upon the unity of the whole prayer,[4] and its properly 'eucharistic' motif. It is now commonly labelled 'The Thanksgiving'.[5] Yet although the whole prayer consecrates, or perhaps because it does, drafters have felt the more free to import references to the work of the Spirit. Undoubtedly they have been influenced here by the way in which the new Roman canons have turned from the 'mechanical' cast of the old one, and make frequent mention of the Spirit.

This can be easily illustrated in the **Eng2-Eng3** family. **SAfr1** inserted into the **Eng2** canon (which it was reworking from its **MLT** form) a prayer for the work of the Spirit in the communicants, and this is continued in **SAfr2**. **Eng3** in its draft form had this feature also, and

[1] See **Amer3** on p.150 below, and cf. the rubrical directions in **Amer1** and **Amer2** (pp.137 and 146 respectively).

[2] The 1662-type **Aus1A** of 1972 retains five manual acts in the narrative, but this is simply being true to its own origins. It can hardly rank as a 'new' rite. **ChilR** retains three manual acts in the narrative—but it is in a separate catagory.

[3] It may be worth noting that **IreR** gave the prayer a heading 'Thanksgiving and Consecration' , whilst **Ire1** calls it 'The Thanksgiving over the Bread and the Wine'. So the term 'consecration' is itself disappearing from prominence, and this could be paralleled elsewhere.

[4] But it raises problems about 'supplementary consecration'—see **MAL** p.17 and pp.31-4 below.

[5] This point can be well made by a glance back to 1928. Then the title 'Thanksgiving' referred to the post-communion prayer of thanksgiving. At Lambeth in 1958 the bishops still referred to the 'consecration', though they allowed that it should be understood as being effected by thanksgiving. In **MAL** **EAUL**, **Eng2**, **Iran**, **IreR**, **LfA** and **Wal**, in some way or other call the eucharistic prayer 'The Thanksgiving' or 'The Great Thanksgiving'. **NZ** calls it 'The Eucharistic Prayer'. Others call it 'The Consecration' or do not have a title at all. Now in this volume the title 'Thanksgiving' is found also in rites from America (**Amer1**, **Amer2** and **Amer3** and the alternative prayers in the **Amer3** appendix), and from Australia (**Aus3** and **Aus4**), neither of which used it before. In addition it is found in rites from countries which had no text in **MAL**— e.g. **CNI**, **Kor1**, **NG**, **SAfr1** and **SAfr2**. **Kuch** adopts the title 'The Eucharistic Prayer'. 'The Consecration' remains only in the traditional **Aus1A** in **BrazR**, and in **ChilR** (where it heads a totally separate section from 'The Thanksgiving'). In **Eng1** in **MAL** the title was 'The Consecration', but it is the **Eng2** term, 'The Thanksgiving', which is found in **Eng1-2A**.

whilst it was before Synod an amendment was passed inserting 'by the power of your Spirit' into the petition that the gifts 'may be to us his body and his blood'.[1] This is now followed in **CNI**.[2] None of these texts amounts to a calling of the Spirit *upon* the elements (like the older epiclesis of Scotland and America, or the dual purpose one of **CSI**[3]), but all give greater prominence to the Spirit than the previous trends had suggested. There may here be the iceberg-tip of a groping after the role of the Spirit in our worship.

With the exceptions of **Aus4** and **ChilR**, which have their own experimental innovations, the structure of the prayer is becoming more and more a matter of consensus, and so familiar as not to need description. It is now characterized by Proper Prefaces,[4] by congregational acclamations after the narrative of institution,[5] by a gently increasing emphasis on the Spirit, already noted, and perhaps on eschatology too.[6] The major variant, apart from the points mentioned above, would seem to be some uncertainty as to whether the 'petition for consecration' (with or without reference to the Spirit) is appropriate in the Western position,[7] and some differing opinions about the sort of verbs to be used in the anamnesis.

---

[1] The mover based his appeal on the Anglican-Roman Catholic Statement on the Eucharist which says: 'Through this prayer of thanksgiving . . . the bread and wine become the body and blood of Christ by the action of the Holy Spirit, so that in communion we eat the flesh of Christ . . . ' (section 10).

[2] The texts may be compared in the pull-out table in Appendix F.

[3] But **CSIR** alters this to a petition that God would 'take us and this bread and wine . . . and make them your own by your Holy Spirit'—see p.287 below.

[4] Thus **NZR** has Proper Prefaces which **NZ** did not, and **Eng3** has a wide selection, where **Eng2** seemed to be moving towards giving them up (see **MAL** p.15). The only ones here without are **Tan**, which keeps the **LfA** invariable pattern, and **Aus3**, which has been superseded by **Aus4** which does have them.

[5] The **CSI-LfA** family has continued these, **Aus4** has introduced them, and the **Eng2-Eng3** family has gone over to them, starting with **SAfr1** in 1969. The main exceptions now to be noted are **WalR** (as this is solely an updating), **Ire1**, **NG** (which is close to **Eng2**), and some of the various American prayers. One of these is of course wholly responsive (it is to be found on p.152 below), but of the other seven five still do not use these particular acclamatory responses. **Aus4** and **CNI** have the acclamations very interestingly placed *after* the anamnesis. There is a good logic, though less precedent, for this.

[6] Once again, **Eng3** is a good instance, but the acclamations in general use also add their weight.

[7] It seems to be in the 'Western' position still in all rites in the **Eng2-Eng3** family (see Appendix F), except for **Aus4**. The **CSI-LfA** family tends to the 'Eastern' position after the anamnesis, as in **CSIR** and **NZR**. The Scottish-American tradition has always been strongly 'Eastern', but two of the new American prayers are 'Western' in this respect (see pp.154-5). There seems also to be a growing class of prayers which do not have an explicit petition relating to the elements at all—amongst them **Aus3**, **Aus4**, **IranR**, **Ire1** and **Tan**.

(iii) *Some Doctrinal Questions*

MAL was produced by a team of avowed evangelicals, partly to show both the active involvement of this wing of Anglicanism in the work of revision (since it was widely reported up till that date that they were opposed to anything which was not 1662) and also to show that the doctrinal direction of revision could no longer be asserted to be all of a uniform 'catholic' sort. In particular the 1960s saw great tensions over petitions for the departed and over the oblation of the elements in the elements in the anamnesis. There were slightly less tense questions relating to the sufficiency of the cross and the nature of the atonement, the special reference of the eucharist to the cross, the language of sacramental realism, the lack of emphasis on sin in modern confessions, the place of the reading of the law, and the desirability of intruding Benedictus qui Venit and Agnus Dei into the eucharistic action. This list could no doubt be lengthened further,[1] but it is the first two matters which have been the sticking-points. They were the subjects of the present writer's dissent from **Eng2** when originally drafted,[2] and they have recurred in a variety of ways in all the new writing of texts since 1964.

The section concerning the departed is a regular feature of the intercessions. It looks as though the compromises worked out in England in 1966-7 have been fruitful elsewhere. Thus **SAfr1** adopted the **Eng2** solution (despite the **Afr** tradition) and so did **Kuch**. Even the frankly catholicizing diocese of Papua New Guinea has not run to excess.[3] As might have been expected the Australian texts do not flirt with the concept, and neither do **ChilR, Ire1**. **Eng3** draws upon the report *Prayer and the Departed*[4] for its text, and the suspicion has grown that, because that particular text comes from the chapter about the *un*faithful departed in *Prayer and the Departed,* the Liturgical Commission was deliberately opening up a new category within the prayers—a category which might well have been highly controversial.[5]

---

[1] An astringent survey of these questions can be found in the Latimer Monograph *Holy Communion* edited by R. T. Beckwith and J. E. Tiller (Marcham 1972).

[2] See **MAL** p.119.

[3] **NG**, which at many points follows **Eng2** exactly, has a different pattern of intercessions, yet even so goes very little beyond **Eng2** on this doctrinal question.

[4] This was a report of the Archbishops' Doctrinal Commission (S.P.C.K. 1971). The relevant text is printed on p.55.

[5] The Liturgical Commission itself went so far as to say that the text was written 'so as not invariably to exclude' the mention of departed other than the faithful (*Commentary on Holy Communion Series* 3, p.16). But on a stricter reading of the whole text, it is controlled by the bidding at the head of the prayer

In **CNI** the same text is introduced by the words 'we remember before you your servants departed this life', and that might be thought to restrict the application more explicitly. In **Eng1-2A** the controversial clause from **Eng1** in the 1928 Prayer for the Church, which was a potent cause of controversy in 1966, has now been omitted.[1] An example of the texts which have caused division may be found in **Kor1,** whilst the American texts are not now so uniformly of the same mould as they have been since 1928.[2] The most sensitive places are perhaps those where an evangelical minority has to struggle with its conscience to use texts imposed by the dominant section of the church or alternatively to settle for an unfashionable 1662. It is perhaps not surprising that some defensiveness on this issue is still to be found by the contributors here from America, Scotland, South Africa and Wales.

The other main issue was the question of offering the elements to God. **Eng2,** after all the debate of 1966-7,[3] reverted to a 1549-type set of words in the anamnesis, 'we make the memorial of his saving death, *etc.*'. Of the other texts of the 1960s in **MAL, AmerR** and **ScotR** conserved the eighteenth century provisions of their respective countries, **Wal** had the 1928 verb 'we . . . set forth the memorial . . .', and **LfA** in its final text brought in an oblation in an indirect way. The others steered well clear of it, and it may well be that, now that it cannot and does not claim unanimity amongst all new Anglican rites, it has ceased to be quite such a live issue. However, it still provides a variety of phenomena in the texts, and should therefore come under scrutiny.

After **Eng2,** further work was done on the exact wording needed. In **MLT** G. J. Cuming translated 'in remembrance of me' at the end of the narrative of institution by 'as a memorial of me'[4] or alternatively 'to recall me' (echoing the earlier **LfA** language adopted by **NZ**). However, in the anamnesis itself he provided 'we commemorate'—a very pregnant translation, which does not seem to have made much further progress. When the South African Committee started from **MLT** in writing

---

'Let us pray for the church and for the world' (and if the bidding in 1662 controlled *its* meaning and application, then the same is true here). The departed are in no case in the world, though the faithful departed are in one sense in the church. Other departed do not seem to be in view in this wording. Cf. pp.41-2 below.

[1] Cf. the text (with variants shown) on p.64 below.
[2] See, e.g., the intercessions on pp.160 and 164-5, and note the comment of the American contributor in footnote 3 on p.127.
[3] For a brief review of this period see **MAL** pp.119-21.
[4] The NEB uses 'memorial' in translating 1 Cor. 11:24-5.

SAfr1, they wrote the anamnesis again from their own first principles, without regard to **MLT** at this point. Hence the classic **Scot-Amer** adjectival clause, 'we . . . celebrate . . . with these thy holy gifts which we now offer unto thee, the memorial . . .', came back (in 'you' form) in **SAfr1**. The American texts, on the other hand, show a more varied emphasis now, and the **Eng3** way through the difficulties has been followed in **CNI**. **Kuch** uses the **LfA** indirect oblation, and **Kor1** and **Mel** reflect an older (and quite undefensive) catholicism. **NZR** has moved on from 'recall' to 'celebrate the memorial', and **IranR**, **Ire1** and **Tan** all stand in direct succession to their own predecessors.

A curious text has arisen in **CSIR**, where an adjectival clause has appeared in the epiclesis, rather than in the anamnesis. Contrary to **CSI**'s own liturgical traditions, it almost looks as though somebody was determined to have this in *somewhere*. In South Africa, **SAfr2** allows the use of three eucharistic prayers, the first reading 'we . . . present before you the one perfect sacrifice', the second being **Eng3** *verbatim,* and the third being the second of the new Roman Catholic prayers. Being based on Hippolytus this last has a straight simple 'we offer you, Father, this life-giving bread, this saving cup'.

Opponents of the oblation would still want to say that the oblation cannot claim (what the texts so often seem to claim) that it is the direct response of obedience to our Lord's command 'do this in remembrance of me'. They still want to say that to offer the elements to God at this point is irrelevant and even disruptive to the eucharistic action. They still point out that it has led to very unsatisfactory theology in the past. They note that no mention is made of such an offering in the 1971 Anglican-Roman Catholic Statement on the Eucharist, signed by theologians of all schools of thought. They believe that no good rationale is available (certainly the second century ones are not favoured or will not serve to-day). But having said all that, it is also true that with the slide away from the narrative of institution as being the 'moment' of consecration, there is little suspicion to-day that the worst of medieval doctrines is implied when texts include an oblation of the bread and cup in the anamnesis. And certainly much progress has been made, perhaps particularly in England and Australia, in finding texts which with a rich biblical content can hold together all but the most obdurate from the two traditional wings of Anglicanism.[1]

---

[1] One odd instance of regression from irenic texts is in the anamnesis of **Can1**, published in 1974. Compared with the relevant point of **CanR** (see **LiE** p.142) it is clearly divisive. Cf. also **MAL** p.193.

There is a small further point to note—'The Offertory'. Attention was drawn in **MAL**[1] to the rising confusion between the offering of money and items of substantial worth to God, and the offering of the elements to God prior to starting the sacramental action. There is a diminishing emphasis on texts to incite the giving of money now that collections are held after the Peace—it would all ring rather strange.[2] Some rites still have no texts to accompany the offering up of the gifts: **Eng2**, for instance, had none in its final text,[3] and was followed by **MLT** and **SAfr1**. **Eng3** was intended to be the same, but General Synod added the extract from 1 Chron. 29 at the second revision stage. Thus **Eng1-2A** in turn has it. The American and Australian rites are also without provision. On the other hand there are nine rites in this volume which do make some use of 1 Chron. 29 and the phrase 'of your own we give you'. What sense is to be made of this? There is a receding nowadays from the theory of Dix that the bringing in of the bread and wine is the first action of the fourfold shape.[4] There is a deliberate avoidance by the Church of England Liturgical Commission of the term 'Offertory' at all. There is the curious warning in the 1969 Pan-Anglican Document[5] that 'care should be taken not to give any impression that the Offertory is an act of oblation in itself'—and yet alongside this there is this array of texts about giving the elements to God. Is there a way out in the preceding words in the Document 'A sentence which looks forward to the eucharistic action may be used: but care . . .'?

If there is a way out, it only brings us back to the question handled earlier about the meaning of making part of the eucharistic action itself an offering of the elements to God. For the Document *seems* to suggest (taking both the quoted sentences together) that the sentence which 'looks forward to the eucharistic action' is looking forward to an 'act of oblation'. If it does so, then it is presumably an oblation of the elements which is in view. And we still ask: *is* that 'the eucharistic action'? However it is far more probable that, despite the Document's warning, the 'Offertory' *will* in fact give an impression that it is 'an act of oblation

---

[1] **MAL** pp.13-14.

[2] The thin collection of 'Offertory Sentences' in Appendix B easily bears out this point.

[3] There had been a use of 1 Chron. 29 in the 'Draft Order' of December 1965, but it was removed (in response to the urging that there were too many 'little bits' in the rite) before the Commission signed it in March 1966.

[4] Thus **Eng3**, to take one example, has two separate rubrics—no. 24 reads *'The bread and wine are brought to the holy table . . .'* and no. 25 reads *'The president takes the bread and wine.'* (The money offerings come under no. 23, quite separately). No. 24 is very clearly *not* the 'taking'.

[5] See p.30 below.

in itself'. The more the elements are conjoined with the money in this action, then the more certain it will be that a muddle will continue here.[1]

If these doctrinal points are worth noting, yet the considerable advance in biblical richness from the first experimental texts of the 1960s is even more worth noting. Neither evangelical nor catholic can complain about a lack of emphasis on the work of our Lord, nor about any evasion of sin,[2] nor about the need for a fuller doctrine of the church, the Spirit, and eschatology. Each of these has been strengthened, the concept of mission has been heightened, and the round of the Church's year has been more deeply and memorably celebrated.[3]

(iv) *Ecumenical Rites*

MAL called ecumenical liturgy 'the coming method of revision',[4] but also forecast delays in the coming of it. This volume bears witness to that. Certainly the united Churches of South India, North India and Pakistan all have ecumenical uses (though a love of 1662 (**Ind**) or **IndR** may still be very strong 'on the ground' in these countries). But there is now no trace of **NUL**, and **EAUL** is only mentioned in these pages in passing—and once to raise an epitaph over it.[5] In America the Consultation on Church Union (COCU) produced a rite in 1968, which is permitted within PECUSA and indeed anticipated its 1970 rites with 'you' form language. But it never had enough ecumenical fervour behind it in the various Churches for it to win widespread acceptance. In South Africa the Church Unity Commission produced a rite in 1972, but it proved doctrinally divisive,[6] and the South African Liturgical Committee which, given a different text, might have chosen to underwrite it, instead went ahead with their own new rite. In England the Joint Liturgical Group published a booklet *Initiation and Eucharist*[7], and this outlines a possible unifying structure. But, in the

---

[1] Thus in the Church of England General Synod debate in July 1972, which led to the inclusion of 1 Chron. 29 after rubric no. 24 (cf. footnote 3 on p.23 above), much of the advocacy related to the stewardship of *money*, and the need to be didactic about it.

[2] Note for instance the reintroduction of the penitential section as a regular Sunday feature in the new American rites, as also the working over of the Decalogue in England (and the original report of 1971 in England made the Decalogue *mandatory* for the Sundays in Lent—but General Synod changed that).

[3] Note not only the new Proper Prefaces in Appendix C, but also the other new 'Proper' material in Appendix D.

[4] **MAL** p.6.

[5] See pp.234-5 and 247 below.

[6] See pp.200-1 below.

[7] S.P.C.K. London, 1972.

flurry of debating and implementing **Eng3**, it has so far gone virtually unnoticed.

It may therefore be fair to say that genuine progress in ecumenical relations on other fronts (particularly when it leads to actual unions) has strong implications for liturgical revision, but that liturgical proposals which outrun the actual desire for union are likely at best to be little more than irrelevant and at worst a conscience-salving substitute for genuine ecumenism.

(v) *Indigenization*

The call of the Dublin meeting of the A.C.C.[1] obviously came too late (and perhaps too equivocally also) to affect the liturgical revision recorded here, and guide it towards genuine indigenization. It must have been the very texts which follow which gave rise to the Council's frustration at simply being caught in an apparently imposed pattern of rites. And it is true that very few signs of genuinely national cultural patterns can be discerned in the actual rites. The tiny hints conveyed by **NG**'s rubric *'Bell, Drum or Rattle'* twice in the eucharistic prayer, or by **Kor1**'s rubric for the Peace *'Each person bows to those standing near him'* are as far as indigenous variants can be traced. Otherwise variants are more likely to reflect questions of churchmanship, or the predilections of a particular strong voice on the body which compiled the rite. It is not at all clear that the Dublin call can itself be implemented properly, and it will be gravely inhibited if the contrary call for 'expert help' from the centre be followed.

(vi) *Flexibility*

The experimental periods set up canonically within many member Churches of the Anglican Communion, as recorded in **MAL,** have not only brought to birth new experimental liturgies. They have also witnessed a growing demand for house communions, alternative intercessions and eucharistic prayers, and a getting away from rigid rubricism and legal-mindedness. Up to a point these desires are reflected in some of the rites which follow. The most flexible provision is that of PECUSA, where **Amer3** is simply an outline structure,[2] and eight eucharistic prayers are available (even including *extempore* or *ad hoc* insertions). In a different way the provision by opening 'Notes' of

---

[1] See p.8 above. It is the *second* quotation from *Partners in Mission* (i.e. that from p.48) which is in view here, but the first is also relevant.

[2] A somewhat fuller 'outline' has also been drafted in North India (cf. p.265 below).

alternative procedures for celebrating the rite, as in **Eng3** and **CNI**, has the same effect though with more restriction. The inclusion of three eucharistic prayers in **SAfr2** can hardly be listed as a help to flexibility, as it was matters of doctrine as much as pastoral sensitivity which seems to have inspired this pattern. It would seem that overall there is either much more official work to come in this field, or, as is canonically allowable in Canada, the alternative materials concerned will remain parochial and diocesan rites, and never achieve the same authorization as is required for inclusion here.[1]

(vii) *Future Trends*

Along with the hardly developed questions of ecumenism, indigenization and flexibility, another factor starts to appear in the contributions to this volume. Just as the experimental periods started roughly simultaneously in many places at once, so there now emerges a simultaneous inchoate quest for the definitive again. It seems that several of the texts here are only technically experimental, and are in fact semi-definitive. A little more use, a little more tinkering, a little more addition of alternatives—and they will be the new definitive rites of the late 1970s. This is overt in the chapters on South Africa and PECUSA, and almost as much so for Australia and New Zealand. Canada will presumably go for a national rite only in order to make it definitive. Chile is incorporating its new rite in a full Prayer Book. Wales is known to be at work on something much fuller than the interim 'study rite' shown here. And in the Church of England not only did the Liturgical Commission use the word 'definitive' when it first published **Eng3**, but General Synod has now passed a resolution asking for the provision of a People's Service Book which would contain authorized texts. None of these moves implies that becoming definitive will be easy, and it may get harder as it gets nearer. But there is no doubt it is a deeply felt desire of many, and it is just breaking surface at a Synodical level at the time of this volume's compilation.

APPENDIXES TO CHAPTER 1

1. The Second Pan-Anglican Document

The Document is self-explanatory, and relates itself to the previous Document, published in **MAL**. Its inclusion of 'Daily Office' provision

---

[1] This is perhaps the point to note the first reference in modern texts to 'The Agape'. This is mentioned in **Amer3** (see p.150 below), and in **CNI** (in the 'Notes' which follow the service). More will doubtless follow on this front.

reflects the discussion at Lambeth 1968, rather than the actual course of liturgical revision since. The idea was already running strongly in South Africa,[1] and has not been overlooked elsewhere. But it has hardly ranked as as important a subject in eucharistic revision as the title of the Document would suggest.

The structure and contents of the eucharist as drafted appear to coincide with the actual work done on the rites which follow. It seems odd to list the Peace as a final item in the Prayers. In no rite does it really appear like this, it is not in fact a time of prayer (in the normal sense) at all, and it belongs more naturally with the sacramental action which follows. Comment on 'The Offertory' has already been made above. The remainder would seem to be unexceptionable, if unexciting.[2]

THE STRUCTURE AND CONTENTS OF THE EUCHARISTIC LITURGY AND THE DAILY OFFICE

(A Report prepared at the request of the Liturgical Consultation held after the Lambeth Conference, August 1968)

The Lambeth Conference of 1958 passed a Resolution (76) which read:
  The Conference requests the Archbishop of Canterbury, in co-operation with the Consultative Body, to appoint an Advisory Committee to prepare recommendations for the structure of the Holy Communion service which could be taken into consideration by any Church or Province revising its Eucharistic rite, and which would both conserve the doctrinal balance of the Anglican tradition and take account of present liturgical knowledge.

No action was taken on this Resolution until the Liturgical Consultation held after the Anglican Congress in Toronto in August 1963 when four people (Archbishop Clark, Primate of Canada; Bishop Sansbury of Singapore; Dr. Massey Shepherd of the Episcopal Church, USA; and Archbishop Brown of Uganda) were appointed to draw up a document suggesting a basic shape or pattern for eucharistic liturgies. The document was circulated to metropolitans and liturgical consultants in March 1965, but it was not studied or used widely.

The Liturgical Consultation held in London after the Lambeth Conference in August 1968 requested Dr. Brown (now Bishop of

---

[1] See **MAL** pages 40-1.
[2] For a fuller and more critical comment see the Article 'The Pan-Anglican Document' by R. T. Beckwith in *The Churchman* January-March 1974. This is of course by the contributor who wrote on the 1965 Document in **MAL**.

St. Edmundsbury and Ipswich) and Dr. Jasper to undertake a revision of the document in the light of the considerable experience of liturgical revision since 1958, in consultation with the other scholars originally concerned. At the same time it was agreed that a similar document should be prepared on the structure of the Daily Office. After due consideration, however, it was thought wise to discuss both questions in a single document. There is nowadays a desire to relate more closely the Daily Office and the Eucharist. Such an arrangement is desirable not only on weekdays, but on Sundays, in those congregations which do not have the Eucharist as their principal act of worship. In many Churches of the Anglican Communion this is the case not from choice, but from necessity, because the number of priests is inadequate. This point is considered in the suggestions made in this document. Sections 1-3 could be used, with little modification, as a Daily Office or a Sunday service without eucharistic celebration: and it could be used either in the morning or in the evening. Experience has already proved this to be a perfectly satisfactory arrangement in a number of places.

Attention should be drawn to the fact that the 1958 Resolution referred specifically to the structure of the Holy Communion service. We have, therefore, concerned ourselves primarily with this aspect in this document: but it is very obvious that the problems of language will also play a large part in the work of liturgical revision for some time to come. There is clearly a desire to use more contemporary forms in all churches, as the work of the International Consultation on English Texts (ICET) indicates. This in itself poses a whole range of new questions, both practical and technical. We believe, however, that the search for contemporary liturgical language should be pursued vigorously; and provided there is a willingness to regard experimental texts as expendable, there is no reason why there should not emerge in the foreseeable future liturgical forms which are truly relevant to the stituations in which they are used.

Finally, we wish to emphasize that, although we have considered very carefully the comments and criticisms of the scholars whom we have consulted and have made several amendments to this document in the light of them, we alone bear the responsibility for what is written here.

Leslie St. Edmundsbury and Ipswich

Ronald Jasper

The Eucharistic Liturgy and the Daily Office

In the full eucharistic rite we identify a number of basic elements in the celebration:

1. The Preparation
2. The Ministry of the Word
3. The Prayers
4. The Offertory
5. The Thanksgiving over bread and wine
6. The Breaking of the Bread
7. The Communion
8. The Dismissal

1. *The Preparation*

  (*a*) The celebrant greets the congregation. This greeting could have reference to the season (e.g. at Easter—V. The Lord is risen. R. Alleluia. Indeed he is risen). This greeting should lead into a prayer asking for the help of God the Holy Spirit (e.g. the Collect for Purity or a seasonable collect).

  (*b*) An act of praise and adoration. The Gloria in Excelsis is very suitable; or a psalm or a hymn (optional on weekdays).

  (*c*) A confession of sins, with absolution or prayer for forgiveness (optional on weekdays). Alternatively, this might be placed with the prayers (No. 3) after the Ministry of the Word.

2. *The Ministry of the Word*

  (*a*) Scripture Readings, including Psalms. Three lessons should be provided, from the Old Testament, Epistles, and Gospels; although it is likely that in many cases only two of the three readings will be used. These readings can be interspersed with psalms, canticles, or hymns.

  (*b*) Sermon (optional on weekdays).

  (c) Creed—either the Nicene Creed or the Apostles' Creed (optional).

3. *The Prayers*

  (*a*) Intercessions with thanksgivings. These may be offered in many forms. A litany form allowing for extemporary prayer and congregational participation is widely appreciated.

  (*b*) A confession of sins, with absolution or prayers for forgiveness—if not used in the Preparation (1) (optional on weekdays).

  (*c*) The Peace.

These first three elements of the service may be used alone, as one of the Daily Offices: and especially when used on Sundays they may be supplemented with an Act of Thanksgiving and Dedication and the Lord's Prayer before the Pax. In this case the first half of the 1662 Blessing might be regarded as an appropriate form for the Pax. When using these elements as either the Morning or the Evening Office, care should be taken to ensure a systematic use of psalmody and a variety of canticles. Psalmody, canticles, and lessons should be used in both the Daily Offices, although not necessarily in equal proportions; and care should be taken to avoid unnecessary duplication of material.

4. *The Offertory*
A sentence which looks forward to the eucharistic action may be used: but care should be taken not to give any impression that the Offertory is an act of oblation in itself.

5. *The Thanksgiving over bread and wine*
The basic elements and progression of this eucharistic prayer are:
  (a) Sursum Corda.
  (b) The proclamation and recital of the mighty acts of God in creation, redemption, and sanctification.
  (c) The Narrative of the Institution.
  (d) The anamnesis of the work of Christ in Death, Resurrection, and and Ascension 'until he come'. It is recognized that this is the most difficult section of the prayer in view of the different doctrinal emphases which are expressed and recognized within the Anglican Communion. The whole concept of anamnesis is, however, so rich in meaning that it should not be impossible to express it in such a way that the needs of everyone are met. Whatever language is adopted should, however, avoid any idea of a propitiatory sacrifice or a repetition of Christ's sacrifice. The 'once for all' character of his work must not be obscured.
  (e) The prayer that through the sharing of the bread and wine and through the power of the Holy Spirit we may be made one with our Lord and so renewed in the Body of Christ.
The whole prayer is rightly set in the context of praise, e.g. Sursum Corda and Sanctus.

6. *The Breaking of the Bread*
This may be done in silence or may be accompanied by suitable words (e.g. 1 Cor. 10:16-17).

7. *The Communion*
  (a) The Communion Devotions. These must not be elaborate or distracting from the main action of the liturgy. The basic devotion

can be the Lord's Prayer alone, the doxology of which suitably
expresses the element of praise at this point.

(*b*) The Communion.

(*c*) The post-communion devotion. This may take the form of a prayer
and/or a hymn or canticle of thanksgiving and dedication: but
whatever material is used should make the point clear that God's
people are to witness and serve as the body of Christ in the world,
strengthened by his grace and looking forward to the fulfilment of
his promise.

8. *The Dismissal*

It may be found appropriate, as a concession to people's traditional
expectation at this point, or for the benefit of non-communicants who
are present, to associate a blessing with the actual words of dismissal.
It is desirable, however, and certainly logical, that no further devotions
should follow the dismissal. This is the final action in the rite.

2. Supplementary Consecration

Wigan in **LiE** omitted all the provisions for Supplementary Consecration from the texts in the volume, and instead gave his own brief
summary of their contents in an Appendix.[1] By the time **MAL** was
published in 1968 it was clear that new concepts of consecration and
of the role of the eucharistic prayer were giving rise to doubts about the
manner of Supplementary Consecration. The tendency was simply to
use previous procedures, either, like 1662, with the sole use of the
requisite half of the narrative of institution, or, like **Scot**, with the
addition of the epiclesis. These procedures would not fit well with the
eucharistic prayers of the 1960s, and the texts were printed in their
respective liturgies in **MAL** and in chapter 2 space was given by the
editor to a discussion of ways of improving the provision.[2] Nevertheless,
where new ideas had arisen, they were often rejected on principles
drawn from previous rites, not from the new ones to which they related.
In New Zealand the 1968 Synod withdrew the provision printed with
NZ in **MAL**, and made new provision, including the 1662 method as an
alternative.[3] In England various bishops tried to impose the 1662
method on **Eng2**, where a rubrical lacuna had given scope for the taking
of more in silence.

---

[1] **LiE** pp.250-2 (second edition 252-4).
[2] **MAL** pp.17-18.
[3] See p.366 below.

The 1968 Lambeth Consultation on Liturgy, as noted in the chapter above, asked the Church of England Liturgical Commission to give further study to the problem. There was already a feeling that *repetition* of either a short part of the whole of the eucharistic prayer was improper. The Church of England Commission had in fact, in the original report containing **Eng2** in April 1966, already said 'we feel that this whole question requires further discussion, and we propose to produce a report at a later date'[1], so that the task was already on their agenda. The matter was complicated, however, by the fact that when the Archbishops remitted it to the Liturgical Commission, they specifically asked for a single provision to be made. The Commission agreed as a matter of principle that what was needed was to *extend the scope of the original Thanksgiving,* not to repeat some part of it. They agreed that more should be added before the original supply of the particular element was exhausted. They agreed it was theologically proper to use an explanatory form of words whilst making the addition, or to do it in silence. But they could *not* agree on which single procedure to propose. Silence was already in use under the **Eng2** lacuna, and was not to be extinguished, whilst a form of words was the procedure appealing to the great majority of the Commission.[2] The report to the Archbishops thus included a minority note, and the Archbishops did not publish or circulate it, but instead referred it to the Doctrinal Commission.[3] The latter Commission accepted the principle of alternatives—a form of words (they altered the Liturgical Commission's proposal) or the use of silence—in an unpublished report of December 1969. The Liturgical Commission accepted this *verbatim,* and printed the provisions in its report containing **Eng3** in its original drafting in September 1971. They defended the alternative as follows:

'. . . As a result [of our deliberations and of consulting the Doctrinal Commission] we suggest the basic principle of bringing additional bread or wine into the sacramental action by associating them with the already consecrated elements, before the supply of the latter

---

[1] *An Order for Holy Communion* (S.P.C.K. London April 1966) p.xi.

[2] The text they proposed was:

If either or both of the consecrated elements prove insufficient, the priest shall return to the holy table and there add to what remains, saying:

Having given thanks to thee, O God, over the bread and the cup in remembrance of our Lord Jesus Christ, we pray that this bread/wine may also be unto us his body/blood.

[3] See D. L. Edwards *Ian Ramsey: Bishop of Durham—A Memoir* (Oxford 1973) pp.90-91.

has been completely exhausted. For this there is good historical precedent.

'The question then remained whether this should be done in silence, or with a brief form of words. In favour of silence it may be said that it causes the least possible disruption to the continuity of the service; while in favour of a form of words, it may be said that it clarifies and defines what is happening and has a certain didactic usefulness. Neither we nor the Doctrine Commission could find any theological objections to either method; but we were unable to agree which should be adopted if only one method were to be provided. We have therefore provided a rubric which permits both methods; but we would not necessarily wish to resist the reduction of these two ways to one should the Synod wish to do this.'[1]

The actual text at that time read as follows:

'35 *If either or both of the consecrated elements are likely to prove insufficient, the president returns to the holy table and adds more, either in silence or with these words :*
>   Having given thanks to you, Father, over the bread and cup, as your Son our Lord Jesus Christ commanded, we receive this bread/wine also as his body/blood.'

However, the option of silence was disliked in Synod, and an amendment to delete it was successfully moved in February 1972.[2] Further discussion before the Steering Committee showed that some wanted a definite citation of our Lord's words (without necessarily having a direct repetition of the narrative of institution). So a borrowing was made from the American provision, and in the second revision stage in July 1972 the form of words above was altered to that which appears in **Eng3** in the next chapter.

Thus the Anglican Communion never got the guidance requested from the Church of England, rather the Church of England went borrowing from elsewhere. Certainly, in **Aus3** (1969) the Australian Commission explored the concept of 'adding' more bread or wine to

---

[1] *A Commentary on Holy Communion Series* 3 (S.P.C.K. London 1971) pp.26-7.

[2] The amendment went through very easily after it was supported by the then Archbishop of Canterbury with these words 'After all, the consecration of bread and wine is one of the most stupendous things that ever happens in the physical world . . . What I shudder from with my whole being is the thought of this reconsecration, by being silent, taking place without the Christian community in the building knowing it is happening.' (*Report of Proceedings of General Synod,* February 1972, Vol. 3 no.1 p.160).

the existing stock (with a brief formula[1]), but they dropped this in 1973 from **Aus4**, and it is castigated gently in passing by the Australian contributor.[2] An uncertain use of repetition remains as an option in America, and as the only provision in **Ire1**. A phrase like 'we set apart this bread and cup' is found in **Aus3**, **CSIR**, **Iran** and **NZR**. No provision at all is found in seven of the rites here. **Aus4** does use repetition—the repetition of the thanks *for* the bread and/or cup which is a distinctive feature of the Australian thanksgiving. **SAfr2** follows the American use, whilst **CNI** follows **Eng3**, and quotes from the first paragraph quoted above from the Church of England Commission's *Commentary* as an explanation.[3]

It is likely that the lacunae and alternatives and copying of each other represent a continuing uncertainty in the various countries. Possibly the paragraphs of the English *Commentary* which have been quoted are the nearest to public advice which the various Commissions will ever receive. The principles are obviously more important than the texts. But it is an open question whether, once the principles are right, we cannot do better in the actual provision made.

[1] See p.342 below.
[2] See p.324 below.
[3] See the rubric on p.279 below.

PART II
THE UNITED KINGDOM AND EIRE

CHAPTER 2

THE CHURCH OF ENGLAND

Constitutional

Eng2[1] was passed for a four-year period of experimental use on 7 July 1967 under the Prayer Book (Alternative and Other Services) Measure 1965.[2] Since 1967 this Measure has first been amended, and secondly superseded.

In 1970 the Church of England began a new phase in church government under the Synodical Government Measure of 1969. The Convocations of the Clergy were reduced in number (from 390 to 250), mostly through the departure of *ex officio* members, and the House of Laity was reduced similarly and joined with the Convocations into a single 'General Synod'. The effects upon liturgical procedure were that agreement was now necessary in *three* separate Houses (Bishops, Clergy, and Laity) when new alternative services were authorized, and not in five (including the division between Canterbury and York) as it had been before. In addition the whole Synod sits as a single body, so that the House of Laity has been unable to exercise the particular separate influence it came to possess in 1966-7; on the other hand its members have been able to table resolutions and amendments direct, and have not had to wait in such cases for the service concerned to go back to the clergy sitting separately before it could be actually amended. The rules of Synodical Government require that liturgical matters must have a 'provisional approval' stage (when a simple majority in the whole Synod suffices) and a 'final approval' (when, under the 1965 Measure as amended, the two-thirds majorities in the three separate Houses have to be gained). Before provisional approval there are two earlier stages in the Synod, and by its own Standing Orders Synod has come to ease the process by appointing a revision committee for particular services. Members of Synod wishing to move amendments may appear before the Committee and talk through the desired change there, often

---

[1] The processes of drafting and authorizing **Eng2** are set out in **MAL,** pp.118-22, and the text of it is in **MAL,** pp.131-40.

[2] The main provisions of this Measure are described in **MAL,** pp.114-5. See also C. O. Buchanan, *Recent Liturgical Revision in the Church of England* (Grove Booklet 14, Grove Books, Bramcote, Nottingham 1973).

getting it into uncontroversial and acceptable form before it reaches the floor of the Synod.[1]

Synodical Government has also meant that from 1 January 1972 the Liturgical Commission has ceased to be an Archbishops' Commission and has become a Commission of Synod. Its members are appointed by the Archbishops still, but with the advice of the Standing Committee of Synod, and on behalf of the Synod. Members appointed or reappointed in January 1972 will serve till 31 December 1975.

The procedures briefly outlined above show how the Synod operated in the authorization of liturgical matters in the period 1970-75. However, with the passing of the Church of England (Worship and Doctrine) Measure 1974,[2] a new situation has dawned. The 1965 Measure is now superseded from the point in 1975 when it comes into force,[3] and Parliament retains no power over the liturgical arrangements of the Church of England (except that the 1662 Prayer Book cannot be abolished without General Synod bringing another Measure before Parliament[4]). With this one limitation Synod can authorize services for any length of time, can amend them at will, and can make them definitive and no longer experimental. The new Canons (which embody the content of the Measure) received Final Approval in Synod in February 1975, and, at the time of going to press, await the Royal Assent and promulgation.

The main period of Eng2—1967-71

Eng2 was authorized originally for four years in 1967, but its form had been largely determined in the years 1964-5. Thus it came just too early for the move from a 'thou' to a 'you' form of address to God. This may well have been for the best, as it is doubtful whether congregations

---

[1] Standing orders were altered slightly in 1973, so that the revision committee now *determines* the form of the text laid before Synod at the Single Revision stage.

[2] The text of the new Measure, with a brief introduction and commentary, is contained in C. O. Buchanan *Supplement for 1973-4 to Recent Liturgical Revision in the Church of England* (Grove Booklet no. 14A, Grove Books 1974).

[3] The Measure passed the House of Lords without a vote on 14 November 1974, and the House of Commons voted 145-45 in favour on 4 December 1974. It gained the Royal Assent on 12 December 1974, and comes into force on a date to be chosen by the Archbishops. It virtually repeals not only the 1965 Measure, but also the famous 1662 Act of Uniformity, the 1872 Act of Uniformity Amendment Act, and several others.

[4] This reserved power for Parliament will read very oddly in parts of the world other than England. And in England itself it is clear that the power is of no account. Any further Measure which gave that last power to Synod would hardly encounter opposition from Parliament (e.g. in the year 2000), and it is much more likely that the power will be conferred long before that in some further disestablishing moves.

would have taken so readily to the rite in the months following its authorization if it had required the further jump into a 'you' form of address. However, even before it was authorized the Liturgical Commission was under pressure to produce more modern forms. In summer 1966 in an 'Additional Introductory Note' to its Report on Morning and Evening Prayer the Commission wrote that it was aware of a desire for modern language, and in December 1966, in the Baptism and Confirmation report[1], the Commission said it was 'engaged in the preparation of texts'. Thus work on the modernization of texts was under way long before the rite of 'language-in-transition' (i.e. **Eng2**) reached authorization.

The first fruit of this work by the Commission was *Modern Liturgical Texts*.[2] In this a series of translations was offered with a 'main purpose' to 'provoke discussion'. The translations were in the first place renderings of traditional liturgical material, such as the Lord's Prayer and Creeds, but they also included an updating of existing *Second Series* services, as entire services. The last of these was **Eng2**, the Communion service. The version there was not produced by the Commission at large but by one man, Canon Geoffrey Cuming.[3] The rite included the Commission's drafts for 'you' form texts of the Lord's Prayer etc., and broke new ground with a neat paraphrase of the Agnus Dei which was later adopted by ICET.[4] It did not of itself much affect later developments in England,[5] but it provided basic texts for ICET when it started work immediately after,[6] and the rite was also very influential upon **SAfr1** in 1969, and through it on **SAfr2** in 1973.[7]

In 1969 a carefully devised questionnaire on **Eng2** was circulated to the parishes in order to provide evidence of reactions as a basis for further drafting. This established that the Old Testament reading was

---

[1] This was the report which led on in 1967 and 1968 to the authorization of Second Series Baptism and Confirmation services.

[2] Published by S.P.C.K. London in August 1968. The Communion rite in it is denominated **MLT** in this volume. See also p.4 above.

[3] This was not of course mentioned at the time, when the compiler remained anonymous, but is now common knowledge.

[4] See the text in ICET 8 on p.398.

[5] It is arguable that the rite could be used legally in 1968 in the Church of England, without authorization, as it only included 'variations which are not of substantial importance' which the minister can make 'at his discretion' under Clause 5 of the Measure. The Dean of Worcester later claimed in Synod to have thus used it for six months when at Oxford (*General Synod: Report of Proceedings*, Vol. 3, No. 1, p.24), but there is no other record of its use.

[6] See pp.10-11 above.

[7] The text of **MLT** can be reconstructed almost entire from **SAfr1**, for the Ante-Communion and the penitential section, with the addition of the eucharistic prayer, which is printed out here in Appendix F.

little used,[1] that the confession was thought to be too slight, that the position of the Lord's Prayer last thing before Communion had passed into popular acceptance, and that the first post-communion prayer was hardly used at all, whilst the second was universally applauded. The 28,000 questionnaires which were processed also gave some evidence from the 'write-in' space left on the backs that a return to some greater emphasis on the atonement was widely desired.

1969 saw another further move by the Commission towards the revision. In 1967 the Joint Liturgical Group had produced a Calendar with eucharistic lectionary for Sundays in *The Calendar and Lectionary*.[2] In 1969 the Church of England Liturgical Commission produced its own report *The Calendar and Lessons*,[3] which took up the previous ecumenical work, edited it, and enlarged it to provide for the *Sanctorale* of the Anglican Calendar, as well as for the extra Sundays needed whilst Easter is still moveable. Psalmody for each occasion was also added, and the Collects from *The Daily Office*[4] included.

In 1970 the ICET texts became available,[5] and time started to run out for **Eng2**. Thus the need for the revision of the text became fairly urgent. A decision was taken at high level not to put the ICET texts before the General Synod (which first met in November 1970) until they could come in the context of the 'Series 3' service.[6] Action was initiated at that first meeting to extend the life of **Eng2** by one year to July 1972, in order to allow time for the work on the revision to be completed.

Meanwhile the Commission itself was changing over in personnel. In 1968 amongst others a lecturer in English from Cambridge, Dr. David L. Frost, was added, whilst between 1967 and 1970 membership was affected by the deaths of E. C. Ratcliff, A. M. Farrer, and K. N. Ross, and by the departure to Jerusalem of J. D. Wilkinson.[7]

---

[1] This was hardly surprising. The 1662 Epistles and Gospels were still being read with the Collect from the 1662 Book. The only existing table of Old Testament readings was those drawn from the C.I.P.B.C. Prayer Book and authorized with *First Series* (**Eng1**) in 1966 (see **MAL** p.121). Most of the clergy were probably unaware of their existence, and so stuck to the easier course of Epistles and Gospels only.

[2] Ed. R. C. D. Jasper (Oxford 1967). See **MAL** p.121. For its overseas influence, see particularly chapter 12 below (footnote 5 on p.198).

[3] S.P.C.K. London 1969. For a more detailed account see C. O. Buchanan, *Recent Liturgical Revision in the Church of England* p.31.

[4] S.P.C.K. London 1969. A discussion of this entrenching of these collects is on pp.4-5 above.

[5] See p.11 above.

[6] See footnote 4 on p.43 below.

[7] The Commission itself noted this factor in 1971 in *A Commentary on Holy Communion Series 3* (S.P.C.K. London) pp.23-4.

The Compilation of **Eng3**, *1970-71*

Inspection will show the new drafting which was done for Series 3.[1] Work on the eucharistic prayer was the most important, and this began in April 1970 by a three-cornered correspondence between Canon Jasper, Kenneth Ross, and the present writer. Progress at most significant points had been already achieved when Kenneth Ross died in June that year, and the Commission was glad to accept the substance of the drafting. Reference was had in the late Autumn to the Doctrinal Commission, and the only notable contribution by that body was the suggestion of 'looking for the *fullness* of his coming in glory' as a way through a drafting problem in the anamnesis[2]. In the last stages of drafting a suggestion from outside the Commission involved the use of 'celebrate' at the crucial point in the anamnesis, and with this the work was done. The eucharistic prayer as it came from the Commission in September 1971 can be seen in the table in Appendix F.

Another sensitive drafting point was the section about the departed in the Prayers (now including thanksgiving as well as petition). The Doctrinal Commission produced a report in January 1971,[3] and the Commission had access to it beforehand. There was no question of continuing the controversial Scottish Litany of **Eng2**,[4] and the sole issue was the drafting of this one section. The matter was slightly more complicated than in 1966-7, as there was now a desire from some to mention the *un*faithful departed in the prayers. The report *Prayer and the Departed* included some discussion of prayer in relation to non-Christians who had died, but added as a suggested text a very minimal 'We commend all men to your unfailing love'. On the Liturgical Commission this form of words was picked up and used in the summary prayer, but the heading to the prayer ('Let us pray for the Church and for the world') does not properly include the unfaithful,[5] and the text

[1] Hereafter called **Eng3**.

[2] The Doctrinal Commission's help on the question of Supplementary Consecration is described above on p.32. Ironically, both that suggestion and the one mentioned here came to nothing, but were replaced in the course of events in Synod later.

[3] *Prayer and the Departed* (S.P.C.K. London 1971). It was accompanied by a monograph by the late Bishop of Durham, Dr I. T. Ramsey, who was chairman of the Doctrinal Commission. This was entitled *Our Understanding of Prayer* (S.P.C.K. London). *Prayer and the Departed* is discussed on p.21 above also.

[4] Apart from the problem it had caused in 1967 (cf. **MAL** p.120), the questionnaires showed it was not in use.

[5] In *A Commentary on Holy Communion Series* 3 the Commission used the very cautious words, 'we have also modified the final section [of the prayers] so as not invariably to exclude the commemoration of other departed apart from the faithful departed' (p.16). But even this is stretching the heading. See also p.21 above.

includes the faithful departed in such a restrained way as to cause little alarm. 'We commend' describes our trustful approach to God, and does not petition him at all.

Three other areas of new work need to be noted. There was, firstly, a serious attempt to simplify the structure and reduce the options. The Decalogue (with the New Testament additions to each commandment) was grouped with the penitential section, and the Comfortable Words became an alternative lead in to the exhortation to confession. The sacramental section (i.e. 'The Communion') started with the mandatory Peace, and, as drafted, the rite then ran as a single text without options from the Peace to the administration.[1] This was designed to make it easy to follow and to have a unifying effect.

The second area of new work was the seasonal provision. There was the two year lectionary, with themes, psalmody, and 'controlling reading' drawn from *The Calendar and Lessons* and mentioned above. But there was also a new and fuller set of 'propers' for major festivals. Proper Prefaces were a very traditional concept, but they had seemed in the liturgies of the 1960s to be fading from the liturgical scene.[2] On the Liturgical Commission, voices were for a time heard to urge that the **Eng2** eucharistic prayer should have its preface slightly enlarged from the few brief Proper Prefaces included, and should then be made invariable. Instead, after various experiments with propers which would accompany the preparing of the Table, the Commission came back to the Preface, and quite deliberately wrote eleven 'proper thanksgivings', often by entirely new drafting.[3] This central provision was flanked by three further categories of propers, all optional and all in some degree innovatory. These were the opening seasonal sentences, the sentences after communion, and the seasonal blessings.[4] The first

---

[1] The sequence does not appear so simple now, as Synod later attached the quotation from 1 Chron. 29 to the rubric at section 24 about bringing the elements to the Table—an addition which is misleading in its position (do we really offer the bread and wine to God here? and do we offer them as elements of real substantial value, which the biblical text teaches?) It is also distracting as an option where no options were meant to be. The later options of the Benedictus qui Venit and the Agnus Dei are printed out *after* the administration at section 34, and can be used anywhere in 'The Communion', i.e. in the sacramental half of the service. Their location was deliberate, so as not to intrude into the main sequence.

[2] The conclusion in **MAL**, '. . . the fuller Preface . . . usually leads to an invariable form . . .' (p.15), may be slightly overstated, but only slightly.

[3] These are set out in the Table in Appendix C, where their use in other rites is also shown.

[4] These are set out in three columns in Appendix D, where their use by **CNI**, and to a lesser extent by **Aus4** and **Irel**, is also shown.

of these paralleled the modern fashion in Morning and Evening Prayer, the second was a working up of an idea mentioned once in passing by the late E. C. Ratcliff, and the third drew upon a medieval concept to be found in traditional 'Benedictionals'.

The third area of new work was the writing of three totally new prayers by Dr. Frost. Two of these were later removed by Synod, and are printed after the service at the end of this chapter. The third, the prayer at section 39, remained with only one word changed by Synod ('Keep' for 'Anchor'). The prayers were a bold and successful attempt to write modern liturgical prose with rich biblical imagery and considerable variety of grammar and sentence structure.[1] The service thus written went to the Bishops in April 1971[2], was approved by them, and was published as a report on 16 September 1971 in a white booklet. The *Commentary* already mentioned was published at the same time.[3] The service received very favourable reviews (apart from the ICET Lord's Prayer[4]). The text as it then stood can be reconstructed from the *apparatus* in the text set out below. This 1971 text passed immediately into use in various places outside England, though it was only available in the 'report' form, which was expensive for a congregational text.[5] In England itself it had of course no authority until it should have been authorized by General Synod under the terms of the Prayer Book (Alternative and Other Services) Measure 1965.

Eng3 *before General Synod*

Synod's first debates on **Eng3** came on 10 November 1971. The general debate went very happily, but when the first revision stage started,

[1] For a fuller discussion, see Dr. Frost's chapter in *The Eucharist To-Day : Studies on Series 3*, ed. R. C. D. Jasper (S.P.C.K. 1974) and his booklet *The Language of Series 3* (Grove Booklet 12, Grove Books 1973).

[2] This was in accordance with a procedure mentioned in **MAL** on p.117. The theory is that the bishops either send the proposals back to the Commission on this private viewing, or they allow them to be published and are prepared to back them in public. History presents a series of exceptions to this, of which **Eng3** is one.

[3] A third report relating in part to **Eng3** was published two months later. This was *The Presentation of the Eucharist* (S.P.C.K. London 1971), but although its copyright is vested in the Liturgical Commission, the Commission takes no responsibility for it.

[4] It was noted above that the ICET texts were not brought before Synod (or anybody else really) from the time of their publication in *Prayers we have in Common* in April 1970 until their inclusion in **Eng3** in September 1971. Minds were not prepared for them, and the correspondence columns of the national newspapers (let alone the Church Press) indicated this very strongly.

[5] Two places which came to the editor's attention, long after the final 1973 text of **Eng3** had been authorized and printed, were Emmanuel Tel Aviv (in Israel) and St. Margaret's Moshi (in Tanzania)!

changes unwelcome to the Commission were put through.[1] In particular the two prayers printed after the service at the end of the chapter were deleted. A laborious day ended with the Synod having only reached the acclamations at section 29. On the other hand, no amendments had been tabled which touched the canon, apart from those relating to the acclamations. The debate was adjourned, and would-be movers of motions or amendments were referred to the Liturgical Steering Committee which sat as a revision committee during that winter.

The completion of that first revision stage took two more afternoons in February 1972. An amendment which would have reintroduced 'memorial' in the anamnesis was then rejected, and the option of silence for further consecration was deleted.[2] The then Archbishop of Canterbury was tempted into saying that he thought the anamnesis was not 'a good piece of liturgical or doctrinal composition',[3] and with this backing the service was referred to the House of Bishops 'for consideration of the theology of the service, particularly in the light of the recent Anglican/Roman Catholic statement on Eucharistic Doctrine and the pastoral problems arising from four Eucharistic Rites concurrently authorized.'[4]

On 9 July 1972 the second revision stage saw further amendments. A report came from the House of Bishops which omitted any mention of the two matters to which particular attention had been drawn, but suggested some small changes. The Steering Committee had also come to agreed amendments, and was accepting others being moved by members of Synod. The broad changes were: the 'Decalogue' and Summary of the Law were moved to an appendix to the service; a re-written confession was introduced keeping some elements of the original one[5] and some of that which had replaced it in November 1971; an optional use of the quotation from 1 Chronicles 29 was attached to section 24;[6] a reference to 'by the power of your Spirit' was added to the 'petition for consecration';[7] the third acclamation was changed;

---

[1] For the reactions of one member of the Commission who was in the gallery that day see D. L. Frost, *op. cit.*, pp.17-22.

[2] For a fuller account see above pp.33-4.

[3] General Synod: *Report of Proceedings*, Vol. 3, No. 1, p.189 (which records the word '*pro*position', surely a misprint).

[4] The Anglican/Roman Catholic Statement on the Eucharist had been released on 31 December 1971. See pp.8-9 above.

[5] Compare the original on p.70 with the final one on p.54-5.

[6] See footnote 3 on p.4 above.

[7] The changes here and in the next two items can be traced out by comparing the two eucharistic prayers in parallel columns beside each other in the Table in Appendix F. This particular change arose from advocacy which relied heavily upon the Anglican/Roman Catholic Statement on the Eucharist.

a new drafting of the anamnesis was accepted; 'the test' became 'the time of trial' in the Lord's Prayer;[1] a new form of supplementary consecration was devised;[2] and some of the seasonal material and notes were slightly altered. On a show of hands the service then obtained 'provisional approval' almost unanimously.

The House of Bishops has the responsibility of deciding the form in which a service provisionally approved shall come before Synod for final approval. On this occasion they changed one word—substituting 'forgives' for 'pardons' in the first line of the absolution for the sake of euphony. The service then came before Synod for 'final approval' on 7 November 1972. It gained its two-thirds majorities in each of three Houses; by 27-0 in the House of Bishops, 148-10 in the House of Clergy, and 123-9 in the House of Laity. The service thus gained a four-year period of trial use from 1 February 1973.[3] One further amendment remained to be made. By an oversight, when the nine-Sunday pre-Christmas season of *The Calendar and Lessons* had been reduced to the four Sundays of Advent (with the preceding five reverting to being the Sundays at the end of the previous year's Trinity season[4]), the readings for those five Sundays had been attached to the wrong years (so that they no longer ran in their own sequence with the four Sundays of the *following* year's Advent season). This was reversed in the Synod session of February 1973, but was of course not included in the copies already printed by then.

Series 1 *and* Series 2 (**Eng1** *and* **Eng2**)

Eng2 was originally due to expire in July 1971, but at the first sessions of the new General Synod in November 1970 and February 1971 provisional and final approval were given to extend this period by one

---

[1] 'Holy' had returned to 'hallowed' in February 1972, but the proposed restoration of 'temptation' had been withdrawn when two Professors of Theology had spoken against it. 'The time of trial' arose from consultations behind the scene, including the members of the Liturgical Commission. Synod was asserting its independence of ICET in altering the Lord's Prayer at all. Paradoxically, Synod's own prayers had been composed and printed with the ICET Lord's Prayer in 1970, and this continued in use at each session of Synod right through to 1975.

[2] See the discussion in ch. 1, pp.34-5 above.

[3] The service was authorized from a point 12 weeks after the debate so that S.P.C.K. and the Privileged Presses could have printed copies available everywhere in time. The green booklets were duly published on 18 January 1973.

[4] This was inevitable as the Prayer Book (Alternative and Other Services) Measure 1965 did not permit experimentation with the Calendar, and a separate Measure would have been needed to alter it. Proposals to change the Calendar were considered by the Synod in February 1974, and remitted to the Liturgical Commission. See footnote 1 on p.6 above.

year, to give time for **Eng3** to be completed. However, action on the Liturgical Steering Committee in Summer 1971 led to Canon Jasper stating in Synod on 10 November 1971, when introducing **Eng3**, that the Committee now thought that **Eng2** ought to run alongside **Eng3** for a substantial period, and would be introducing proposals to this effect. This policy arose from the realization that, quite apart from any delays encountered in authorizing **Eng3**, it would be unwise to let **Eng2** expire the day **Eng3** was authorized. Worshippers needed reassurance that no gun would be held at their heads to go over to **Eng3** on a set day; if they did not get this, then Synod might conceivably reject **Eng3** altogether, and, even if it did not, the introduction of the new rite would certainly be a cause of considerable friction. Thus in February 1972 the Steering Committee brought forward a proposal for an extension of **Eng2** from July 1972 to 27 November 1976. This was given provisional approval without debate or amendment at that session of Synod, and final approval came on 9 July 1972.[1]

Eng1 was originally authorized for a seven-year period from 7 November 1966,[2] so that its authorization was due to lapse in November 1973. An inquiry round diocesan Liturgical Committees in 1971-2 suggested it was not widely in use, but sufficiently so for there to be resentment if it were to be withdrawn. Thus a proposal was brought before Synod in July 1973 for an extension of its period to 31 December 1979. This gained provisional approval then, and came to Synod again on 6 November 1973 for final approval. As it still contained the 1928 Prayer for the Church (including very explicit petitions for the departed), and also the old problem of self-oblation in the canon, it was still technically controversial, though recognized by all to be a fading use. It was passed on final approval by 23 to nil in the House of Bishops, 114 to 13 in the House of Clergy, and 90 to 25 in the House of Laity, though without debate.

The 'Intermediate Rite' (**Eng1-2A**)

In his speech on 10 November 1971 mentioned above, Canon Jasper also looked forward to the point where **Eng1** and **Eng2** could be

---

[1] The date is of some interest, especially as it was a Sunday, the first ever Sunday sitting of Synod. In fact the previous extension from July 1971 to July 1972 ran out on midnight the night before (or possibly 24 hours before that), so that on that Sunday morning (alone in the years from July 1967 to November 1976) **Eng2** was not legal. Final approval came in the afternoon.

[2] For a description of the debates and controversies leading up to this see **MAL** pp.115-7. The text is on **MAL** pp.123-31.

combined in a single rite as a course midway between 1662 and **Eng3** for those who wanted it. This point became part of Synod's policy when in July 1973, in a debate on 'The Future Course of Liturgical Revision',[1] the resolution was passed 'That the General Synod would welcome an opportunity to consider the desirability of replacing Series 1 and Series 2 Holy Communion with a single rite'. The Liturgical Commission was instructed to take in hand the editing of this 'intermediate rite'.

The Liturgical Commission worked on this project through 1973 and into the early part of 1974. The rite included the major features of **Eng1** and **Eng2** as alternatives at most points, but was based on the structure of **Eng2**. The less used alternatives from **Eng1** were quietly dropped. At points where **Eng1** had proved sensitive in 1966 small changes were made. Thus the prayer about the departed in the 1928 form of the Prayer for the Church lost one phrase, and the self-oblation in the **Eng1** canon was also removed, and the resultant ending of the canon was then half-way between the two alternatives set out in parallel columns in **Eng1**.[2] The question arose as to whether material already incorporated uncontroversially in **Eng3** could not be employed in this newly refurbished rite, but cautious counsels prevailed when it came to the canon. The **Eng2**-type intercessions benefitted at several points from both structure and contents of the **Eng3** provision, and this later modern rite was also laid under contribution in the opening Notes, the texts from 1 Cor. 10 at the Breaking of the Bread, the Words of Administration, and the provision for supplementary consecration. Finally the complete set of high seasonal material from **Eng3** was incorporated—with the interesting proviso that the 'you' form of address to God had to be translated backwards into 'thou' form in six of the Proper Prefaces to go with the **Eng2**-type Thanksgiving. The text thus compiled was accepted by the House of Bishops in September 1974, and was published as a Report on 2 January 1975. It was on the agenda of General Synod for the February 1975 session, but was not reached. As it needs successive sessions for its various stages, it cannot now begin its course till November 1975 after the next elections to General Synod. The text as here presented is as it appears

---

[1] This is the title of a report of the Standing Committee published by the Church Information Office (GS 161). In addition to the above resolution it included resolutions about producing a whole range of 'Series 3' services, and the provision of a 'People's Service Book' which would contain the new services in a single handy form.

[2] See **MAL** pp.128-9.

in GS 217, the report of the Liturgical Commission to General Synod. It could be amended in the revision committee or at the revision stage, whenever those come, and has no authorization in 1975 in its form below. Whether, when and if it is authorized, General Synod will in fact rescind the existing **Eng1** and **Eng2** is wholly unclear.

THE ENGLISH SERIES 3 LITURGY 1973 (Eng3)

[The numbering here is original. The official text is printed in two colours, with black used for liturgical text, for rubrics indicating posture, and speakers (e.g. 'All'), and for the marginal numbers for mandatory parts of the service. Blue is used for most cross-headings, for rubrics (other than for posture and speakers), and for marginal numbers for optional parts of the service. Italics are not used at all, except for the mention of topics in the Prayers, and for the marginal listing of the seasons with the Proper material. The 1971 text, as it came from the Liturgical Commission prior to revision in Synod, is indicated by an *apparatus* where necessary. In nos. 39ff. the numbering was different in 1971, as rubric no. 38 was an addition at the time of revision in Synod, and to that extent references to the text read slightly differently in 1971, but no further attention is drawn to that here.]

AN ORDER FOR HOLY COMMUNION

It is provided in Canon B12 'Of the Ministry of Holy Communion' that only those who have been episcopally ordained priest shall consecrate the holy sacrament of the Lord's Supper.
1971: OMIT

NOTES

1 *POSTURE. Wherever a certain posture is particularly appropriate, it is indicated in the left-hand margin. At all other points local custom may be established and followed.*

2 *SAYING AND SINGING. Where rubrics indicate that a section is to be 'said', this must be understood to include 'or sung' and vice versa.*

3 *SEASONAL MATERIAL. The proper thanksgivings* (28) *are obligatory; but the seasonal sentences* (1, 37) *and the seasonal blessings* (45) *are optional. The use of one portion of the optional material does not necessitate the use of the other portions.*

4   *SERIES 2 MATERIAL. During the initial period of experiment, it is permitted to use in certain sections the texts prescribed in Holy Communion Series 2 (excluding Appendix 2) instead of the texts printed here. These sections are: the Salutation (3), the Collect for Purity (4), the Gloria in Excelsis (5), the responses to the Gospel (11), the Nicene Creed (13), the Prayers (15), the Comfortable Words (17), the Confession (18), the Prayer of Humble Access (20), the Sursum Corda (26),[1] the Lord's Prayer (31), the Words of Administration (33), the Anthems (34), and the final prayer after communion (40). Where parts of the service are also sung to well-known musical settings, it is also permitted to use the words for which these settings were composed.*

1971: *(excluding Appendix 2)*] OM
    the Sursum Corda (26),] OM
    the Words of Administration (33),] OM

5   *THE KYRIES (5). The Kyries may be said or sung in English or Greek. In penitential seasons it is desirable that this section should be used in preference to Gloria in Excelsis.*

6   *THE GLORIA IN EXCELSIS (5). This canticle is also appropriate at sections 2, 10, or 41.*

7   *THE COLLECTS (6). The Collects are either those appointed in The Book of Common Prayer or those appended to Holy Communion Series 1.*

8   *THE LESSONS (7, 9, 11). The Lessons should be announced in the order: book, chapter, verse. They should be either those set out in Tables 1-3 appended to Holy Communion Series 3, or those in the Book of Common Prayer, or any other lessons which are authorized for use in the Church of England. It should be noted that the three lessons from the Old Testament and the New Testament in these tables form a coherent whole. But when only two lessons are used, the Old Testament lesson and the Gospel should be used during Advent and the last five weeks of Trinity; the Epistle and the Gospel should be used during the rest of Trinity and Whitsun, and either the Old Testament lesson or the Epistle should be be read with the Gospel from Christmas until the end of Easter.*

1971: *It should be noted . . . Gospel from Christmas*] When the lessons of Table 1 appended to Series 3 are used and only two lessons are read, the Epistle should be omitted during Advent and the last five weeks of Trinity; the Old Testament lesson should be omitted during the rest of Trinity and Whitsun; and either the Old Testament lesson or the Epistle may be omitted from Christmas

---

[1] [['The Sursum Corda (26)'* did not appear in the first printing but it was part of the text authorized, and was omitted in error.]]

9   *THE SERMON* (12). *A sermon should be preached at* (12) *whenever possible; but it is not necessary at every service.*

10   *THE PRAYERS* (15). *The introduction to the specific subjects of prayer is not restricted to the printed forms* 'we give thanks for', 'we pray for', 'we commemorate'. *Other forms may be used at the discretion of the minister provided they are clearly addressed to God. It is desirable that the subjects of prayer should be expressed briefly.*
1971: *It is desirable . . . briefly*] OM

11   *THE PEACE* (22). *The president may accompany the words of the Peace with a handclasp or similar action: and both the words and the action may be passed through the congregation.*

⟦1971 has a note 12, as follows (and the next two are renumbered accordingly):
12 *THE THANKSGIVING* (26-29). *During the Thanksgiving the president may be joined by any other priests who are present.*⟧

12   *A SERVICE WITHOUT COMMUNION. When there is to be no communion, the minister reads the service as far as the absolution* (19) *and then adds the Lord's Prayer* (31), *the General Thanksgiving, and other prayers at his discretion, ending with the Grace. When such a service is led by a deacon or lay person,* 'us' *is said instead of* 'you' *in the Absolution* (19).

13   *HYMNS, NOTICES, OFFERINGS OF THE PEOPLE. Points are indicated for the singing of hymns, the publication of banns of marriage and other notices, and the collection and presentation of the offerings of the people, but if occasion requires, there are other points at which they may occur.*

⟦1971 has: *HYMNS. Various points are indicated for the singing of hymns; but if occasion requires they may be sung at other points also.*⟧

AN ORDER FOR HOLY COMMUNION
1   *SEASONAL SENTENCES*

⟦The 14 Seasonal Sentences which follow are to be found in Appendix D. 1971 has no provision for All Saints, but allocates this sentence to Saints' Days and omits the following one⟧

THE WORD AND THE PRAYERS
THE PREPARATION

2   *At the entry of the ministers a sentence* (p. . . . ⟦i.e. no. 1⟧) *may be used and a hymn, a canticle, or a psalm may be sung.*
⟦1971 inverts the order of this rubric⟧

3 *The minister may say*
> The Lord be with you.
>
> *All*   **And also with you.**

4 *The following prayer may be said*
> *All*   **Almighty God, to whom . . . [CF 1] . . . Christ our Lord. Amen.**
>
> [1971 omits the rubric above this prayer]

5 *The Kyries may be said.*
> Lord, have mercy.
>
> **Lord, have mercy.**
>
> Lord, have mercy.
>
> Christ, have mercy.
>
> **Christ, have mercy.**
>
> Christ, have mercy.
>
> Lord, have mercy.
>
> **Lord, have mercy.**
>
> Lord, have mercy.

Or the canticle Gloria in Excelsis may be said.
> *All*   **Glory to God . . . [ICET 4] . . . God the Father. Amen.**

6 *The collect of the day.*

THE MINISTRY OF THE WORD

7 *Sit*
> *The Old Testament lesson. At the end there may be said*
>
> *Reader*   This is the word of the Lord.
>
> *All*   **Thanks be to God.**
>
> 1971: *there may be said] the reader says*
> > *Reader]* OM
> > *All* **Thanks be to God]** OMIT
>
> [And similarly at no. 9 below]
>
> *Silence may be kept.*

8 *A psalm may be said.*

9 *The Epistle. At the end there may be said*
> *Reader*   This is the word of the Lord.
>
> *All*   **Thanks be to God.**
>
> [1971 has the same variants as at no. 7 above]
>
> *Silence may be kept.*

10 *A canticle, a hymn, or a psalm may be sung.*
    Stand
    The Gospel. When it is announced
    All   **Glory to Christ our Saviour.**
    At the end the reader says
              This is the Gospel of Christ.
    All   **Praise to Christ our Lord.**

    Silence may be kept.

12 *Sit*
    The sermon.
    At the end silence may be kept.

13 *Stand*
    The Nicene Creed is said, at least on Sundays and greater Holy Days.
    All   **We believe in one God . . . ⟦ICET 3⟧ . . . world to come.**
              Amen.
              (and the Son)] OM BRACKETS

THE PRAYERS

14 *Banns of marriage and other notices may be published; the offerings of the*
    people may be collected; and a hymn may be sung.

15 *Intercessions and thanksgivings are offered by the president or by some other*
    person. These may be introduced by biddings.
    1971: *These may be introduced by biddings.*] OM
    It is not necessary to include specific subjects in any section of the following
    prayer.

    The set passages may also follow one another as a continuous whole,
    without versicles and responses.

    Minister Let us pray for the Church and for the world; and let us thank
                God for his goodness.
                Almighty God, our heavenly Father, who promised through
                your Son Jesus Christ to hear us when we pray in faith:
                We give thanks for/we pray for
                the Church throughout the world . . .
                our own Church, our diocese and bishop . . .
                any particular work of the Church . . .

    Silence may be kept.

Strengthen your Church to carry forward the work of Christ; that we and all who confess your Name may unite in your truth, live together in your love, and reveal your glory in the world.

Lord, in your mercy

All **Hear our prayer.**

We give thanks for/we pray for

the nations of the world . . .
our own nation . . .
all men in their various callings . . .

Silence may be kept.

Give wisdom to all in authority, especially Elizabeth our Queen; direct this nation and all nations in the ways of justice and of peace; that men may honour one another, and seek the common good.

Lord, in your mercy

All **Hear our prayer.**

We give thanks for/we pray for

the local community . . .
our families and friends . . .
particular persons . . .

Silence may be kept.

Give grace to us, our families and friends, and to all our neighbours in Christ; that we may serve him in one another, and love as he loves us.

Lord, in your mercy

All **Hear our prayer.**

We pray for

the sick and the suffering . . .
those who mourn . . .
those without faith . . .

We give thanks and pray for

all who serve and relieve them . . .

Silence may be kept.

Comfort and heal all those who suffer in body, mind, or spirit; give them courage and hope in their troubles; and bring them the joy of your salvation.

Lord, in your mercy

All **Hear our prayer.**

We commemorate
the departed, especially . . .

Silence may be kept.

We commend all men to your unfailing love, that in them your
will may be fulfilled; and we rejoice at the faithful witness of
your saints in every age, praying that we may share with them
in your eternal kingdom.
Lord, in your mercy

All **Accept these prayers
for the sake of your Son,
our Saviour Jesus Christ. Amen.**

16 *The minister may say the Commandments (pp.... [i.e. in the Appendix
after the service]) and silence may be kept after the responses; or the
Summary of the Law may be said (p.... [i.e. in the Appendix after the
service]).*

[1971 omits this rubric, and instead has: *At least on Ash Wednesday and the
five Sundays following, the minister says these commandments; and silence may be
kept after the responses.* The text which is printed in the Appendix after the
service then follows.]

17 *Minister* God so loved the world that he gave his only Son, Jesus Christ,
to save us from our sins, to be our advocate in heaven, and
to bring us to eternal life.

Let us therefore confess our sins, in penitence and faith, firmly
resolved to keep God's commandments and to live in love and
peace with all men.

Or he says one or more of these sentences:

Hear the words of comfort . . . [CF 4] . . . expiation of our sins.

After which he says:

Let us therefore . . . [as above] . . . with all men.

18 *Kneel*

Silence may be kept.

All **Almighty God, our heavenly Father,
we have sinned against you and against our fellow men,
in thought and word and deed,
in the evil we have done
and in the good we have not done,
through ignorance, through weakness,
through our own deliberate fault.**

We are truly sorry and repent of all our sins.
For the sake of your Son, Jesus Christ, who died for us,
forgive us all that is past;
and grant that we may serve you in newness of life
to the glory of your Name. Amen.

[1971 has as its Confession the first of the 'Deleted Prayers' printed
at the end of this chapter]

19 *President* Almighty God, who forgives . . . [CF 5] . . . Jesus Christ our
Lord.

  All   **Amen.**

1971: *President*] *Minister*
       forgives] pardons

20 *All may say*

We do not presume . . . [CF 6] . . . he in us. Amen.

[1971 has as an alternative the second of the 'Deleted Prayers' printed
at the end of this chapter]

THE COMMUNION

THE PEACE

21 *Stand*

President We are the Body of Christ. In the one Spirit we were all
baptized into one body. Let us then pursue all that makes for
peace and builds up our common life.

22 *The president gives the Peace to the congregation saying:*
The peace of the Lord be always with you.

  All   **And also with you.**

THE TAKING OF THE BREAD AND WINE

23 *A hymn may be sung, and the offerings of the people may be collected and
presented.*

24 *The bread and wine are brought to the holy table, and this sentence may be
used:*

**Yours, Lord, is the greatness, the power, the glory, the
splendour, and the majesty; for everything in heaven and
on earth is yours.
All things come from you, and of your own do we give
you.**

1971: *and this sentence . . .* **do we give you**] OM

25 *The president takes the bread and wine.*

THE THANKSGIVING

26 *The president says,*

The Lord is here.

All **His Spirit is with us.**

President Lift up your hearts.

All **We lift them to the Lord.**

President Let us give thanks to the Lord our God.

All **It is right to give him thanks and praise.**

27 *President* It is not only right, it is our duty and our joy, at all times and in all places, to give you thanks and praise, holy Father, heavenly King, almighty and eternal God, through Jesus Christ, your only Son, our Lord;

For he is your living Word; through him you have created all things from the beginning, and formed us in your own image;

Through him you have freed us from the slavery of sin, giving him to be born as man, to die upon the cross, and to rise again for us;

Through him you have made us a people for your own possession, exalting him to your right hand on high, and sending upon us your holy and life-giving Spirit.

28 *Proper Thanksgivings*

And now we give you thanks,

[The Proper Prefaces which follow here are to be found in Appendix C]

29 Therefore with angels and archangels, and with all the company of heaven, we proclaim your great and glorious Name, for ever praising you and saying:

Holy, holy, holy Lord,
God of power and might,
Heaven and earth are full of your glory.
Hosanna in the highest.

President Accept our praises, heavenly Father, through your Son, our Saviour Jesus Christ; and as we follow his example and obey his command, grant that by the power of your Spirit these gifts of bread and wine may be to us his body and his blood;

For in the same night that he was betrayed, he took bread; and after giving you thanks, he broke it, gave it to his disciples, and said, 'Take, eat; this is my body which is given for you. Do this in remembrance of me.' Again, after supper he took the cup; he gave you thanks, and gave it to them, saying, 'Drink this, all of you; for this is my blood of the new Covenant, which is shed for you and for many, for the forgiveness of sins. Do this, as often as you drink it, in remembrance of me.'

All **Christ has died:**
Christ is risen:
Christ will come again.

President Therefore, heavenly Father, with this bread and this cup we do this in remembrance of him: we celebrate and proclaim his perfect sacrifice made once for all upon the cross, his resurrection from the dead, and his ascension into heaven; and we look for his coming in glory. Accept through him, our great high priest, this our sacrifice of thanks and praise; and as we eat and drink these holy gifts in the presence of your divine majesty, renew us by your Spirit, inspire us with your love, and unite us in the body of your Son, Jesus Christ our Lord.

With him, and in him, and through him, by the power of the Holy Spirit, with all who stand before you in earth and heaven, we worship you, Father Almighty, in songs of everlasting praise:

All **Blessing and honour and glory and power be yours for ever and ever. Amen.**

Silence may be kept.

[The Thanksgiving of the 1971 service is set out in Appendix F in this volume]

THE BREAKING OF THE BREAD

30 *The president breaks the consecrated bread, saying:*
We break this bread
to share in the body of Christ.

All **Though we are many, we are one body,**
because we all share in one bread.

THE GIVING OF THE BREAD AND THE CUP

31 *President* As our Saviour has taught us, so we pray:

  All   **Our Father in heaven ... [ICET 1] ... and for ever. Amen.**

     holy] hallowed
     test] time of trial
     [1971 has no variants from ICET 1]

32 *President* Draw near with faith. Receive the body of our Lord Jesus Christ which he gave for you, and his blood which he shed for you. Remember that he died for you, and feed on him in your hearts by faith with thanksgiving.

33 *The president and the other communicants receive the holy communion. At the administration the ministers say to each communicant,*

  The Body of Christ keep you in eternal life.
  The Blood of Christ keep you in eternal life.

The communicant replies each time,

  Amen.

and then receives.

34 *During THE COMMUNION these and other hymns and anthems may be sung :*

  Blessed is he . . . [ICET 5(b)] . . . the highest.
  Jesus, Lamb of God . . . [ICET 8] . . . give us your peace.

35 *If either or both of the consecrated elements are likely to prove insufficient, the president returns to the holy table and adds more, with these words :*

  Having given thanks to you, Father, over the bread and the cup according to the institution of your Son, Jesus Christ, who said, 'Take eat; this is my body', (*and/or* 'Drink this; this is my blood',) we pray that this bread/wine also may be to us his body/blood, and be received in remembrance of him.

  [1971 has rubric and text as found on p.33 above]

36 *Any consecrated bread and wine which is not required for purposes of communion is consumed at the end of the administration, or after the service.*

AFTER COMMUNION

37 *A seasonal sentence may be said.*

[The 11 seasonal sentences which follow are to be found in Appendix D.]

Silence may be kept.

38 *Either or both of the following prayers are said.*

1971 OMITS

39 *President* Father of all, we give you thanks and praise, that when we were still far off you met us in your Son and brought us home. Dying and living, he declared your love, gave us grace, and opened the gate of glory. May we who share Christ's body live his risen life; we who drink his cup bring life to others; we whom the Spirit lights give light to the world. Keep us in this hope that we have grasped; so we and all your children shall be free, and the whole earth live to praise your Name; through Christ our Lord.

All   **Amen.**

1971: *President*] *One of the ministers may say:*
Keep] Anchor

40 *All*   **Almighty God . . . ⟦CF 8⟧ . . . praise and glory. Amen.**

41 *A hymn or canticle may be sung.*

42 *The President may say this or the appropriate seasonal blessing.*
The peace of God . . . ⟦CF 9⟧ . . . with you always.

All   **Amen**

43 *President* Go in peace and serve the Lord.

All   **In the name of Christ. Amen.**

44 *The Ministers and people depart.*

45 *Seasonal Blessings*

⟦The 10 seasonal blessings which follow are to be found in Appendix D. Each ends 'And the blessing . . .' in order to be run on as no. 42 above (see CF 9). In 1971 the Lent Blessing reads 'Christ bestow upon you the spirit of holy discipline to deny yourself . . . etc.' The others are unchanged.⟧

APPENDIX: *THE COMMANDMENTS*

⟦In 1971 the Commandments come in the main text at no. 16. In the eighth commandment 1971 reads '. . . do honest work that you may be able to give . . .'⟧

Minister Our Lord Jesus Christ said, If you love me, keep my commandments: happy are those who hear the word of God and keep it. Hear then these commandments which God has given to his people, and take them to heart.
I am the Lord your God: you shall have no other gods but me. You shall love the Lord your God with all your heart, with all your soul, with all your mind, and with all your strength.

All   **Amen. Lord, have mercy.**

Minister You shall not make for yourself any idol.
God is spirit, and those who worship him must worship in spirit and in truth.

All **Amen. Lord, have mercy.**

Minister You shall not dishonour the name of the Lord your God.
You shall worship him with reverence and awe.

All **Amen. Lord, have mercy.**

Minister Remember the Lord's day and keep it holy.
Christ is risen from the dead; set your minds on things that are above, not on things that are on the earth.

All **Amen. Lord, have mercy.**

Minister Honour your father and mother.
Live as servants of God: honour all men; love the brotherhood.

All **Amen. Lord, have mercy.**

Minister You shall not commit murder.
Do not nurse anger against your brother; overcome evil with good.

All **Amen. Lord, have mercy.**

Minister You shall not commit adultery.
Know that your body is a temple of the Holy Spirit.

All **Amen. Lord, have mercy.**

Minister You shall not steal.
You shall work honestly and give to those in need.

All **Amen. Lord, have mercy.**

Minister You shall not be a false witness.
Let everyone speak the truth.

All **Amen. Lord, have mercy.**

Minister You shall not covet anything which belongs to your neighbour.
Remember the words of the Lord Jesus: It is more blessed to give than to receive. Love your neighbour as yourself, for love is the fulfilling of the law.

All **Amen. Lord, have mercy.**

THE SUMMARY OF THE LAW

[1971 omits the Summary of the Law entirely]

Minister Our Lord Jesus Christ said . . . [CF 3] . . . greater than these.

All **Amen. Lord, have mercy.**

THE ENGLISH 'SERIES 1 AND SERIES 2 REVISED' LITURGY 1975 (Eng1-2A)

⟦This service is in its report form, prior to its revision and authorization. It reproduces many features of **Eng1** and **Eng2**, and can only be reconstructed by reference to **MAL**. The numbering is original.⟧

AN ORDER FOR HOLY COMMUNION

NOTES

1 *POSTURE Wherever a certain posture is particularly appropriate, it is indicated in the left-hand margin. At all other points local custom may be followed.*

2 *SAYING AND SINGING Where rubrics indicate that a section is to be 'said', this must be understood to include 'or sung' and vice versa.*

3 *SEASONAL MATERIAL The proper prefaces (28, 31) are obligatory; but the seasonal sentences (1, 42) and the seasonal blessings (51) are optional. The use of one portion of the optional material does not necessitate the use of the other portions. On any occasion for which no seasonal sentence is provided, the priest may use a suitable sentence of his own choice.*

4 *1662 MATERIAL It is permitted to use 1662 text of the Gloria (6), the Creed (14), the Intercession (17, 18), the Confession (20), the Absolution (21), and the Prayer of Humble Access (23) instead of the texts printed here.*

5 *SERIES 2 MATERIAL It is permitted to use the Series 2 text of the Confession (20), the Absolution (21), the Breaking of the Bread (34), the Post-communion prayer (46), and the Dismissal (49) instead of those provided here.*

6 *THE KYRIES (5) The Kyries may be said or sung in English or Greek either three, six, or nine times.*

7 *THE GLORIA IN EXCELSIS (6) This canticle is also appropriate at sections 2, 11, and 47.*

8 *THE COLLECTS (7) The collects are either those appointed in the Book of Common Prayer or those appended to this service.*

9 *THE LESSONS (8, 10, 12) The lessons should be announced in the order: book, chapter, verse. They should be either those set out in Tables 1-3 appended to Holy Communion Series 3, or those in the Book of Common Prayer together with those appended to this service.*

10 *THE SERMON (13) A sermon should be preached at (13) whenever possible; but it is not necessary at every service.*

11 *THE PEACE (25) The priest may accompany the words of the Peace with a handclasp or similar action; and both the words and the action may be passed through the congregation.*

12 *THE PRAYER OF INTERCESSION (17-18) AND THE THANKS-GIVING (27-32) The use of Intercession A(17) does not presuppose the use of Thanksgiving A(28-30). Either prayer of intercession may be used with either thanksgiving.*

13 *THE THANKSGIVING A(28f) The Thanksgiving (A) may end after the words, 'Do this, as oft as ye shall drink it, in remembrance of me', in which case the people then say* **Amen.**

14 *A SERVICE WITHOUT COMMUNION When there is to be no communion, the minister reads the service as far as the absolution (21) and then adds the Lord's Prayer (23), the General Thanksgiving, and other prayers at his discretion, ending with the Grace. When such a service is led by a deacon or lay person, 'us' is said instead of 'you' in the absolution (21).*

15 *HYMNS, NOTICES, OFFERINGS OF THE PEOPLE, AND THE PLACING OF THE BREAD AND WINE Points are indicated for the singing of hymns, the publication of the banns of marriage and other notices, the collection and presentation of the offerings of the people, and the placing of the bread and wine upon the holy table; but if occasion requires, there are other points at which they may occur.*

SEASONAL SENTENCES

1 ⟦The Seasonal Sentences which follow are those of **Eng3** without any alterations. They are set out in this volume in Appendix D⟧

THE WORD AND THE PRAYERS

THE PREPARATION

2 *At the entry of the ministers a sentence (p.... ⟦i.e. no. 1⟧) may be used; and a hymn, a canticle, or a psalm may be sung.*

3 *The minister may say,*
> The Lord be with you.
All **And with thy spirit.**

4 *The following prayer may be said.*
All **Almighty God, unto whom . . . ⟦MAL CF 2⟧ . . . our Lord. Amen.**

5 *One of the following may be used: either the Ten Commandments, or our Lord's summary of the Law, or the Kyries in English or Greek. The text of these appears in the Appendix (p.... ⟦i.e. after the service⟧).*

6 *The canticle Gloria in Excelsis may be said.*
> **Glory be to God on high . . . ⟦MAL CF 5⟧ . . . God the Father. Amen.**
> **Thou that takest . . . upon us]** OM[1]
> **most high] the Most High**

7 *The collect of the day*

THE MINISTRY OF THE WORD

8 *Sit*
A lesson from the Old Testament may be read. At the end silence may be kept.

9 *A psalm may be said.*

---

[1] ⟦This line is not actually included in the printing of the Gloria in Excelsis in the Common Forms in **MAL** p.346. But this was an error (see p.421 below), and references to this Common Form are made throughout **MAL**, as here, as though the Gloria in Excelsis had been printed there in its 1552, 1662, and **LiE** Common Form text.⟧

10 *A lesson from the Old or New Testament shall be read. At the end silence may be kept.*

11 *A canticle, a hymn, or a psalm may be sung.*

12 *Stand*
A lesson from the Gospels shall be read. When it is announced,
All **Glory be to thee, O Lord.**
At the end of the Gospel,
All **Praise be to thee, O Christ.**
Silence may be kept.

13 *Sit*
The sermon

14 *Stand*
The Nicene Creed is said, at least on Sundays and greater Holy Days.
All **I believe in one God . . . ⟦MAL CF 6⟧ . . . world to come. Amen.**

PRAYERS OF INTERCESSION

15 *Banns of marriage and other notices may be published; the offerings of the people may be collected and presented; and a hymn may be sung.*

16 *Intercessions are offered by the priest or by some other person. These may be introduced by biddings.*
It is not necessary to include specific subjects in any section of the following prayers.
The set passages may follow one another as a continuous whole, without the versicles and responses.

Let us pray for the whole Church of God in Christ Jesus, and for all men according to their needs.

INTERCESSIONS

17 *Either A*
Almighty and everliving God . . . ⟦**MAL** CF 8⟧ . . . our only mediator and advocate. **Amen.**

AFTER EACH PARAGRAPH EXCEPT THE LAST ADD
Lord, in thy mercy
Hear our prayer.
INSTEAD OF THE INDENTED RUBRIC THERE IS A REFERENCE TO A FOOTNOTE
WHICH READS *If the offerings of the people have not been presented these words are omitted.*
knowledge of thy truth] knowledge of thy love
beseeching thee to grant them everlasting light and peace] OM
high praise and hearty thanks] praise and thanks

18 *Or B*

Almighty God, who hast promised . . . ⟦As in **Eng2**, no. 14, **MAL**
pp.132-3, with variants as shown⟧ . . . in thy eternal kingdom.
Lord, in thy mercy
**Accept these prayers for the sake of thy Son, our Saviour Jesus
Christ. Amen.**

> THE ORDER IN EACH SECTION IS: RUBRIC, SET TEXT, VERSICLE AND RE-
> SPONSE (NOT, AS IN **Eng2**, RUBRIC, VERSICLE AND RESPONSE, SET TEXT)
> *and (again) a short period of silence may be kept; after which he
> may say] Silence may be kept* THROUGHOUT
> we who confess] we and all who confess
> *and especially . . . Queen; for all men] for this kingdom, and for all
> men*
> Direct this nation] ADD BEFORE THIS Give wisdom to all in authority,
> bless Elizabeth our Queen, and direct
> ADD NEW THIRD SECTION *Here he may pray for the local community; for
> families, friends, and particular persons. Silence may be kept.* Give
> grace . . . ⟦as in **Eng3**, no. 15, on p.53 above⟧ . . . he loves us.

PRAYERS OF PENITENCE

19 *The minister says either*

> (Ye that do truly . . . ⟦**MAL** CF 9⟧ . . . upon your knees.
>
> > THE BRACKET IS CLOSED AFTER 'ways' AND REFERENCE IS MADE TO A
> > FOOTNOTE WHICH SAYS *The words in brackets may be omitted.*

or   Seeing we have . . . ⟦as in **Eng2**, no. 17, **MAL** p.133⟧ . . .
heavenly Father.

20 *Kneel*

> *The minister and people make the following confession*
>
> **Almighty God . . .** ⟦as in **Eng2**, no. 18, **MAL** p.134 with an
> addition⟧ . . . **of thy Name. Amen.**
>
> > **through our own fault** IS MOVED UP TO END THE SECOND LINE, AND A
> > NEW FIFTH LINE IS ADDED **We are heartily sorry and repent of all
> > our sins.**

21 *The priest says the absolution*

> Almighty God . . . ⟦CF 5⟧ . . . Christ our Lord. **Amen.**

22 *One or more of the Comfortable Words may be said by the priest or by one
of the other ministers*

> Hear what comfortable . . . ⟦**MAL** CF 12⟧ . . . our sins
> saith] says THRICE

23 *The following prayer may be said.*

> **We do not presume . . .**⟦**MAL** CF 13⟧ . . . **he in us. Amen.**
> **property] nature**
> **that our sinful bodies . . . precious blood and]** OM

THE COMMUNION

THE PEACE

24 *Stand*

The priest may say,

We are the body . . . ⟦as in **Eng3**, no. 21, p.55 above⟧ . . .
bond of peace.

25 *The priest may give the Peace to the congregation, saying,*
The peace of the Lord be always with you.

All **And with thy spirit.**

THE PREPARATION OF THE BREAD AND WINE

26 *A hymn may be sung, and the offerings of the people may be collected and presented if this has not already been done.*

27 *The bread and wine are brought to the holy table, and this sentence may be said.*

Thine, O Lord, is the greatness and the power
and the glory and the victory and the majesty.
All that is in heaven and earth is thine.
All things come of thee, O Lord,
and of thine own do we give thee.

THE THANKSGIVING

28 *Either A*

The priest says

The Lord be with you.
And with thy spirit.
Lift up your hearts.
We lift them up unto the Lord.
Let us give thanks unto the Lord our God.
It is meet and right so to do.
It is very meet, right and our bounden duty, that we should at all times, and in all places, give thanks unto thee, O Lord, Holy Father, Almighty, Everlasting God

Here follows the Proper Preface

⟦The Proper Prefaces which follow here are those for **Eng1** to be found in **MAL** Appendix C. There are some tiny changes recorded in Appendix C here⟧

Therefore, with angels and archangels, and with all the company
of heaven, we laud and magnify thy glorious name; evermore
praising thee and saying,
Holy, holy, holy, Lord God of hosts
heaven and earth are full of thy glory.
Glory be to thee, O Lord most high. (Amen.
Blessed is he that cometh in the Name of the Lord:
Hosanna in the highest).

*The priest says the Prayer of Humble Access, if it has not already been
said : and the people may say it with him.*

The Priest continues,

All glory be to thee, almighty God, our heavenly Father, who
of thy tender mercy . . . [as in **Eng1**, **MAL** pp.127-9, with the
longer of the two endings beyond the narrative of institution
as the only form, but with variants as shown] . . . world
without end.

> IN THE INDENTED RUBRICS SYMBOLS, NOT LETTERS, ARE USED FOR
> REFERENCE.
>
> IN THE FIFTH INDENTED RUBRIC OMIT (*be it chalice or flagon*)
>
> OMIT THE RUBRIC AFTER in remembrance of me AND *either* AND *or* AND
> CONTINUE WITH LEFT-HAND COLUMN
> And here we offer and present . . . sacrifice unto thee] OMIT
> humbly beseeching . . . benediction] THIS COMES AS A SEPARATE
> SENTENCE AFTER . . . pardoning our offences, AND IS INTRODUCED We
> pray that all we . . .

29 *All*   **Amen.**

30 *The priest and people together may say the Lord's Prayer*

Priest As our Saviour Christ has commanded and taught us, we are
bold to say,

All   **Our Father, who art . . .** [MAL CF 1] **. . . for ever and**
ever. Amen.

> in earth] **on earth**
> them that] **those who**

Or B

31 *The priest says*

The Lord be with you.
And with thy spirit.
Lift up your hearts.
We lift them up unto the Lord.
Let us give thanks unto the Lord our God.
It is meet and right so to do.

It is very meet . . . 〚as in **Eng2**, **MAL**, p.135, but without any Proper Prefaces between paragraphs〛 . . . and life-giving Spirit.

Here follows the Proper Preface

And now we give thee thanks

〚The Proper Prefaces which follow are those for **Eng3**, but with 'you' 'your' changed into 'thou' 'thee' 'thy' and verb forms amended accordingly. They are set out in 'you' form in Appendix C as for **Eng3**〛

Therefore with angels . . . 〚as in **Eng2**, **MAL**, pp.135-6, but with symbols instead of letters to refer to indented rubrics〛 . . . world without end.

32 *All*   **Amen.**

33 *This anthem may be said:*

**Blessed is he that cometh in the name of the Lord.
Hosanna in the highest.**

THE BREAKING OF THE BREAD

34 *The priest breaks the consecrated bread, and the following may be said,*
Priest The bread which we break,
is it not a sharing of the Body of Christ?
All   **Though we are many, we are one Body,
for we all partake of the one bread.**

35 *The priest may give the Peace to the people, if it has not already been given saying,*
The peace of the Lord be always with you.
All   **And with thy spirit.**

36 *This anthem may be said.*
O Lamb of God . . . 〚MAL CF 14〛 . . . thy peace

THE GIVING OF THE BREAD AND THE CUP

37 *The priest and the people may say the Lord's Prayer, if it has not already been said.*
Priest As our Saviour . . . 〚as above at no. 30〛 . . . **for ever and ever. Amen.**

38 *The priest and the other communicants receive the holy communion*
The communion may be administered in one of the following ways:
either (a)
One of the ministers delivers the bread to each communicant, saying
> The Body . . . ⟦CF 7(a)⟧ . . . with thanksgiving.

and one of the ministers delivers the cup to each communicant, saying,
> The Blood . . . ⟦CF 7(b)⟧ . . . thankful

or (b)

The priest first says to all the communicants,
> Draw near and receive the Body of our Lord Jesus Christ, which was given for you, and his Blood which was shed for you. Take this in remembrance that Christ died for you, and feed on him in your hearts by faith with thanksgiving

One of the ministers then delivers the bread to each communicant, saying,
> The Body of Christ.

or   The Body of Christ preserve your body and soul unto everlasting life.

or   The Body . . . ⟦CF 7(a)⟧ . . . unto everlasting life.

One of the ministers then delivers the cup to each communicant, saying,
> The Blood of Christ.

or   The Blood of Christ preserve your body and soul unto everlasting life.

or   The Blood . . . ⟦CF 7(b)⟧ . . . unto everlasting life.

The communicant may reply each time,
> **Amen,**

and then he receives.

39 *During the administration hymns and anthems may be sung.*

40 *If either or both of the consecrated elements are likely to prove insufficient* . . . ⟦as in **Eng3**, no. 35, p.58 above⟧ . . . in remembrance of him.

41 *Any consecrated bread and wine which is not required for purposes of communion is consumed at the end of the administration, or immediately after the service.*

AFTER COMMUNION

42 *A seasonal sentence may be said.*

⟦The seasonal sentences which follow are those for **Eng3** without any alterations. They are set out in Appendix D⟧

Silence may be kept.

43 *The priest and people shall say the Lord's Prayer, if it has not already been said.*

44 *Either or both of the following prayers shall be said:*

45 *Priest* O Lord and heavenly Father, we most heartily thank . . . [**MAL** CF 18] . . . world without end. **Amen.**

> thy dear Son . . . so to assist] thy dear Son. Through him we offer and present unto thee, O Lord, ourselves, our souls and bodies, to be a reasonable, holy, and living sacrifice unto thee; most humbly beseeching thee, so to assist
> Ghost] Spirit

46 *All* **Almighty God** . . . [CF 8] . . . **praise and glory. Amen.**
> you . . . your] thee . . . thy THROUGHOUT

47 *The canticle Gloria in Excelsis may be sung if it has not been used already: or some other suitable canticle or hymn may be sung.*

48 *The priest may say this or the appropriate seasonal blessing.*
> The peace of God . . . [CF 9] . . . with you always. **Amen.**

49 *The priest dismisses the people, saying,*

Priest Go in peace and serve the Lord.

All **In the name of Christ. Amen.**

50 *The ministers and people depart.*

51 *Seasonal blessings*
> [The seasonal blessings which follow are those of **Eng3** without any alterations. They are set out in Appendix D]

APPENDIX

THE TEN COMMANDMENTS

God spake these words . . . [**MAL** CF 3 without the bracketed portions] . . . **in our hearts, we beseech thee.**

OUR LORD'S SUMMARY OF THE LAW

Our Lord Jesus Christ said . . . [**MAL** CF 4(b)] . . . **write both these thy laws in our hearts, we beseech thee.**

THE KYRIES

Lord, have mercy.	Kyrie eleison.
Lord, have mercy.	**Kyrie eleison.**
Lord, have mercy.	Kyrie eleison.
Christ, have mercy.	**Christe eleison.**
Christ, have mercy.	Christe eleison.
Christ, have mercy.	**Christe eleison.**
Lord, have mercy.	Kyrie eleison.
Lord, have mercy.	**Kyrie eleison.**
Lord, have mercy.	Kyrie eleison.

THE DELETED PRAYERS

⟦The two prayers which follow were new compositions written especially for Series 3, and were part of the Commission's original report of September 1971. They were both deleted by Synod in November 1971, as recorded in the introduction to the service above. They are included here for the purposes of information, and are not part of the service⟧

THE CONFESSION

Father eternal, Giver of light and grace,
we have sinned against you and against our fellow men,
in what we have thought,
in what we have said and done,
through ignorance, through weakness,
through our own deliberate fault.
We have wounded your love,
and marred your image in us.
We are sorry and ashamed,
and repent of all our sins.
For the sake of your Son, Jesus Christ, who died for us,
forgive us all that is past,
and lead us out from darkness
to walk as children of light. Amen.

THE ALTERNATIVE 'HUMBLE ACCESS'

Most merciful Lord,
your love compels us to come in.
Our hands were unclean,
our hearts were unprepared;
we were not fit
even to eat the crumbs from under your table.
But you, Lord, are the God of our salvation,
and share your bread with sinners.
So cleanse and feed us
with the precious body and blood of your Son,
that he may live in us and we in him;
and that we, with the whole company of Christ,
may sit and eat in your kingdom. Amen.

CHAPTER 3

THE EPISCOPAL CHURCH OF SCOTLAND

1637 and after

THE pedigree of the Scottish Liturgy (**Scot**), as printed in the Scottish Prayer Book of 1929 (and in **LiE**) and since, has been traced by Colin Chapman in the relevant chapter of **MAL**. The rite has been modified through three centuries and in particular in 1764. 'This was the service which Bishop Seabury took with him to America, and is the basis of the American Liturgy' (**Amer**).[1] In the nineteenth century, and up to the present, **Scot** has been paralleled in Scottish use by the 'English Office' **ScotE**. Thus the Scottish and English Communion Services are printed in the SPB, and until 1966, **Scot** was used in the majority of congregations. A few employed **ScotE** only, and a number used both at different service times.

In 1966 the College of Bishops authorized for permissive use a new or experimental Liturgy (**ScotR**[2]). Basically this revised service is **Scot** with the permitted variations, introduced between 1960 and 1966, incorporated. It was issued as a booklet, commonly referred to as 'the wee grey bookie', and has been widely used in probably two-thirds of the congregations in the Province. Its features (enumerated in **MAL** pp.148-49) are a reduction in the total length of the service, and a change in the order, in particular the Confession and Intercession come before the Consecration. The language and doctrinal slant are not affected, and it is therefore a very conservative revision.

Further experimentation

It was predictable that the 'Grey Bookie' of 1966 would be widely used and gain, on the whole, a favourable reception, particularly in congregations which previously had used **Scot** exclusively. Some were irritated (naturally enough in the early stages) by the small changes, by the order, or by the omissions or additions. Some clergy and congregations did not use the experimental service because they were wedded to **Scot** as printed in the SPB, and did not see the point of changing to a booklet

---

[1] **MAL,** p.145.
[2] Printed in full in **MAL,** p.151.

which in general was very similar to their familiar and much loved Liturgy. Others have not used it because they had not previously used **Scot,** but (in a few cases) **ScotE** only.[1] Yet again, others were dissatisfied with the 1966 Liturgy because they wanted a more radical revision and modernization, or (as it has turned out) importation from England.

Liturgical revision is the responsibility of the Provincial Synod which is a body representing the whole Church and including all the Bishops and a proportion of clergy and laity. The Synod meets annually in the Autumn, and has a five-year 'life' after which the seven Diocesan Synods (clergy only) and Councils (clergy and laity) again elect their representatives. The Provincial Synod has a Liturgical Committee which in recent years has met three times a year and reports annually to the Synod. Thus 'A Bishop may permit for Liturgical experiment such variations in the services . . . as may be authorized by the College of Bishops after consultation with Liturgical Committee of the Provincial Synod' (Canon XXII.8).

At the 1968 Provincial Synod, the Primus (Chairman) announced that experimentation, especially with **ScotR,** was to continue and it was agreed that Dioceses and Congregations should send in comments on current liturgical views for the Liturgical Committee and Bishops to consider. This was done by means of a questionnaire referred to below.

Quite unexpectedly, there was a question at the Synod as to whether **Eng2** could be used in Scotland. The Primus answered that the Bishops could not agree to this because it would mean a fourth Liturgy in use. But clearly the mind of the Synod was for greater freedom amid the 'thousands of variations' already. A 'straw' vote was taken on a motion to allow the use of **Eng2.** In the first Chamber (Bishops) the vote was 3 for and 3 against, and in the second Chamber the motion was carried by 27 votes to 26. Historically this may well be seen to be a visible turning-point in the official councils of the Church on the whole subject of liturgical revision. Following the matter being raised in this way, the Bishops authorized **Eng2** for experimental use, where it was desired.

In April 1969, the Primus announced 'additions to the existing Variations authorized for experimental use in the Liturgy' (see Appendix 1 to this chapter) including material from **Eng2.**

[1] In the past there have been strong canonical safeguards which made it difficult for a congregation to swing from one of the traditional Liturgies to the other.

Questionnaire

A questionnaire was circulated throughout the Province to collect reactions to **ScotR** and other experiments. October 1970 witnessed the report to the Provincial Synod of the results of the questionnaire to which some 250 congregations had replied, out of a possible total of 340. This showed that **ScotR** was preferred to **Scot** by three-quarters of those who replied. Other substantial opinions gleaned from the questionnaire were: many would prefer the Confession to come later in the Service, rather than in the opening section; likewise many were dissatisfied with the form of Confession, being too 'thin' or general. Some would like to use the Gloria at the end of the Service. There was a substantial desire for the optional use of the Summary of the Law and, to a lesser extent, for the Ten Commandments in the place of the Kyries, and for the optional use of the Comfortable Words. Many expressed a desire for more 'freedom and adaptability' in the Inter-cessions and for further forms to be allowed. A fair proportion (namely 96 as against 123) would prefer a new Consecration prayer to be drawn up, and an even larger number would like to have a shorter one.

On the more general question (which had not previously been studied in Scotland) of the language of the Liturgy, the questionnaire showed that the Church was equally divided between those wishing to retain the traditional language, and those who wanted it modernized.

The study of the replies to this questionnaire led the Liturgical Committee and the Bishops to decide to allow a longer period of experimentation and not to propose one official Liturgy for the Province, as had previously been thought a desirable goal. **ScotR** was therefore reprinted in August 1970 (hereafter called **ScotRR**) and now contains Notes about permitted variations and an Appendix of Alternative Forms (see Appendix 2 to this chapter). The new 'grey bookie' took account of the views of the Church as a whole, reflected in the replies to the questionnaire.

Of the use of **Eng2** in Scotland, the questionnaire revealed that in 1970, 58 congregations had used it, some with frequency. A majority of these liked it and approved its order and length. Some suggested its language should be up-dated.

At the Synod in October, 1970, it was agreed to allow the use of two new alternative Sunday lectionaries, namely the 2-year cycle of the Church of England Liturgical Commission (the 'Orange book' of 1969), and the 3-year cycle of the Roman Catholic Church.

The Situation since 1970

For two and a half years from the Provincial Synod of October 1970 until the Spring of 1973, the official position regarding eucharistic experimentation remained fairly static. The attitude of many could be summed up in a phrase used by the Primus, 'that for the time being we should rest with the Liturgies that we have'. The report of the 1970 Synod in *Scan* (the Provincial News Magazine) in November added, 'This meant that in Scotland for the time being there are authorized the SL of 1929 [**Scot**], the EO of 1662 [**ScotE**], the new edition of the Grey Book containing a number of permitted variations [**ScotRR**], and also the English Series 2 Communion Service [**Eng2**], which, as the Primus pointed out, is a variation of the accepted English rite. While there was certainly a weariness with change, yet the Synod seemed to recognize that we could not stand still. Bishop Neil Russell [Assistant Bishop of Edinburgh] pointed out that liturgical change probably needs to be understood as part of the ferment of the Spirit by which God is renewing His Church.'

The number of eucharistic forms which are permitted in the S.E.C. was further increased in 1973. In addition to the four mentioned above, the College of Bishops authorized the experimental use of:

The Church of England Series 3 [**Eng3**][1]

The eucharistic prayers B and D in the American 'Green Book'[2]

Then a further turning point was reached. In 1974 the Diocesan Synod of St. Andrews, Dunkeld and Dunblane requested that the Liturgical Committee should 'proceed with a major revision of Eucharistic Liturgical Use'. At the Provincial Synod on 8 October 1974 this was carried by 3 to 1 in the First Chamber (of Bishops), but defeated 32-25 in the Second Chamber (of Clergy and Laity). The Episcopal Church is not easily to be moved away from its traditionalisms.

Survey

The impression gained from six of the seven dioceses is one of cautiousness. The diocese of Edinburgh alone has done serious work on

---

[1] The Primus indicated at the Provincial Synod in October 1973 that this was authorized on the grounds that it was a modification of **Eng2**.

[2] [Apparently these prayers are only to be used under strictly controlled conditions. It should be noted that the two prayers permitted (nos. 99 and 102 in the American rites in chapter 7) are in the 'you' form of address to God. Thus presumably they should be used with **Eng3**, and not with the other, 'thou' form, rites authorized in Scotland. On any reckoning, there is an interesting historical appositeness about the fact that the Scottish Episcopalians, who exported their own rite to America with Samuel Seabury in the 1780s, should now be prepared to import back the latest linear descendants from their own liturgical ancestry. Editor]

liturgical experimentation at the diocesan level, and even there the Bishop's letter to his clergy (April 1973) had to be as concerned to allay fears as to encourage boldness. The Edinburgh Liturgical Committee had earlier reported in February 1972 that half the Congregations were experimenting seriously, while the others betrayed 'a considerable degree of ignorance and confusion in the minds of both clergy and laity about what "Liturgy" is and is for. Opinions and practises seem to be rooted more in non-liturgical, non-theological factors, such as personal likes and dislikes, personal defensiveness and authoritarianism, changes of fussy details in the pursuit of modernity or of tradition'. Little has changed since then.

In other dioceses, especially in the country districts and in the Highlands, and, to a lesser extent in the Aberdeen diocese, there seems even more conservatism. It is fair to conclude that the real ferment and clash of attitudes in the use of eucharistic forms is yet to come for the bulk of Episcopalian Congregations.

It is difficult to analyse precisely 'who uses what'[1]. A majority (perhaps 60%) still use exclusively either **Scot** or **ScotR** (or **ScotRR**). A few (say 10%) use **ScotE** (basically 1662). The rest (some 30%) use at different service times both Scottish and English rites. Apparently only in the Glasgow and Edinburgh dioceses is there regular use made of **Eng2**, and this in only about twelve congregations (some 4% of the total number of charges). There is also now a growing use of **Eng3**, following study and preliminary use of it in some of the more 'go-ahead' places. Worthy of individual mention is that St. Mary's Cathedral, Edinburgh, have changed from **ScotR** to **Eng2** for their main Sunday morning Eucharist. Further it is not possible to say what proportion of those who use **Scot** (exclusively or shared with **ScotE**) are using it in the revised form (**ScotR** or **ScotRR**).[2] At a guess, well over half of such Congregations use the Grey Book, and this is certainly the rite normally used on Diocesan and Provincial occasions.

Alongside the use of the experimental Liturgies, the impact of the Liturgical Movement has been felt, as in most other parts of the Anglican Communion. So, whereas in the mid-fifties, Westward position was known in only one or two Churches, now in probably half,

[1] The facts and figures quoted here are gathered from a study of the 1973 SEC Year Book, but some of the information it contains is likely to be out-of-date. (The contributor gratefully acknowledges the research done by Mrs. Elspeth Grant.)

[2] Most congregations using this rite have the 1970 **ScotRR** Edition. (This is obtainable from the S.P.C.K. Bookshop, 7 Drumsheugh Place, Edinburgh).

the celebrant faces the people over the Table. The rest still use East-ward position.[1] Again, the Table being in the nave or at the entrance to the chancel, either as a permanent fixture or moveable, has been a feature introduced in some places during the past decade. A lead has been taken in these respects in new church buildings, in the student world, in Edinburgh Theological College, and in some Cathedrals. The SEC having been in the past a monochrome 'Catholic' Province, the Eucharist as the 'main' Sunday service has been the norm in perhaps 70% or 80% of the Congregations. Now others are following suit. The general loosening up brought in by the Liturgical Movement is being felt ever more widely.

Prognosis

With the rapid and universal change in matters liturgical, how are things likely to move in Scotland? Answer: Slowly. That is about all that can be said. Perhaps the reader has gleaned from this chapter that both at official decision-making level, and at the Congregational practical level, many are reluctant to 'modernize'. Yet some 'radicals' are impatient for change, especially in the 'southern' dioceses of Glasgow, Edinburgh and St. Andrews. The tensions then are likely to persist, and in a generally conservative atmosphere, we may find that slow change and compromise are the order of the day. However, one important aspect of Scottish life in general, and in the Episcopal Church in particular, is the wish 'to do things together and to do the same'. This attitude can be seen in the desire in the recent past to work towards 'one Liturgy for Scotland'. However, this dream seems to be shattered by recent trends and the number of alternatives available and used at the present time.

It might be that the possibility of having a new SPB will continue to recede, and perhaps be lost sight of altogether amid the many coloured 'wee bookies'. What effect this will have on the health and vitality of the Church at large and the individual members of Congregations, not to mention the unity of the Church, will have to be left to others to guess! It is enough to say that the possible future unifying effect of **Eng2** and **Eng3**, to say nothing of the ecumenical prospects, may in the end of the day be seen to be more important than the much treasured and long used SL—unless this can be revised in such a way that it can be used in the nineteen-eighties. Some would like to see it put through a theological as well as a liturgical and linguistic revision.

---

[1] 'North Side' is unheard of, except at St. Thomas', Edinburgh and St. Giles', Glasgow.

APPENDIX 1

EXPERIMENTAL LITURGY
(April 1969)

The College of Bishops has agreed to the following additions to the existing Variations authorized for experimental use in the Liturgy, under Canon XXIII.8.

1. The Kyries and the Gloria in Excelsis may be used as alternatives.
2. For the Intercession, as an alternative to the Prayer for the Church or the Litany, the Intercession from the Service of Holy Communion Alternative Series II of the Church of England may be used.
3. If it is desired to shorten the Prayer of Consecration the paragraphs after that containing the Epiclesis may be reduced in length as follows:
   'We earnestly desire thy fatherly goodness, mercifully to accept this our sacrifice of praise and thanksgiving. . . . And here we offer and present unto thee O Lord, ourselves, our souls and bodies, to be a reasonable, holy and living sacrifice unto thee, beseeching thee . . . to accept this our bounden duty and service, through Jesus Christ our Lord; by whom and with whom, in the unity of the Holy Ghost, all honour and glory be unto thee, O Father Almighty, world without end, **Amen**'.
4. For the words of administration the formula 'The Body of Christ' and 'The Blood of Christ' may be used as in Alternative Series II.
5. Where it is desired, the Bishop may authorize the Service of Holy Communion Alternative Series II for experimental use.

APPENDIX 2

ScotRR (1970)

ScotRR is distinguished from **ScotR** in the following ways:

(A) There is an opening page of *NOTES*. These allow the use of material in the *APPENDIX* (see below), the omission of material bracketed in the text, and the omission of other parts under certain precise conditions. The Gloria in Excelsis may be used at the end of the service.

(B) In the text brackets are placed round where they were in **ScotR** and also round the versicles and responses in no. 3 of **ScotR** (**MAL** p.152), except the first words of all, and the confession and absolution. In the eucharistic prayer they are placed round 'most humbly beseeching thee . . . benefits of his passion' and 'that all we who shall . . . sacrifice; yet we beseech thee' (**MAL** pp.157-8). In the Dismissal the salutation is omitted and brackets are placed round 'Go forth in peace. **Thanks be to God'.** Many of the very skeletal rubrics are amplified, and a brief post-communion thanksgiving is included (cf. **MAL** p.159). Hymns, Psalms or Canticles are permitted by rubric in four places. The Scottish Litany, omitted from the main text, appears in the *APPENDIX*.

(C) There is added the following after the service:

APPENDIX

ALTERNATIVE FORMS

1 *THE CONFESSION AND ABSOLUTION*
Almighty God, . . . [**MAL** CF 10] **. . . Christ our Lord. Amen.**
Almighty God, . . . [**MAL** CF 11] . . . Christ our Lord. **Amen.**
Our Lord Jesus Christ said: Hear, O Israel . . . [**MAL** CF 4(b)] . . . law and the prophets.

People. **Lord, have mercy upon us, and write all these thy laws in our hearts, we beseech thee.**

2 *THE INTERCESSION*
The Second Shorter Litany
Let us beseech . . . [The Litany from **ScotR, MAL** pp.153-4, now removed from the main text and placed in this appendix] . . . for the faithful departed.

The Litany may close with a prayer

Or THE INTERCESSION may be made in the following or similar form
Let us pray for the whole state . . . [The intercession from **Eng2, MAL** pp.132-3] . . . our Saviour Jesus Christ. **Amen.**

3 *AT THE OFFERTORY*
At the offering of the Bread and Wine these prayers may be said:
C. Blessed art thou, Lord, God of all creation; through thy goodness we have this bread to offer, which earth hath given and human hands have made: it will become for us the bread of life.

P. **Blessed be God for ever.**

C. Blessed art thou, Lord, God of all creation; through thy goodness we have this wine to offer, fruit of the vine and work of human hands: it will become our spiritual drink.

P. **Blessed be God for ever.**

CHAPTER 4

THE CHURCH IN WALES

THE period between 1968 and 1975 has witnessed the appearance of no genuinely new eucharistic rite in the Province of Wales. The one and only new rite the Welsh Church has ever produced is the experimental rite of 1966 (**Wal**)[1]. The experimental period is to last ten years from that date, and during this period the only other rite authorized for use is that of 1662. This is why **Eng2** and **Eng3** have never been used in the parish churches of the Province. It is the next revision that will be regarded as definitive and for inclusion in the BCP of the Church in Wales.

In the meanwhile reactions to **Wal** are being tested; a detailed questionnaire has been sent to every parish and at the time of writing there seems little desire to change from **Wal**. In the same way the accompanying modern English Language version (**WalR**) must be essentially regarded as part of the Liturgical Commission's attempt to gauge the reaction of the Province to the ICET forms of the Lord's Prayer, the Nicene Creed, Gloria, Sanctus, Benedictus and Agnus Dei, and to prepare the way for the possibility of the second definitive rite being produced in modern English. **WalR** is primarily intended to be a study document. It is not recommended for use, except in the very limited context of a study group, and this is why it contains no rubrics or headings.

WalR was completed in the summer of 1970, approved for publication by the Welsh bishops in Holy Week 1971 and published in March 1972. The above stipulations about its use were made by the bishops in Holy Week 1971. Although the study period will presumably end with the authorization of the definitive rite, correspondence with the Liturgical Commission's secretary on the subject dwindled away by Summer 1973.

The original guiding principle of those responsible for this version was to effect a 'straight' translation of **Wal,** and to include the relevant ICET material. This does not mean just the retention of traditional language in a much simpler form, as would seem to be the case in

---

[1] [The text of **Wal** is printed out in **MAL**, pp.163-72. The main principles of compilation of **Wal** are common to **WalR** also (apart from the modern English), and these are not restated here.—Editor.]

Eng2. Neither does it mean simply using the language that is most commonly used today, whatever the loss may be in terms of rhythm and beauty, as would seem to be the case in the vernacular version of the Roman Mass. Liturgical language needs to be dignified, rhythmic and evocative, as well as clear and doctrinally sound.

But a 'straight' translation is not only very difficult to achieve; it sometimes proves impossible, and sometimes it may even be deemed to be undesirable. At the same time variations in doctrinal and liturgical nuance are bound to emerge. That the compilers were not content with a mere reproduction of the original text in simpler language becomes immediately apparent in their versions of the Collect for Purity and the Confession. 'From whom no secrets are hid' is omitted from the Collect, and into the Confession comes the novel insertion of a reference to the sins of omission. Again, one observes the significant substitution of a plea for forgiveness expressed in the first person plural for an absolution expressed by the priest to the congregation. Is it proper to deduce from such a change that the Eucharist itself is to be regarded as the remission of sins which this prayer anticipates?

The two forms of Intercession allow for much greater variety in the choice of prayer topics, but the wording and division of the two final petitions reveal again the 'exclusive'[1] character of the Welsh revision i.e. prayers for the dead are made obligatory. The 'saints' in this context, as opposed to 'servants' who have died in the faith, are those for whom we give thanks and praise, and in whose fellowship we rejoice. Yet by a strange anomaly this is by no means made apparent in the words that immediately precede the Sanctus. There we have 'hosts of heaven' for 'all the company of heaven'. This is not modern English on any reckoning and seems to be more like a straight translation of the Latin. If this is so, we are left with both an unnecessary qualification of the preceding reference to angels and an unfortunate omission of the 'saints' as part of the whole company with whom we worship.

Changes in the Eucharistic Prayer are minimal and consist in the main of a marked simplification of the text, as in, for example, the sentence: 'he made one perfect sacrifice for the sin of the world', which omits atonement language that is Anselmian and post-Scriptural, and, in keeping with the Gloria, refers to 'sin' rather than 'sins'. Another example of simplification is in the omission of epithets when the

---

[1] This categorization is used by R. T. Beckwith in *Prayer Book Revision and Anglican Unity* (Church Book Room Press 1967). His other two categories are entitled 'Divisive' and 'Unitive'.

'passion, resurrection and ascension' are mentioned. But the words of invitation to receive the consecrated elements call for comment in that they are far from being a 'straight' translation. The rubric in **Wal** reads: '*The Priest shall receive . . . and then proceed to administer . . . first saying*'. The **WalR** version is: 'Come, let us receive'. This only makes sense if the celebrant receives *after* extending the invitation to the congregation, as is the sequence in **Eng3.** The only other radical change is to be found in the form of words of administration. These are certainly not a mere transposition into modern English but the abbreviated form, plus response, that we find in **Eng2**:'The body/blood of Christ. **Amen.**'

There is also a modern Welsh language version of the Welsh version of **Wal.** This has been in the hands of the members of the Liturgical Commission since January 1973, but it has not yet been authorized for publication. Its appearance is being delayed pending the publication of the new Welsh Bible, when particular interest will be shown in the translation of the Lord's Prayer and the words of Institution that it will contain. Suffice it to say at this stage that the disparity between modern and traditional language is not so marked in Welsh as it is in English. The Welsh version for the most part is not a translation of **WalR** but is a simple updating of the Welsh version of **Wal.** This, in addition to having a number of detailed textual variations from **WalR,** particularly in the Collect for Purity, the Confession and the Creed, it does contain headings (but still no rubrics).

The coming of modern English in **WalR** has inevitably had repercussions on other services. The English used in the new Burial service is partially in this style—that in the new Marriage service almost entirely so. The new Burial service also bears upon a question mentioned above, as the petitions for the departed in it are significantly optional. Whether this principle will be invoked as **WalR** is in turn revised into its second and definitive form remains to be seen.

THE WELSH MODERN ENGLISH STUDY
LITURGY 1972 (WalR)

[There are no rubrics in this study rite. It is probable that the slightly inconsistent use of brackets and double brackets indicate alternative and optional items, but no guidance is given on this point. They are reproduced as in the original rite. The numbering is editorial.]

THE HOLY EUCHARIST

1 In the name of the Father, the Son and the Holy Spirit. **Amen.**

2 Let us pray.
Almighty God,
   to you all hearts are open
   and all desires known:
Purify our thoughts through your Holy Spirit,
   that we may love you with heart and mind,
      and praise you as we ought;
         through Jesus Christ our Lord. **Amen.**

3 Lord, have mercy on us.
Christ, have mercy on us.
Lord, have mercy on us.

4 Let us confess our sins to God.
Almighty God, Father of our Lord Jesus Christ,
we confess that we have sinned
in our thoughts and our words.
in what we have done and in what we have failed to do.
We are truly sorry for our faults.
Have mercy on us, Father;
forgive us our sins,
and help us to lead a new life in your service
and to make known your glory;
through Jesus Christ our Lord. Amen.

5 May almighty God have mercy on us,
   forgive us and set us free from our sins;
   may he strengthen us in goodness,
   and keep us in eternal life;
   through Jesus Christ our Lord. **Amen.**

6 ((**Glory to** . . . ⟦ICET 4⟧ . . . **Father. Amen.**))

7 The Lord be with you.
His Spirit be with us.
Let us pray.
COLLECT(S) OF THE DAY

8 *(OLD TESTAMENT LESSON)*
The reading from . . .

9 *EPISTLE*

10 *(PSALM)*

11 The Holy Gospel according to Saint . . .
Glory to you, Lord.
GOSPEL
Praise to you, Lord Christ.

12 *(SERMON)*

13 ((**We believe** . . . ⟦ICET 3⟧ . . . **come. Amen.**))
(**and the Son**) OM BRACKETS

14 ((*NOTICES, ETC.*))

15 Let us pray for the whole Church of Christ, and for all men according
to their needs.

((*EITHER*

That God may send his Spirit to
guide the universal Church into
the way of truth and love, that
all who call themselves Christians
may maintain the unity of the
Spirit in the bond of peace;

Let us pray to the Lord.
Lord, hear our prayer.

For all bishops, priests and
deacons, and especially N. our
Bishop that by word and example
they may proclaim God's true and
living word and administer his
holy sacraments;

Let us pray to the Lord.
Lord, hear our prayer.

OR))

Father in heaven, grant that all
who believe in you may be united
in your truth, live together in your
love, and reflect your glory in the
world.
(*Here the priest may mention
special objects of prayer in the field
of Christian unity, and a silence
may be kept*).

Lord, hear us.
Lord, graciously hear us.

Give grace to our Bishop N. and
to all other ministers of your
Church, that they may truly
proclaim your word and rightly
administer your sacraments.

For all Christian people, and especially the family of God in this place (*or* parish, college, etc.), that he may give us grace to live worthy of our calling, in obedience to his commands;

Let us pray to the Lord.
Lord, hear our prayer.

For those who govern the nations of the world, and especially Elizabeth our Queen and all in authority under her, that God in his wisdom may direct them in the ways of justice and peace;

Let us pray to the Lord.
Lord, hear our prayer.

For the leaders and people of Wales, that we may live together in the fear of God and in brotherly love;

Let us pray to the Lord.
Lord, hear our prayer.

For all who are in trouble, sorrow, need, sickness, or distress of any kind, that trusting in God's love they may find hope and strength and be comforted: and especially for . . . ;

Let us pray to the Lord.
Lord, hear our prayer.

That God's servants who have died in faith, especially . . . may have everlasting light and peace;

Let us pray to the Lord.
Lord, hear our prayer.

(*Here he may mention special objects of prayer, referring to the ministry, and a silence may be kept*).
Lord, hear us.
Lord, graciously hear us.

Bless your people everywhere, particularly in this place, that they may serve you faithfully all their days.
(*Here he may mention special objects of prayer referring to the people of God, and a silence may be kept*).
Lord hear us
Lord, graciously hear us.

Direct this and every nation in the ways of justice and peace, that we may honour all men and seek the common good.
(*Here he may introduce special objects of prayer for the nations of the world, the Queen, Government and people of the United Kingdom, or the Welsh people and their leaders. A silence may be kept*).
Lord, hear us.
Lord, graciously hear us.

Save and comfort those who suffer and help them to put their trust in your love.
(*Here he may mention those in special need, and a silence may be kept*).
Lord, hear us.
Lord, graciously hear us.

We praise God's holy name for his grace and glory shown through all the saints, and pray that, rejoicing in their fellowship and following their example, we may have a place with them in his eternal kingdom.

Hear us, Father, for the sake of Jesus Christ, our only mediator and advocate; to him, with you and the Holy Spirit, be honour and glory for ever. Amen.

Hear us as we commend to your keeping those who have died in faith, and grant them everlasting light and peace.
(*Here departed persons may be specially mentioned, and a silence kept*).

Lord, hear us.
Lord, graciously hear us.

Finally, we give you thanks and praise for all your saints. Glad of their fellowship and striving to follow their example, we ask you to grant us with them a share in your eternal kingdom.

Hear us, Father, through Jesus Christ your Son. To him, with you and the Holy Spirit, is all honour and glory, now and for ever. Amen.

16 The Lord's peace be with you:
His peace be with us always.
(*Offertory sentence*).

((All things come from you, Lord:
And we give you what is your own)).

17 The Lord be with you:
And also with you.

Lift up your hearts:
We lift them up to the Lord.

Let us give thanks to the Lord our God:
It is right to give him thanks and praise.

It is indeed right, it is our privilege and duty,
 to give you thanks always and everywhere,
  Holy Father, all-powerful and everliving God,

[There follows a Proper Preface in the Study text, and this is a sample of those which follow the service in an appendix and are printed here in Appendix C].

And so with the company of angels and all the hosts of heaven
we proclaim the glory of your name,
and join in their unending hymn of praise:
Holy, holy, holy Lord, God of power and might,
heaven and earth are full of your glory.
  Hosanna in the highest.
Blessed is he who comes in the name of the Lord.
  Hosanna in the highest.

Almighty God, our heavenly Father,
  we thank you and praise you
    for creating heaven and earth and all that is in them,
      making man in your own image.
We thank you for your great love
  in giving us your only Son, Jesus Christ,
    to be made man, live on earth,
      and suffer death for our redemption.
By his death on the cross,
  he made one perfect sacrifice for the sin of the world;
  and he commands us to commemorate that death
    until he comes again.
And so we ask you, Father,
  to sanctify these gifts of bread and wine,
    that as we receive them
      according to the commandment of our Saviour Jesus Christ,
    we may truly share in his most precious body and blood.
On the night when he was betrayed,
    he took bread,
    and when he had given thanks,
    he broke it,
    and gave it to his disciples, saying:
  'Take this and eat; this is my body, given for you:
    do this as a memorial of me'.
In the same way after supper
    he took the cup,
    and when he had given thanks,
    he gave it to them and said:
  'Drink from it, all of you; for this is my blood of the new
    covenant, shed for many for the forgiveness of sins:
    do this, whenever you drink it, as a memorial of me'.

Therefore, Father we commemorate
  his passion, resurrection and ascension,
    as he has commanded;
  rejoicing in his gift of the Holy Spirit,
    we look for his coming again with power and glory;
  and, together with all your people,
    we set before you
      this bread of eternal life
      and this cup of everlasting salvation.
We ask you to accept our offering of thanks and praise.
Grant to us and all your church
  forgiveness of sins
    and renewal of life;
  may all who share in this holy communion
    be filled with grace and blessing;
  and be numbered with your saints in the everlasting glory
    of the Lord Jesus Christ:
Through him and with him,
  in the unity of the Holy Spirit,
  all honour and glory are yours,
    almighty Father,
    for ever and ever.
      Amen.

18 We break this bread:
and we share in the body of Christ.

19 (**Lord, we come to your table,**
  trusting in your mercy
  and not in any goodness of our own.
We are not good enough
  to pick up the crumbs under your table.
  But it is your nature always to have mercy.
Grant that we may so eat the flesh and drink the blood
  of your Son, Jesus Christ,
  that we may live for ever in him,
    and he in us. Amen.)

20 Let us say with confidence the prayer our Saviour taught us:
Our Father in heaven . . . [ICET 1] . . . for ever. Amen.

21 Come, let us receive the body and blood of our Lord Jesus Christ, given
for us, and feed on him in faith with thanksgiving.
>The body of Christ. **Amen.**
>The blood of Christ. **Amen.**

22 **Jesus, Lamb of God . . .** ⟦ICET 8⟧ **. . . give us your peace.**

23 Give thanks to the Lord, for he is good:
His love is everlasting.
We thank you, Father,
>for giving us the body and blood of your Son
>>in this holy sacrament,
through which we, the members of his mystical body,
>are assured of the hope of eternal life.
And we offer ourselves to you,
as a living sacrifice;
keep us in this holy fellowship
and help us to do all the good works you have designed for us:
through your Son, Jesus Christ,
who, in the unity of the Holy Spirit,
lives and reigns with you,
one God for ever. Amen.

24 The Lord be with you:
And also with you.
Go out into the world in peace:
In the name of Christ. Amen.

CHAPTER 5

THE CHURCH OF IRELAND

Background

THE first revision of the 1662 Book of Common Prayer undertaken by the Church of Ireland after disestablishment in 1870 took seven years to complete. The next very modest revision which commenced in 1909 was not completed until seventeen years had passed. When a Liturgical Commission was set up in 1962 it aimed to have ready for 1970 (the centenary year of disestablishment)[1] a revision of the Prayer Book. Progress has been slower than anticipated and the Draft Revised Service of Holy Communion (**IreR**)[2] which was originally authorized for a three year period of experimental use in 1967 has had to wait until 1972 for a successor. What has now become reform of the Liturgy is a far more complex operation than revision. It is no longer the work of an advisory committee proposing minor alterations to the General Synod for authorization but an involvement of the whole Church. This requires time for consultation and discussion at Parish level as well as a continuing contact with the developments of reform in other Churches. **IreR** had been preceded by a Draft Service in 1965 issued for discussion and comment. There followed in 1968 the publication of Six Study Outlines[3] and in 1969 a Questionnaire composed by the Holy Communion sub-committee and sent to all Incumbents to test reaction to the use of the Service in the Parishes. By 1971 a Communications sub-committee had been formed to devise ways and means of maintaining as close a contact as possible between the worshipping community and the revising committee. This was followed by the appointment of a Liturgical Adviser in each Diocese by the Bishop. As a result there is a far more effective communications link than that provided by the sending of Questionnaires.

Authorization

The General Synod in May 1971 had before it a draft of the proposed 1972 Service of Holy Communion included in the Report of the Liturgical Advisory Commission. Following criticisms and the rejection of the report at General Synod by a very narrow lay vote (Clergy; 69 for,

---

[1] Vincent Ryan *Irish Anglicanism* 1869-1969, p.182.
[2] The text of this is in **MAL**, pp.179-88.
[3] J. E. Greer *Six Study Outlines* (Dublin University Press, 1968).

21 against: Laity; 58 for, 61 against)[1], an amended Draft was approved
by the House of Bishops and authorized for study use in October 1971.
A copy of this service together with a letter from the Primate, an
Explanation of the Service, and a Commentary, was sent in November
via the Liturgical Advisors to every Clergyman and General Synodsman
of the Church. In the months immediately preceding the Synod of 1972
the service was used throughout the Dioceses in special gatherings of
clergy, synodsmen, and other groups. After making small corrections
and additions the House of Bishops authorized the general use of
Holy Communion 1972 from the first Sunday in Advent, 3 December
1972, for a period of seven years. Throughout the period 1971-2 the
Holy Communion sub-committee took note of the work in the field
of Liturgy being undertaken by other Churches and particularly by
fellow-members of the Anglican Communion. One representative of the
Committee, the Dean of Lismore, is a member of the International
Consultation on English Texts and is also an observer for the Church of
Ireland at the Church of England Liturgical Commission. The gradual
extension of the period for experimental use, which was first three
years, then five and now seven, underlines this involvement in depth by
so many in the work of reform. Their participation has set the pace
at which progress is made, and has dictated the change from the original
plan of completing a definitive revision by 1970.

Sources

The influence of this variety of sources can be detected when a comparison is made between the 1967 Draft and the latest 1972 Service.
Quite early on it was decided to accept the ICET agreed Liturgical
Texts wherever they were applicable to Holy Communion. This in
turn required a more radical approach to the language used throughout
the Service. Compare for instance the opening words of the two
Litany forms of Intercession.

1967 (IreR)

Almighty and everliving God, graciously accept our prayers, we beseech
thee.
People.   **Lord, hear our prayer.**
For the peace that is from above, and for the salvation of all mankind, let
us pray to the Lord.
People.   **Lord, hear our prayer.**

1972 (Ire1)

Almighty and everliving God, hear the prayers which we offer in faith:
For peace and for the salvation of all men, Lord in your mercy,
People.   **Hear our prayer.**

[1] *Journal of the General Synod* 1971, p.cxiv.

On the other hand usage and familiarity decided that changes in the wording and structure of such prayers as the Collect for Purity and the Prayer of Humble Access should be minimal. Quotations from Holy Scripture in 1967 followed the Revised Standard Version and where phrases in the Prefaces were based on Scripture Texts this version was the norm. Now a much freer use of translations has been accepted and most of the modern versions have been consulted. Sometimes a quotation may be direct from one version; in other instances it may combine phrases from several.

The recognition that revision should not be divisive has influenced the Church of Ireland revisers against any kind of 'go-it-alone' policy. When the post-Lambeth Consultation produced its guidelines for structure in the Pan-Anglican document 'The Structure and Contents of the Eucharistic Liturgy and the Daily Office' the Church of Ireland commission recognized their importance.[1] Indeed it is remarkable how closely **IreR** had been in line with their suggestions. The main changes in the shape of **Ire1** that reflect this document are to be seen: (1) in the substitution of praise in the form of the Gloria in Excelsis for the commandments at the opening of the Service, and the summary of the Law and the alternative use of the commandments transferred to the Penitential preparation for Communion after the Prayers of the Church: (2) in setting the Fraction after the Thanksgiving and the Lord's Prayer immediately before Communion and in the outline of the ending which consists of the brief post-Communion devotion and Dismissal.

As well as following the Pan-Anglican Document, and employing the ICET texts, the Commission has kept the work of the Church of England Commission particularly in view. The text of the Ten Commandments (with New Testament Comment) resembles **Eng3**, but has roots also in the 1926 Irish Prayer Book's provision for Ash Wednesday. The Comfortable Words come in the English position, before confession. The Peace, the Offertory and the Taking of the Bread and Wine follow the English pattern in several respects. The whole concept of four actions is now much clearer, though the retention of manual acts at the Narrative of Institution in the Thanksgiving provides a link with the past expression of these actions in **Ire** and **IreR.** The English wording has been used at many points, in order to give a common text in a worldwide context.

---

[1] [See pages 27-31 above—Editor.]

One final contribution from Ireland's own previous texts came when General Synod debated the first draft in 1971. Then representations were made that the 1662 words of administration should be retained, and these were re-introduced as an alternative at 29b.

Significant Changes

Some further differences between **IreR** and **Ire1** deserve attention. Of the two intercessions in each, the litany form is common to both, but the old 'Church Militant' type has given way to a form based on that in **Eng2**, which gives scope for extempore inclusion of particular needs. The Thanksgiving too is altered. The reference to creation introduces an oblique mention of the Fall ('more wonderfully *restored* him'). The anamnesis includes the hope of Christ's coming ('looking for the coming of his kingdom'). And the petition for the benefits of reception omits the forgiveness of sins (which is the traditionally stated benefit) and replaces it with emphasis upon the role of the Spirit in giving unity, communion, and perseverance. There is also a rich profusion of seasonal blessings for the great Festivals. However, the Long Exhortations which still appeared in **IreR** in an appendix have been omitted. The typography has been improved, with a return to red for rubrics, and with varying types used to indicate headings of the different sections and the congregational parts of the service.

The Lectionary

There was an experimental lectionary authorized in 1968[1], and its five-year period expired in 1973. The English Joint Liturgical Group's proposals form the basis of a new Table of lessons put before General Synod and accepted in 1973, and collects in modern English have now been composed to accompany the readings. Thus the theme and readings for each Sunday will normally be common to both the Church of England and the Church of Ireland.

Evaluation

With the acceptance that reform of the liturgy, like that of the Church itself, is an ongoing process, no-one would now pronounce this or that liturgical text 'final' or 'definitive'. Nevertheless in **Ire1** there appears to be a pattern which will be stable for some time to come. Seven years of use and experiment will give plenty of opportunity to judge its merits and test its soundness.

---

[1] This is described in some detail in **MAL** pp.178-9.

THE IRISH LITURGY 1972 (Ire1)

[The numbering in this service is original, except for the three appendixes, where it is editorial. The 'Directions' below come on a separate page of the booklet, and precede the title of the service.]

DIRECTIONS

1   *Every confirmed person should, after careful preparation, communicate regularly and frequently.*

2   *It is the duty of every parishioner to contribute generously, according to his means, to the maintenance of the worship of God, to the spread of the Gospel, and to works of charity.*

3   *The Minister and Churchwardens decide on the disposal of the offertory alms. If they disagree, the Ordinary shall make the decision.*

4   *The Holy Table, at the time of the Communion, is to have a fair linen cloth on it.*

5   *When the Old Testament Lesson and Psalm are used in this Order the service is to be regarded as the equivalent of Morning or Evening Prayer and Holy Communion.*

6   *On occasions sanctioned by the Ordinary, this Order may begin with the Collect of the Day.*

7   *The Holy Communion is not to be celebrated unless there is at least one person present to communicate with the priest.*

8   *If any of the consecrated Bread and Wine remains it is to be consumed reverently by the priest (and by other communicants if necessary). This may be done either when all have communicated, or after the Blessing—in which case the consecrated elements are to remain, covered with a linen cloth, on the Holy Table from the time of the Communion until after the Blessing.*

9   *The priest is to say or sing the Service audibly and clearly.*

10   *Whenever a certain posture is particularly appropriate, it is indicated thus—'Stand' or 'Kneel'. At other points local custom may be established and followed, including the provision of opportunity to withdraw before the Communion for those who wish to do so.*

AN ORDER FOR THE CELEBRATION OF

THE HOLY COMMUNION

1 *Stand*
 Priest The Lord be with you
 People **And also with you.**

2 *Priest*
 Almighty God . . . ⟦CF 1⟧ . . . Lord. **Amen.**
  hid] hidden

3 *All say or sing,*
 Glory to God . . . ⟦ICET 4⟧ . . . **Father. Amen.**

4 *Priest* Let us pray.
 The Collect of the Day, and any other prayer appointed or permitted, is said.

THE MINISTRY OF THE WORD

5 *Sit*
 A LESSON. One of the Old Testament Lessons appointed for the day, or part of it, may be read, and the reader says,
 The Lesson is written in . . . in the . . . chapter, beginning at the . . . verse.
 At the end of the reading he says,
 This is the word of the Lord.

6 *After the Lesson one of the appointed Psalms, or a part of it, is said or sung.*

7 *THE EPISTLE. The reader of the Epistle says,*
 The Epistle is written in the . . . in the . . . chapter, beginning at the . . . verse.
 At the end of the reading he says,
 This is the word of the Lord.

8 *A canticle, hymn or anthem may follow.*

9 *Stand*
 THE GOSPEL. The minister who is to read the Gospel says,
 The Holy Gospel is written in the Gospel according to . . . in the . . . chapter . . . beginning at the . . . verse.

10 *Then is said or sung,*
 Glory to Christ our Saviour.
 At the end of the reading the minister says,
 This is the Gospel of Christ.
 Then is said or sung,
 Praise to Christ our Lord.

11 *When there is a sermon, it is preached here.*

12 *Stand*

All say or sing the Nicene Creed.

We believe . . . ⟦ICET 3⟧ **. . . world to come. Amen.**

(and the Son))] OM BRACKETS

13 *Banns of Marriage and notices may be read here.*

14 *The offerings of the people may be collected and a hymn may be sung.*

THE PRAYERS OF THE CHURCH (*First Form*)

15a *Kneel*

The priest, or some person appointed by him, says,

Let us pray.

Almighty and everliving God, hear the prayers which we offer in faith:

For peace and for the salvation of all men,

> Lord, in your mercy,

People   **Hear our prayer.**

For the one holy catholic and apostolic Church, and for the unity of all Christian people,

> Lord, in your mercy,

People   **Hear our prayer.**

For bishops, priests and deacons, and especially for N. our bishop,

> Lord, in your mercy,

People   **Hear our prayer.**

For those who learn and those who teach the Christian faith,

> Lord, in your mercy,

People   **Hear our prayer.**

For all who live and work in this parish,

> Lord, in your mercy,

People   **Hear our prayer.**

For families and for those who live alone,

> Lord, in your mercy,

People   **Hear our prayer.**

For the sick and afflicted,

> Lord, in your mercy,

People   **Hear our prayer.**

For all in authority, and especially for (*N.I.* Elizabeth our Queen) (*R.I.* our President),

> Lord, in your mercy,
People **Hear our prayer.**

For those who work for peace, justice and righteousness throughout the world,

> Lord, in your mercy,
People **Hear our prayer.**

For . . .

> Lord, in your mercy,
People **Hear our prayer.**

Mindful of the holy apostles and martyrs, and of all your servants departed this life in your faith and fear, we commend ourselves, and one another, and our whole life to you, Lord God, through Jesus Christ our Saviour. **Amen.**

THE PRAYERS OF THE CHURCH (*Second Form*)

15b *Kneel*

The priest, or some person appointed by him, says,

Let us pray.

Almighty God, our heavenly Father, who promised through your Son Jesus Christ, to hear the prayers of those who ask in faith: Hear our prayer for your Church in all the world, for this diocese and for N. our bishop:

(*Here he may pray for any particular need of the Church*)

Grant that we, and all who confess your Name, may be united in your truth, live together in your love, and reveal your glory in the world.

> Lord, in your mercy,
People **Hear our prayer.**

We pray for the nations of the world, for this country, for (*N.I.* Elizabeth our Queen) (*R.I.* our President) and for all in authority.

(*Here he may pray for any particular need*)

Guide the people of this land, and of all the nations, in the ways of justice and peace; that men may honour one another and serve the common good.

> Lord, in your mercy,
People **Hear our prayer.**

We pray for the sick, the poor and those in trouble.
(*Here he may pray for the needs of particular persons*)
Save and comfort those who suffer, that they may hold to you through
good and ill, and trust in your unfailing love.

> Lord, in your mercy,

People   **Hear our prayer.**

We bless your holy Name for all your servants who have died in faith.
Grant that we may share with them the joys of your eternal kingdom.

> Lord, in your mercy,

People   **Hear our prayer.**

Accept these our prayers, merciful Father, for the sake of your Son, our
Saviour Jesus Christ. **Amen.**

PENITENCE

16a   *The priest says,*

Hear what our Lord Jesus Christ said:

You shall love the Lord your God with all your heart, and with all your
soul, and with all your mind. This is the first and great commandment,
and the second is like it, You shall love your neighbour as yourself. On
these two commandments depend all the law and the prophets.

A new commandment I give to you, that you love one another; even as I
have loved you, that you also love one another.

People   **Amen, Lord have mercy.**

or

16b   *On Ash Wednesday, and at other times at his discretion, the priest says,*

Hear these commandments of God to his people:
I am the Lord . . . [Then as in the Appendix to **Eng3** on pp.59-60, with
the omission noted and with people's response after the fourth and
tenth Commandments only.] . . . **Amen, Lord have mercy.**
Remember the words . . . to receive] OM
[The eighth commandment is in the **Eng3** 1971 form.]

17a   *The Priest or one of the ministers, says,*

God so loved the world that he gave his only Son, Jesus Christ, to save
us from our sins, to plead for us in heaven, and to bring us to eternal
life.

or

17b *He may say,*

Hear what our Saviour Christ says . . . ⟦CF 4⟧ . . . the propitiation of our sins.

who labour] that travail
give you rest] refresh you
only Son, that whoever believes] only-begotten Son to the end that all who believe
saying is true and worthy of full acceptance] is a true saying and worthy by all men to be received
anyone does] any man
life eternal] eternal life

18 *Then he says,*

Let us therefore confess our sins in penitence and faith, firmly resolved to keep God's commandments and to live in love and peace with all men.

19 *All say together,*

Almighty God, our heavenly Father,
we have sinned in thought and word and deed,
and in what we have left undone.
We are truly sorry, and we humbly repent.
For the sake of your Son, Jesus Christ,
have mercy on us and forgive us;
that we may walk in newness of life
to the glory of your Name. Amen.

20 *The priest, or the bishop if he is present, says,*

Almighty God have mercy on you . . . ⟦CF 5⟧ . . . Christ our Lord.
Amen.

21 *All may say together,*

We do not presume . . . ⟦CF 6⟧ . . . he in us. Amen.

THE COMMUNION

22 *Stand*

The priest at the holy table says,

      The peace of the Lord be always with you.

People   **And also with you.**

THE OFFERTORY

23 *The priest says one or more of the following sentences. The proper sentence is used when one is provided.*

⟦Both the Common Sentences, which follow here, and the Proper Sentences, which come after the end of the service, are to be found in Appendix B.⟧

24 *A hymn may be sung. The alms of the people are brought to the Lord's Table. The bread and wine for Communion are placed on the Lord's Table. All may say together,*

Lord, yours is the greatness,
and the power and the glory,
and the victory and the majesty;
For all things come from you,
and of your own we give you.

1 Chron. 29:11, 14

THE TAKING OF THE BREAD AND WINE

25 *The Priest takes the bread and wine.*

THE THANKSGIVING OVER
THE BREAD AND WINE

26 *Stand or Kneel*

Priest	The Lord be with you.
People	**And also with you.**
Priest	Lift up your hearts.
People	**We lift them up to the Lord.**
Priest	Let us give thanks to the Lord our God.
People	**It is right to give him thanks and praise.**

Priest

Father, almighty and everliving God,
at all times and in all places
it is right for us to give you thanks and praise:

When there is a proper preface (pages . . . ⟦i.e. no. 32⟧) it follows here.
⟦The Proper Prefaces, which come after the end of the service, are to be found in Appendix C.⟧

And so with all your people,
with angels and archangels,
and with all the company of heaven,
we proclaim your great and glorious Name,
for ever praising you and saying:

Holy, holy, holy Lord,
God of power and might,
Heaven and earth are full of your glory.
Hosanna in the highest.

Father, you are the blessed One,
the creator and sustainer of all things;
You made man in your own image,
and more wonderfully restored him
when you freed him from the slavery of sin;
For in your love and mercy
you gave your only Son Jesus Christ to become man
and suffer death on the cross to redeem us;
He made there the one complete and all-sufficient sacrifice
for the sins of the whole world:
He instituted, and in his Holy Gospel commanded us
to continue, a perpetual memory of his precious
death until he comes again:
On the night that he was betrayed he took bread;
and when he had given thanks to you, he broke it,
and gave it to his disciples, saying,

The priest   Take, eat,
lays his hand
on the bread   this is my Body which is given for you;
      Do this in remembrance of me:
In the same way, after supper he took the cup;
and when he had given thanks to you,
he gave it to them, saying,

The priest   Drink this, all of you,
lays his hand
on the cup   for this is my Blood of the new covenant,
      which is shed for you and for many
      for the forgiveness of sins;
      Do this, as often as you drink it,
      in remembrance of me:
Father, with this bread and this cup
we do as Christ your Son commanded:
We recall his passion and death,
we celebrate his resurrection and ascension,
and we look for the coming of his kingdom:
Accept through him this our sacrifice
of praise and thanksgiving;
and as we eat and drink these holy gifts,
grant, by the power of the life-giving Spirit,
that we may be made one in your holy Church
and partakers of the Body and Blood of your Son,
and that he may dwell in us and we in him:

Through the same Jesus Christ our Lord,
by whom, and with whom, in the unity of the Holy Spirit,
all honour and glory are yours, Almighty Father,
for ever and ever. **Amen.**

THE BREAKING OF BREAD

27 *As the priest breaks the bread he says,*
The bread which we break
is a sharing in the Body of Christ.
We being many are one bread, one body,
for we all share in the one bread.

THE GIVING OF THE BREAD AND WINE

28 *The priest says,*
As our Saviour Christ has taught us, so we pray,
Our Father in heaven . . . ⟦ICET 1⟧ . . . for ever. Amen.
holy] **hallowed**
the test] **temptation**
The Lord's Prayer may be said in the old form.

9a *The priest says,*
Draw near and receive the Body of our Lord Jesus Christ, which he
gave for you, and his blood which he shed for you.
Remember that he died for you,
and feed on him in your hearts by faith with thanksgiving.
*The priest and the other communicants receive the consecrated bread and
wine.*

Each communicant is given the consecrated bread and wine with the words,
The Body of Christ keep you in eternal life.
The Blood of Christ keep you in eternal life.
The communicant replies each time,
Amen.
and then receives.

or

9b *The following words are said as the priest and the other communicants
receive the consecrated bread and wine :*
The Body . . . ⟦CF 7(a)⟧ . . . thanksgiving.
The Blood . . . ⟦CF 7(b)⟧ . . . thankful.
everlasting] **eternal** TWICE
Hymns or anthems may be sung during the Communion.

30 *Kneel*

The priest says,

Let us pray.

All say together,

Almighty God . . . ⟦CF 8⟧ **. . . praise and glory. Amen.**

A period of silence may be kept.

31 *The priest, or the bishop if he is present, says,*

The peace of . . . ⟦CF 9⟧ . . . our Lord.

On the occasions for which a seasonal blessing is provided (pages . . . ⟦i.e.
no. 32⟧*) it is used in place of* The peace of God . . . *The priest always ends
with the words,*

And the blessing of God . . . ⟦CF 9⟧ . . . always. **Amen.**
among] with

APPENDICES

32   1. *THE PROPER SEASONAL OFFERTORY
SENTENCES, PREFACES, AND BLESSINGS*

⟦There follows an appendix containing Proper Offertory Sentences (which are
to be found here in Appendix B), Proper Prefaces (which are to be found
here in Appendix C), and Proper Blessings (which are to be found here in
Appendix D).⟧

33   2. *WHEN THE CONSECRATED ELEMENTS
ARE INSUFFICIENT*

*If the consecrated bread proves insufficient, the priest returns to the Lord's
Table, takes bread, and says,*

Father, almighty and everliving God,
hear the prayer and thanksgiving which we offer
through Jesus Christ our Lord,
who, on the night that he was betrayed, took bread;
and when he had given thanks to you, he broke it,
and gave it to his disciples, saying,

The priest   Take, eat,
lays his hand   this is my Body which is given for you;
on the bread
                  Do this in remembrance of me.

*If it is necessary to consecrate in both kinds, the priest takes wine, and
continues,*

In the same way, after supper he took the cup;
and when he had given thanks to you,
he gave it to them, saying,

The priest   Drink this, all of you,
lays his hand
on the cup   for this is my Blood of the new covenant
           which is shed for you and for many
           for the forgiveness of sins;
           Do this, as often as you drink it,
           in remembrance of me.

For the blessing of the cup only, the priest says,

Father, almighty and everliving God,
hear the prayer and thanksgiving which we offer
through Jesus Christ our Lord, who after supper took the cup;
and when he had given thanks to you,
he gave it to them, saying,

The priest   Drink this, all of you,
lays his hand
on the cup   for this is my Blood of the new covenant
           which is shed for you and for many
           for the forgiveness of sins;
           Do this, as often as you drink it,
           in remembrance of me.

34   3. *THE COMMUNION OF THE SICK*

[This Appendix consists of two rubrics about what parts may be omitted in such
cases.]

PART III
THE AMERICAS

CHAPTER 6

THE ANGLICAN CHURCH OF CANADA

Background to the 1970s

As was noted in **MAL,** a conservative revision of the eucharist (**CanR**[1]) was adopted by the Canadian Church in 1959, and was received with enthusiasm. It passed into use throughout the country, was translated into the requisite languages, and replaced the previous rite completely. In 1965 General Synod started to look forward to the production of a Prayer Book in modern English, and gave the task of preparation to its Committee on the Revision of the Book of Common Prayer.[2] At the same time General Synod resolved that each Bishop should be able to permit in his own diocese what were called 'various exploratory liturgical uses'. The Committee's own contribution to this move was to produce a set of 'Guidelines' for local experiment.[3] It did not see its task as the immediate drafting of a national liturgy, but rather as the promoting of a healthy use of the experimental period.

Most of the Bishops dealt with liturgical experiment in letters to their clergy. In the diocese of Toronto, for example, Bishop George Snell issued 'Interim Guidelines for Liturgical Experimentation' in November 1968. This was a booklet prepared by his Liturgical Commission and containing considerable background material and a reading list, as well as guidelines both for using **CanR** more imaginatively, and also for using experimental liturgies. Some other diocesans also used this booklet, adding their own covering letters.

A typical set of such directions is to be found in the 'Guidelines for Liturgical Development' issued by the House of Bishops of the ecclesiastical Province of British Columbia in March 1970. After a preamble with recommendations for study, these 'Guidelines' proceed as follows:

---

[1] This rite is printed in **LiE** pp.136-44. The earlier Canadian recension of 1662 (**Can** dated 1918) is presented in **LiE** as a variant on 1662 in the apparatus to '1662 and Related Rites' pp.26-37.

[2] In the 'restructuring' of General Synod in 1969, this Committee has now become the Doctrine and Worship Committee.

[3] These 'Guidelines', which are very general, are printed in *Lambeth Conference* 1968 : *Preparatory Information* (S.P.C.K 1968), pp.52-5.

1 Before engaging in experimental worship, the parish should inform and consult with its diocesan concerning its plans.

2 The rites selected for experimental use should be confined in the first instance to those already authorized for use in Canada or elsewhere in the Anglican Communion, e.g. New Zealand, English 'Series Two', Qu'appelle, new American liturgy etc.[1]

3 Any particular rite should be tried out for a definite period in consultation with the Bishop and not just used once or twice.

4 Throughout the period of experiment the regular services must be maintained since the Book of Common Prayer is our standard. No one should be deprived of services to which he is accustomed and which he desires.

5 There should be good preliminary preparation to acquaint the parishioners with the nature, object and methods of experimental worship.

6 Announcement of the use of any particular experimental form should be accompanied by a brief introduction and a few explanatory comments.

7 Every participant in an experimental service must be supplied with a copy of the rite that is being used.

8 Discussion and evaluation of the rite as an act of worship must follow its use and be reported to the Bishop.

In general, Bishops have informed their dioceses what rites they would permit, and although there is obviously a considerable variety among them, a controlled experimentation has become possible almost everywhere.

General Reactions in the Church

Partly in order to discover broad feelings about **CanR** after a decade of use, and partly to discover how the experimental period was affecting parish life, the present writer sent a questionnaire in September 1970 to the General Secretary of the Church, and to the Liturgical Commissions and other representatives of the twenty-eight dioceses. Just over half the dioceses replied (as did the General Secretary), and they include a cross-section from Toronto to the Arctic and from East to West.

The response showed that dissatisfaction with **CanR** because of its conservatism is very widespread among the clergy (35% in one diocese), but not as much among the laity. The dissatisfied urge that language

---

[1] ['New Zealand' here means the 1966 rite (**NZ**), 'new American Liturgy' means the 1967 rite (**AmerR**). For Qu'appelle see below.—Editor.]

must be modern, the meaning of ceremonial clearer, the 'feel' of worship more joyous, and the understanding of the corporate nature of the sacrament much stronger. They further add that the laity tend to be conservative largely because they have known nothing but **CanR.** Those satisfied with **CanR** do not think it important that it has a 'shape' and language out of accord with modern scholarship. But it is true that the dissatisfied tend to make their wishes known, while the satisfied say nothing until something unwelcome is being forced upon them. Curiously enough, there is no strong evidence that the young want change and the old do not. Rather, both young and old, clergy and laity, are found on each side of the debate. Overall, there *is* a dissatisfaction with the existing forms, and the experimental period has come at the right time.

Actual Experimentation

The questionnaire enables three different advances upon the previous 'uniformity' situation to be charted. These are adaptations of **CanR,** the use of Anglican rites from elsewhere, and experimentation with diocesan or local rites.

a Adaptation of **CanR** This rite has been adapted by making a clearer distinction between the service of the Word, and the service of the Sacrament. Much greater lay participation is introduced throughout. In particular congregational responses are used to break up the two very long monologues—the Prayer for the Church and the canon. The conservative will often go this far without protest. A bolder step is found in Paul Gibson's *Say What You Mean*[1] which is basically one man's rendering of **CanR** into modern English, with further small changes.

b Use of Rites from elsewhere Among rites from elsewhere, the ones most frequently mentioned by Bishops as being acceptable are **Eng2, NZ** and **AmerR. Eng3** is now being added to Bishops' lists, and is coming into use. **LfA** has been sanctioned in at least one diocese. Other rites are mostly unknown. But 'authorizing' or listing by the Bishop does not mean a rite is in use. The questionnaire revealed that **Eng2** is popular (though occasional adverse comment on the quality of its English was found), and **NZ** has won considerable praise. Others, even if listed, do not enjoy much actual use. It is too early yet to see the impact of **Eng3.**

---

[1] Dept. of Religious Education of the Anglican Church in Canada (1966).

c Diocesan or Local Rites Some diocesan Liturgical Commissions (or equivalent bodies) have compiled their own liturgies. Of these the Qu'appelle Liturgy is the best known and most frequently used throughout Canada.[1] Thus, while not more than half a dozen dioceses have their own liturgies, most Bishops have approved the use of Qu'appelle. In a few cases genuinely local preparation of a liturgy has been encouraged; for a time this was particularly true of the diocese of Kootenay.[2] The situation there is the more interesting because there are in the diocese a number of parishes operating under 'shared ministry' agreements. In these parishes the pastor may be either an Anglican or a United Churchman and he leads the worship of combined congregations. Thus it is appropriate to have considerable liturgical initiative allowed to the local Church, although the Bishop's approval still is needed for experimental rites.

Progress at the National Level

In October 1970 the Office of the General Secretary of General Synod stated that the 'Task Force on Common Liturgical Texts' had recommended the adoption of the ICET texts in all new liturgies.'[3] Another 'Task Force' on 'The Expansion of Minimal Liturgical Forms' was then discussing what these minimal forms are, and what expansion of them should be left to the local congregation in the perspective of liturgical renewal. The General Secretary's Office also stated that the Doctrine and Worship Committee of General Synod would be 'undertaking to prepare a Canadian modern language liturgy following the outline prepared by inter-Anglican scholars together with the basic outline as agreed upon by the United Church/Anglican Commission.' That might be said to be the genesis of **Can1**. The Committee also made recommendations to General Synod on the reform of the initiation Liturgies, and these revised liturgies are constructed so as to fit together with the eucharist with a minimum of dislocation to the latter.

The making of **Can1**

The rite produced by the Doctrine and Worship Committee was used once at the 1973 session of the General Synod and debated there.

---

[1] The Great Thanksgiving of the Qu'appelle Liturgy is appended to this chapter, as a sample of a diocesan rite.

[2] The Great Thanksgiving of 'The Kootenay-Boundary Rite' (drawn up by the Kootenay-Boundary Regional parish centred on Trail, British Columbia) is appended to this chapter as a sample of a well-known parish rite.

[3] Many of the new liturgies came from the period 1965-70, before ICET texts were available.

However, it was not adopted. The Committee was instructed to rewrite the text. This has been done, and during the period of rewriting it has been used in its many varying forms in the parishes of committee members across Canada. It was published in its rewritten form in July 1974, with a view to its authorization by General Synod in June 1975. Meanwhile, it has the same status as any local or diocesan rite (or, say, **Eng3**), that is, it may be permitted for experimental use by any diocesan bishop. It is possible that in 1975 it may be rejected by Synod;[1] if this should happen it is doubtful whether bishops would continue to allow its use. However, the Committee is hopeful that this will not be the case, as the reaction to the the rite has been favourable in those parishes where it has been used during the rewriting period.

The rite follows the general outline of the structure document, as the Committee was instructed to do. As was to be expected, it uses the 'you' form of address to God, and the latest form of the ICET texts.[2]

The penitential section comes before rather than after the Ministry of the Word, in spite of all that can be said for the later position, on the ground that this enables the service to be combined with Morning Prayer or Holy Baptism with less disruption and duplication.

The Great Thanksgiving draws its opening salutation from **Eng3**, but its wording in general is original. It is old-fashioned, and, to some, controversial in its oblation of the elements[3] in the anamnesis, and in the epiclesis upon the elements which follows immediately. The division into lines of the Great Thanksgiving and the Post-Communion is very poorly done.

The meaning of the Saints Day Proper Preface is obscure. It should be revised. We do not run the race *because* of the existence of the 'cloud of witnesses'.

What the General Synod of 1975 will decide can only be guessed. One guess is that it will authorize the experimental use of the rite across Canada for a period of years, probably with a few amendments, and during that period it will be reassessed. Probably this rite should

---

[1] It might also be amended. In either case the text here presented would be immediately out of date, and would also be a rite which had never had national authorization. It is for this reason that it is printed here with the safeguarding formula.

[2] i.e. the 1974 forms, which are to be found in the *apparatus* to the 1971 texts in Appendix A.

[3] [See the discussion on p.23 above—Editor.]

be viewed as one further step in General Synod's development of a definitive rite which is acceptable to all.[1]

AN ALTERNATIVE CANADIAN LITURGY, 1974 (Can1)

⟦The text of the Canadian Liturgy which follows is at the time of going to press a report from a committee, which is explained by the relevant authorities of the Anglican Church of Canada thus:

'This alternative Eucharistic Liturgy was prepared by the Doctrine and Worship Committee at the request of the General Synod of the Anglican Church of Canada for report back to that body at its next meeting in 1975.

'In the interim period Bishops of the Anglican Church of Canada may authorize its use within their particular jurisdiction.'

The numbering here is editorial.⟧

1 DIRECTIONS FOR THE SERVICE

1. *The preparation and liturgy of the word, to the end of the intercession, together with other appropriate hymns and prayers, may be used as a separate service when the eucharist is not celebrated.*

2. *Holy baptism or the first part of morning prayer may take the place of all that precedes the offertory.*

3. *For the preparation, one of the confession and absolution, the kyries, or the gloria in excelsis shall normally be used, either or both of the others being omitted as appropriate. However, when this service is combined as in (2), this direction is superseded.*

4. *The kyries may be used in nine-fold form.*

5. *The lessons should be announced in the order: book, chapter, verse. The old testament lesson and the epistle should normally be read by lay persons. In the absence of a deacon, a priest or lay person may read the gospel.*

---

[1] **Can1** can be obtained from the Anglican Book Centre, 600 Jarvis Street, Toronto, M4Y 2J6, Canada. Attention is also drawn to three other publications of the Anglican Church of Canada, obtainable from the same source. These are:
  Gibson, Paul: *Say What You Mean*—background material on liturgical revision and a modern English version which is substantially the Canadian 1959 rite.
  Lods, Kirby, et al: *Experiment and Liturgy*—essays on worship and experiment, and the experimental Algoma, Qu'Appelle and Kootenay-Boundary Liturgies plus two other experiments.
  ed. Kirby: *Words and Action*—new forms of the liturgy in Canada and the U.S.A., mostly non-Anglican.

6. *An alternative cycle of lessons to those provided in the Book of Common Prayer may be used as authorized by the ordinary.*

7. *An appropriate reading from a non-scriptural source, if approved and authorized by the ordinary, may replace either the old testament lesson or the epistle. In such case the versicle* 'This is the lesson' *shall be used.*

8. *Banns of marriage and other notices may be given either before the intercessions, after the greeting of the peace, or at the beginning or end of the service as convenient.*

9. *The intercessions may be led by a deacon or lay person, and other members of the congregation may add their own intercessions following each bidding, according to local custom.*

10. *The greeting of the peace may occur at the place provided, or before the intercession or the communion.*

11. *The priest (or bishop if he is present) may give a blessing prior to the dismissal.*

12. *Standing, sitting or kneeling may follow local custom except that all stand for the gospel, and for the gloria in excelsis and the creed when used.*

13. *The saying or singing of parts of the service may follow local custom.*

THE HOLY EUCHARIST

THE PREPARATION

2 *At the entrance of the ministers a psalm, a portion of a psalm, or a hymn may be used.*

3 *Priest:* Blessed be God: Father, Son and Holy Spirit.

   People: **And blessed be his kingdom, now and forever. Amen.**

4 *All:* **Almighty God . . . ⟦CF 1⟧ . . . Christ our Lord. Amen.**

5 *Priest:* My brothers and sisters, as we prepare ourselves to celebrate these holy mysteries, let us confess our sins.

   Silence may be kept.

6 *All:* **Almighty God, our heavenly Father,**
   we have sinned
   in thought and word and deed:
   we have not loved you with our whole heart,
   we have not loved our neighbours as ourselves.
   We pray you of your mercy,
   forgive us all that is past;
   and grant that we may serve you
   in newness of life
   to the glory of your name. Amen.

7 *Priest:*   Almighty God have mercy upon you, pardon and deliver you from all your sins and keep you in life eternal.

   All: **Amen.**

8 *All:*   **Lord, have mercy**   **Kyrie eleison**
   Christ, have mercy   *or*   **Christe eleison**
   Lord, have mercy   **Kyrie eleison**

9   **Glory to God . . . ⟦ICET 2⟧ . . . God the Father. Amen.**

THE LITURGY OF THE WORD

10 *Priest:*   The Lord be with you.

   People: **And also with you.**

   Priest: Let us pray . . . *The collect of the day.*

11 *Reader:*   *The old testament lesson.*

   Reader: This is the word of the Lord.

   All: **Thanks be to God.**

   Silence may be kept.

12 *Reader:*   *The epistle.*

   Reader: This is the word of the Lord.

   All: **Thanks be to God**

   Silence may be kept.

13 *A psalm, a portion of a psalm, a hymn or a canticle may be used.*

14 *Deacon:*   The holy gospel of our Lord Jesus Christ according to . . .

   All: **Glory to you, Lord Christ.**

   The deacon reads the gospel.

   Deacon: This is the gospel of the Lord.

   All: **Praise to you, Lord Christ.**

   Silence may be kept.

15 *A sermon or homily is preached at least on sundays and holy days.*

16 *The creed may be omitted on weekdays which are not holy days.*

   All: **We believe in one God . . . ⟦ICET 3 with '1974' variants⟧**
   . . . the world to come. Amen.
   (and the Son)⟧ OM BRACKETS

THE INTERCESSION

17 *Intercessions and thanksgivings are offered using biddings such as the following:*

   Leader: Let us pray for the church, and for all people according to their needs.

Almighty God, you have promised to hear the prayers of those who ask in faith, therefore
We pray for the church:

Here, particular intercessions may be offered by the leader and others.

Leader: O Lord, renew your church:
All: **In faith, hope and love.**
Leader: We pray for the world:

Here, particular intercessions may be offered by the leader and others.

Leader: Give peace, O Lord, in all the world;
All: **And guide us in the way of truth and justice.**
Leader: We pray for those in need:

Here, particular intercessions may be offered by the leader and others.

Leader: Have compassion, O Lord, on all in need;
All: **That they may know your unfailing love.**
Leader: Rejoicing in the fellowship of all the saints, we commemorate those who have died and are at rest:

Here, particular intercessions may be offered by the leader and others.

Leader: Make your servants to be numbered with your saints;
All: **In glory everlasting.**
Leader: Grant these our prayers, O Father, for the sake of your son, our Saviour Jesus Christ.
All: **Amen.**

THE LITURGY OF THE EUCHARIST

18 *Priest:* The peace of the Lord be always with you.
People: **His peace be with you.**

The priest and people may greet one another using some appropriate gesture and words of peace.

19 *The bread and wine and other gifts and offerings of the people are placed on the altar, during which time a hymn may be sung.*

Priest: The Lord is here.
People: **His Spirit is with us.**
Priest: Lift up your hearts.
People: **We lift them to the Lord.**
Priest: Let us give thanks to the Lord our God.
People: **It is right to give him thanks and praise.**
Priest: It is right, and a good joyful thing always and everywhere to give thanks to you, Father almighty, creator of heaven and earth:

Here is said or sung a proper preface when appointed.

[The Proper Prefaces, which are printed at the end of the service, are to be found here in Appendix C.]

Therefore we praise you,
joining our voices with angels and archangels,
with the heavenly chorus, and with the hymn
of all creation
proclaiming in unending song the glory of your name.

All :   **Holy, holy, holy Lord,**
God of power and might,
Heaven and earth are full of your glory.
Hosanna in the highest.

Priest :   All blessing and glory are yours almighty God
our heavenly Father,
for in your infinite love you created all things
and when we turned away from you in sin you sent
your son Jesus Christ
to take our human nature, to live and die as one
of us, to reconcile us to you, the God and Father
of all.
On the night he was handed over to suffering and death,
our Lord Jesus Christ took bread;
and when he had given thanks to you,
he broke it, and gave it to his disciples,
and said, 'Take this and eat it:
this is my body, which is given for you.
Do this for the remembrance of me.'
After supper he took the cup of wine;
and when he had given thanks, he gave it to them,
and said, 'Drink this, all of you:
this is my blood of the new covenant,
which is shed for you and for many
for the forgiveness of sins.
Whenever you drink it, do this for the
remembrance of me.'

All :   **Christ has died.**
Christ is risen.
Christ will come again.

Priest : Wherefore, O Father, recalling his death, proclaiming
his resurrection and ascension, and looking to his
coming in glory, we celebrate the memorial
of our redemption as we offer this bread and this
cup of new and unending life in him. Sanctify these
gifts by your Holy Spirit, that they may be for your
people the body and blood of your Son.
Receiving them, may we serve you faithfully, be
made one body in your Son, and share in your eternal
kingdom.
Through Jesus Christ our Lord, by whom, with whom,
and in whom, in the unity of the Holy Spirit,
all honour and glory is yours, almighty Father, now
and forever.

All : **Amen.**

20 *Priest :* In the words our Saviour gave us; let us pray:

All : **Our Father in heaven . . .** [ICET 1 with '1974' variants]
. . . now and forever. Amen.

21 *Here the priest breaks the bread.*

22 *Priest :* The gifts of God for the people of God.

*The ministers receive the sacrament in both kinds, and then deliver it to
the people.*

The bread and the cup are given with these words :
The body (blood) of Christ given (shed) for you.

The communicant may respond.
Amen.

23 *During the communion, hymns or anthems may be sung.*

24 *Priest :* Let us pray.

29 *All :* **Almighty God, we thank you for the new life
which you have given us.
Send us out now in the power of your Spirit
to love and serve you and to be the
instruments of your peace;
Through Jesus Christ our Lord, to whom with
you and the same Spirit be all honour and
glory, now and forever. Amen.**

26 *Deacon or*

Priest :   Go forth in the peace of Christ.

People :   **Thanks be to God.**

27 *Proper Prefaces*

⟦The Proper Prefaces which are printed out here in the service are to be found in Appendix C⟧.

TWO CANONS

1 THE QU'APPELLE LITURGY (1969 edition)

Priest :   The Lord be with you.

People :   **And with you also.**

Priest :   Lift up your hearts.

People :   **We lift them up to the Lord.**

Priest :   Let us give thanks.

People :   **We give thanks to the Lord our God.**

Priest :   Truly it is right
That we should give thanks to you
At all times and in all places,
O Lord, Holy Father, Almighty, Eternal God,
Creator and preserver of all things.

(*Here an appropriate preface may be said.*)

Therefore we join our voices
With all the company of heaven,
and all the powers of creation,
In the endless song of praise:

All :   **Holy, holy, holy**
Lord God of hosts,
Heaven and earth are full of your glory.
The highest glory is yours, O Lord.
Blessed is he who comes in your name.
The highest glory is yours.

Priest :   Lord, God, Creator and Father,
We thank you for the gift of your Son,
Jesus the Christ.
We give thanks that he has become one of us,
sharing our life.

We give thanks that we are becoming one with him,
sharing his life.
Give us then, Father, through this Eucharist,
The true life and presence of our Lord:
Who, in the same night that he was betrayed,
Took bread;
And when he had given thanks,
He broke it
And gave it to his disciples, saying,
'Take, eat, this is my body given for you.
Do this and know that I am with you.'[1]
Then after supper he took the cup;
And when he had given thanks,
He gave it to them saying,
'Drink this, all of you;
This is the new agreement between God and man,
Made in my blood.
Do this, as often as you drink it,
And know that I am with you.'
And so, Father,
We remember Christ's death, his resurrection, his ascension,
his sending of the Holy Spirit.
And rejoicing in his presence in the world,
We look for his coming again in glory.
Accept, Lord, our sacrifice
And send on us here
And on this Eucharist
The Holy Spirit of love and peace and strength.
Through Jesus Christ, our Lord,
By whom and with whom,
In the unity of the Holy Spirit,
We praise you, our Father, throughout all ages,
World without end.

People: **Amen.**

(*After a short period of silence, the priest shall say*)

Priest: The cup of blessing which we bless:

People: **It is a sharing of the Blood of Christ.**

---

[1] [cf. the next Canon, and the footnote on page 121.]

Priest :	The bread which we break:
People :	**It is the Communion of the Body of Christ.**
Priest :	We who are many are one Body:
People :	**For we are all partakers of the one Bread.**
Priest :	Let us pray.
All :	**Our Father in heaven**
	Your name be honoured;
	Your kingdom come,
	Your will be done,
	On earth as it is in heaven.
	Give us today our daily bread,
	Forgive us the wrong we have done,
	As we forgive those who have wronged us,
	And do not bring us to the test,
	But save us from evil.
	For the kingdom is yours,
	And the power and the glory,
	Forever. Amen.

2 THE KOOTENAY-BOUNDARY LITURGY

(*We remain standing*)

Priest :	The Lord is with you.
People :	**And with you.**
Priest :	Lift up your hearts:
People :	**We lift them to the Lord.**
Priest :	Let us give thanks to our Lord God:
People :	**It is right that we should.**
Priest :	It is our joy and our salvation that we should at all times and in all places give thanks to you, O Father, holy and eternal God, Creator and Sustainer of all things . . .

(*An extra preface may be inserted here*)

	. . . therefore, with all creation, that which is seen and that which is unseen, we praise your name, O Father, saying:
All :	**Holy! Holy! Holy! Lord God of Hosts.**
	Heaven and Earth are full of thy glory.
	Glory be to thee, O Lord most high.
	Blessed is he that cometh in the name of the Lord.
	Hosanna in the highest.

(*The eucharistic consecration is the action of God in Christ, gathering the complex creation to himself and declaring it to be his Body.*)

Priest :   Hosanna indeed to you, Creator and Father, for the gift of your Son, Jesus the Christ.

We give thanks that he has become one with us, living our life. We give thanks that we are becoming one with him, living his life.

Give us then, Father, the true life and presence of our Lord; who in the same night that he was betrayed, took bread; and when he had given thanks he broke it and gave it to his friends and followers, saying,

'Take, eat, this is my Body given for you'.

Then after supper he took the cup, and when he had given thanks, he gave it to them, saying,

'This is the New Covenant in my Blood which is shed for you. Do this and know that I am with you.'[1]

All :   **Therefore, Father, remembering Christ's death and resurrection, his ascension and his sending of the Holy Spirit; we stand before you rejoicing, and waiting for the consummation of all things in Christ.**
Accept, Lord, his sacrifice and ours.
And send on us here
and on our Eucharist now
your Spirit of love and joy and fellowship. Through Jesus Christ our Lord, by whom and with whom, in the unity of the Holy Spirit, we praise you, our Father throughout all ages and world without end.

Amen!

(*The reply of all present*)

(*We kneel*)

---

[1] ⟦This rendering of *eis ten emen anamnesin* is curiously paralleled by the translation which appears in **Mel** on page 385 below. Can there possibly be any interdependence of texts between the praish of Trail, B.C. Canada and the Province of Melanesia?⟧

CHAPTER 7

THE PROTESTANT EPISCOPAL CHURCH OF THE UNITED STATES OF AMERICA

The 1967 Rite (AmerR)

AmerR,[1] the rite which was authorized for three years of experimental use by the General Convention of 1967, received wide and varied trial throughout the American Episcopal Church. In 1968 the Standing Liturgical Commission circulated questionnaires designed to evaluate its reception. There was a broad welcome for placing the sermon after the Gospel, for the hymn 'Christ our Passover . . .', for the greater flexibility (including the possibilities in the use of the Peace), and for the wider congregational participation and the role of the laity.

However, the Commission had to report four areas of concern which they unearthed. Firstly, there was a suspicion abroad that the Commission was imposing the liturgy on the church, regardless of its view.[2] The status of the service had not been understood by everybody—i.e. it was a trial to be used as a *step* in revising the 1928 Prayer Book rite (**Amer**[3]), not itself an automatic replacement for that rite. Secondly, concern was expressed over the minimising of the 'Penitential Order'.[4] Thirdly, the new intercessions were viewed by some as cumbersome. Fourthly, the disappearance of the 'priestly blessing' at the close of the service was disliked. And in addition there was criticism of the language of the Creed,[5] and of the loss of the Prayer of Humble Access.

At the same time the Commission concluded that certain deep-seated trends in the church should be noted when revision came about. There existed simultaneously both strong attachment to the traditional language of the Book of Common Prayer, *and* a widespread desire for a thorough modernization of that language, in keeping with Roman

---

[1] For introduction and text see **MAL** pp.195-229.
[2] This is set out in their official report to the 1970 General Convention.
[3] The text of this rite is printed in **LiE**, pp.52-61, showing variants in the 1790 and 1892 orders.
[4] This was made optional on all but five occasions in the year, and was printed separately as an appendix.
[5] In particular the Creed was expressed in the plural ('We believe') and daringly omitted the *filioque*, after Eastern Church practice.

Catholic and other developments. There was also a growing request for a wide latitude for experiment with new and flexible forms of eucharistic liturgy, to meet the needs of informal situations such as camps, and house-groups. Undergirding all these trends was a growing concern among Episcopalians of all backgrounds to see the eucharist as the central act of worship in the parish. The Liturgical Commission recognized this concern as a unifying factor of no mean consequence.

A first interim step to meet these needs was made possible in 1969. The General Convention, which is usually triennial, met in a Special Convention (only for the second time in its history) at South Bend Indiana that year. Though social issues dominated the meeting, the occasion was used to approve a 'Schedule of Variations and Substitutions' prepared by the Commission in response to the concerns voiced in the replies to the questionnaires.[1] These encouraged more frequent and flexible use of the penitential order, provided an optional form for the intercessions, permitted the use of a blessing at the close, and allowed other small variations. From the Commission's point of view, however, the main task was to be a thorough working over the whole of the eucharistic rite, and the production of a new full-scale report.

Prayer Book Studies 21 (**Amer1, Amer2, Amer3**)

This new report was published as *Prayer Book Studies* 21 in 1970,[2] in time for the General Convention. The demands being laid on the Commission were met by the provision of two full communion services (one with three, one with two, eucharistic prayers) and a skeletal 'Order of Celebration'. The Commission is careful to say 'Each intends to do the same thing'.[3] Though their forms of language may differ, and the roles they best serve may vary, yet all three conform to the two Pan-Anglican documents on the structure of a eucharistic rite.[4] The services were duly accepted by the 1970 General Convention at Houston

[1] This Schedule is printed in *Prayer Book Studies* 21 (Church Hymnal Corporation, New York, 1970) pp.42-47.

[2] See footnote 1 above. It should be noted that whilst this work on the eucharist was going on, a whole further series of *Prayer Book Studies* was being produced—nos. 18-24 cover proposals for Initiation, the Pastoral Offices, the Lectionary, the Psalter, the Daily Offices and the Ordinal, apart from the eucharist, and were all published in 1970. When adopted by the General Convention the services concerned were then reprinted without commentary or introduction in *Services for Trial Use* (Church Hymnal Corporation, New York, 1971), 639 pages long and nicknamed 'the green book' from its cover.

[3] *Prayer Book Studies* 21 p.11.

[4] The first Document was published in *Prayer Book Studies XVII* and in **MAL** pp.22-32. The second is in *Prayer Book Studies* 21 and in this volume on pp.27-31. It is also published in *Partners in Mission* (S.P.C.K. London 1973).

and were authorized without amendment for a three-year trial use. The 1967 rite (**AmerR**) did not lapse, but it will be obvious that virtually all its contents are also contained within the framework of the new rites.

The three services are so laid out that much of the material of the liturgy is interchangeable between them. Thus the opening notes 'CONCERNING THE CELEBRATION OF THE EUCHARIST' appear before both **Amer1** and **Amer2**, whilst the material in the various appendixes, i.e. 'Forms of Intercession' 'Offertory Sentences' 'Proper Prefaces' and 'Additional Directions and Suggestions', relates to all three rites, though in some cases giving a choice between 'Traditional' and 'Contemporary' wording.[1]

The First Service (**Amer1**)

The first service conserves the spirit and language of **Amer** but in the pattern of **AmerR**.[2] Thus the Gloria in Excelsis comes at the beginning, the sermon precedes the Creed, the various options are permitted for the Intercession, and the standard (1928-type) prayer has been expanded to include non-Christian rulers and also our stewardship of creation. An alternative confession of a very simple character, based on Psalm 51, is added, and the Comfortable Words are placed *between* the confession and absolution.[3] The position of the Offertory is adapted to the current fashion in structure, and the rubrics seem to provide for a procession with the elements as well as with the money. The eucharistic prayer follows 1928 very closely, though each of the actual omissions or alterations deserves critical consideration. As alternatives the 1967 (**AmerR**) eucharistic prayer slightly adapted, or a shortened version of the one in the main text, may be used. Again the changes may be significant.

The breaking of the bread predictably becomes a section in its own right, and the conclusion of the Prayer of Humble Access is minutely altered. After communion the wording 'feed us who have duly received these holy mysteries' becomes (after 1549) 'feed us in these holy mysteries'. Finally two choices of blessing and three possible other forms of dismissal conclude the service. Thus, although the 'thou' form

---

[1] [This material is labelled '**Amer1-3**' in this volume, to indicate its availability for all three of the 1970 services—Editor.]

[2] A thorough analysis of all the differences between **Amer** and **Amer1** may be found in 'The Prayer Book Liturgy and the Proposed Revision' J. M. McCready *St. Luke's Journal of Theology,* 1973.

[3] This is of course the position in Hermann's *Consultatio* at Cologne in 1545 (and is therefore the original position). In latter days it has been emulated in **CSI**, cf. **CSIR** on pp.282-3 below. The Comfortable Words are optional here.

of address to God is retained,[1] a flexible modern structure is given to the traditional material.

The Second Service (**Amer2**)

This service starts not from the 1928 rite (**Amer**) but from the 1967 one (**AmerR**). The modernization required is therefore not in the field of structure so much as in that of language (for **AmerR** was still in the 'thou' form) and flexibility. 1967 had been criticized for only going half-way towards a modern service, and the job is now completed. The International texts are used wherever possible and the rest of the language conforms to this kind of modernity and style. The service carries further the note of joy of **AmerR,** and it also incorporates the flexibility permitted under the 1969 Schedule of variations. The differing forms of intercession seem very appropriate for **Amer2**, and in particular the congregational participation and the introduction of topical material are points of advance on **AmerR**'s still rather rigid provision. As with **Amer1**, the Peace is added to the earlier rite at the end of the Prayers.

The Communion is also slightly restructured, with the sections pointing up the four-fold shape. The Offertory Procession is again envisaged in the rubrics, as in **Amer1**. 'The Consecration' of 1967 is now 'The Great Thanksgiving'. But the notable change is in the wording of the Thanksgiving. Only the Narrative of Institution remains unaltered—the wordiness of the old is turned into a brief, and poetic new. The Narrative itself is now followed by the congregational acclamations (which were first found in America in the 'COCU'[2] rite). The theology of the old prayer is retained— including the offering of the gifts godward, made now a main sentence, and not just an adjectival clause. The epiclesis still calls for the sanctifying of the elements by the Spirit. But overall the note of thanksgiving dominates in a new way. A more traditional alternative is provided by the putting of the Thanksgiving from **AmerR** into a 'you' form.

In 'The Breaking of the Bread' section, the use of 1 Cor. 5:7 ('Christ our Passover') is made an option, as is the second part of the invitation.

---

[1] This means that the International texts (ICET Common Forms, cf Appendix A) are not employed in **Amer1**, with the sole exception of the Creed, which does not address God directly at all and is therefore used (in the interests of a common usage where possible).

[2] Consultation on Church Union, mentioned on pages 204-5 of **MAL.** The COCU rite was published in 1968 and therefore lay before the Committee when they were preparing the 1970 rites.

The latter retains the oddity of **AmerR** 'Christ gives himself for you', which seems to change the historical emphasis of the rite considerably.[1] The administration includes as an alternative set of words 'The Body of Christ, the Bread of heaven' and 'The Blood of Christ, the Cup of salvation' from the COCU rite. The service ends with one of two brief prayers, each with a missionary note, and a blessing or other form of dismissal. The rite is a careful advance on **AmerR**, still well within the American Episcopal liturgical tradition, but also thoroughly modern.

An Order for Celebrating the Holy Eucharist (**Amer3**)

The third rite is a mere skeleton of a eucharist, in which the Great Thanksgiving is the only prescribed textual element. The rite is intended for special occasions and not for the regular Sunday or weekday worship of a parish church. It is intended to spring naturally and with careful preparation out of the life of informal Christian gatherings. The demand for freedom and spontaneity, so prevalent in America to-day, the growing number of those who are finding new life in Jesus Christ outside the institutional church, and the desire on the part of many to express their newfound faith in a sacramental and liturgical way—all of these factors have led to this innovative and far-sighted liturgical proposal. The rationale makes clear that its success depends upon its responsible use.

As the Eucharistic Prayers are the only texts provided, it is here that interest will lie. The rubric allows the Eucharistic Prayer from either **Amer1** or **Amer2** or one of four further prayers. Of these last four, the first two are brief and traditional in form. The third is longer and is responsive, like a litany. The fourth is notable for the opportunity it gives for the priest to extemporize a portion of the Great Thanksgiving. **Amer3** requires maturity and involvement from all the participants.

Evaluation

The Commission itself claimed to keep five major concerns in the forefront of its thinking when preparing these three rites: clarity, contemporaneity, flexibility, consistency, and ecumenicity[2]. These principles provide clear criteria for assessing the rites.

Clarity has been sought by a more exact translation of biblical words, particularly the almost pedantic 'for the remembrance of me' in the Narrative of Institution, and the use of the ICET texts in traditional

---

[1] But note the change made in 1973, cf pp.128-9 below.
[2] *Prayer Book Studies* 21 pp.9-11

liturgical material. Whether at times this is *wholly* achieved is a matter for debate, but the rites are a great advance on the previous American uses.

Contemporaneity is achieved by modern language, and even **Amer1** has good scope for this. **Amer2** is most obviously contemporary, and **Amer3** meets the *mood* of the times, in a way often more relevant than updating the language could be. The post-communion prayers lay greater emphasis on service, and the concluding note 'rejoicing in the power of the Spirit' hints at a sensitivity to the neo-Pentecostal revival. It is still a question whether the Commission has responded sufficiently to the new voices raised within the Church. But on the other hand they have aroused considerable protest simply by including the Lord's Prayer in its ICET form.[1]

On the third principle cited, the need for *flexibility* arose partly because in **AmerR** 'A major problem with the prayer of Intercession was its lack of variety and flexibility'.[2] The Schedule of Variations of 1969 went some way to meet this, the provisions of 1970, already noted, go much further.[3] But the need ran deeper, and has been met more fully. The whole idea of producing three services at once, the various choices within them, and the actual format of **Amer3**:—all these attest to the Commission's thoroughness in meeting the needs. If no other evidence were available, the very existence in the book of *eight* Eucharistic Prayers would speak eloquently of this thoroughness.

Consistency was necessary if the three rites were each to 'do the same thing'.[4] The Commission looked to the structure to unify the three rites, and the basic structure can be seen at a glance in **Amer3**. The 'four-fold shape of the liturgy', to quote Dix, emerges there, with 'Prepare the Table' being the Taking, 'Make Eucharist' being the Thanksgiving, 'Break the Bread' and 'Eat and Drink Together' being the self-explanatory last two actions. However, when the actions are found in **Amer1** and **Amer2**, a more stylized 'Offertory' is built up from the 'Taking'. A sentence about offerings is read. Repre-

---

[1] The protest became so persistent that the Executive Council of the Church then authorized an interim use of the traditional Lord's Prayer in **Amer2** after *Sevices for Trial Use* was published. The 1973 printing includes it.

[2] *Prayer Book Studies* 21 p.15.

[3] A by-product—or was it a genuine concern of the Commission?—has been the provision, for the first time since **Amer** was authorized in 1928, of forms of prayer which so pray about the departed as to respect the consciences of the Episcopalians who value the Church's reformed heritage. The forms are numbers IV and VI. Did the Commission read Peter Moore's final comment in **MAL** p.205 and respond to it?

[4] *Prayer Book Studies* 21 p.11.

sentatives of the congregation bring up the elements (mandatorily if the rubrics are obeyed). This kind of 'offering' seems a departure from the simple preparing of the table. It also seems to neglect the advice of the Pan-Anglican Document 'Care should be taken not to give any impression that the offertory is an act of oblation in itself'.[1]

Another smaller point of inconsistency arises in the use of capitals for the elements. In **Amer1** and **Amer2** capitals appear for 'Bread' and 'Wine' once the Great Thanksgiving has begun. In **Amer3** this is not done. Similarly the word 'altar' appears in the rubrics of the first two rites, but not in the third—'holy table' was the usual (but not invariable) term in **Amer.** One is left to wonder why these small changes were made—and made inconsistently. But overall, the Commission has undoubtedly achieved its aim. Though the three rites are very different, there is a logical connection and progression from the one to the other, and all three stand together as diverse expressions of the same liturgical tradition.

On the fifth principle, the texts have come into use at a time when the Episcopal Church has been involved in ever widening *ecumenical* contacts. The General Convention of October 1973 voted to continue participation in COCU, and also to endorse the agreed Anglican/ Roman Catholic Statement on the Eucharist. The three liturgies reflect this growing ecumenical concern. The rationale in *Prayer Book Studies* 21 does suggest that items 'restored' because they will be helpful in ecumenical contacts, have in fact been justified on the basis that they are 'ancient'. Among such items are the absence of the filioque (as in **AmerR**), the litany form of the intercession, the offering of the elements to God, and the invitation to communion ('The Gifts of God for the People of God'). Again, it is a varied list, and the items may or may not be valued for their own sakes, or for their ecumenical importance. But their basis for inclusion would seem in fact to be neither, but rather their antiquity.

The General Convention 1973

When the General Convention met in October 1973, the three services from 1970 were to be re-authorized, but in addition the Convention had before it a report from the Standing Liturgical Commission recommending certain changes and optional variations in them. These were in most cases to add further flexibility to the rites, though the

[1] See p.30 above.

increasing emphasis on penitence shows that the dropping of this element to five times a year in **AmerR** had caused considerable reaction, which even the 1970 provisions did not meet. The 'thou' form of the Lord's Prayer was inserted into **Amer2**, and this also looks somewhat like a reaction, and the dismay about the words of invitation mentioned above was met by the inclusion of 'Christ gave himself for you' (getting away from the present tense usage). When the services were subsequently printed in a new book[1] the text of all three was left virtually unchanged, and a schedule added at the beginning. The actual changes emerge clearly in the texts as edited here.

The Liturgical Commission also proposed to the General Convention a timetable 'to bring the revision to an orderly conclusion'. This meant that the Commission would be reviewing all comment on its services in the years 1973 to 1975. It would then complete a draft of 'A Proposed Book of Common Prayer' to be in the hands of all Bishops and Deputies six months before the opening of the 1976 General Convention (i.e. by March or April 1976). The 1976 Convention would entrench two whole days for consideration of this draft Book, and would give it approval for a three year period. Then in 1979 the next General Convention would be able to make it the permanent new Book of Common Prayer of the Episcopal Church.

In the light of these timetable proposals a resolution was moved from the floor to ensure that the original **Amer** (of 1928) was included in the future Prayer Book. This was defeated, and the Commission's proposals were then adopted as the Episcopal Church's official policy in Prayer Book revision.

---

[1] *Authorized Services* 1973, published by the Church Hymnal Corporation and known as 'the Zebra book' because of its striped cover.

THE AMERICAN EXPERIMENTAL LITURGIES
1970/1973 (Amer1, Amer2, Amer3)

⟦This text is taken from *Services for Trial Use* (Church Hymnal Corporation, New York, 1971) and from *Authorized Services* 1973 (Church Hymnal Corporation, 1973). These two books set out the three services as authorized in 1970, and as amended and authorized again in 1973. The 1973 'Schedule' below contains virtually all the changes made, and is self-explanatory. A very few other changes have been incorporated into the actual text of the services, and where this is so there is a sign □ in the margin (i.e. in nos. 16, 25, 38, 42, 68, 70, 74, 75, 85, 87, 94, 104, 113, 116, 121, 125, 126, 127, 128, 131, 132, 133, 137, 138, 142, 143, 144) and an *apparatus* below shows the extent of the changes. The numbering is editorial, and runs right through the three services, as they have so much in common. As in **LiE** and **MAL,** American spelling ('succor' 'Savior' etc.) has been Anglicized. Because the first two rites are basically revisions of **Amer** and **AmerR** respectively, frequent reference back to the text of these two rites has been used, especially in the forms of the Great Thanksgiving. The Appendix material common to all three services is cited in this volume as '**Amer1-3**'.⟧

1   **SCHEDULE OF OPTIONAL CHANGES AND VARIATIONS IN THE HOLY EUCHARIST** ⟦1973 only⟧

As indicated in the Preface[1], the General Convention of 1973 authorized for further use throughout this Church, the rites published in *Services for Trial Use,* either in the form in which they appear in that publication or with certain optional changes and variations listed in the Annex appended to the enabling Resolution.

Wherever feasible the authorized changes have been inserted in the text in the following pages. All such changes are marked with the symbol e.g. □ in the margin.

In a number of cases, however, inserting the authorized changes or variations would have involved extensive resetting of pages with resulting increase in the cost of this pew edition. In other cases, inserting the variations would have impaired their optional character.

All such optional changes and variations not included in the text are listed below, and the symbol ■ appears in the margin to identify the place where the optional variation may be introduced:

⟦In the list which follows, each provision in the original includes words like 'On p.31, replace . . .'. For obvious reasons these are changed here to 'In no. . . . , replace . . .' etc.⟧

[1] ⟦i.e. The Preface to *Authorized Services* 1973⟧

(1) In no. 6, replace 'Hear the words of our Lord Jesus Christ' by the words 'Hear what our Lord Jesus Christ saith.'

(2) In the rubric before *The Gloria*, no. 8, after the words *'some other song of praise is sung or said'* insert the following: *'in addition to, or in place of, the foregoing.'*

(3) Amend the rubric in no. 17 to read as follows: *'A Confession of Sin, as in no. 22 or in no. 47 is to be said here, or at one of the other places appointed. If the Confession is omitted, a penitential petition is to be included in the Intercession.'*

(4) In the Great Thanksgiving in no. 29, after the words ' . . . he took bread; and when he had given thanks,' insert the phrase 'to thee.'

(5) In the prayer following 'Christ our Passover . . .' in no. 33, replace all that follows the words 'Grant us therefore, gracious Lord,' by the following: 'so to eat the flesh of thy dear son Jesus Christ and to drink his blood, that we may evermore dwell in him and he in us. **Amen.**'

(6) In no. 41, insert in the words over the Bread the phrase, 'to thee', after 'had given thanks.'

(7) Immediately after the Nicene Creed, in no. 65, replace the present rubric by the following, *'A Confession of Sin is to be said here, or after the Intercession, or before the beginning of the Service. If the Confession is omitted, a penitential petition is to be included in the Intercession.'*

(8) In the rubric under **'THE PRAYERS'**, in no. 69, replace the second line by the following: *'The Universal Church, its members, and its mission.'*

(9) In no. 78, in the words following 'The Gifts of God for the People of God' replace the word 'gives' by the word 'gave', to read '. . . that Christ gave himself for you . . .'

(10) In Eucharistic Prayer B, no. 102, replace the two lines, 'In the same way, he took the cup . . .,' by the following: 'After supper, he took the cup, gave thanks, and said.'

(11) In Eucharistic Prayer C, no. 104, replace the two lines beginning, 'In the same way, after supper . . .', by the following: 'After supper, he took the cup of wine, gave thanks, and said "Drink this, all of you." '

(12) In Eucharistic Prayer D, no. 105, replace the two lines beginning 'in the same way, after supper . . .,' by the following: 'After supper, he took the cup of wine, gave thanks, and said "Drink this, all of you." '

(13) In the rubric under **'FORMS OF INTERCESSION'**, no. 107, replace the second line by the following: *'The Universal Church, its members, and its mission.'*

(14) Under **'FORMS OF INTERCESSION'**, no. 107, insert a new rubric to read, *'The forms of intercession which follow may be adapted, provided that prayer is always offered for the intentions listed.'*

(15) In Intercession II, no. 111, change the final sentence of each bidding to read, 'Pray, brothers and sisters . . .,' and add a footnote as follows: *'Any other suitable words may be substituted.'*

(16) In Intercession V, no. 121, immediately following the petition, 'For those in positions of public trust,' add a new, asterisked, petition, 'For all who live and work in this community, especially . . . we pray to you, O Lord.'

(17) In the second Invitation, no. 144, replace the clause, '. . . Christ gives himself for you,' by the clause, '. . . Christ gave himself for you . . .'

2   ## CONCERNING THE CELEBRATION

The Holy Eucharist is the principal act of Christian worship on the Lord's Day.

At all celebrations of the Liturgy, it is fitting that the presiding Minister, whether bishop or priest, be assisted by other priests, and by deacons and lay persons.

When the Bishop is present, it is his prerogative as the chief sacramental minister of the Diocese to be principal celebrant at the Lord's Table, and to preach the Gospel.

It is appropriate that other priests present stand with the presiding Minister at the altar, and join with him in the consecration of the gifts, in breaking the Bread, and in distributing Communion.

A deacon, when present, should read the Gospel and lead the Prayer of Intercession. Deacons should also serve at the Lord's Table, preparing and placing on it the elements of bread and wine, and assisting in the ministration of the Sacrament to the People. In the absence of a deacon, his duties may be performed by an assisting priest.

Lay persons appointed by the presiding Minister should normally be assigned the reading of the Lessons which precede the Gospel; and in the absence of a deacon, they may lead the intercession.

The Order for Morning or Evening Prayer may be used in place of all that precedes the Offertory, provided that a lesson from the Gospel is always included and that the Intercession conforms to the directions on page . . . ⟦i.e. no. 107⟧.

Additional Directions and Suggestions for the Ministers will be found on page . . . ⟦i.e. nos. 136-48⟧.

THE HOLY EUCHARIST

3   ### FIRST SERVICE ⟦Amer1⟧

4 *A Psalm, Hymn, or Anthem may be sung during the entrance of the Ministers.*

5 *The People being assembled, the Priest, standing, says*
Almighty God, unto whom . . . ⟦CF 1⟧ . . . Christ our Lord. **Amen.**
your . . . you] thee . . . thy THROUGHOUT

6 *Then the Ten Commandments (page ... [i.e. no. 42]) may be said, or the*
   following
   ■Hear the words of our Lord Jesus Christ:
   Thou shalt . . . **[MAL CF 4(a)]** . . . and the Prophets.

7 *Here is sung or said*
   Lord, have mercy upon us.   Kyrie eleison.
   Christ, have mercy upon us. *or* **Christe eleison.**
   Lord, have mercy upon us.   Kyrie eleison.
   or this
   Holy God,
   Holy and Mighty,
   Holy Immortal One,
   Have mercy upon us.

8 ■*When appointed, the following Hymn or some other song of praise is sung*
   or said, all standing
   Glory be to God on High . . . **[MAL CF 5]** . . . **Father. Amen.**
   in earth] on earth
   Jesu Christ] Jesus Christ
   Thou that takest away . . . **mercy upon us]** OM[1]

9   THE PROCLAMATION OF THE WORD OF GOD

10 *The presiding Minister says to the People*
            The Lord be with you.
   Answer   **And with thy spirit.**
   Priest   Let us pray.

11 *The Collect of the Day*
   The people respond **Amen.**

12 *The Lessons*
   The people sit. One or two lessons, as appointed, are announced and read.
   [See page ... [i.e. no. 138] for forms for announcing and ending Epistles
   and other Lessons.]

13 *A Psalm, Hymn, or Anthem may follow each Lesson.*

14 *Then, all standing, the Deacon or a priest reads the Gospel, first saying*
   The Holy Gospel of our Lord Jesus Christ according to . . .
   The People respond **Glory be to thee, O Lord.**
   At the end of the Gospel, the Deacon says
   The Gospel of the Lord.
   The people respond **Praise be to thee, O Christ.**

   [1] [This reflects an error in **MAL** Common Forms, where the extra line of
   Cranmer is omitted, but should not be. See Appendix G, p.421 below].

15 *The Sermon*

16 *On Sundays and other festivals there follows, all standing*

THE NICENE CREED

□*The version of the Creed in the Book of Common Prayer may be used in place of the following :*
We believe . . . ⟦ICET 3⟧ **. . . world to come. Amen.**
(and the Son)] ᴏᴍ
⟦1970 places the rubric after the Creed and reads *'preceding'* for *'following'*⟧.

17 ■*A confession of sin may be said here (pages . . . or . . .* ⟦i.e. nos. 21-2 or 47-8.⟧)

18 ### THE PRAYERS

19 *Intercession is offered according to the following form, or according to one of those provided on pages . . .* ⟦i.e. nos. 106-135⟧

The Deacon, or some other person appointed, says
Let us pray for Christ's Church and the world.

After each paragraph of this prayer, the People may make an appropriate response as directed by the Minister.

Almighty and everliving God, who has taught us to make prayers, and supplications, and to give thanks to all men: Receive these our prayer which we offer unto thy Divine Majesty, beseeching thee to inspire continually the Universal Church with the spirit of truth, unity, and concord; and grant that all those who do confess thy holy Name may agree in the truth of thy holy Word, and live in unity and godly love.

Give grace, O heavenly Father, to all Bishops and other Ministers, [especially . . .], that they may, both by their life and doctrine, set forth thy true and lively Word, and rightly and duly administer thy holy Sacraments.

And to all thy People give thy heavenly grace; and especially to this congregation here present; that, with meek heart and due reverence, they may hear, and receive thy holy Word; truly serving thee in holiness and righteousness all the days of their life.

We beseech thee also, to rule the hearts of those who bear the authority of government in this and every land [especially . . .], and to lead them to wise decisions and right actions for the welfare of mankind, and for the peace of the world. Grant to all people, Lord, the will and the wisdom to be good stewards of the riches of creation, that we neither selfishly waste nor wantonly destroy thy handiwork.

And we most humbly beseech thee, of thy goodness, O Lord, to comfort and succour all those who, in this transitory life, are in trouble, sorrow, need, sickness, or any other adversity, [especially . . .].

And we also bless thy holy Name for all thy servants departed this life in thy faith and fear, [especially . . .], beseeching thee to grant them continual growth in thy love and service, and to give us grace to follow their good examples, that with them we may be partakers of thy heavenly kingdom.

Grant these our prayers, O Father, for Jesus Christ's sake, our only Mediator and Advocate. **Amen.**

20 *If there is no celebration of the Communion, or if a priest is not available, the Service is concluded as directed on page . . . [i.e. no. 140].*

21 *CONFESSION OF SIN*

The Deacon or Priest says the following, or the Exhortation on page . . . [i.e. no. 43].

Ye who do . . . [**MAL** CF 9] . . . to Almighty God, devoutly kneeling.

lead a new] lead the new
and take this holy sacrament to your Comfort] OM

22 *The People kneel. A period of silence may be kept; after which one of the Ministers leads the People in this General Confession:*

Father almighty, Lord of heaven and earth:
we confess that we have sinned against thee
in thought, word, and deed.
Have mercy upon us, O God,
according to thy loving kindness;
In thy great goodness,
do away our offences,
and cleanse us from our sins;
For Jesus Christ's sake. Amen.

or this

Almighty God . . . [MAL CF 10] . . . Christ our Lord. Amen.

23 *The Minister may then say*
Hear the Word of God to all who truly turn to him:
Come unto me, all ye that travail . . . ⟦**MAL** CF 12⟧ . . . Christ the righteous; and he is the perfect offering for our sins, and not for ours only, but for the sins of the whole world. [1 *St. John* 2:1-2]

So God] God so
Hear also what St. Paul saith] OM
Jesus Christ] Christ Jesus[1]
Here also what Saint John saith]OM

24 *The Bishop, if he is present, or the Priest, stands and says this Absolution :*
Almighty God . . . ⟦**MAL** CF 11⟧ . . . our Lord. **Amen.**

sins to all them] sins to all those

25 *THE PEACE*
□*Here (or at one of the other places suggested on page . . . ⟦i.e. no. 141⟧), the Priest may say to the People, all standing*
⟦*1970 omits 'all standing'*⟧
The Peace of the Lord be always with you.
Answer **And with thy spirit.**
Then the Ministers and People may greet one another in the Name of the Lord.

26 **THE CELEBRATION OF THE HOLY COMMUNION**

27 *The Priest, standing at the Holy Table, begins the Offertory with this or some other Sentence of Scripture :*
Ascribe to the Lord the honour due to his name; bring offerings and come into his courts. (*Psalm* 96:8)

28 *During the Offertory, a Psalm, Hymn, or Anthem may be sung. Representatives of the Congregation bring the People's offerings of bread and wine, and money or other gifts, to the Deacon or Priest. The People stand while the offerings are presented and placed on the Altar.*

29 *THE GREAT THANKSGIVING*
The People remain standing. The Priest faces them, and sings or says
The Lord be with you.

People **And with thy spirit.**
Priest Lift up your hearts.
People **We lift them up unto the Lord.**
Priest Let us give thanks unto our Lord God.
People **It is meet and right so to do.**

---

[1] ⟦This reflects an error in **MAL** Common Forms. See Appendix G, p.421⟧.

Then, facing the Holy Table, the Priest proceeds

It is very meet, right, and our bounden duty, that we should at all times, and in all places, give thanks unto thee, O Lord, Holy Father, Almighty, Everlasting God.

On all Sundays, and other occasions when a Proper Preface is appointed, it is sung or said here.

[The Proper Prefaces, which come after the end of the service, are to be found in Appendix C].

Therefore with Angels and Archangels, and with all the company of heaven, we laud and magnify thy glorious Name; evermore praising thee, and saying,

Priest and People

Holy, Holy, Holy, Lord God of Hosts:
Heaven and earth are full of thy glory.
Glory be to thee, O Lord Most High.

Here may be added

Blessed is He that cometh in the Name of the Lord:
Hosanna in the highest!

The people may kneel

Then the Priest continues

All glory . . . [As in **Amer** (1928) to be found in **LiE** pp.58-9, with variants as shown] . . . world without end. **Amen.**

(by his one oblation of himself once offered)] OM BRACKETS
oblation and satisfaction] OM
Drink ye all of this] Drink this, all of you
Testament] Covenant
according to the institution of thy dearly beloved Son, our Saviour Jesus
    Christ] OM
these thy gifts and creatures] these gifts
in remembrance of his death and passion] OM
[There are no indented rubrics concerning manual acts, but the following rubric comes after ' . . . until his coming again': *At the following words concerning the Bread, the Priest is to hold it, or lay his hand upon it. And at the words concerning the Cup, he is to hold, or lay his hand upon, the Cup and any other vessel containing wine to be consecrated.*
In 1973 a ■ is in the margin opposite 'he took bread; and when he had given thanks,']

30 And now, as our Saviour Christ hath taught us, we are bold to say,

People and Priest

Our Father, who art . . . [MAL CF 1] . . . and ever. Amen.

in earth] on earth
them that trespass] those who trespass
the power] and the power

31 *The Breaking of Bread*
A period of silence is kept, during which the Priest breaks the consecrated Bread.

32 *Then may be sung or said*
(Alleluia.) Christ our Passover is sacrificed for us:
Therefore let us keep the feast. (Alleluia.)
From Ash Wednesday until Easter Eve, Alleluia is omitted; and may be omitted at other times except during Easter Season.

33 *The following prayer may be said:*
We do not presume . . . ⟦**MAL** CF 13⟧ . . . he in us. **Amen.**

so to eat the flesh . . . and that we may] so to partake of the Body and Blood
of thy dear Son Jesus Christ, that we may be cleansed from all our sins, and may
⟦In 1973 there is a ■ in the margin here⟧

34 *The Ministers receive the Sacrament in both kinds, and then immediately deliver it to the People.*
The Bread and the Cup are given to the communicants with these words, or with the words on pages . . . ⟦i.e. no. 144⟧.
The Body . . . ⟦CF 7(a)⟧ . . . thanksgiving.
The Blood . . . ⟦CF 7(b)⟧ . . . thankful.

you . . . your] thee . . . thy THROUGHOUT

During the ministration of Communion, Psalms, Hymns, or Anthems may be sung.

35 *After Communion the Priest says*
Let us pray.
He then says this prayer. The people may repeat it with him.
Almighty and everliving God . . . ⟦**MAL** CF 18⟧ . . . world without
end. **Amen.**

vouchsafe to] OM
who have duly received these holy] in these holy
which is the blessed] the blessed
thy everlasting] thine everlasting
by the merits of the most precious death and passion of thy dear Son] OM
most humbly] humbly

36 *The Bishop, if present, or the Priest, gives the blessing*
The Peace of God . . . ⟦CF 9⟧ . . . always. **Amen.**

passes] passeth
Spirit] Ghost
among] amongst

or

The Blessing of God Almighty, the Father, the Son, and the Holy Spirit, be upon you, and remain with you for ever. **Amen.**

37 *The Deacon (or Priest) may then dismiss the People*

Go forth into the world
rejoicing in the power of the Spirit.
Thanks be to God.

or

Go in peace to love and serve the Lord.
Thanks be to God.

or

Let us go forth in the Name of Christ.
Thanks be to God.

38 □*From Easter Day through the Day of Pentecost,* **'Alleluia, Alleluia'** *may be added to any of the Dismissals or to the Response.*
〚1970 omits〛

39   OTHER FORMS OF THE GREAT THANKSGIVING
which may be used in place of the Prayer in the preceding Rite.

40   I

[*From the Liturgy of the Lord's Supper,* 1967. 〚**AmerR**〛].

After the Sursum Corda and Sanctus, the Priest continues

All glory . . . 〚As in **AmerR** no. 29, **MAL**, pp. 211-2〛 . . . world without end. **Amen.**

〚There are no indented rubrics concerning manual acts, but after '. . . his coming again' the same rubric as in no. 29 occurs.〛

41   II

After the Sursum Corda and the Sanctus, the Priest continues

All glory . . . 〚as in no. 29 above with one further variant〛 . . . world without end. **Amen.**

〚This prayer is identical with that in the rite except:
most humbly beseeching . . . our offences] and to accept us, our souls and bodies, in union with our Saviour Jesus Christ, a reasonable, holy, and living sacrifice unto thee; beseeching thee to make us one body with him, that he may dwell in us, and we in him;
Rubrics are set out as in the rite. In 1973 a ■ is in the margin opposite '. . . after he had given thanks'.〛

42   **THE DECALOGUE**

The Ten Commandments and their responses may be substituted for the Summary of the Law, or may precede it, the People kneeling.
God spake these words . . . ⟦**MAL** CF 3 omitting the sections in brackets⟧ . . . covet.

☐**Lord have mercy upon us, and write all these thy laws in our hearts, we beseech thee.**
Six days . . . thy God] OM
witness] witness against thy neighbour.
⟦1970 has the tenth response identical with the first nine—perhaps by mistake⟧

The Minister may then proceed directly to the Hymn, 'Glory be to God on High', or to the Salutation and Collect of the Day.

43   **AN EXHORTATION**

which may be used, in whole or in part, either during the Liturgy or at other times. In the absence of a deacon or priest, this Exhortation may be read by a lay person. The People stand or sit
Beloved in the Lord:
Our Saviour Christ, on the night before he suffered, established the Sacrament of his Body and Blood: as a sign and pledge of his love, for the continual remembrance of the sacrifice of his death, and for a spiritual sharing in his life. For in those holy Mysteries we are made one with Christ, and Christ with us; we are made one body in him, and fellow-members one of another.

Having in mind, therefore, his great love for us, and in obedience to his command, his Church renders to Almighty God our heavenly Father never-ending thanks:

for the creation of the world,
for his continual providence over us,
for his love for all mankind, and

for the redemption of the world by our Saviour Christ, who took upon himself our flesh, and humbled himself even to death on the Cross, that he might make us the children of God by the power of the Holy Spirit, and exalt us to everlasting life.

But if we are to share rightly in the celebration of those holy Mysteries, and be nourished by that spiritual Food, we must remember the dignity of that holy Sacrament. I therefore call upon you to consider how Saint Paul exhorts all persons to prepare themselves carefully before eating of that Bread and drinking of that Cup.

For as the benefit is great, if with penitent hearts and living faith we receive the holy Sacrament; so is the danger great, if we receive it improperly, not recognizing the Lord's Body. Judge yourselves therefore, my brothers, lest you be judged by the Lord.

Examine your lives and conduct by the rule of God's commandments, that you may perceive wherein you have offended in what you have done or left undone, whether in thought, word, or deed. And acknowledge your sins before Almighty God, with full purpose of amendment of life, being ready to make restitution for all injuries and wrongs done by you to others; and also being ready to forgive those who have offended you, in order that you yourselves may be forgiven. And then, being reconciled with your brothers, come to the banquet of that most heavenly Food.

And if in your own preparation, you cannot quiet your conscience, but need help and counsel, then go to a discreet and understanding Priest, and open your grief to him: that you may receive the benefit of Absolution and spiritual counsel and advice; to the removal of scruple and doubt, the assurance of pardon, and the strengthening of your faith.

To Christ our Lord who loves us, and washed us in his own blood, and made us a kingdom of priests to serve his God and Father: to him be glory in the Church evermore. Through him let us offer continually the sacrifice of praise which is our bounden duty and service, and, with faith in him, come boldly before the Throne of grace [and humbly confess our sins to Almighty God].

44   A PENITENTIAL ORDER

This Order may be used immediately before the Liturgy (in which case the Collect for Purity is to be omitted), or as a separate service.

When used separately, a Sermon or the Exhortation on page . . . [i.e. no. 43] may follow the Sentences; and then, after the confession of sin, the service may be concluded with suitable prayers, and the Grace.

45 *The Minister begins with this sentence :*
Grace to you and peace from God our Father and the Lord Jesus Christ. [*Philippians* 1:2]

46 *He then adds one or more of the following :*
If we say that we have no sin, we deceive ourselves, and the truth is not in us. But if we confess our sins, God, who is faithful and just, will forgive us our sins and cleanse us from all unrighteousness. [1 *John* 1:8-9]
Since we have a great high priest who has passed through the heavens, Jesus, the Son of God, let us with confidence draw near to the throne

of grace, that we may receive mercy and find grace to help in time of
need. [*Hebrews* 4:14]

Jesus said,

The first commandment is this: 'Hear, O Israel: The Lord your God
. . . ⟦CF 3⟧ . . . greater than these [*Mark* 12:29-31].

You shall] OM
This is the first commandment] OM

Then follows a confession of sin.

47   *CONFESSION OF SIN* [*For use with the First Service*]
The Minister says

Let us confess our sins against God and our neighbour.

A period of silence may be observed.

48 *Minister and People*

Most merciful God,
We confess that we have sinned against thee
in thought, word and deed:
we have not loved thee with our whole heart;
we have not loved our neighbours as ourselves.
We pray thee of thy mercy
forgive what we have been,
amend what we are,
direct what we shall be;
that we may delight in thy will,
and walk in thy ways,
through Jesus Christ our Lord. Amen.

or

Father Almighty, Lord of heaven and earth:
We confess that we have sinned against thee
in thought, word, and deed.
Have mercy upon us, O God,
according to thy loving kindness;
In thy great goodness,
do away our offences,
and cleanse us from our sins;
for Jesus Christ's sake. Amen.

49 *The Bishop, if present, or the Priest stands and says*

The Almighty and merciful Lord grant you Absolution and Remission
of all your sins, true repentance, amendment of life, and the grace and
consolation of his Holy Spirit. **Amen.**

50   *CONFESSION OF SIN* [*For use with the Second Service*]

The Minister says
Let us confess our sins against God and our neighbour.

A period of silence may be observed.

51 *Minister and People*
Most merciful . . . [As the first confession at no. 48 above, but replacing **'thee'** and **'thy'** with **'you'** and **'your'** throughout] . . . **Christ our Lord. Amen.**

52 *The Bishop, if present, or the Priest stands and says*
Almighty God have mercy on you, forgive you all your sins, through our Lord Jesus Christ; strengthen you in all goodness, and by the power of the Holy Spirit, keep you in eternal life. **Amen.**

THE HOLY EUCHARIST[1]

53   **SECOND SERVICE** [Amer2]

A Psalm, hymn, or Anthem may be sung during the entrance of the Ministers.

The People being assembled, and all standing, the Priest says
Blessed be God: Father, Son, and Holy Spirit.

People
And blessed be his Kingdom, now and for ever. Amen.

From Easter Day through the Day of Pentecost, in place of the above, he says
Alleluia! Christ is risen.

People   **The Lord is risen indeed. Alleluia!**

54 *The Priest may say*
Almighty God to you . . . [CF 1] . . . our Lord. **Amen.**
whom] you

55 *When appointed, the following Hymn or some other song of praise is sung or said, all standing*
Glory to God . . . [ICET 4] . . . **God the Father. Amen.**

56 *On other occasions the following is used*
Lord, have mercy. . . . [as at no. 7 above] . . . **Have mercy upon us.**

----

[1] [Note that **'CONCERNING THE CELEBRATION'** set out before the 'First Service' is reprinted before the 'Second Service' but is omitted in this editing of the rites]

57   **THE PROCLAMATION OF THE WORD OF GOD**

58 *The presiding Minister says to the People*
The Lord be with you
Answer **And also with you.**
Priest Let us pray.

59 *The Collect*
The People respond **Amen.**

60 *The Lessons*
The People sit. One or two Lessons, as appointed, are announced and read.
See page . . . ⟦i.e. no. 138⟧ for forms for announcing and ending Epistles and
other Lessons.

61 *A Psalm, Hymn, or Anthem may follow each Lesson.*

62 *Then, all standing, the Deacon or a priest reads the Gospel, first saying*
The Holy Gospel of our Lord Jesus Christ according to . . .
The People respond **Glory to you, Lord Christ.**
At the end of the Gospel, the Deacon says
The Gospel of the Lord
The People respond **Praise to you, Lord Christ.**

63 *The Sermon*

64 *On Sundays and other festivals there follows, all standing*
                  THE NICENE CREED
We believe . . . ⟦ICET 3⟧ **. . . world to come. Amen.**
(and the Son)] OM

65 ■*A confession of sin may be said here, or after the Intercession.*

66   *CONFESSION OF SIN*
The minister says
Let us confess our sins against God and our neighbour.
A period of silence may be observed.

67 *Minister and People*
Most merciful . . . ⟦as at no. 51 above⟧ **. . . our Lord. Amen.**

68 *The Bishop, if present, or the Priest stands and says*
☐Almighty God . . . ⟦as at no. 52 above⟧ . . . eternal life. **Amen.**
⟦1970 omits 'our', presumably by mistake, as it is in *Prayer Book Studies* 21.⟧

69   **THE PRAYERS**
Here Prayer is offered with intercession for

■*The Universal Church and all its members*
The Nation and all in authority
The welfare of the world

The concerns of the local community
Those who suffer and those in any trouble
The departed (with commemoration of a saint when appropriate)
See pages . . . ⟦i.e. nos. 106-135⟧ *for various forms of Intercession.*

70   *THE PEACE*
□*Here (or at one of the other places suggested on page . . .* ⟦i.e. no. 141⟧*),*
the Priest may say to the People, all standing
⟦1970 omits 'all standing'⟧
             The Peace of the Lord be always with you.
Answer **And also with you.**
Then the Ministers and People may greet one another in the Name of the
Lord.
If there is no celebration of the Communion, or if a priest is not available,
the Service is concluded as directed on page . . . ⟦i.e. no. 140⟧*.*

71   **THE CELEBRATION OF THE HOLY COMMUNION**

72 *The Priest, standing at the Holy Table, begins the Offertory with this or*
some other Sentence of Scripture:
Ascribe to the Lord the honour due to his Name; bring offerings and
come into his courts. [*Psalm* 96:8]

73 *During the Offertory, a Psalm, Hymn, or Anthem may be sung.*
Representatives of the Congregation bring the People's offerings of bread and
wine, and the money or other gifts, to the Deacon or Priest. The People
stand while the offerings are presented and placed on the Altar.

74   *THE GREAT THANKSGIVING*
The People remain standing. The Priest faces them, and sings or says
Priest   The Lord be with you.
People   **And also with you.**
Priest   Lift up your hearts.
People   **We lift them up to the Lord.**
Priest   Let us give thanks to the Lord our God.
People   **It is right to give him thanks and praise.**
Then, facing the Holy Table, the Priest proceeds
It is right, and a good and joyful thing, always and everywhere to
give thanks to you, Father Almighty, Creator of heaven and earth:
On all Sundays, and on other occasions when a Proper Preface is appointed,
it is sung or said here.
⟦The Proper Prefaces which come after the three services are to be found here
in Appendix C⟧

Therefore we praise you,
joining our voices with angels and archangels
and with all the company of heaven
who for ever sing this hymn
to proclaim the glory of your Name:

Priest and People
Holy, holy, holy Lord, God of power and might,
heaven and earth are full of your glory.
Hosanna in the highest.
Blessed is he who comes in the name of the Lord.
Hosanna in the highest.

The People may kneel.

Then the Priest continues
Holy and gracious Father,
in your infinite love you made us for yourself;
and when we fell into sin
and became subject to evil and death,
you, in your mercy, sent Jesus Christ,
your only and eternal Son,
to share our human nature,
to live and die as one of us
to reconcile us to you,
the God and Father of all.

He stretched out his arms upon the Cross,
and offered himself, in obedience to your will,
a perfect sacrifice for all mankind.

At the following words concerning the Bread, the Priest is to hold it, or lay his hand upon it. And at the words concerning the Cup, he is to hold, or lay his hand upon, the Cup and any other vessel containing wine to be consecrated.

On the night he was handed over to suffering and death,
our Lord Jesus Christ took bread;
and when he had given thanks to you,
he broke it, and gave it to his disciples,
and said, 'Take this and eat it:
This is my Body, which is given for you.
Do this for the remembrance of me.'

After supper he took the cup of wine;
and when he had given thanks, he gave it to them,
and said, 'Drink this, all of you:
This is my Blood of the new Covenant,
which is shed for you and for many
for the forgiveness of sins.
Whenever you drink it, do this for the remembrance of me.'

☐Therefore, Father, we recall the mystery of faith:

Priest and People
Christ has died,
Christ is risen,
Christ will come again.
The Priest continues
We celebrate the memorial of our redemption, O Father,
in this sacrifice of praise and thanksgiving,
and we offer you these Gifts.
Sanctify them by your Holy Spirit
to be for your people the Body and Blood of your Son,
the holy food and drink of new and unending life in him.
Sanctify us also
that we may faithfully receive this holy Sacrament,
and serve you in unity, constancy, and peace;
and at the last day bring us with all your saints
into the joy of your eternal kingdom.

All this we ask through your Son Jesus Christ:
By him, and with him, and in him,
in the unity of the Holy Spirit
all honour and glory is yours, Almighty Father,
now and for ever.
Amen.
⟦1970 omits the line 'Therefore . . . of faith'⟧

75 As our Saviour Christ has taught us, we now pray,
People and Priest

| ☐**Our Father who art** . . . ⟦as at no. 30 above⟧ . . . **ever and ever. Amen.** | **Our Father** . . . ⟦ICET 1⟧ . . . **for ever. Amen.** |

⟦1970 omits **MAL** CF and has ICET form only⟧

76   *THE BREAKING OF THE BREAD*
A period of silence is kept, during which the Priest breaks the consecrated Bread.

77 *Then may be sung or said*
(Alleluia.) Christ our Passover is sacrificed for us:
Therefore let us keep the feast. (Alleluia.)
From Ash Wednesday until Easter Eve, Alleluia is omitted; and may be omitted at other times except during Easter Season.

78 *Facing the People, the Priest says the following Sentence of Invitation:*
The Gifts of God for the People of God.

■*He may add:* Take them in remembrance that Christ gives himself for you, and feed on him in your hearts by faith, with thanksgiving.

79 *The Ministers receive the Sacrament in both kinds, and then immediately deliver it to the People.*
The Bread and the Cup are given with these words, to which the communicant may respond, **Amen.**
The Body [Blood] of our Lord Jesus Christ keep you in everlasting life.

or this

The Body of Christ, the Bread of heaven.
The Blood of Christ, the Cup of salvation.

80 *During the ministration of Communion, Psalms, Hymns, or Anthems may be sung.*

81 *After Communion, the Priest says*
Let us pray

People and Priest
Eternal God, Heavenly Father,
you have accepted us as living members of your Son
our Saviour Jesus Christ,
and you have fed us with spiritual food
in the Sacrament of his Body and Blood.
Send us now into the world in peace,
and grant us strength and courage
to love and serve you
with gladness and singleness of heart. Amen.

or this

82 **Almighty and everliving God,**
   you have fed us with the spiritual food
      of the most precious Body and Blood
      of your Son, our Saviour Jesus Christ;
   You have assured us, in these holy Mysteries,
      that we are living members
      of the Body of your Son,
      and heirs of your eternal kingdom.
   And now, Father, send us out
      to do the work you have given us to do,
   To love and serve you
      as faithful witnesses of Christ our Lord.
   To him, to you, and to the Holy Spirit,
      be honour and glory now and for ever. Amen.

83 *The Bishop, if present, or the Priest, may bless the People.*

84 *The Deacon (or Priest) may dismiss them with these words:*
Go forth . . . [As at no. 37 above (three choices)] . . . **Thanks be to God.**

85 □*From Easter Day through the Day of Pentecost,* **'Alleluia, Alleluia'** *may be added to any of the Dismissals and the Response.*
[1970 omits]

86 **ANOTHER FORM OF THE GREAT THANKSGIVING**
[*Based on the Liturgy of the Lord's Supper,* 1967 [**AmerR**]]
After the Sursum Corda and the Sanctus, the Priest continues
All glory is yours, Almighty . . . [As in **AmerR** and at no. 40 above, but with variants as shown] . . . O Father Almighty, now and for ever. **Amen.**
thy . . . thee . . . thine] you . . . you . . . your/yours THROUGHOUT
Creator of Heaven and earth, who didst make us] You made us
thou of thy tender mercy didst give] you gave
Who made] He made
once offered] OM
perpetual] OM
In the same way also] OM
Wherefore . . . do celebrate . . . these thy holy Gifts . . . unto thee] Therefore . . . celebrate . . . these holy Gifts . . . to you.
And herewith we . . . to accept] And with these Gifts, O Lord, we offer to you ourselves, for this is our duty and service, And we pray you, in your goodness and mercy, to accept
We pray thee, gracious Father, of thine almighty power to bless] Gracious Father, in your almighty power bless
the same Jesus] Jesus
[There are no indented rubrics concerning manual acts, but after 'his coming again' the same words as in no. 29 occur.]

87 □*The Eucharistic Prayer C (page* ... ⟦i.e. no. 104⟧) *may be used as an alternative*
⟦1970 OMITS⟧

88 ⟋ **AN ORDER FOR CELEBRATING
THE HOLY EUCHARIST** ⟦Amer3⟧
*which may be used on occasions other than the principal services on sunday[1]
and other feasts of our lord*

89 **ORDER OF THE CELEBRATION**
*This order requires for its effective use careful preparation by all the
worshippers so that all may understand what takes place and their own
part in the celebration.*
*The use of silence, movement, and music will depend on the nature of the
particular occasion.*

90 *THE PEOPLE AND PRIEST*
91 *GATHER IN THE LORD'S NAME*
92 *PROCLAIM AND RESPOND TO THE WORD OF GOD*
*the proclamation and response may include, in addition to a reading from
the gospel, other readings, song, talk, dance, instrumental music, other art
forms, silence.*
93 *PRAY FOR THE WORLD AND THE CHURCH*
94 *EXCHANGE THE PEACE*
□*here or elsewhere in the service.*
⟦1970 omits⟧
95 *PREPARE THE TABLE*
*some of those present prepare the table; the bread, the cup of wine, and
other offerings, are placed upon it.*
96 *MAKE EUCHARIST*
*the great thanksgiving is said by the priest in the name of the gathering,
using one of the eucharistic prayers provided. In the course of the prayer,
he takes the bread and cup into his hands, or places his hand upon them.*
the people respond—**amen!**
97 *BREAK THE BREAD*
98 *EAT AND DRINK TOGETHER*
*the body and blood of the lord are shared in a reverent manner; after
all have received, any of the sacrament that remains is then consumed.*

99 *When a common meal or agape accompanies the celebration, it follows here.*

---

[1] ⟦Apparently as a matter of principle, no capitals are used in this order here,
or in any directions from no. 91 to no. 98 inclusive. Even the headings are in
lower case in the original.⟧

00 **EUCHARISTIC PRAYERS**

*In making the Eucharist, the Priest uses one of the Eucharistic Prayers
from the First or Second Service, or one of the following.*

01 **A**

*After a suitable invitation by the Priest, and a response by the People, the
Priest gives thanks as follows:*

We give thanks to you, O God our Creator;
You are worthy of praise from every creature you have made.
For in these last days you have sent your only Son
to be the Saviour and Redeemer of the world.
In him, you have forgiven our sins,
and made us worthy to stand before you.
In him, you have brought us out of darkness into light
out of error into truth,
out of death into life.

On the night he was handed over to suffering and death,
our Lord Jesus Christ took bread;
and when he had given thanks to you,
he broke it, and gave it to his disciples,
and said, 'Take this and eat it:
This is my Body, which is given for you.
Do this for the remembrance of me.'

After supper he took the cup of wine,
and when he had given thanks, he gave it to them,
and said, 'Drink this, all of you:
This is my Blood of the new Covenant,
which is shed for you and for many
for the forgiveness of sins.
Whenever you drink it, do this for the remembrance of me.'

Remembering his death and resurrection,
we offer in thanksgiving this Bread and this Cup.
And we pray you to send your Holy Spirit
upon this Offering and upon your People,
to change us, and to make us one in your kingdom.
To you be praise and honour and worship
through your Son Jesus Christ
with the Holy Spirit
for ever and ever.
Amen.

102   B

After a suitable invitation by the Priest, and a response by the People,
the Priest gives thanks as follows :
We give you thanks, O Father,
for the goodness and love
which you have made known to us in creation,
in the calling of Israel,
in the words of the prophets,
and, above all, in Jesus your Son:

Who, on the night before he died for us,
took bread and gave thanks;
he broke it and gave it to his disciples, and said:
'This is my body which is for you:
do this for my memorial.'

■In the same way,
he took the cup after supper and said:
'This cup is the new Covenant in my Blood.
Whenever you drink it,
do this for my memorial.'

Remembering now his suffering and death,
and celebrating his resurrection,
and looking for his coming again
to fulfill all things according to your will,
we ask you, Father,
through the power of the Holy Spirit,
to accept and bless these Gifts.
Make us one with your Son in his sacrifice,
that his life may be renewed in us.

And therefore, Father, through Jesus your Son,
in whom we have been accepted and made your children,
by your life-giving Spirit
we offer our grateful praise and say:

103 *People and Priest*
Our Father . . .

104   C

In the following Prayer, the italicized lines [printed here in **bold** not
italic] *are spoken by the People.*
The Lord be with you.
And also with you.

Lift up your hearts.
We lift them up to the Lord.
Let us give thanks to the Lord our God.
Let us praise him for his goodness now and for ever.
God of all Power, Ruler of the Universe,
you are worthy of glory and praise.
Glory to you for ever and ever.

At your command all things came to be,
the vast expanse of interstellar space,
galaxies, suns, planets in their courses,
and this fragile earth, our island home:
By your will they were created and have their being.

From the primal elements you brought forth the race of man,
and blessed us with memory, reason, and skill;
you made us the rulers of creation.
But we turned against you, and betrayed your trust;
and we turned against one another.
Have mercy, Lord, for we are sinnners in your sight.

Again and again, you called us to return.
Through prophets and sages you revealed your righteous Law;
and in the fulness of time, you sent your only Son,
born of a woman, to fulfil your Law,
to open for us the way of freedom and peace.
By his blood, he reconciled us.
By his wounds, we are healed.

☐And, therefore, we praise you,
joining with the heavenly chorus,
with prophets, apostles, and martyrs,
and with men of every generation who have looked to you in hope:
to proclaim with them your glory,
in their unending hymn:
Priest and People
Holy, holy, holy Lord, God of power and might,
heaven and earth are full of your glory.
   Hosanna in the highest.
Blessed is he who comes in the name of the Lord.
☐   **Hosanna in the highest.**
[1970 has square brackets round the thirteen lines above]

The Priest continues

And so, Father, we who have been redeemed by him,
and made a new people by water and the Spirit,
now bring before you these gifts.
Sanctify them by your Holy Spirit
to be for us the Body and Blood
of Jesus Christ our Lord.

On the night he was betrayed,
he took bread, said the blessing,
broke the bread, and gave it to his friends,
and said, 'Take this and eat it.
This is my Body, which is given for you.
Do this for the remembrance of me.'

■In the same way, after supper, he took the cup,
and said 'Drink of this, all of you.
This is my Blood of the new Covenant,
which is poured out for you and for all mankind
for the forgiveness of sins.
Whenever you drink it, do this for the remembrance of me.'

Priest and People

**When we eat this Bread
and drink this Cup,
we show forth your death, Lord Christ,
until you come in glory.**

Priest

Lord God of our Fathers,
God of Abraham, Isaac, and Jacob,
God and Father of our Lord Jesus Christ:
open our eyes to see your hand at work in the world about us.
Deliver us from the presumption of coming to this Table
for solace only, and not for strength;
for pardon only, and not for renewal.
Let the grace of this Holy Communion
make us one body, one spirit in Christ,
that we may worthily serve the world in his name.

Risen Lord, be known to us in the breaking of the Bread.

Accept these prayers and praises, Father,
through Jesus Christ, our great High Priest,
to whom with you and the Holy Spirit,
your Church gives honour, glory, and worship,
from generation to generation.
Amen.

05   **D**

Priest   The grace of our Lord Jesus Christ and the love of God and
           the fellowship of the Holy Spirit be with you all.
or   The Lord be with you.
People   **And also with you.**
Priest   Lift up your hearts.
People   **We lift them up to the Lord.**
Priest   Let us give thanks to the Lord our God.
People   **It is right to give him thanks and praise.**
The Priest begins the Prayer with these or similar words :
Father, we thank you and we praise you . . .

*He gives thanks for God's work in Creation and his revelation of himself
to men.*

He may recall before God the particular occasion being celebrated.

He may incorporate or adapt the Proper Preface of the day.

[*If the Sanctus is to be included he leads into it with these or similar words :*
And so we join the saints and angels
in proclaiming your glory as we sing (say),
Holy, holy, holy Lord . . .]

*Here he praises God for the salvation of the world through Jesus Christ
our Lord.*

He then continues with these words
And so, Father, we bring you these gifts.
Sanctify them by your Holy Spirit
to be for your People the Body and Blood
of Jesus Christ our Lord.

On the night he was betrayed,
he took bread, and said the blessing,
broke the bread, and gave it to his friends,
and said, 'Take this and eat it.
This is my Body, which is given for you.
Do this for the remembrance of me.'

■In the same way, after the supper, he took the cup,
and said 'Drink of this, all of you.
This is my Blood of the new Covenant,
which is poured out for you and for all men
for the forgiveness of sins.
Whenever you drink it, do this for the remembrance of me.'

Father, we now celebrate the memorial of your Son.
By means of this holy Bread and Cup,
we show forth the sacrifice of his death
and we proclaim his resurrection
until he comes again.

Gather us by this Holy Communion
into one Body in your Son Jesus Christ.
Make us a living sacrifice of praise.

By him, and with him, and in him,
in the unity of the Holy Spirit
all honour and glory is yours,
Almighty Father,
now and for ever.
Amen.

106   **FORMS OF INTERCESSION** [Amer1-3]

107 *Prayer is offered with intercession for*

■*The Universal Church and all its members*
The Nation and all in authority
The welfare of the world
The concerns of the local community
Those who suffer and those in any trouble
The departed (with commemoration of a saint when appropriate)

■

*If a confession of sin is not said at the service, a form of Intercession
containing a penitential petition should be chosen. [For example : I, V, or
VII.]*

*The Priest may introduce the Prayers with a sentence of invitation
related to the Season or the Proper of the Day.*

*When a briefer form of Prayer is desired, some or all of the petitions
marked with an asterisk may be omitted.*

08 **I**

Deacon or other leader

With all our heart and with all our mind, let us pray to the Lord, saying, 'Lord, have mercy'.

*For the peace from above, for the loving kindness of God, and for the salvation of our souls,

let us pray to the Lord.

Lord have mercy.

〚This versicle and response is printed out after each brief paragraph down to 'reproach'〛

For the peace of the world, for the welfare of the holy Church of God, and for the unity of all mankind,

For our Bishop, and for all the clergy and people,

For our President, for the leaders of the nations, and for all in authority

For this city (town, village, . . .), for every city and community, and for those who live in them,

*For seasonable weather, and for an abundance of the fruits of the earth,

*For the good earth which God has given us, and for the wisdom and will to conserve it,

*for those who travel on land, on water, in the air, or through outer space,

For the aged and infirm, for widows and orphans, and for the sick and suffering,

For the poor and oppressed, for prisoners and captives, and for all who remember and care for them,

For all who have died in the hope of the resurrection, and for all the departed,

*For deliverance from all danger, violence, oppression, and degradation,

*For the absolution and remission of our sins and offences,

*That we may end our lives in faith and hope, without suffering and without reproach,

*Defend us, deliver us, and in *thy* compassion protect us, O Lord, by *thy* grace.

Lord, have mercy.

In the communion of Saints, let us commend ourselves, and one another, and all our life, to Christ our God.

To *thee*, O Lord our God.

09 *A brief silence is then observed.*

110 *The Priest concludes with the following or some other prayer :*
Lord Jesus Christ; *who hast* given us grace at this time with one accord
to make our common supplication; and *hast* promised that when two
or three are agreed together in *thy* Name *thou wilt* grant their requests;
Fulfil now, O Lord, our desires and petitions, as may be best for us;
granting us in this world knowledge of *thy* truth, and in the world to
come life everlasting; through *thy* mercy, O Christ, to whom with
the Father and the Holy Spirit be honour and glory for ever and ever.
Amen.

111

II

*In the course of the silence after each bidding, the People offer their own
prayers, either silently or aloud.*

I ask your prayers for God's people throughout the world: for our
Bishop(s) . . . ; for this gathering; and for all ministers and people.
■Pray, brothers, for the Church.
Silence.

I ask your prayers for peace among men; for goodwill among nations;
and for the well-being of all people.
■Pray, brothers, for justice and peace.
Silence

I ask your prayers for the poor, the sick, the hungry, the oppressed, and
those in prison.
■Pray, brothers, for those in any need or trouble.
Silence

I ask your prayers for all who seek God, or a deeper knowledge of him.
■Pray, brothers, that they may find and be found of him.
Silence.

I ask your prayers for the departed [especially . . .].
■Pray, brothers, for those who have died.
Silence.

*Members of the congregation may ask the prayers or the thanksgiving
of those present.*
★I ask your prayers for . . .
★I ask your thanksgiving for . . .
■Give thanks, brothers, for God's great goodness.
Silence.

Praise God for those in every generation in whom Christ has been honoured [especially . . . whom we remember today]. And pray that we may have grace to glorify Christ in our own day.

Silence.

¶12 *The Priest adds a concluding collect.*

¶13

III

(*Traditional Form*)

After the Priest's invitation to prayer, the Leader and People pray responsively.

Father, we pray for thy holy Catholic Church:
That we may all be one.

Grant that every member of the Church may truly and humbly serve thee:
That thy Name may be glorified by all people.

We pray for all Bishops, Priests and Deacons:
That they may be faithful stewards of thy holy mysteries.

We pray for all who govern and hold authority in the nations of the world:
That there may be peace and justice among men.

May we seek to do thy will in all that we undertake:
That we may be blest in our works.

Have compassion on those who suffer from any grief or trouble:
That they may be delivered from their distress.

Grant rest eternal to the departed:
Let light perpetual shine upon them.

We praise thee for all thy saints who have entered into joy:
May we also come to share in thy heavenly kingdom.

☐Let us pray for our own needs and those of others.
〚1970 adds after 'pray' the words 'in silence'〛

114 *Silence*

115 *The Priest concludes with this or some other collect:*

Almighty God, the fountain of all wisdom, who knowest our necessities before we ask, and our ignorance in asking: We beseech thee to have compassion upon our infirmities; and those things which for our unworthiness we dare not, and for our blindness cannot ask, mercifully give us for the sake of thy Son Jesus Christ our Lord. **Amen.**

116   **III**

(Contemporary Form)

After the Priest's invitation to prayer, the Leader and People pray responsively.

Father, we pray . . . [As in form III above, no. 113, with variants noted below] . . . **your heavenly kingdom.**

thy . . . thee] you . . . you THROUGHOUT
thy holy mysteries] your Word and Sacraments.
May we seek] Give us courage
Grant rest . . . departed] Give to the departed eternal rest
light perpetual] your light
upon them] upon them for ever

☐Let us pray for our own needs and those of others.

[1970 adds after 'pray' the words 'in silence']

117 *Silence.*

118 *The Priest concludes with this or some other collect:*

Almighty God, to whom our needs are known before we ask, help us to ask only what accords with your will; and those good things which we dare not, or in our blindness cannot ask, grant us for the sake of your Son, Jesus Christ our Lord. **Amen.**

119   **IV**

The Leader may expand any paragraph with specific petitions. A short period of silence follows each paragraph. The periods of silence may be concluded as follows:

Lord, in your mercy
Hear our prayer.

120 Let us pray for the whole Church of God in Christ Jesus, and for all men according to their needs.

Silence.

Grant, Almighty God, that we who confess your Name may be united in your truth, live together in your love, and show forth your glory in the world.

Silence.

Direct this and every nation into the ways of justice and peace, that we may honour all men, and seek the common good.

Silence.

Save and comfort those who suffer, that they may hold to you through good and ill, and trust in your unfailing love.

Silence.

Remember, Lord, those who have died in the peace of Christ, and those whose faith is known to you alone, and deal with us and them according to your great mercy.

Silence.

Grant these our prayers, O merciful Father, for the sake of your Son, our Saviour Jesus Christ. **Amen.**

21   V

Deacon or other leader
In peace, let us pray to the Lord, saying
                    'Lord, have mercy'
    or   'Kyrie eleison'.
□For the holy Church of God, that it may be filled with truth and love, and be found without fault at the Day of your Coming, we pray to you, O Lord.
⟦1970 has the later bidding 'For the peace of the world' first in order⟧
Here and after every petition the People respond:
        Kyrie eleison.
    or   **Lord, have mercy.**
For *N.* our Presiding Bishop, for *N.* (*N.*) our own Bishop(s), for all Bishops and other Ministers, and for all the holy People of God, we pray to you, O Lord.

★For all who fear God and believe in his Christ, that our divisions may cease and all may be one as you, Lord, and the Father are one, we pray to you, O Lord.

★For the mission of the Church, that in faithful witness it may preach the Gospel to the ends of the earth, we pray to you, O Lord.

★For those who do not yet believe, and for those who have lost their faith, that they may receive the light of the Gospel, we pray to you, O Lord.

□For the peace of the world, that a spirit of respect and forbearance may grow among nations and people, we pray to you, O Lord.
⟦1970 has this bidding first of all⟧

For those in positions of public trust, [especially . . .], that they may serve justice, and promote the dignity and freedom of all men, we pray to you, O Lord.

■. . .

*For a blessing upon the labours of men, and for the right use of the riches of creation, that mankind may be freed from famine and disaster, we pray to you, O Lord.

For the poor, the persecuted, the sick, and all who suffer; for refugees, prisoners, and all who are in danger: that they may be relieved and protected, we pray to you, O Lord.

For this Congregation; for those who are present, and for those who are absent, that we may be delivered from hardness of heart, and show forth your glory in all that we do, we pray to you, O Lord.

*For our enemies and those who wish us harm; and for all whom we have injured or offended, we pray to you, O Lord.

*For ourselves; for the forgiveness of our sins, and for the grace of the Holy Spirit to amend our lives, we pray to you, O Lord,

For all who have commended themselves to our prayers: for our families, friends, and neighbours; that being freed from anxiety, they may live in joy, peace, and health, we pray to you, O Lord.

*For . . . , we pray to you, O Lord.

For all who have died in the faith of Christ, that, with all the saints, they may have rest in that place where there is no pain or grief, but life eternal, we pray to you, O Lord.

Rejoicing in the fellowship of [the ever-blessed Virgin Mary, (*blessed N.*) and] all the saints, let us commend ourselves, and one another, and all our life to Christ our God.

To you, O Lord our God.

122 *Silence.*

123 *The Priest says this doxology:*

For yours is the Majesty, O Father, Son, and Holy Spirit; yours is the kingdom and the power and the glory, now and for ever. **Amen.**

or else he concludes with this or some other prayer:

O Lord our God, accept the fervent prayers of your people; in the multitude of your mercies, look with compassion upon us and all who turn to you for help: For you are gracious, O lover of men; and to you we give glory, Father, Son and Holy Spirit, now and for ever. **Amen.**

124

VI

The specific petitions that are indented may be adapted by addition or omission, as appropriate, at the discretion of the Minister. The collects which follow each period of silent prayer are customarily said by the Priest. Each collect is printed twice : first in contemporary and then in traditional language.

125 *Deacon or other leader*

Let us pray for all men everywhere according to their need, and for the people of God in every place.

□Let us pray for the Catholic Church of Christ throughout the world;
〚1970 adds 'especially,'〛

    For its unity in witness and service

    For all Bishops and other Ministers

      and the people whom they serve

    For *N.,* our Bishop, and all the people of this Diocese

    For all Christians in this community

    For those preparing to be baptized (particularly, . . .)

that God will confirm his church in faith, increase it in love and preserve it in peace.

Silence.

Almighty and everlasting God, by whose Spirit the whole company of your faithful people is governed and sanctified: Receive our prayers which we now offer before you for all members of your holy Church, that in their vocation and ministry they may truly and devoutly serve you, to the glory of your Name; through our Lord and Saviour Jesus Christ. **Amen.**

Almighty and everlasting God, by whose Spirit the whole body of the Church is governed and sanctified: Receive our supplications and prayers, which we offer before thee for all members of thy holy Church, that every member of the same, in his vocation and ministry, may truly and godly serve thee; through our Lord and Saviour Jesus Christ. **Amen.**

126 Let us pray for all nations and peoples of the earth, and for those in □authority among them;
〚1970 adds 'especially,'〛

    For *N.,* the President of the United States

    For the Congress and the Supreme Court

For the Members and representatives of the United Nations
For all who serve the common good of men
that by God's help they may seek justice and truth, and live in peace and concord.

Silence.

Almighty God, from whom all thoughts of truth and peace proceed: We pray you to kindle in the hearts of all men the true love of peace; and guide with your pure and peaceable wisdom those who take counsel for the nations of the earth, that in tranquillity your kingdom may go forward, until the earth is filled with the knowledge of your love; through Jesus Christ our Lord. **Amen.**

Almighty God, from whom all thoughts of truth and peace proceed: Kindle, we pray thee, in the hearts of all men the true love of peace; and guide with thy pure and peaceable wisdom those who take counsel for the nations of the earth; that in tranquillity thy kingdom may go forward, till the earth is filled with the knowledge of thy love; through Jesus Christ our Lord. **Amen.**

127 □Let us pray for all who suffer, and are afflicted in body or in mind;
[1970 adds 'especially,']

For the hungry and the homeless, the destitute and the oppressed
For the sick, the wounded, and the crippled
For those in loneliness, fear, and anguish
For those who face temptation, doubt, and despair
For prisoners and captives, and those in mortal danger
For the sorrowful and bereaved

that God in his mercy will comfort and relieve them, and grant them the knowledge of his love, and stir up in us the will and patience to minister to their needs.

Silence.

Gracious God, you see all the suffering, injustice, and misery which abound in this world. We implore you to look mercifully upon the poor, the oppressed, and all who are burdened with pain and sorrow. Fill our hearts with your compassion, and give us strength to serve them in their need, for the sake of him who suffered for us, our Saviour Jesus Christ. **Amen.**

Gracious God, who seest all the suffering, injustice, and misery which abound in this world: We beseech thee to look mercifully upon the poor, the oppressed, and all who are burdened with pain and sorrow.

Fill our hearts with thy compassion, and give us strength to serve them in their need, for the sake of him who suffered for us, our Saviour Jesus Christ. **Amen.**

128 Let us pray for all who, whether in ignorance or in disbelief, have not
☐received the gospel of Christ;
⟦1970 adds 'especially,'⟧

    For those who have never heard the word of Christ
    For those who have lost their faith
    For those hardened by sin or indifference
    For the contemptuous and the scornful
    For those who are enemies of the Cross of Christ, and persecutors
      of his disciples

that God will open their hearts to the truth, and lead them to faith and obedience.

Silence.

Merciful God, who made all men and hate nothing that you have made; nor do you desire the death of a sinner, but rather that he should be converted and live: Have mercy upon all who know you not as you are revealed in the Gospel of your Son. Take from them all ignorance, hardness of heart, and contempt of your Word. Bring all men home, good Lord, to your fold, so that they may be one flock under the one shepherd, your Son Jesus Christ our Lord. **Amen.**

Merciful God, who hast made all men, and hatest nothing that thou hast made, nor desirest the death of a sinner, but rather that he should be converted and live: Have mercy upon all who know thee not as thou art revealed in the Gospel of thy Son. Take from them all ignorance, hardness of heart, and contempt of thy Word; and so bring them home, blessed Lord, to thy fold, that they may be made one flock under one shepherd, Jesus Christ our Lord. **Amen.**

129 Let us commit ourselves to our God, and pray for the grace of a holy life, that, with all who have departed this world and have died in the faith, we may be accounted worthy to enter into the fullness of the joy of our Lord, and receive the crown of life in the day of resurrection.

Silence.

O God of unchangeable power and eternal light: Look favourably on your whole Church, that wonderful and sacred mystery. By the tranquil operation of your providence, carry out the work of man's salvation. Let the whole world see and know that things which were cast down are now being raised up, and things which had grown old are being made new, and that all things are being renewed to the perfection of him through whom all things were made, your Son our Lord Jesus Christ, who lives and reigns with you, in the unity of the Holy Spirit, one God, for ever and ever. **Amen.**

O God of unchangeable power and eternal light: Look favourably upon thy whole Church, that wonderful and sacred mystery; and by the tranquil operation of thy providence, carry out the work of man's salvation. Let the whole world see and know that things which were cast down are being raised up, and things which had grown old are being made new, and that all things are being renewed unto the perfection of him through whom all things were made, thy Son our Lord Jesus Christ, who liveth and reigneth with thee in the unity of the Holy Spirit, one God, for ever and ever. **Amen.**

130   **VII**

The Leader and People pray responsively
In peace, we pray to you, Lord God:
For all people in their daily life and work;
For our families, friends, and neighbours, and for those who are alone.
For this community, the nation, and the world;
For all who work for justice, freedom and peace.
For the just and proper use of your creation;
For the victims of hunger, fear, injustice and oppression.
For all who are in danger, sorrow, or any kind of trouble;
For those who minister to the sick, the friendless, and the needy.
For the peace and unity of the Church of God;
For all who proclaim the gospel, and all who seek the Truth.
For Bishops and other Ministers, [especially for *N.* our Presiding Bishop, and *N.* (*N.*) our Bishop(s)];
For all who serve God in his Church.
For the special needs and concerns of this congregation.
Those present may add their own petitions.
Hear us, Lord;
For your mercy is great.

131 We thank you, Lord, for all the blessings of this life.
The People may add their own thanksgivings
We will exalt you, O God our King;
And praise your Name for ever and ever.

We pray for all who have died, that they may have a place in your eternal kingdom.

□*The People may add their own petitions*
⟦1970 adds '[especially . . .]' after 'died' and omits this rubric⟧

Lord, let your loving kindness be upon them;
Who put their trust in you.

132*We pray to you also for the forgiveness of our sins.
□*Silence may be kept*
⟦1970 omits this rubric⟧

Leader and People
Have mercy upon us, most merciful Father:
In your compassion forgive us our sins,
    known and unknown, things done and left undone:
And so uphold us by your Spirit
that we may live and serve you in newness of life,
    to the honour and glory of your Name.

33 □*The Priest concludes the prayers with an absolution or a suitable collect.*
⟦1970 omits 'an absolution or'⟧

134 *CONCERNING THE COLLECT AT THE PRAYERS*
When a Collect concludes the Intercession, a suitable one is selected, such as :
(a) a collect appropriate to the Season or occasion being celebrated ;
(b) a collect expressive of some special need in the life of the local congregation ;
(c) a collect for the mission of the Church ;
(d) a general collect such as the following :

135 Lord, hear the prayers of your people; and what we have asked faithfully, grant that we may obtain effectually, to the glory of your Name; through Jesus Christ our Lord. **Amen.**

Heavenly Father, you have promised to hear what we ask in the Name of your Son: We pray you, accept and fulfil our petitions, not as we ask in our ignorance, nor as we deserve in our sinfulness, but as you know and love us in your Son, Jesus Christ our Lord. **Amen.**

Almighty and eternal God, ruler of all things in heaven and earth: Mercifully accept the prayers of your people, and strengthen us to do your will; through Jesus Christ our Lord. **Amen.**

Hasten, O Father, the coming of your Kingdom; and grant that we your servants, who now live by faith, may with joy behold your Son at his coming in glorious majesty; even Jesus Christ, our only Mediator and Advocate. **Amen.**

Lord Jesus Christ, you said to your Apostles, 'Peace I give to you; my own peace I leave with you': Regard not our sins, but the faith of your Church, and give to us the peace and unity of that heavenly City where, with the Father and the Holy Spirit, you live and reign now and for ever. **Amen.**

O God, you have brought us near to an innumerable company of angels, and to the spirits of just men made perfect: Grant us during our earthly pilgrimage to abide in their fellowship, and in our heavenly country to become partakers of their joy; through Jesus Christ our Lord. **Amen.**

God grant to the living—grace;

to the departed—rest;

to the church, the nation, and all mankind—peace and concord;

and to us and all his servants—life everlasting. **Amen.**

⟦1970 omits the last three Collects, which were contained in *Prayer Book Studies* 21, but this is clearly an error. 1973 restores them without symbols or explanation.⟧

⟦The original places Offertory Sentences, music for the Sursum Corda and Proper Prefaces next. The Offertory Sentences and Proper Prefaces are to be found here in Appendixes B and C.⟧

136   ADDITIONAL DIRECTIONS AND SUGGESTIONS

The Holy Table is spread with a clean white cloth during the celebration.

A Psalm, or part of a Psalm, may be sung or said at the places indicated in the Services. The addition of Gloria Patri is optional.

On occasion, and when appropriate, instrumental music may be used in place of a Psalm, Hymn, or Anthem.

137   *The Beginning of the Service*

When the Litany is sung or said immediately before the Eucharist, the Prayer of Intercession may be omitted. The Litany may be concluded with the Kyries, in which case the Eucharist begins with the Salutation and Collect of the Day.

In the First Service, the Priest may preface the Collect for Purity with an Opening Sentence from Morning or Evening Prayer.

The Decalogue (page ... ⟦i.e. no. 42⟧) with its responses may be used before the Summary of the Law and Kyries, or in place of them.

The Kyrie eleison, or 'Lord, have mercy', may be sung or said in three-fold, six-fold, or nine-fold form. The Trisagion, 'Holy God', may be sung or said three times.

Gloria in excelsis is sung or said from Christmas Day through the Feast of the Epiphany; on Sundays from Easter Day through the ☐Day of Pentecost, on all the days of Easter Week, and on Ascension Day; and at other times as desired; but it is not used on the Sundays or ordinary weekdays of Advent or Lent. Te Deum laudamus is not used on the Sundays or ordinary weekdays of Lent.

⟦1970 omits 'on all the days of Easter week'⟧

The Collect of the Day is said by the Bishop or Priest presiding at the celebration. With few exceptions, there is only one Collect at this point.

138   *Concerning the Lessons*
It is desirable that the Lessons which precede the Gospel be read from a lectern.

Lessons are announced in the following manner:
'A Reading from [*Name of Book*]',
or 'The Word of God, written in [*Name of Book*]',
(A citation in the following words may be added:
'chapter . . . , beginning at the . . . verse.')

After each Lesson, the reader may say,
'Here ends the Lesson (Reading, Epistle).'

☐Or he may say, 'The Word of the Lord'; and the People respond
'Thanks be to God.'

⟦1970 omits these two lines⟧

It is desirable that the Gospel be read from the pulpit or a lectern or from the midst of the Congregation.

When a significant portion of the Congregation is composed of persons whose native tongue is other than English, the Gospel may be read in that language by a reader appointed by the Priest, either in place of, or in addition to, the Gospel in English.

A Hymn may be sung before or after the Sermon.

The Nicene Creed may be omitted, except on Sundays and major Feasts.

Directions concerning the Prayer of Intercession will be found on page . . . ⟦i.e. no. 107⟧.

139   *The Confession of Sin*
A confession of sin is a normal part of the Service, but may be omitted on appropriate occasions. It may be said before the Liturgy begins; or before or after the Prayer of Intercession. When a confession is used, the Peace should not precede it. When the Confession is omitted, a form of Intercession containing a penitential petition should be chosen.

140   *When there is no Communion*
If there is no Communion, all that is appointed through the Prayer of Intercession may be said. (The Confession of Sin under such circumstances should be said before the Service begins or before the Intercession). A Hymn or Anthem may then be sung, and the offerings of the People received. The Service may then conclude with the Lord's Prayer; and with either the Grace or a Blessing, or with the exchange of the Peace.

In the absence of a priest, all that is described above (except for the Absolution and Blessing) may be said by a deacon, or if there is no deacon, by a lay-reader specially licensed by the Bishop.

141   *At the Peace and Offertory*
The greeting, 'The Peace of the Lord be always with you', is addressed
to the entire assembly. In the exchange between individuals which may
follow, any appropriate words of greeting may be used.
The greeting of Peace may take place:
1. Before the Offertory Sentence.
2. Before the Prayer of Intercession.
3. Before the ministration of the Sacrament (before or after the
   Sentence of Invitation.)
Necessary announcements may be made after the Creed, or before the
Offertory (before or after the Peace), or at the end of the Service, as
convenient.
It is appropriate that the Deacon and other assisting ministers make
ready the Table for the celebration, preparing and placing upon it the
bread and cup of wine. (In preparing the chalice it is customary to
add a little water.)

142   *Alternative Acclamations at the Great Thanksgiving*
One of the following alternative acclamations may be used in the course
of the Great Thanksgiving:
A. **We remember his death;**
   We proclaim his resurrection;
   We await his coming in glory.
☐B. **When we eat this Bread and drink this Cup,**
   we proclaim the Lord's death,
   until he comes in glory.
     ⟦1970 reads **'we proclaim your death, Lord Christ,**
                 until you come in glory.'⟧

143   *At the Breaking of the Bread*
☐At the Breaking of the Bread, in place of, or in addition to, 'Christ our
Passover,' some other appropriate Psalm, Hymn, or Anthem may be
used.
⟦1970 omits 'or in addition to' and 'Psalm, Hymn, or'⟧

If the number of communicants requires the use of additional chalices,
it is convenient that Wine which had been consecrated in a flagon
be poured into them at the time of the Breaking of the Bread.

144   *At the Ministration of the Sacrament*
In the First Service, at the ministration of the Sacrament, the following
procedure may be used:
1. Before receiving Communion himself, the Priest says to the
   People:
   The Body and Blood of our Lord Jesus Christ, given for you,
   preserve your bodies and souls unto everlasting life. Take this
   in remembrance that Christ died for you, and feed on him in
   your hearts by faith, with thanksgiving.
2. The Gifts are then ministered with these words:
   The Body [Blood] of our Lord Jesus Christ. (**Amen.**)
☐   The Gifts may also be ministered with the words of administration
      from the Second Service.
      ⟦1970 omits⟧

or he may use this Invitation:
   The Gifts of God for the People of God.

or this Invitation:
   The Gifts of God for the People of God: Take them in remem-
■ brance that Christ gives himself for you, and feed on him in your
   hearts by faith, with thanksgiving.

While the People are coming forward to receive Communion, the presiding Minister receives the Sacrament in both kinds. The bishops, priests, and deacons at the Holy Table then communicate, and after them the People.

Opportunity shall always be given to every communicant to receive the consecrated Bread and Wine separately. But the Sacrament may be received in both kinds simultaneously, in a manner approved by the Bishop.

When the presiding Minister is assisted by a deacon or another priest, it is customary for the President to minister the consecrated Bread and the assistant the Chalice. When several deacons or priests are present, some may minister the Bread, others the Wine, as the President may appoint.

145   *The Consecration of Additional Elements*

If the Consecrated Bread or Wine does not suffice for the number of communicants, the Priest is to consecrate more of either or both, by saying,

HEAR US, O HEAVENLY FATHER, AND WITH THY (YOUR) WORD AND HOLY SPIRIT BLESS AND SANCTIFY THIS BREAD [WINE] THAT IT, ALSO, MAY BE THE SACRAMENT OF THE PRECIOUS BODY [BLOOD] OF THY (YOUR) SON JESUS CHRIST OUR LORD, WHO TOOK BREAD [THE CUP] AND SAID, 'THIS IS MY BODY [BLOOD]'. **Amen.**

or else he may consecrate more of both kinds, saying again the Prayer of Consecration, beginning with the words which follow the Sanctus, and ending with the Invocation.

146   *The Ministration of Communion by a Deacon*

When there is no priest available, a deacon may be appointed to distribute Holy Communion from the reserved Sacrament in the following manner:

After the Intercession (and the receiving of the People's offerings), the Deacon reverently places the holy Sacrament on the altar.

The Lord's Prayer is then said, the Deacon first saying, 'Let us pray in the words which our Saviour Christ has (*hath*) taught us.'

And then, omitting the breaking of the Bread, he proceeds with what follows in the Liturgy (page . . . [i.e. no. 32] or . . . [i.e. no. 77]) as far as the end of the Prayer after Communion, after which he dismisses the People.

147   *The Conclusion of the Service*

If any of the consecrated Bread or Wine remain, apart from any which may be required for the Communion of the sick or of others who for weighty cause could not be present at the celebration, the Priest (or Deacon) and other communicants shall reverently eat and drink the same, either immediately after the Communion of the People or after the Dismissal.

A hymn of praise may be sung before or after the Prayer after Communion.

From Easter Day through the Day of Pentecost, Alleluia may be added to any of the Dismissals in the following manner:

'Go in peace to love and serve the Lord. Alleluia, alleluia.

Thanks be to God. Alleluia, alleluia.'

148   *The Music of the Liturgy*

In the Second Service, the texts of the Kyrie eleison, Gloria in excelsis, Nicene Creed, and Sanctus given in the Book of Common Prayer may be substituted for the ICET versions when a musical setting composed for the Prayer Book wording is being used.

Musicians are encouraged to write new music for the Services, and especially for the ICET and other new texts.

CHAPTER 8

THE CHURCH OF THE PROVINCE OF THE WEST INDIES

IN the West Indies the 1959 rite (**WInd**[1]) is still the standard liturgy for the Province. In December 1970 the Liturgical Committee, under the chairmanship of the Bishop of Barbados, was asked to produce a draft of a revised liturgy. A draft was drawn up, still proceeding on fairly traditional lines, and in particular keeping to the style of English, and in broad terms to contents also, of **WInd**. There was no use of ICET texts, and no introduction of the 'you' form of address to God.

The draft was laid before Synod in June 1972, but the Synod remitted the task of supervising a period of experiment to a new Provincial Liturgical Commission, and the draft eucharist has proceeded no further.

The other parts of Central America fall within the PECUSA Province IX, and in *Partners in Mission*[2] there is a statement that for this Province '*Las Santa Eucharistia* was published [in 1971], containing the full Spanish text of three experimental eucharistic rites . . .'. The jurisdiction, the date, and the quantity all conspire to interpret this statement. But lest it should mislead, it should be recognized that this book is simply a Spanish translation in a handsome format of the three American rites of 1970 (**Amer1, Amer2, Amer3**). These are to be found in the immediately preceding chapter to this.

---

[1] The text of this is printed in **LiE** pp.178-85 (first edition pp.175-82).
[2] *Partners in Mission* (S.P.C.K. 1973) p.84.

CHAPTER 9

THE EPISCOPAL CHURCH OF BRAZIL

THE Brazil Experimental Liturgy of 1967 (**Braz**), which was printed in translation in **MAL**[1], has continued in use in the Province. However, the Liturgical Commission of the Provincial Synod (consisting of seven members) has worked on and produced a further Portuguese liturgy for the Province (here given the code **BrazR**), and this was authorized for initial use in 18 parishes at the Synod in 1972. It was originally produced in duplicated form, but the Synod of 1973 authorized its publication in printed form, and the new booklet contains daily offices and baptismal rites also. The Proper Prefaces from **Braz**, which did not appear in the duplicated form, are now set out in the printed edition.[2]

The most distinctive feature of **BrazR** is its structure. It is unique amongst Anglican rites in placing the Intercessions before the Ministry of the Word. On the other hand it shows certain signs of reaction compared with **Braz**—for example, Humble Access, which was omitted in **Braz** (perhaps in dependence upon **AmerR**), has reappeared, and the Gloria in Excelsis returns (remarkably) to a 1662 (or **Amer**) position in the post-communion. The restoration of the Decalogue (missing from **Braz**) and of the traditional words of administration provides further instances. However, the eucharistic prayer represents an advance on that American tradition, which was so apparent in the canon of **Braz**. The acclamations after the narrative of institution, the re-wording (and improvement) of the anamnesis, and the deletion of the 'heaven altar' are among the many evidences of a critical working over of the traditional forms previously used. **BrazR** thus suggests the point at which other families of rites have cross-fertilized with the Scottish-American pedigree.

---

[1] See **MAL** pp. 220-29.
[2] In **MAL** these were translated (along with the rest of **Braz**) into a 'Thou' form of address to God. It seemed unnecessary to translate them anew into a 'You' form, and they are here only described, rather than set out, in appendix C.

THE BRAZIL EXPERIMENTAL LITURGY 1972 (BrazR)

[The text below is a translation from the Portuguese made by the editor and Mr. S. Robertson. The style of Portuguese is unchanged from that in **Braz** in 1967, but a 'You' form of address to God in translation has altered the English text. In particular the Creed, Lord's Prayer etc. are much closer to the traditional English forms than to the ICET forms which are here cited. The numbering is editorial.]

CELEBRATION OF THE HOLY EUCHARIST
AND ADMINISTRATION OF HOLY COMMUNION

PREPARATION

1 *A Psalm or a hymn may be sung.*

2 *The Celebrant may say:*
Come, let us celebrate with praise and thanks the Sacrament of the New and Eternal Covenant, which proclaims the Last Supper and declares the Death and Triumph of the Lord, and his living presence in the holy mysteries of his Body and Blood, in the midst of his people to whom the same Lord gives his word 'I am the living bread which comes down from heaven; if anyone eats of this bread he shall live forever'.
Celebrant: Blessed be God: Father, Son and Holy Spirit.
People: **Both now and for evermore.**

COLLECT FOR PURITY

3 *Celebrant:* Almighty God, to whom . . . [CF 1] . . . through Jesus Christ our Lord.
People: **Amen.**

4 *Then the Celebrant reads the Ten Commandments, and the People reply:*
Lord, have mercy, (etc., etc.)
[The full text **'Lord, have mercy upon us, and incline our hearts to keep this law'** is printed out after each of the first nine commandments below.]

DECALOGUE

Celebrant: God spoke these words and said . . . [CF 2] . . . you shall not covet.
People: **Lord, have mercy upon you, and write all these your laws in our hearts, we beseech you.**

5 *Or he says:*
Hear what our Lord Jesus Christ says: You shall love the Lord your God with all your heart and with all your soul and with all your mind. This the first and great commandment. And the second is like it, You shall love your neighbour as yourself. On these two commandments hang all the Law and the Prophets.

Celebrant : Lord, have mercy upon us
People : **Christ, have mercy upon us.**
Celebrant : Lord, have mercy upon us.

6 *The Celebrant or another Minister says :*
Let us humbly confess our sins to Almighty God.
or
You, who do truly and earnestly repent of your sins and live in love
with your neighbour, and are resolved to live a new life walking in
the ways of the Lord; draw near with faith, make your confession to
Almighty God, and, trusting in his pardon, take this Holy Sacrament.

7 *All kneeling, a few moments meditation may be kept in silence.*
All : **Almighty God, our Father,**
we acknowledge and confess our many sins,
which we have committed in our thoughts, words, deeds
and omissions,
against you, against our neighbour, and against ourselves.
Grant us true repentance,
and for the love of your Son, our Lord Jesus Christ,
forgive us all that is past,
and give us grace to serve you
for the honour and glory of your name. Amen.

8 *The Celebrant, or the Bishop when he is present, says :*
Almighty God, our Heavenly Father, who, in his great mercy, has
promised pardon of sins to all those who, with true repentance and
living faith, turn to him, pardon and loose you from all your sins,
confirm and strengthen you in all goodness, and keep you in the way
of life eternal; through the mediation of Jesus Christ, our Lord.
People : **Amen.**

INTERCESSION

9 *Celebrant :* We present to you now, Heavenly Father, our prayers for
the Church of your Son Jesus Christ and for all whom you have created.
People : **Hear us, Lord.**
Celebrant : Father, guide all Christians in the way of the visible unity
of the Church, that there may be one flock and one Shepherd.
People : **Hear us, Lord.**
Celebrant : We pray to you for Bishops (especially *N.* our Bishop),
Presbyters, Deacons and all the people of God.
People : **Hear us, Lord.**

Celebrant : We beseech you also that there may be justice and peace in all the world and we ask for Brazil and those who govern it.

People : **Hear us, Lord.**

Celebrant : Lord, give your help to those who are in distress or sickness, (especially . . .) and to the poor and oppressed.

People : **Hear us, Lord.**

Celebrant : We entrust to your mercy, God of love, all those who have departed this life (remembering to-day especially . . .).

People : **Hear us, Lord.**

Celebrant : Finally receive our thanks for all your saints (commemorating especially this day *N.*) and we ask you that, rejoicing in their fellowship, following their good examples, and encouraged by their prayers, we may share with them in your kingdom.

People : **Hear us, Lord.**

10 *Note that, in place of this Intercession, there may be used one of the authorized litanies, extemporary prayer or silent prayer.*

11 *The Celebrant says or sings next the COLLECT OF THE DAY.*

LITURGY OF THE WORD

12 *The following are read, the OLD TESTAMENT LESSON and the EPISTLE set for the day, and these are announced as follows :*
The Word of God written in the Book of . . ., chapter . . ., beginning to read at verse . . .
One of the two lessons may be omitted.

13 *There may be said or sung a Psalm, a portion of a Psalm, or a hymn, or a period of silence for meditation may be observed after each lesson.*

14 *The appointed Presbyter or Deacon reads or sings the GOSPEL set for the day, first saying :*
The Word of God from the Holy Gospel according to . . ., chapter . . . , beginning at verse . . .
Note that, when the Gospel is announced, there is said or sung by all :
Glory be to you, Lord.
After the reading of the Gospel, there is said or sung by all :
Praise be to you, Christ.

15 *There follows the SERMON, before which a canticle or hymn may be sung.*

16 *Then next there is recited the Nicene Creed (or the Apostles' Creed), which may be omitted for midweek celebrations, except on Festivals.*

I believe in one God . . . ⟦ICET 3⟧ **. . . world to come. Amen. (and the Son)]** OM BRACKETS

or this

APOSTLES' CREED

I believe in God . . . ⟦ICET 2⟧ **. . . life eternal. Amen.**

LITURGY OF THE SACRAMENT

OFFERTORY

17 *The Celebrant begins the Offertory, reading one of the following Sentences:*

Let us present to the Lord the offerings of our life and work.

We thank and praise you, Lord God of the Universe, for all things and at all times. Everything comes from you, and what we give we have received at your hand.

Yours, Lord, is the greatness, the power, the glory and the majesty, for everything which exists in the heaven and the earth are yours. Glory and honour be given to you, Lord.

18 *The Bread and the Wine, together with the Offerings in money, are duly placed on the Altar, preferably being brought by persons from the congregation.*

19 *During the Offertory, a Psalm or Hymn may be sung or said.*

CONSECRATION

20 *Celebrant:* The Spirit of the Lord be with you.

People: **And also with you.**

Celebrant: Lift up your hearts.

People: **We lift them up to the Lord.**

Celebrant: Let us give thanks to our Lord God.

People: **It is meet and just to do so.**

Celebrant: It is indeed meet, just and right, at all times and in all places to give you thanks, Lord, Holy Father, Almighty and Eternal God:

There follows the Proper Preface.

⟦The Proper Prefaces of **Braz** are printed after the rite, and are described here in Appendix C.⟧

On Sundays which do not have a Proper Preface:

Through the mediation of Jesus Christ our Lord, who on this day overcame death, and, through his glorious resurrection, opened to us the gates of eternal life.

Celebrant: Therefore, with the faithful who rest in him and with all the glorious company of heaven, we praise and magnify your Holy Name, evermore praising you and saying:

All: **Holy, Holy, Holy, Lord God of the Universe. Heaven and earth are full of your glory. Glory be given to you, Lord most High.**

Celebrant: Blessed is he who comes in the name of the Lord.

All: **Hosanna in the highest.**

Celebrant: All glory and thanks be given to you, Father, God of infinite power and love, by all creation and by us mortals made in your own image: because, when we had been corrupted by sin, through your mercy you sent your only Son Jesus Christ to our help, and he for our redemption took our human nature upon him and suffered death upon the cross; and also because he, by the one oblation of himself, made a perfect complete and sufficient sacrifice for the sin of the whole world. At that time the Lord Jesus, in the night in which he was betrayed, took Bread, and when he had given thanks he broke it and gave it to his disciples, saying: Take, eat, this is my Body, which is given for you; do this in remembrance of me. Then, after the supper, he took the Cup, and when he had given thanks he gave it to them, saying: Drink this all of you, for this is my Blood of the New Covenant, which is given for you and for many for the forgiveness of sins. Do this, whenever you drink it, in remembrance of me.

Celebrant and People: **Your Death, Lord, we proclaim. Your Resurrection we confess. And your coming we await. Even so, come, Lord Jesus.**

Celebrant: Therefore, Father, following the command of your Son, we commemorate until he comes his life, passion, death, resurrection and ascension and give you thanks for the innumerable blessings which we receive through him.

And here, Lord, we present you to the offering of ourselves. And we humbly beseech you to accept this our sacrifice of praise and thanks, and to be pleased to bless and sanctify with your Holy Spirit both this Bread and this Wine, that we, clothed in your grace and heavenly blessing, may be united with Christ in your Holy Church; Through the same your Son, our Lord, by whom and with whom, in the unity of the Holy Spirit, all honour and glory be to you, Father Almighty, through the ages and for ever.

People: **Amen.**

21 *Celebrant:* As our Saviour Christ has taught us, we are bold to say:
All: **Our Father in heaven . . . [ICET 1] . . . now and for ever. Amen.**

BREAKING OF THE BREAD

22 *The Celebrant then breaks the consecrated bread, keeping a moment of silence, after which may be said:*
Celebrant: The Bread which we break is the communion of the Body of Christ and the Cup which we bless is the communion of the Blood of Christ.
People: **We all, though many, are one body.**

23 *The Greeting of Peace may then be given with the words:*
Celebrant: The peace of the Lord be always with you.
People: **And also with you.**

24 *Then may be said or sung the following (or another appropriate hymn).*
Celebrant: Lamb of God, you take away the sins of the world, Son of God.
People: **Establish us in your Kingdom.**
Celebrant: Lamb of God, you take away the sins of the world, Son of God
People: **Shine your light into our night.**
Celebrant: Lamb of God, you take away the sins of the world, Son of God
People: **Let your people live in peace.**

25 *Or there may be said:*
We do not presume . . . [CF 6] . . . grant us, therefore, that we may so partake of this sacrament that we may be fed with the precious Body and purified with the precious Blood of Jesus Christ; and that we may evermore dwell in him and he in us. Amen.

COMMUNION

26 *The Celebrant receives the Holy Communion and then administers it to the people, saying to each one as he gives the Bread:*
The Body of our Lord Jesus Christ, which was given for love of you, keep your body and soul unto life eternal, and be thankful.
Response: **Amen.**
As he gives the Cup:
The Blood of our Lord Jesus Christ, which was shed for love of you, keep your body and soul unto life eternal, and be thankful.
Response: **Amen.**

27 *The Celebrant may then consume the Bread and Wine which remain, and continue as follows:*
Celebrant: Let us pray.

AFTER COMMUNION

28 *The following prayer may be said by all:*
Celebrant and People: **Almighty and Eternal God, we give you heartfelt thanks that, through these holy mysteries, you deign to feed us with the Body and Blood of your Son, Jesus Christ, and to keep us in his mystical Body, which is the blessed communion of all faithful people, and do make us participants in your eternal Kingdom. And we beseech you, Father, that through your grace, we may continue in your Holy Church, and do all those good works which you have prepared for us; through the same Jesus Christ, our Lord, who lives and reigns, in the unity of the Holy Spirit, one God, for ever and ever. Amen.**

29 *On Festivals the following Hymn may be sung, except that it is omitted during Lent and Advent and for Memorial Services; note that for the Gloria in Excelsis may be substituted any appropriate hymn.*

GLORIA IN EXCELSIS

30 **Glory to God in the highest . . . ⟦ICET 4⟧ . . . God the Father. Amen.**

DISMISSAL

31 *Celebrant:* Go in the peace of Christ. Be brave and strong in testifying of the Gospel to all men. Serve the Lord with gladness.
People: **In the power of the Holy Spirit.**
Celebrant and People: **Alleluia.**

32 *Note that, after this dismissal, the Celebrant, or the Bishop if he is present, adds one of the following blessings, with the people kneeling.*

And the Blessing of God Almighty, the Father, the Son, and the Holy Spirit, be with you all and remain with you always.

The Lord bless you and keep you. The Lord make his face to shine upon you and be merciful to you. The Lord lift up the light of his countenance upon you, and give you peace, now and for ever.

The God of peace, who brought again from the dead our Lord Jesus Christ, the great Shepherd of the sheep, through the blood of the eternal covenant, make you perfect in all good works to do his will, working in you as seems pleasing in his sight; through Jesus Christ, to whom be the glory throughout all ages.

And now the Blessing of our Lord remain with all his people of all tongues and nations; the Lord give his mercy to all who seek it; the Lord comfort all those who suffer and sorrow; the Lord hasten his coming and give us the fulness of his peace.

May the love of God unite us; may the joy of God inspire us; may the peace of God embrace us; may the courage of God uphold us; and the Blessing of God, Father, Son and Holy Spirit, rest upon us all always.

People : **Amen.**

⟦In the printed booklet there then follow 'General Rubrics' which are an almost exact repetition of those in **Braz** (**MAL** pp.220-1). The form of supplementary consecration remains unchanged (an epiclesis alone), but the form of administration by intinction condenses the new words of administration thus: 'The Body and Blood of our Lord Jesus Christ, which were given for love of you, keep your body and soul unto life eternal, and be thankful.'⟧

CHAPTER 10

THE ANGLICAN CHURCH OF CHILE[1]

The History of Revision since 1968

IT was within the context of rapid social change under a left-wing government pledged to give maximum participation of the people in the task of governing that a considerable amount of liturgical material in Spanish has been produced. The work was done mainly by the Liturgical Commission working in the Valparaiso region. Their work includes among others, services of Sunday Worship, Baptism, Confirmation, Holy Communion, Holy Matrimony and the Burial of the Dead, and they were bound together in a loose-leaf book called *Anglican Services of Worship,* which was then authorized for experimental use throughout Chile. No specific time limit was set for the experiment.

The book in fact contained two alternative rites of Holy Communion. The first was that produced by the Liturgical Commission working in the Cautin and Malleco region in the South to which extensive reference (as **Chil**[2]) was made in **MAL.** This went into experimental use initially in two congregations, but its use became more widespread on its formal inclusion in *Anglican Services of Worship.*

In 1968 the Northern Commission produced a text which was also authorized for experimental use, and this became the second rite in the service book. Both services have been used with much appreciation in both areas of Chile where the Anglican Church thrives.

However, in 1970 it became necessary to work towards incorporating all the services into a more permanent form, with the addition of an Ordinal, a service of Exorcism, a service of Betrothal, a new Lectionary, etc. The decision was taken to produce a new service of Holy Communion, incorporating elements from both Chilean rites. This *Book of Common Prayer, and Anglican Church Manual* has now (October 1973) been authorized by the Bishop for use throughout the diocese. It is the revised service appearing in that book which receives attention here.

---

[1] As in **MAL,** only one country of the diocese of Chile, Bolivia and Peru is included. Bolivia and Peru, along with the Eastern South American countries, report no new eucharistic services.

[2] See **MAL,** pages 239-44.

It must be mentioned in passing that **Eng2** was not used in any except two of the English-speaking chaplaincy churches in the Diocese. The influence of this rite on present revision in Chile will be discussed later.

The 1973 *Revised Service* (**ChilR**)—*Introduction*

Experience has shown that people with limited educational attainments have been confused by the rubrical material incorporated in the service. The solution to this seemed to be to provide an Introduction to the service, which would be printed in the Prayer Book itself, but not on the service cards which would be used by the majority of the people attending the celebration. These cards are exact replicas of the service, using the same type setting as the Prayer Book.

The purpose of the Introduction is twofold. First, to show some of the principles followed in the drawing up of the rite. The Introduction speaks for itself. 'The order shows a certain number of simplifications and minor changes from other Anglican services in use elsewhere in the world. In using them, there has been no wish to abandon the normal practice merely to be novel and to show our independence, but simply a constant desire to be intelligible, biblical and relevant to the needs of a young church in Latin America. The use of Greek and Latin titles, such as Kyrie, Gloria in Excelsis etc. has been abandoned, for the reasons already mentioned . . . The service has the official authorization of the Diocesan Bishop. This implies a general doctrinal standard and uniformity in the different congregations, though this is not intended to mean a legalistic adherence to each detail of the service, but rather to provide a basis for flexibility and variation'.

The second purpose is to give guidance to the clergy as they prepare for the service. This in essence is the rubrical material, and deals with such subjects as the use of silence and music, the bodily postures to be adopted at different points in the service, the preparation of the Holy Table with a clean white cloth, the position of the Table in the church building, the preparation of the bread and the cup, and the manner of consecrating extra bread and wine should it become necessary. It also covers those parts of the service where there can be flexibility. For example, the Peace (in Chile called the Holy Kiss or the Love Embrace) is not included as a formal part of the service itself. However in the Introduction the pastor is advised how and when to incorporate this. 'This can be included during paragraph 5 (Repentance) before the congregational response, or before paragraph 13 (Dismissal).'

In a service in which wide variations are possible within the basic structure, to be used in congregations which vary from sophisticated fashion-conscious Chileans to remote country groups composed of indigenous people, and taking place in church buildings which vary from a simple hut with a mud floor crowded with people to a magnificent building like an English parish church, it was felt that one of the keys to a meaningful act of worship is the way in which the presbyter prepares the liturgical material and adapts it to his people in their setting.

Main Features of **ChilR**

The new service derives its basic structure and theological emphasis from the 1662 rite. One major departure from this is the Decalogue, which along with other alternative biblical material is placed in the penitential section as a means to helping the congregation in its self-examination and subsequent confession of sins.

The 1968 rite produced by the Northern Chile Commission followed **Eng2** fairly closely in the Thanksgiving, with thanks being offered for all the mighty acts of God in creation and redemption. The 1973 service has reverted to the 1662 order: Sursum Corda, Proper Preface (omitted in 1968), Sanctus, and Prayer of Humble Access. The 1968 Thanksgiving has not been lost from sight, however, and appears printed later on in the Prayer Book. The Introduction to the Service of Holy Communion suggests that on occasion it be used as an alternative.

The Institution follows closely the 1968 Northern rite, which in this instance used words strongly reminiscent of 1662 in reference to the Cross, and also employs biblical phrases from Isaiah 53 that lay stress on the sacrificial work of Christ in his death. The quotation from Revelation 5, 'Worthy is the Lamb', in which the whole congregation joins, strengthens this, and serves the additional purpose of breaking up the Prayer of Consecration, the second part of which recounts the Institution based on the 1 Corinthians account. The presbyter's hand is not laid on the elements, and as he administers them he uses the 1552 form of administration.

The Conclusion and Dismissal show a further departure from the 1662 order, though the Gloria in Excelsis (in slightly shortened form) is retained. The main emphasis here is the response of praise and glad commitment to serve Christ in the world. The prayer of self-offering in **Eng2** has been used here.

The use of 1662 as a basis in no way precludes flexibility in the conduct of the service. For example, the section 'Prayers', while providing a Litany which owes much to **Eng2,** can be used in a variety of different ways, as the Introduction to the Service envisages. It allows for the practice of extempore prayer, which is a meaningful and proven mode of prayer throughout the Chilean Church. The Introduction also suggests to the minister preparing the service that he might use the Litany, set out in another part of the Prayer Book, which is in fact based on the *Liturgy of the Lord's Supper,* authorized for experimental use by the 1967 General Convention of the PECUSA **(AmerR).** It remains to be seen whether this will prove as meaningful to the Chilean church as the more deeply-rooted custom of extempore prayer.

Congregational response will also be quick and appropriate, particularly in the use of 'Amen'. This has been specifically introduced as the congregation's answer to the minister's invitation to hear the Word of God, and also after 'The Lord be with you' during the Dismissal, but it is more than likely that the congregation will respond in this and other ways quite spontaneously at other points during the service.

The readings from Scripture (which include one from the Old Testament) will generally follow those set in the Diocesan Lectionary. A recent production, this is unusual in that it is based on the calendar rather than on the ecclesiastical year, and pays close attention to Chilean national festivals. The readings will be taken by laymen or deacons from the 1960 De Valera Revision of the Scriptures (from which all Scripture quotations in the service are taken), and the prayers will be taken by different members of the congregation. This means that the presbyter, while guiding the service through its various phases, is much less of a central figure in the service, and his principal part lies in the sections Consecration and Administration.

Scripture quotation is also employed as a form of congregational response at different points in the service, and in places that are novel in the Holy Communion service. One of these comes at the beginning of the section The Word of God (from Matthew 13:9) after the Minister invites the people to hear the Scriptures. Again when the people are called to self-examination, their response is 'Search me, O God, and know my heart . . ., (Psalm 139:23). Later, during the Consecration, the congregation breaks the sequence with the ejaculation of praise 'Worthy is the Lamb that was slain . . .' (Rev. 5:12).

Associated Liturgical Material

The new *Book of Common Prayer and Anglican Church Manual* contains certain novel features closely related to the rite of Holy Communion. These are optional and can be used either by congregations or by individuals. First there is a Service of Preparation for the Holy Communion derived largely from the Church of Scotland *Book of Common Order*. It is suggested that it be used either the night before the celebration or in the morning of the same day. Next follow two Exhortations, for which the Commission has gone to the Latimer House monograph *Holy Communion and its Revision*.[1] These are included with the suggestion that they be read in church before the main church festivals or in the Service of Preparation. These are followed by a Guide to Personal Preparation for the Lord's Supper. At the end of the book appear three short forms of service which could be used on less formal occasions, or as a fitting conclusion to some other form of activity in which the congregation has participated, such as a Quiet Day.[2]

Conclusion

At the time of writing it is uncertain how the rite will be received in the Anglican congregations in Chile. Although it has a more permanent form than **Chil,** yet there may need to be time given to yet further revision, as its suitability to the Chilean cultural and historical context is put to the test.

In his letter commending the Prayer Book and Manual to the Diocese, the Bishop recognizes that 'we are not to imagine that this is the last word in Liturgy, but merely the latest expression for the present moment'. The ability to sense and incorporate local reaction and to take advantage of the flexibility provided for in the service will be essential to its future.

[1] Edited R. T. Beckwith and J. E. Tiller (Marcham 1972).
[2] These have their origin in Grove Booklet No. 16, *Alternative Eucharistic Prayers* by Derek Billings (June 1973). The services translated, adapted and included are text 4 (alternative 1), text 6 (alternative 2), and text 7 (alternative 3).

THE CHILE LITURGY 1973 (ChilR)

⟦This liturgy was compiled in modern Spanish, and has been translated by Sr Balmore Garcia, the editor, and Bishop Bazley. In the original the numbering is by sections only, and that numbering is here retained (1 *PREPARATION,* etc.) whilst editorial numbering is added to the left-hand margin also.⟧

THE ORDER FOR THE ADMINISTRATION OF THE HOLY SUPPER

1 *PREPARATION*

1 *Hymn or Psalm.*

2 *All (kneeling or sitting):*

Our Father in heaven ... ⟦ICET 1⟧ ... for ever. Amen.

3 *Minister:*   Almighty God, to whom ... ⟦CF 1⟧ ... our Lord. **Amen.**

4 *Special prayer for the day.*

2 *THE WORD OF GOD*

5 *Minister:*   Brothers, let us hear the Word of the Lord.

  All: **Amen. He who has ears to hear, let him hear.**

6 *Reading of the Old Testament and/or Epistle.*

7 *Hymn or Psalm—optional (it can be sung here or after the readings).*

8 *Reading of the Gospel.*

9 *All Stand.*

  Minister: Let us confess the faith that God has given us in the words of the Creed (called 'Nicene').

  All: **We believe ... ⟦ICET 3⟧ ... world to come. Amen. (and the Son)]** OM BRACKETS

10 *Sermon (and notices).*

3 *OFFERING*

11 *(As an alternative the collection may be received during the last hymn). Whilst the collection is being made, some texts may be read or a hymn may be sung.*

  ⟦The Offertory Sentences which follow here are to be found in Appendix B.⟧

12 *The offering is dedicated with this prayer.*

  Blessed be your glorious name. Everything is yours, and of what we have received from your hand we now give back to you. Sanctify and multiply this offering for the extension of your kingdom, and for the glory of your Son Jesus Christ our Lord. **Amen.**

4 *PRAYERS*

13 *After each petition the leader may have a period of silence and/or may add specific petitions referring to : (a) the Church, (b) This Nation or others; (c) Those who suffer. As an alternative, other forms of prayer may be used.*

Minister : (*a*) Almighty God, who of your goodness have promised to hear the prayers of those who ask in faith:
Grant that we and all those in every place who confess your name may be guided by your word and united by your Holy Spirit in truth and love, as we fearlessly proclaim your gospel.

Minister : Lord, in your mercy

All : **Hear our prayer.**

Minister : (*b*) Direct this nation and every nation towards peace and justice; guide our President and all who are in authority; reform our society, and free all men from selfishness and covetousness.

Minister : Lord, in your mercy

All : **Hear our prayer.**

Minister : (*c*) Help and comfort all those who suffer that they may trust wholly in you, as you assure them of your steadfast love and protection in all their troubles.

Minister : Lord, in your mercy

All : **Hear our prayer.**

Minister : (*d*) Accept our thanks for those who have departed this life in your faith; we ask that you will give us grace so to follow their good examples that we may share with them in your eternal kingdom.
(*Some specific names may be mentioned*)

All : **Hear our petitions, Father, and accept our thanks through our Lord and Saviour Jesus Christ. Amen.**

14 *Hymn (This may be sung after the Declaration of Forgiveness (7)). The minister places the bread and wine on the Lord's table.*

5 PENITENCE

15 *Minister :* Our Lord Jesus Christ instituted the Lord's Supper to remind us of his death for our sins, and to give us spiritual nourishment. We should not share in it without first examining ourselves and sincerely repenting of our sins, and we should be in love with our neighbours and intend to lead a new life. Let us search our hearts according to the commandments of God.

16 *All* (*kneeling or sitting*) :

Search me, God, and know my heart;
try me and know my thoughts,
and see if there is any wicked way in me,
and lead me to the way everlasting.

The minister chooses A, B or C

17 A THE TEN COMMANDMENTS (*Exodus* 20)

Minister : God spoke all these words . . . [CF 2] . . . shall not covet.

The congregation responds as follows after each commandment, or as indicated by the minister :

Lord, have mercy upon us, and incline our hearts to keep your laws.

[Omitting the bracketed parts in nos. 2 and 4, but including 'against your neighbour' in no. 9.]

All : **Lord, have mercy upon us, and write all these commandments in our hearts by your Holy Spirit.**

18 B THE SUMMARY OF THE LAW (*Matthew* 22:37-40)

Minister : The Lord Jesus Christ said: 'You shall love . . . [CF 3] . . . yourself. On these two commandments hang all the law and prophets.'

first] first and great
is this] is like it

19 C *ALTERNATIVE READINGS*

> *The Beatitudes* (*Matthew* 5:3-12)
> *The More Excellent Way* (1 *Corinthians* 13:1-7)
> *The Works of the Flesh and the Fruit of the Spirit*
> (*Galatians* 5:16-24)

One of these readings can be read with the following response:

All: **Lord, have mercy upon us, and teach us to walk in your path.**

6 CONFESSION

20 *All:* **Almighty God, creator of all things and judge of all men,**
we confess before you the evil we have done;
and we acknowledge that we have not done the things we ought to have done.
We have sinned in thought and word and deed.
Heavenly Father, have mercy upon us,
for we deserve your wrath and condemnation.
We repent of all our sins, and ask your forgiveness through Jesus Christ our Lord. Amen.

7 DECLARATION OF FORGIVENESS

21 *Presbyter:* Almighty God, who of his great goodness has promised to forgive the sins of those who with sincere repentance and true faith turn to him; have mercy upon you(us), forgive your(our) sins and deliver you(us) from them, keep you(us) from falling and present you(us) spotless before his glory with great joy, through Jesus Christ our Mediator. **Amen.**

22 *The presbyter or minister says* (*optionally*):

Brothers, now you have repented, hear the divine promises, and rejoice in eternal salvation.
The Lord Jesus Christ says 'Come to me . . . ⟦CF 4⟧
. . . our sins, and not for ours only but also for the sins of the whole world.'

8 THANKSGIVING

23 *All stand.*

Presbyter :	Lift up your hearts
All :	**We lift them up to the Lord**
Presbyter :	Let us give thanks to the Lord our God
All :	**It is right and just to do so**
Presbyter :	It is indeed right and just that at all times and in all places we should give you thanks, Lord, holy Father, almighty and eternal God, through Jesus Christ your only Son:

Here may be included the specific praise appropriate to the Christian Calendar.

[The Proper Prefaces which follow here are to be found in Appendix C.]

Therefore with angels and archangels, and with all the company of heaven, we praise and magnify your glorious name, for ever praising you and saying:

Holy, holy, holy,
Lord God of hosts;
heaven and earth are full of your glory,
glory be to you, Lord most high. Amen.

9 APPROACHING THE TABLE

24 *All :* **We do not presume . . . [CF 6] . . . he in us. Amen.**

10 CONSECRATION

25 *Presbyter :* Glory be to you, almighty God, our heavenly Father, because in your great mercy you delivered up your only Son Jesus Christ to suffer death upon the cross for our redemption. He was offered once for all time, and made there a single, perfect and sufficient sacrifice and propitiation for the sins of the whole world. He was wounded for our transgressions, he was bruised for our iniquities; the punishment for our peace was upon him, and with his stripes we are healed. All we like sheep have gone astray, but you have laid on him the sin of us all.

All : **Worthy is the Lamb who was slain;**
To him who sits upon the throne and to the Lamb
be the praise, and honour, the glory, and the power,
for ever and ever. Amen.

Presbyter :

(a) Here he takes the bread in his hands.
(b) Here he breaks it.
(c) Here he takes the cup into his hands.

We also give you thanks, merciful Father, that our Lord Jesus instituted this sacrament and commanded us to continue it until his coming again. He, in the same night that he was betrayed, took bread (*a*), and having given thanks, broke it (*b*) and said: 'Take, eat; this is my body which is given for you. Do this in remembrance of me.' In the same way, after supper he took the cup (*c*) and said: 'This cup is the new covenant in my blood. Do this as often as you drink it in remembrance of me'.

All :

Christ, we proclaim your death,
we confess your resurrection,
we look for your coming.
Glory be to you. Amen.

11 *SHARING AT THE TABLE*

26 *Presbyter :*　Brothers, share with faith in the communion of the body and blood of Christ.

27 *As he gives the bread he says :*

Take and eat this in remembrance that Christ died for you; feed on him in your heart by faith with thanksgiving.

As he gives the cup he says :

Drink this in remembrance that Christ's blood was shed for you, and be thankful.

12 *CONCLUSION*

28 *All :*

Almighty God, we glorify you because you deign to feed us with spiritual food.
In thanksgiving we offer you all our being as a living sacrifice.
Send us into the world
in the power of your Holy Spirit
as witnesses and workers
for your praise and glory.
Amen.

29 *All :*

Glory to God . . . ⟦ICET 4⟧ . . . God the Father. Amen.

30 *A hymn may be sung.*

13 *DISMISSAL*

31 *Presbyter :*   The Lord be with you.

All :   **Amen. God bless you.**

Presbyter :   (*The congregation kneeling or sitting*)
The God of peace, who brought again from the dead our Lord Jesus Christ, that great shepherd of the sheep, by the blood of the eternal covenant, make you fit in every good work to do his will, working in us what is pleasing to him through Jesus Christ, to whom be glory for ever and ever. **Amen.**

33 *The service may end here or else be concluded with the following dismissal :*

Presbyter :   Brothers, stand and let us go to serve the Lord.

All :   **Amen. We will serve the Lord. Alleluia!**

APPENDIX

ALTERNATIVE THANKSGIVING

It is truly right and just that at all times and in all places we give you thanks, O Lord, holy Father, almighty and eternal God.

You, at the beginning, created man, and placed him over the works of your hands.

You, when he rebelled, showed him mercy, setting apart a people for your glory, making the covenant with him, and freeing him from Egypt.

You, when we had added iniquity to iniquity, sent your only Son, who humbled himself to the death of the Cross to save sinners.

You, when Jesus had perfected our salvation, raised him up from the dead, exalted him on high, and poured out upon his church the Holy Spirit.

PART IV
AFRICA

CHAPTER 11

THE CHURCH OF THE PROVINCE OF SOUTH AFRICA

The 1969 Rite (SAfr1)

IN **MAL** Peter R. Akehurst reported on the reception of **LfA** in South Africa, and went on at the end of the chapter to write of a provincial 'quest . . . for a basic eucharistic structure' with the 'intention . . . to incorporate the provisions for the daily services into the synaxis'.[1] This was a shorthand way of saying that the Liturgical Committee was responding to two specific requests from the House of Bishops:

1. 'To provide alternative forms of Morning and Evening Prayer, particularly for the clergy who are obliged to say them daily.'
2. 'To provide a new Communion service, shorter in some respects than that of the South African Prayer Book, using more modern language, and exhibiting more fully the insights of the current, world-wide liturgical revival.'[2]

The rite which worked out these principles was authorized by the Synod of Bishops and published in 1969, and is here reprinted as **SAfr1**. It has certain distinctive features of its own, though it is based on **Eng2** (and on the modernized version of **Eng2** contained in *Modern Liturgical Texts* here called **MLT**[3]). In particular it went beyond **Eng2** in four respects: in allowing the synaxis to fulfil the role of the daily office; in allowing the communion from both **Afr** and 1662 to be used with the new synaxis; in addressing God as 'you' throughout (except in Collects and Canticles); and in introducing by rubric periods of silence after the Scripture readings and after communion.

The new role of the synaxis helped the rite to depart from 1662 and **Afr,** (and indeed from **Eng2**), and to follow **LfA** in putting the penitential section at the beginning of the service. This meant that when the communion from **Afr** or 1662 was to be used with the synaxis, the service went directly from 'Offertory' to Sursum Corda.

---

[1] **MAL,** p.40.
[2] *Proposed Alternative Forms of the Daily Offices of Morning and Evening Prayer and the Holy Communion* (Liturgical Committee C.P.S.A. 1969), p.2.
[3] Church of England Liturgical Commission (S.P.C.K. 1968). See pp.4 and 9 above.

In its modern language the rite was at a very early experimental stage. The forms of *Modern Liturgical Texts* were followed almost *verbatim* in the synaxis, except in the Gloria in Excelsis and Creed, where the texts of the Roman Catholic I.C.E.L.[1] were employed. In the communion itself no new forms were needed, of course, for the **Afr** and 1662 provision, as these remained in their original form. In the new eucharistic prayer 'A', the true prayer of the new rite, the **Eng2** form, itself the outcome of prolonged debate and amendment in England,[2] was not followed *verbatim*.[3] An oblation of the elements was restored to it, following the **Afr** pattern. This caused a major problem for the evangelical minority, who, although they desired to use the new rite, were unable in conscience to do so—for in the pew copies for liturgical use only the new eucharistic prayer 'A' was printed.[4] The objection to petitions for the departed was respected in a minimal way, by using the **Eng2** text in the intercessions.

The rite was intended for four years' experimental use from 26 October 1969,[5] and was commended by the House of Bishops to be used in this way.

Reactions to **SAfr1**

Criticisms of the rite were specifically requested, and were studied by the Liturgical Committee. Parishes and individuals submitted comments, and some recurrent themes started to appear. Attention was being focussed on the modern language, the loss of the 'devotions' from **Afr,** the small number of Proper Prefaces (these were simply the **Eng2** quartet), and the poverty of Office II (the one which could not be used as the synaxis).

In 1971 questionnaires were produced by the Committee, under the direction of Professor H. L. Watts, a statistics expert. All the clergy

---

[1] See p.391, in Appendix A. No text of the Lord's Prayer was printed.
[2] See **MAL,** pp.118-21.
[3] [A comparison of the eucharistic prayers of **Eng2, MLT** and **SAfr1** is afforded by Appendix F.—editor.]
[4] It was from one point of view an improvement that 1662 gained recognition as a genuine *South African* rite printed out in the report of the Committee, as shown above. But it was, and is also, still, the official rite of the Province, which should need no further 'recognition'. 1662 is used in its entirety by a few parishes, but it has to be acknowledged that, even if it is made available with a modern language synaxis, it does not blend well with it.
[5] The starting date was determined by the lectionary, which derived from the English two-year Sunday pattern and included nine Sundays before Christmas. This date, therefore, was the beginning of a lectionary year. See *The Calendar and Lectionary,* ed. R. C. D. Jasper (O.U.P. London 1967).

were asked in one questionnaire about the functioning of the combined synaxis and office.

Another questionnaire with comprehensive coverage was sent by Diocesan Bishops to selected groups throughout the Province (and could also be requested by any parish, group, or individual). Others were employed for different language groups and their specific problems. The results were computerized and correlated by Dr. E. Higgins of Rhodes University.

The African language groups' replies were among the most exciting. They wanted more freedom of expression in terms of their own culture, and more use of informal prayer and congregational participation. They also wanted a litany type of intercession, and alternative eucharistic prayers (which **SAfr1** did not really provide). Other groups echoed these requests. The printing and layout were also criticized. As a result of the comments on language, a linguistics expert, Professor L. W. Lanham, had already been appointed to the Committee in 1971.

The theological criticisms were the hardest to correlate. From a statistical point of view Dr. Higgins reported a wide 'scatter', with different standpoints cancelling each other out. Opinions obviously had to be weighed rather than tabulated. For instance, on the one hand Canon F. C. Synge accused the rite of Pelagianism in that the self-offering after communion was 'another sacrifice'. On the other hand, evangelicals expressed their inability to use the words in the eucharistic prayer 'with these gifts which we offer to you'. The Evangelical Fellowship of Anglican Churchmen submitted a resolution which stated that these words changed 'what should be in the *first* instance a sacrament of grace manwards into a Godward sacrifice'.[1] This particular resolution also noted a regular problem with all eucharistic rites based on **Eng2**: 'We would like to see the once-for-all nature of the Atonement re-stressed as in Series 3'.[2] By contrast, the more 'catholic'-

---

[1] Resolution of the Annual Conference of E.F.A.C. in September 1971 submitted to Liturgical Committee in March 1972. A similar but independent line was taken by the editor of this volume who was asked to submit a comment on the theology of the rite and wrote, 'This is not to say that the whole *rite* is "man-ward", for obviously if we are giving thanks we are offering these thanks to God. We do offer the sacrifice of praise and thanksgiving. We do later offer ourselves. We may earlier offer money. All our worship is all the time offered to God, but the sacramental elements are offered by God to us' (memorandum submitted in June 1972).

[2] Citation of Series 3 (**Eng3**) was of course from its original report form of September 1971. The text of that eucharistic prayer is to be found in Appendix F, but on this point it does not differ from the final text.

minded churchmen (who are the majority in the Province) tended to feel that **SAfr1** was insufficiently sacrificial.

Early Stages in Compiling **SAfr2**—*The Collects*

In the period of considering the returns from the questionnaires, the Committee felt that the first task lay in the linguistic field. Soon after **SAfr1** passed into use the International Consultation on English Texts produced its proposals, and it was clear that these would be incorporated entire. In addition a complete set of modern collects was required, and a subcommittee of the Rev. R. E. B. Taylor, Professor Lanham, and the present writer was appointed to prepare them. Various points of principle had to be settled: for instance, the relative clause was retained, and the alternative 'you have' form rejected; the relative clause uses the third person ('God, who has . . . ' not 'God, who have . . .'). The starting point for supplying modern English collects was the provision made in **SAfr1**. This in turn was based on those set out in *The Daily Office* by the English Joint Liturgical Group (S.P.C.K. London 1968) and *The Calendar and Lessons* by the Church of England Liturgical Commission (S.P.C.K. London 1969). For saints' days the original models were those in **Afr**. In over forty cases it was impossible to adapt existing collects, and entirely new ones were written, which stand closer to the 'theme' of the Sunday than many of those in **SAfr1**. The modernized Collects were published in 1972 as *Modern Collects* (S.P.C.K./C.P.S.A.).

The Liturgy of the Church Unity Commission (1972)

At this point a new factor came onto the scene. Church Unity discussions had proceeded for some time between the Church of the Province, the Methodist Church of South Africa, the United Congregationalist Church of Southern Africa, and three Presbyterian Churches. The Church Unity Commission independently prepared a united liturgy, and published in August 1972 a full report *Sunday Worship : A Suggested Form*. This included three eucharistic prayers, each of which was doctrinally controversial. Two had in various ways the oblation of the elements in the anamnesis, and the third (based, like the Roman Catholic Prayer II, on Hippolytus), also followed the Roman Catholic prayer in asking God to bring the departed 'into the light of your presence'.

The present writer commented in a report presented to the Provincial Committee at its meeting in November 1972: 'It is very disappointing to see the oblation of the eucharistic elements reappearing in the same controversial form. Even though baptized, we are still utterly dependent upon God's grace and mercy manwards. This should be reflected in the direction of the sacramental movement and is the very thing which becomes the constant motive for the Church's eucharist.' The form of prayer for the departed in the third eucharistic prayer was also challenged. Non-liturgical Churches might not be so sensitive to these features, but amongst Anglicans, quite apart from between the denominations, they would not be a means of unity.[1]

For reasons differing from one member to another the Committee generally agreed in November 1972 that the C.U.C. rite, although it meets many of the requests resulting from the questionnaires, is not the equivalent of the liturgy that would have been produced on that basis. The Committee recommended, and the Synod of Bishops the same month endorsed, that the rite should not become the new experimental rite of the Province, but that it should be recommended for use on ecumenical occasions and for the purposes of study.

The Writing of **SAfr2**

The Committee, starting from this discussion, were from then on determined to provide a rite that was peace-keeping and consistently modern. It was recognized this might, in the South African situation, mean the provision of alternatives at some points for the sake of one group or another, but this was accepted. Thus the catholic desire for more 'sacrificial' material was to be met both with optional 'offertory' prayers and with an optional canon taken from the *Ordo Missae,* in fact Eucharistic Prayer II of the Roman rite. But at the same time evangelicals were to be comprehended with a modern rite in which they could in conscience find an acceptable route through the liturgy.

On the Liturgical Committee, Canon John Rowland was asked to produce a rough draft of a rite containing the following features:

1. Four alternative prayers for the Church—one of which was to be a litany from the 'Africanization' Committee, one a revision of the form

---

[1] One might instance the contrast between the form of petition for the departed quoted opposite, and the more cautious non-controversial drafting in the Church of England Doctrinal Commission's report *Prayer and the Departed* (S.P.C.K. London 1971). This report was in fact treated as helpful by the Liturgical Committee.

in **SAfr1** (i.e. drawn from **Eng2** via **MLT**), one based on **NZR**, and one free prayer.

2. Three alternative eucharistic prayers—one to be a revision of Prayer 'A' in **SAfr1** (for which a subcommittee was appointed), another to be **Eng3** unamended, and a third to be the most suitable of the new Roman Catholic prayers.

At the following meeting in March 1973 the structure was endorsed and the wording was redrafted. Partly at the instigation of the Episcopal Synod, in May 1973 further changes were made[1] (though by the decision to use texts from elsewhere certain parts were obviously not open for alteration). One instance of this was that prayers for the faithful departed in any controversial form were to be optional in the Prayers of the Church (and in the morning and evening offices). Another was that the 'offertory' prayers at the 'Taking' were also made optional, in order to allow the interpretation that this section is to be seen as 'The Laying of the Table'. This sort of flexibility enabled the text to achieve the result which had been kept steadily in view—that the rite should be truly comprehensive.

The Provincial Synod received the rite in November 1973, and gave it 'general approval', without debating or dividing over details. The Committee then had the task of redrafting further in the light both of the Synod discussion, and also of other comments sent in. The Committee met again in November 1973 and February 1974, and made many minute changes (often of presentation only). None of these affected the rite's essential character. The final proposals then came before the Synod of Bishops in May 1974, and were authorized from 1 January 1975. The rite is published with new forms of Morning and Evening Prayer under the title, *Liturgy* 1975.

---

[1] The material had now grown to a book, entitled *Liturgy* 1973, and including not only the eucharist (with its several options), but also Morning and Evening Prayer in fairly traditional form, as separate offices. Much variety was allowed in these, including free prayer. The book also contained 'The Manual for the Ministry of the Word', providing a complete lectionary for every day of the year. It also had a 'Commentary' on the services. Morning and Evening Prayer followed the parallel course to Holy Communion, before authorization in final form in *Liturgy 1975*.

THE SOUTH AFRICAN
EXPERIMENTAL LITURGY 1969 (SAfr1)

⟦The liturgy has one 'Office' or Ante-Communion, followed by a choice of three different texts of the Communion. The Office itself is labelled 'Office 1' because a second office is also printed in the original report *Proposed Alternative Services of the Daily Offices of Morning and Evening Prayer and the Holy Communion* (The Liturgical Committee of the Church of the Province of South Africa 1969), but the second office is not to be used as Ante-Communion. The numbering is set out in the report, and runs on from the first office through the first communion and into the second office. It is not however used for the second and third communions, and for them the numbering here is editorial.⟧

OFFICE 1
SYNAXIS OR ANTE-COMMUNION

(*This may be used independently or in conjunction with the Holy Communion*).

PRAISE

1 *At the entry of the Minister a hymn may be sung.*

2 *When the Minister has come to his place, he says,*
> Praise the Lord, Praise the name of the Lord;
> *Answer.* **Praise it, you servants of the Lord.**

> *Minister.* You that stand in the house of the Lord;
> *Answer.* **In the courts of the house of our God. Praise the Lord.**

3 *Then all say,*
> **Glory to God in heaven:**
> **Peace and grace to his people on earth.**
> **We praise you for your great glory,**
> **We worship you, we give you thanks,**
>   **Lord God, heavenly King,**
>   **almighty God and Father.**
> **Lord Jesus Christ, Lamb of God,**
> **Lord God, only Son of the Father,**

You take away the sin of the world:
  have mercy on us.
You sit at the right hand of the Father:
  hear our prayer.
You alone are the Holy One,
You alone are the Lord,
You alone are the Most High,
  Jesus Christ,
  with the Holy Spirit
  in the glory of the Father. Amen.

PENITENCE

4 *Then is said,*

> God, Almighty, you see into our hearts, you know our desires, and nothing can be kept secret from you; purify our thoughts with your Holy Spirit, so that we may love you with all our hearts and praise you as we ought, through Jesus Christ our Lord.

5 *The Minister then says,*

> If we say we have no sin in us,
> we are deceiving ourselves
> and refusing to admit the truth;
> but if we acknowledge our sins,
> then God who is faithful and just
> will forgive our sins and purify us
> from everything that is wrong.
> Let us search our hearts in silence.

6 *After the silence the Minister and people say together,*

> Almighty God, our heavenly Father,
> We have sinned against you
> through our own fault,
> in thought, and word, and deed,
> and in what we have left undone.
>   For the sake of your Son, Christ our Lord,
> forgive us all that is past;
> and grant that we may serve you
> in newness of life
>   to the glory of your name.

7 *If the Priest is present, he says,*

> Almighty God have mercy on you,
> pardon your sins, and set you free from them;
> confirm and strengthen you in all goodness,
> and keep you in eternal life; through Jesus Christ
> our Lord. **Amen.**

THE WORD OF GOD

8   The Spirit of the Lord be with you.
> **And also with you.**

Let us pray.

9 *The Collect of the Day.*

10 *Then follow the readings from Scripture. The Psalm and the lesson from the Gospels are always read. But on days other than Sundays and the Greater Holy Days the lesson from either the Old or the New Testament may be omitted. If the lesson read is from the Old Testament, the Psalm precedes this reading. The Canticle always precedes the Gospel. After each lesson, except the Gospel when it is followed by the Sermon, a period of silence is kept, that the people may think upon the Word of God.*

11   THE LESSON FROM THE OLD TESTAMENT

12   THE PSALM

13   THE LESSON FROM THE NEW TESTAMENT

14   A CANTICLE

15   *When the Gospel is announced, the people answer :*
> **Glory to you, Lord.**
                        THE GOSPEL

16   *And at the end of the Gospel, the people answer :*
> **Praise to you, Christ.**

17   THE SERMON

18 *On Sundays and Greater Holy Days the Nicene Creed is said, if the Eucharist follows; but if there is no Eucharist, the Apostles' Creed.*

THE NICENE CREED

We believe . . . ⟦ICET 3, with ICEL variations⟧ **. . . world to come. Amen.**

THE APOSTLES' CREED

I believe in God . . . ⟦ICET 2, with ICEL variations⟧ **. . . everlasting life. Amen.**

THE PRAYERS

19 *The Prayers of the Church are then offered by the Priest, or by another Minister.*

Let us pray for the whole Church of God in Christ Jesus, and for everyone according to his need.

God, Almighty, you have promised to hear the prayers of those who ask in faith.

Lord, in your mercy.

Answer. **Hear our prayer.**

Here he may pray for the Church throughout the world, and especially for the diocese and its bishop; for any particular need of the Church: and a short silence is kept; after which he may say,

Grant that we who believe in you may be united in your truth, live together in your love, and reflect your glory in the world.

Lord, in your mercy.

Answer. **Hear our prayer.**

Here he may pray for the nations of the world, and especially for this country and those in authority here; for all men in their various callings; and again a short period of silence is kept, after which he may say,

Direct this and every nation in the ways of justice and peace, that we may honour all men, and seek the common good.

Lord, in your mercy,

Answer. **Hear our prayer.**

Here he may pray for the sick, the poor, and for those in trouble; for the needs of particular persons; and again a short period of silence is kept; after which he may say,

Save and comfort those who suffer, and help them to put their trust in your love, knowing that it will not fail them in their distress.

Lord, in your mercy,

Answer. **Hear our prayer.**

Here he may commemorate the departed and commend them by name; and again a short period of silence is kept; after which he may say,

> Hear us as we remember those who have died in faith, and grant us with them a share in your eternal kingdom.
>
> Lord, in your mercy,
> *Answer.* **Hear our prayer.**

20 *At the end of the prayers he says,*

> In your mercy, Father, do what we ask for your Son Jesus Christ's sake. **Amen.**

21 *Or the Prayers of the Church may be said as one continuous prayer.*

THE CONCLUSION

(if there is no Holy Communion to follow)

[Nos. 22-24 are then directions for concluding the Office when it stands on its own. The Lord's Prayer (22) is followed by an optional hymn and collection (23), and a choice of one of six collects and one of six endings (24)—one of the endings being the Grace, and the other five ascriptions. Nos. 25 and 26 do not seem to exist at all.]

THE HOLY COMMUNION
(A) BASED ON SERIES II [Eng2]

(as outlined for experimental use in the Church of England)

THE TAKING OF THE BREAD AND WINE

27 May the peace of the Lord be with you always:
> **And also with you.**

28 *The priest takes bread and wine, and places them on the holy table.*

29 *A collection may be taken and presented, and a hymn sung.*

THE THANKSGIVING

30 *The Priest says:*

The Spirit of the Lord be with you:
And also with you.

Lift up your hearts;
We lift them up to the Lord.

Let us give thanks to the Lord our God.
That is right and fitting.

It is right and fitting, and indeed our duty, always and everywhere to give thanks, Lord and heavenly Father, God almighty and eternal, through Jesus Christ, your only Son, our Lord;

Because through him you have created everything from the beginning, and formed us in your own image;

Through him you ransomed us from the slavery of sin, when you gave him to be born as a man, to die on the cross, and to rise again for us;

During Christmastide insert here :[1]

For by the power of the Holy Spirit he took human form from the Virgin Mary his mother; and that without spot of sin, to make us clean from all sin;

During Passiontide insert here :[1]

For being found in human form he humbled himself, and became obedient to death, even death on a cross; therefore you raised him from the dead, and gave him the name that is above every name;

During Eastertide insert here :[1]

For he is the true Passover Lamb who was offered for us, and has taken away the sin of the world; who by his death has abolished death, and by his rising again has restored to us eternal life:

Through him you claimed us as your own people when you enthroned him with you in heaven, and through him sent out your Holy Spirit, the giver of life;

From Ascension Day to the Saturday after Pentecost insert here :[1]

For by the gift of that Spirit you have empowered your people to preach the Gospel among the nations, and to serve you faithfully as priests of your kingdom:

---

[1] [As in **Eng2** in **MAL,** these very short few Proper Prefaces are included here. They are not included in Appendix C.]

Through him therefore, with angels and archangels, and with all the company of heaven, we acclaim you and declare the greatness of your glory: we praise you now and for ever saying:

Holy, holy, holy Lord God of hosts;
Heaven and earth are filled with your glory;
Blessed is he who comes in the name of the Lord:
Hosannah in the highest.

Hear us, Father through your Son Christ our Lord; through him accept our offering of praise; and grant that these gifts of bread and wine may be to us his Body and Blood;

For on the night that he was betrayed he took bread, and when he had given you thanks, he broke it, and gave it to his disciples saying, Take this and eat; this is my body which is given for you; do this in remembrance of me. So too after supper he took the cup, and when he had given you thanks, he gave it to them, saying, Drink of it, all of you; for this is my blood of the new covenant, which is shed for you and for many that your sins may be forgiven; whenever you drink it, do this in remembrance of me.

His death, Father, we show forth, his resurrection we pro-
claim, his coming we await. Glory to you, Lord most high.

And so, holy Father, we your people celebrate here before your divine majesty, with these your gifts which we offer to you, the memorial of Christ's saving death, his rising from the dead, and his ascending to the glory of heaven; and we look for the coming of his kingdom. Gracious Lord, we pray you in your goodness to bless and sanctify us through the Holy Spirit, by whom, in these holy mysteries, we are united with you and one another in your son, our living Lord and Saviour. Accept this, our duty and service, and mercifully grant that as we eat and drink, these holy things, we may be filled with your grace and blessing: through Jesus Christ our Lord, by whom and with whom in the unity of the Holy Spirit, all glory and honour be given to you, Almighty Father, by the whole company of earth and heaven, throughout all ages, now and for ever.

31 **Amen.**

32 *Then the priest says:*

As Christ has taught us, we are bold to say:

The Lord's Prayer

THE BREAKING OF THE BREAD

33 *The Priest says:*

The bread which we break,
is it not a sharing of the Body of Christ?
We, who are many, are one body
for we all partake of the one bread.

34 *Then he breaks the consecrated bread.*

35 *Then all say together:*

**Jesus, Lamb of God, taking away the sins of the world,
have mercy upon us.**

**Jesus, Lamb of God, taking away the sins of the world,
have mercy upon us.**

**Jesus, Lamb of God, taking away the sins of the world,
give us peace.**

THE COMMUNION

36 *Then the priest says:*

Draw near in faith. Receive the Body of our Lord Jesus Christ,
which was given for you, and his Blood which was shed for you;
and feed on him in your heart in faith and thanksgiving.

37 *After the priest and other ministers have received the Sacrament he administers it to the people, saying to each communicant:*

The Body of Christ *and* The Blood of Christ.

and each communicant replies:

Amen.

38 *Or else the priest says:*

The Body . . . ⟦CF 7(a)⟧ . . . in faith and thanksgiving
The Blood . . . ⟦CF 7(b)⟧ . . . and be thankful
to everlasting life⟧ for eternal life TWICE

39 *Meanwhile hymns or anthems may be sung.*

40 *After the people have received, a period of silence may be kept.*

CONCLUSION

41 *Then may be said:*

Almighty and eternal God, we thank you for feeding us in these
holy mysteries with the Body and Blood of your Son, our Saviour
Jesus Christ, and for keeping us by this Sacrament in the Body
of your Son which is the company of all faithful people. Help us,

we pray, to persevere as living members of that holy fellowship, and to grow in love and obedience according to your will through Jesus Christ our Lord, who lives and reigns with you and the Holy Spirit, God for ever and ever. **Amen.**

42 *Then shall be said:*

God Almighty,
we offer you our souls and bodies,
to be a living sacrifice
through Jesus Christ our Lord.
Send us out into the world
in the power of your Spirit
to live and work
to your praise and glory. Amen.

43 *The priest may say:*

The peace of God . . . ⟦CF 9⟧ . . . always. **Amen.**

44 *Then is said:*

Go in peace in the name of the Lord.

Thanks be to God.

45 *What remains of the consecrated bread and wine which is not required for purposes of Communion shall be consumed immediately after all have communicated, either by the Priest, or by one of the other Ministers while the Priest continues the service; or it shall be left upon the Holy Table until the end of the service, and then consumed.*

⟦Nos. 46-61 are 'Office II' which 'is not to be used in conjunction with Holy Communion'.⟧

62   **THE HOLY COMMUNION**

(B) FROM THE SOUTH AFRICAN PRAYER BOOK ⟦Afr⟧

63   *OFFERTORY*

⟦There follow from **LiE Afr** nos. 12-13, Offertory sentences, rubrics, and prayer over the elements.⟧
⟦The Intercession (**Afr** nos. 14-15) and Preparation (**Afr** nos. 16-19) are omitted here, having come in the Ante-Communion above.⟧

64   *CONSECRATION*

⟦There follow **Afr** nos. 20-27.⟧

65   *COMMUNION*

⟦There follow **Afr.** nos. 28-29.⟧

66 *THANKSGIVING*

[There follow **Afr** nos. 30 and 32. The Gloria in Excelsis (**Afr** no. 31) is omitted here, having come in the Ante-Communion. The rubric (**Afr** no. 33) is also omitted.]

The post-communion collects, the proper prefaces and the rubrics[1] have not been reproduced here. It is doubtful whether they need be, as this book will have to be read in conjunction with the S.A.P.B. (for the collects for the Greater Holy Days, for example).

67 **THE HOLY COMMUNION**
(C) FROM THE BOOK OF COMMON PRAYER [1662]

68 *Then shall the priest . . .* [As in 1662 in **LiE**, no. 12] *. . . in his discretion.*

[Two sentences follow: 'Let your light . . . heaven' (Matthew 5) and 'Lay not up . . . through and steal' (Matthew 6)—Nos. 1 and 2 in Appendix B in **LiE**]

69 *After which the Priest shall proceed, saying :*
Lift up your hearts.

[There follow **LiE** 1662 nos 21-34. No Proper Prefaces are printed out, the Gloria in Excelsis (no. 33) is omitted, having come in the Ante-Communion, and there are no final rubrics at all.]

THE SOUTH AFRICAN LITURGY 1975 (SAfr2)

[This service is authorized from 1 January 1975. The numbering is original to the rite.]

THE HOLY EUCHARIST

[In the Report accepted by the Synod of Bishops in May 1974 the whole report is entitled 'THE HOLY EUCHARIST and MORNING AND EVENING PRAYER 1975'. This title is followed by rubrics which cover the whole set of services, of which the relevant ones are reproduced here. Then the further title of the eucharistic rite follows as below.]

---

[1] [These are not printed out here in **LiE** either, but they cover several pages of Appendixes in the South African Prayer Book (1954).]

THE RUBRICS

I GENERAL

1 ⟦This refers to bold type for congregational parts⟧.

2 An asterisk (*) against a marginal number in the text indicates that the whole section is optional.

II THE EUCHARIST AND THE OFFICES

1 *The Lessons* are announced in the order: book, chapter, verse.

2 *State Prayers:* Appropriate alterations to prayers for the State are to be made in dioceses outside the Republic of South Africa.

3 *Silences:* At the discretion of the Priest silences may be introduced at appropriate places in the services: they are recommended after the Lessons and where indicated.

4 *Hymns and Acts of praise* may be introduced at appropriate places in the services.

5 *Musical Settings:* Traditional versions of the Gloria, the Lesser Litany, the Creed, the Sursum Corda, the Sanctus, the Agnus Dei, and the Canticles may be substituted when a musical setting composed for them is being used. In the Second Eucharistic Prayer, (66) may be replaced by (55) of the First Eucharistic Prayer.[1]

6 *Notices:* The service shall not be interrupted by the publication of notices except immediately before or after the Prayers, (26, 136, 182).

III THE EUCHARIST

1 *Lay Participation:* The parts assigned to the Priest, apart from the opening Greeting and Act of Praise (2, 4), the Absolution (16), the Collect (18) and from the Peace (41) to the end, may at his invitation be performed by lay persons.

2 *The Lesser Litany* (11) may be used as set or in any other traditional form.

3 *The Collect* (18): On Sundays, other Great Festivals, Festivals and other special days, the Collect of the Day may be said at the beginning or the end of the Word of God (17).

---

[1] ⟦66 is simply six lines of dialogue—the Salutation and Sursum Corda from **Eng3**.⟧

4 *The Prayers* (26): (i) The Prayers may include thanksgiving as well as intercession.

(ii) The biddings, which should be brief, are addressed to God, e.g., 'Father, we give you thanks . . .'

'Lord we ask you . . .'

(iii) In the first form of the Prayers of the Church (28), one or more sections may be omitted.

5 *The Peace* (41): The words of the Peace may be accompanied by a handclasp or other suitable action.

6 *The Preparation of the Gifts* (48): Gifts for the needs of the Church and of the poor may be brought to the altar with the bread and wine by members of the congregation. If it is more convenient the alms may be accepted after the bread and wine.

7 *Disposal of the Elements:* What remains of the consecrated bread and wine which is not required for the purposes of Communion shall be consumed immediately after all have communicated, either by the Priest, or by one of the other Ministers while the Priest continues the service; or it shall be left upon the Holy Table until the end of the service, and then consumed.

[There then follow the rubrics of 'The Offices' and of 'The Word of God'. The latter include provision for the lectionary (e.g. the permission to omit one lesson on weekdays), psalmody, and the use of hymns in place of canticles at the eucharist, but they also refer to the use of the Bible at the Offices.]

THE HOLY EUCHARIST

The Liturgy for the Proclamation of the Word of God

and

Celebration of the Holy Communion

1 *GREETING*

2 The Lord be with you
And also with you

3 *PRAISE*

4 Praise the Lord
Praise him you servants of the Lord
You that stand in the house of the Lord
Praise the Name of the Lord

5 *Then is said the following, which may be omitted in Lent.*

6 **Glory to God . . .** ⟦ICET 4⟧ **. . . God the Father. Amen.**

7   *PREPARATION*

8 My brothers and sisters★, let us ask God's help in preparing ourselves
to celebrate the holy mysteries.

9 ★*(At the discretion of the Priest these words may be omitted or other
words, such as 'friends', may be used.)*

10 **Almighty God to whom . . .** ⟦CF 1⟧ **. . . Christ our Lord.**

11★Lord, have mercy
   Lord, have mercy

   Christ, have mercy
   Christ, have mercy

   Lord, have mercy
   Lord, have mercy

12 *At least on Ash Wednesday and the five Sundays following, the Ten
Commandments (116) are said:*

13 Let us call to mind our sins.

14 *Silence may be kept. Then is said,*

15   **Almighty God, our heavenly Father**
         In penitence we confess
            that we have sinned against you
            through our own fault
         in thought, word, and deed
         and in what we have left undone.
         For the sake of your Son, Christ our Lord
         forgive us all that is past
         and grant that we may serve you
            in newness of life
         to the glory of your name.

16 Almighty God, have mercy on us; pardon our sins and set us free from
them; confirm and strengthen us in all goodness and keep us in eternal
life; through Jesus Christ our Lord.
        Amen

17   *THE WORD OF GOD*
18   THE COLLECT OF THE DAY
Let us pray.
After the prayer
   Amen

19   THE LESSON FROM THE OLD TESTAMENT
The Old Testament Lesson is written in . . .
After the reading,
This is the word of the Lord
Thanks be to God

20   PSALM

21   THE LESSON FROM THE NEW TESTAMENT
The New Testament Lesson is written in . . .
After the reading,
This is the word of the Lord
Thanks be to God

22   CANTICLE OR HYMN
23   THE GOSPEL
Listen to the Good News proclaimed in . . .
Glory to Christ our Saviour
After the reading,
This is the Gospel of Christ
Praise to Christ our Lord

24   (THE SERMON)
25   *THE NICENE CREED*
is said at least on Sundays, other Great Festivals and Festivals.

26 **We believe . . .** [ICET 3] **. . . world to come. Amen.**
   (and the Son)] OM BRACKETS

                    THE PRAYERS

27 *The Prayers of the Church are offered in one of the four forms following.*

28 | A |

As we celebrate the Holy Eucharist to the glory of God and in thanksgiving for his mercies, let us pray for his Church in Christ Jesus and for
all men according to their needs.
Almighty God, our heavenly Father, who promised through your Son
Jesus Christ to hear us when we pray in his name;

29 We pray for your Church throughout the world and especially for this diocese, and for N. our bishop (*and other needs of the Church*).
Silence may be kept.
Give your Church power to proclaim the Gospel of Christ; and grant that we and all Christian people may be united in truth, live together in your love, and reveal your glory in the world.
Lord, in your mercy
Hear our prayer

30 We pray for the world (and especially . . .)
Silence may be kept.
Give to all a reverence for the earth as your creation, that they may rightly use its resources in the service of their fellow men and to your honour and glory.
Lord, in your mercy
Hear our prayer

31 We pray for all nations and especially for this country and those in authority (*and other particular needs of the nations*).
Silence may be kept.
Give wisdom to those in authority; direct this and every nation in the way of justice and peace; so that men may honour one another and seek the common good.
Lord, in your mercy
Hear our prayer

32 We pray for our families and friends and all others with special claims upon us (and especially . . .)
Silence may be kept.
Give grace to all whose lives are closely linked with ours; that we may serve Christ in them and love one another as he loves us.
Lord, in your mercy
Hear our prayer

33 We pray for all who are in trouble, sorrow, need, sickness or any other adversity (and especially . . .)
Silence may be kept.
To all who suffer give courage, healing and a steadfast trust in your love.
Lord, in your mercy
Hear our prayer

34 We remember all who have died (and especially . . .)
Silence may be kept.

We bless and praise you for all your saints; for the Blessed Virgin Mary, mother of our Lord, for the patriarchs, prophets, apostles and martyrs (especially . . . whom we remember today). And we commend all men, the living and the dead, to your unfailing mercy.
Lord, in your mercy

35 **Accept these our prayers for the sake of your Son, our Saviour, Jesus Christ.**
The service continues at 41.

36 B

Particular intentions may be mentioned before this prayer but it is said without interpolation.

37 Almighty God, we are taught by your Apostle, St. Paul, to pray for all men.

We ask you to receive our prayers for the universal Church, that it may know the power of your Spirit, and that all Christian people may agree in the truth of your Holy Word and live in unity and godly love.

We pray for your servant N., our bishop, and for all other ministers of your Word and Sacraments, that by their life and teaching your glory may be revealed and all men drawn to you.

Guide and prosper, we pray, all who strive for the spread of your Gospel, and enlighten with your Spirit all places of work, learning and healing.

We pray for your servant, the State President, and for all who have authority and responsibility among the nations that, ruling with wisdom and justice, they may promote the peace and well-being of all their peoples.

To all your people in their different callings give your heavenly grace, and especially to this congregation, that they may hear your holy Word with reverent and obedient hearts, and serve you truly all the days of their life.

We ask you, Father, that your love and compassion may strengthen and comfort all who are in trouble, sorrow, need or sickness.

We praise and thank you for all your saints, especially for the Blessed Virgin Mary, the mother of Jesus Christ our Lord, (for . . . whom we remember at this time), and for all the great heroes of the faith in every generation; and we remember before you all your servants who have died, praying that we may enter with them into the fulness of your unending joy.
Grant this, holy Father, for Jesus Christ's sake.
Amen.
The service continues at 41.

38 $\boxed{\text{C}}$

Particular intentions may be mentioned before this prayer but it is said without interpolation.

39 Father, we are your children, your Spirit lives in us and we are in your Spirit: hear us, for it is your Spirit who speaks through us as we pray;
Lord hear us

Father, you created the heavens and the earth: bless the produce of our land and the works of our hands;
Lord hear us

Father, you created man in your own image: teach us to honour you in our fellow men;
Lord hear us

Father, you provide for all men: grant good rains for our crops;
Lord hear us

Father, you inspired the prophets of old: grant that your Church may faithfully proclaim your truth to the world;
Lord hear us

Father, you sent your Son into the world: reveal him to others through his life in us.
Lord hear us

Lord Jesus, you called the apostles to be fishers of men: bless the bishops of this Province especially N. our bishop and all other ministers of your Church:
Christ hear us

Lord Jesus, for your sake men and women forsook all and followed you: call many to serve you in Religious Communities and in the ordained ministry of your Church;
Christ hear us

Lord Jesus, you called men and women to be your disciples: deepen in each of us a sense of vocation;
Christ hear us

You prayed that your Church may be one: unite all Christians so that the world may believe you have sent us;
Christ hear us

You forgave the thief on the cross: bring all men to penitence and reconciliation;
Christ hear us

You gave us your peace: bring the people of this world to live in brotherhood and concord;
Christ hear us

You taught us through Paul, your apostle, to pray for all kings and rulers: bless and guide all who are in authority;
Christ hear us

You were rich yet for our sake became poor: move those who have wealth to share generously with those who are poor;
Christ hear us

You sat among the learned, listening and asking them questions: inspire all who teach and all who learn;
Christ hear us

You cured by your healing touch and word: heal the sick and bless all who minister to them;
Christ hear us

You were unjustly condemned by Pontius Pilate: strengthen our brothers who are suffering injustice and persecution;
Christ hear us

You lived as an exile in Egypt: be with all migrant workers and protect their families;
Christ hear us

You open and none can shut: open the gates of your kingdom to those who have died without hearing your Gospel;
Christ hear us

You have been glorified in the lives of innumerable saints: give us strength through their prayers to follow in their footsteps;
Christ hear us

Father, we know that you are good and that you hear all those who call upon you: give to us and to all men what is best for us so that we may glorify you through your Son, Jesus Christ our Lord, who is alive and reigns with you and the Holy Spirit, one God, now and for ever.
Amen.

The service continues at 41.

40 | D |

The Priest and congregation may offer free and spontaneous Prayers for the Church which will be concluded by the Priest using either a collect or by introducing a chorus, or by some other suitable method.

41   ## THE PEACE

42 *One of the following sentences may be read.*

(43 Listen to the words of our Saviour Jesus Christ. I give you a new commandment: love one another. As I have loved you, so are you to love one another. If there is this love among you, then all will know that you are my disciples.)

(44 If, when you are bringing your gift to the altar, you remember your brother has a grievance against you, leave your gift where it is before the altar. Go, make your peace with your brother, and only then come, and offer your gift.)

(45 We for our part have crossed over from death to life; this we know, because we love our brothers. The man who does not love is still in the realm of death.)

46 *The Peace is given according to local custom.*

47 The peace of the Lord be with you always
Peace be with you

48   ## THE PREPARATION OF THE GIFTS

49 *★Accepting the alms,*
Blessed are you, Lord, God of all creation. Through your goodness we have this money to offer, the fruit of our labour and of the skills you have given us. Take us and our possessions to do your work in the world.
Blessed be God for ever

50 *★Taking the bread,*
Blessed are you, Lord, God of all creation. Through your goodness we have this bread to offer, which earth has given and human hands have made. For us it becomes the bread of life.
Blessed be God for ever

51 *★Taking the wine,*
Blessed are you, Lord, God of all creation. Through your goodness we have this wine to offer, fruit of the vine and work of human hands. For us it becomes the cup of salvation.
Blessed be God for ever

52 *In place of the three foregoing prayers the Priest may say,*

53 *Yours, Lord, is the greatness, the power, the glory, the splendour, and the majesty; for everything in heaven and on earth is yours. All things come from you, and of your own do we give you.
Amen

54   *THE GREAT THANKSGIVING*

55   THE FIRST EUCHARISTIC PRAYER

The Lord be with you
And also with you
Lift up your hearts
We lift them up to the Lord
Let us give thanks to the Lord our God
It is right to give him thanks and praise

56 It is right and indeed our duty and joy, Lord and heavenly Father, God almighty and eternal, always and everywhere to give thanks through Jesus Christ, your only Son our Lord;

Because through him you have created everything from the beginning and formed us in your own image;

Through him you delivered us from the slavery of sin, when you gave him to be born as man, to die on the cross and to rise again for us;

Through him you claimed us as your own people when you enthroned him with you in heaven, and through him sent out your Holy Spirit, the giver of life;

57 (*PROPER PREFACE :* and now we give you thanks . . . *See pp.* . . .
               [i.e. no. 115])

[The Proper Prefaces, which are printed after the end of the service, are to be found in Appendix C]

58 Through him therefore, with angels and archangels, and with all the company of heaven, we acclaim you and declare the greatness of your glory; we praise you now and for ever saying:

59   **Holy, holy, holy Lord,**
          God of power and might
          heaven and earth are full of your glory.
          Hosanna in the highest
          Blessed is he who comes in the name of the Lord.
          Hosanna in the highest.

60 Hear us, Father, through your Son Christ our Lord; through him accept our offering of thanks and praise, and send your Holy Spirit upon us and upon these gifts of bread and wine so that they may be to us his body and his blood.

For on the night that he was betrayed he took bread, and when he had given you thanks, he broke it, and gave it to his disciples saying, 'Take this and eat; this is my body which is given for you; do this in remembrance of me.'

So too after supper he took the cup, and when he had given you thanks, he gave it to them saying, 'Drink of it all of you; for this is my blood of the new covenant, which is shed for you and for many for the forgiveness of sins; whenever you drink it, do this in remembrance of me.'

61 Let us proclaim the mystery of faith

Christ has died
Christ is risen
Christ will come again.

OR

62 Let us acclaim the victory of Christ

Dying you destroyed our death
Rising you restored our life
Lord Jesus, come in glory.

63 And so, Holy Father, we your people celebrate and, with these your gifts, present before you the one perfect sacrifice of Christ our Lord, his rising from the dead and his ascending to the glory of heaven.

Gracious Lord, accept us in him, unworthy though we are, so that we who share in the body and blood of your Son may be made one with all your people of this and every age.

Grant that as we await the coming of Christ our Saviour in the glory and triumph of his kingdom, we may daily grow into his likeness; with whom, and in whom, and through whom, by the power of the Holy Spirit, all glory and honour be given to you, almighty Father, by the whole company of earth and heaven, throughout all ages, now and for ever.

64 *Here shall the people say:*
Amen.

The service continues at 93.

65   *THE SECOND EUCHARISTIC PRAYER*

66-76 〚There follows the entire Thanksgiving of **Eng3,** from the Salutation to the Doxology, exactly as printed above on pp.55-7〛

The service continues at 93.

77   *THE THIRD EUCHARISTIC PRAYER*

78 The Lord be with you
And also with you
Lift up your hearts
We lift them up to the Lord
Let us give thanks to the Lord our God
It is right to give him thanks and praise

79 Father, it is our duty and our salvation, always and everywhere to give you thanks through your beloved Son, Jesus Christ.

80 (*PROPER PREFACE :* And now we give you thanks . . . *See pp.* . . . 〚i.e. no. 115〛)

〚The Proper Prefaces which are printed after the end of the service are to be found in Appendix C.〛

81   *Or if no Proper Preface is appointed*

He is the Word through whom you made the universe, the Saviour you sent to redeem us.
By the power of the Holy Spirit he took flesh and was born of the Virgin Mary.
For our sake he opened his arms on the cross; he put an end to death and revealed the resurrection.
In this he fulfilled your will and won for you a holy people.

82 And so we join the angels and the saints in proclaiming your glory as we say:

Holy, holy, holy Lord,
God of power and might
heaven and earth are full of your glory.
Hosanna in the highest.
Blessed is he who comes in the name of the Lord.
Hosanna in the highest.

83 Lord, you are holy indeed, the fountain of all holiness. Let your Spirit come upon these gifts to make them holy, so that they may become for us the body and blood of our Lord, Jesus Christ.

84 Before he was given up to death, a death he freely accepted, he took bread and gave you thanks. He broke the bread, gave it to his disciples, and said: 'Take this, all of you, and eat it: this is my body which will be given up for you.'

85 When supper was ended, he took the cup. Again he gave you thanks and praise, gave the cup to his disciples, and said: 'Take this, all of you, and drink from it: this is the cup of my blood, the blood of the new and everlasting covenant. It will be shed for you and for all men so that sins may be forgiven. Do this in memory of me.'

86 Let us proclaim the mystery of faith.

87 **Christ has died**
   Christ is risen
   Christ will come again

   OR

88 **Dying you destroyed our death**
   rising you restored our life
   Lord Jesus, come in glory

   OR

89 **When we eat this bread and drink this cup**
   we proclaim your death, Lord Jesus
   until you come in glory

   OR

90 **Lord, by your cross and resurrection**
   you have set us free.
   You are the Saviour of the world.

91 In memory of his death and resurrection, we offer you, Father, this life-giving bread, this saving cup.
   We thank you for counting us worthy to stand in your presence and serve you. May all of us who share in the body and blood of Christ be brought together in unity by the Holy Spirit.
   Lord, remember your Church throughout the world; make us grow in love, together with N. our bishop, and all the clergy.
   Remember our brothers and sisters who have gone to their rest in the hope of rising again; bring them and all the departed into the light of your presence.
   Have mercy on us all; make us worthy to share the eternal life with Mary, the virgin mother of God, with the apostles, and with all the saints who have done your will throughout the ages.

May we praise you in union with them, and give you glory through your Son, Jesus Christ.

Through him, with him, in him, in the unity of the Holy Spirit, all glory and honour is yours, almighty Father, for ever and ever.

92 *Here the people say:*

Amen.

93 THE BREAKING OF THE BREAD

94 *The Priest breaks the consecrated bread, saying:*

95 The bread which we break,
   is it not a sharing of the body of Christ?
   We, who are many, are one body
   for we all partake of the one bread.

96 ★**Jesus, Lamb of God** . . . ⟦ICET 8⟧ . . . **give us your peace.**

97 THE COMMUNION

98 As Christ has taught us we are bold to say:

99 **Our Father in heaven** . . . ⟦ICET 1⟧ . . . **for ever. Amen.**
   holy] hallowed
   test] time of trial

100 *Silence may be kept.*

101 ★**We do not presume** . . . ⟦CF 6⟧ . . . **he in us.**

102 Draw near and receive the body of our Lord Jesus Christ which he gave for you, and his blood which he shed for you. Feed on him in your hearts by faith with thanksgiving.

103 *The Priest first receives the Sacrament, after which it is administered to the other ministers and the people.*

104 *Minister:* The body of Christ
   Amen

   Minister: The blood of Christ
   Amen

OR

105 *Minister:* The body of our Lord Jesus Christ, which was given for you, keep you in eternal life. **Amen.**

   Minister: The blood of our Lord Jesus Christ, which was shed for you, keep you in eternal life. **Amen.**

106 *After the people have received, a period of silence may be kept.*

107   CONCLUSION

108 Give thanks to the Lord for he is gracious
His mercy endures for ever

109 ★Almighty and eternal God, we thank you for feeding us in these holy
mysteries with the body and blood of your Son, our Saviour Jesus
Christ; and for keeping us by this Sacrament in the Body of your
Son, the company of all faithful people. Help us to persevere as
living members of that holy fellowship, and to grow in love and
obedience according to your will; through Jesus Christ our Lord, who
lives and reigns with you and the Holy Spirit, God for ever and ever.
Amen

110   **Father almighty**
we offer ourselves to you
as a living sacrifice
in Jesus Christ our Lord.
Send us out into the world
in the power of the Holy Spirit
to live and work
to your praise and glory.

111 ★The peace of God . . . [CF 9] . . . with you always. **Amen.**

112 Go in peace to serve the Lord
In the name of Christ. Amen.

From Easter Day to the Saturday after the Day of Pentecost,

113 Go in peace to serve the Lord, Alleluia, Alleluia.
In the name of Christ. Amen. Alleluia, Alleluia.

114   THE CONSECRATION OF
ADDITIONAL ELEMENTS

If the consecrated bread or wine does not suffice for the number of com-
municants, the Priest is to consecrate more of either or both, by saying :
Hear us, heavenly Father, and with your Word and Holy Spirit bless
and sanctify this *bread/wine* that it, also, may be the sacrament of the
precious *body/blood* of your Son Jesus Christ our Lord, who took
bread/the cup and said, 'This is my *body/blood.'* **Amen.**

Or else he may consecrate more of both kinds, saying again the words of
the Eucharistic Prayer, from after the Sanctus up to but not including
the Acclamation.

115   *PROPER PREFACES*

which are said on Sundays, other Great Festivals, Festivals and other occasions. The Preface to be used is that related to the Collect of the day.
[There then follow the Proper Prefaces, which are to be found in Appendix C.]

116   *THE TEN COMMANDMENTS*

Hear the commandments which God has given to his people, and take them to heart.

I am the Lord your God . . . [CF 2, without bracketed parts, and with **'Amen'** responsive to each commandment] . . . not covet the possessions of others. **Amen.**

> for yourself any graven image . . . and worship them] anything your idol and worship it.
> take the name of the Lord your God in vain] make wrong use of the name of the Lord your God.
> to keep holy the sabbath day] the Lord's day and keep it holy; you have six days to do your work.
> your mother] OM your
> bear] give

CHAPTER 12

THE CHURCH OF THE
PROVINCE OF CENTRAL AFRICA

Provincial Policy

THE Province of Central Africa as a whole has not been vigorous in liturgical experiment. In 1972 the Provincial Liturgical Commission disbanded in favour of diocesan and national committees. The reasons are twofold—the needs of the dioceses vary widely and the problems in meeting, including the cost are a deterrent. Communication is now maintained at a Provincial level through the appointment of Bishop Mark Wood as 'Provincial Liturgical Consultant'.

In his 1972 report to Provincial Synod, the Provincial Liturgical Consultant pointed to three questions needing consideration. The first was whether liturgical committees should simply respond to felt need to take the initiative in making worshippers consider their needs. (The fact that there was no general discussion of his report suggests there is not much felt need at present.) Secondly, and connected with this, whether any effort should be made to introduce English liturgical texts at this time. The third matter concerned the Provincial Calendar. Following from this third question, new collects are at present being considered for those Holy Days and Saint's Days for which no collect is yet provided in the Central Africa Prayer Book. The aim of the collect is to pinpoint the reason for which the saint is being commemorated. Notes are also included to enable the Celebrant to introduce the saint's history briefly.[1]

In addition to the Central Africa Service (**Afr**) for which there are thirty permitted variations,[2] there are authorized at present for experi-

---

[1] Leonard Kamungu may serve as an example.
Leonard Kamungu, Priest, 1913: The first Nyasa priest, ordained in 1909 in Likoma Cathedral, who was called to leave his own country and people to go as a missionary to Northern Rhodesia where his quiet manner and fervent prayer and apostolic zeal converted many and left an enduring memory of holiness.
Collect: Almighty God You called Leonard Kamungu to be a priest in Your Church and win many souls for Christ; help us to follow his good example of holiness and zeal and to bring Your Good News to those who have not yet heard it: through Jesus Christ our Lord.
[2] This is the 1929/1954 South African rite, included in **LiE** (pp.73-81) as **Afr**, and adopted into the Central African Prayer Book in 1962 (see **MAL**, pp. 42-6). The permitted variations are appended to this chapter.

mental use in the Province, **LfA, Eng2,** and the 1969 South African alternative form (**SAfr1**).[1] **Eng3** has also now been authorized by Episcopal Synod. It is up to the separate dioceses what use they in fact allow these services. Each country tends to its own common use. In Botswana it is almost exclusively **Afr.**

Malawi

The old Nyasaland Liturgy (**Nyas**)[2] went out of use in 1963-4, when the Central Africa Prayer Book had been authorized and was becoming available in vernacular languages. At that stage **Afr** was slightly modified, particularly by the Prayer for the Church having responses between paragraphs. Since then two further diocesan revisions of the same liturgy have been completed, the variations receiving the approval of the Provincial Episcopal Synod.

The 1968 revision brought the Gloria in Excelsis to follow the Kyries, added an Old Testament lesson, reversed Creed and sermon,[3] changed the 'Offertory' to the 'Placing of the Gifts' between the Preparation of the People and the Consecration, and completely replaced the intercession. The new intercession owes to **Eng2** both its bidding ('Let us pray for the whole Church of God . . .') and its responsive 'Lord in thy mercy **Hear our prayer'.** But the petitions are more like the short sentences of **CSI** or **LfA.** In the Communion the Preparation of the People includes 'Seeing we have a great high priest . . .' from **Eng2,** and mutual confession from **LfA.**[4] The Consecration was unaltered, but the Breaking of the Bread has become a separate section (including the Agnus Dei). The Peace had already been added before Humble Access in 1964, but the short words of administration from **Eng2** were now inserted. After Communion a short Dismissal was simply the the second post-communion prayer from **Eng2** with the blessing, interspersed with three versicles and responses.

This rite was authorized by the diocesan synod in 1969, and a further small addition was then made before the present rite was

---

[1] See above pp.203-11.

[2] An English translation of this is in **LiE** pp.145-161.

[3] Though this was an option allowed in **Afr** right from its early days in the 1920s, very untypically of its times.

[4] This is the *middle* column of the mutual confessions in **LfA** in **MAL,** pp.58-9.

approved in 1971. After the narrative of institution, acclamations were
added as follows:

**Lord, by thy cross and resurrection
thou hast made us free.
Thou art the Saviour of the world.**

The 1971 rite is published among other ways in a bilingual English
and Chichewa version, and as can be seen it represents a considerable
advance on **Afr**. One is left to wonder, however, when modern English
will be adopted, or the **Afr** canon revised.

In 1971 the revised liturgy was also incorporated into the Malawi
Prayer Book, where it is kept company by **LfA** (known tactfully in
Central Africa as The Liturgy of 1964—*Ukaristia wa* 1964[1]). The
latter is more in use for vernacular non-sacramental services in the
absence of a priest on Sundays than for the full eucharist, but in
English it is used in the townships and educational institutions.

Zambia

As in Malawi, so the old diocesan rite in Zambia (**Rhod**)[2] came to an
end in 1963-64. Zambia in turn has followed its own policy of revising
the basic **Afr** rite. A diocesan service of Holy Communion was issued
in 1968; this simply contained **Afr** with one or two minor variants
(e.g. the permitting of the Gloria in Excelsis at the beginning of the
service) but with virtually no wording changed. It is a bilingual rite,
with the Chibemba text put on the right-hand pages of the booklet,
facing the English.

In 1973 the Bishops (the diocese of Zambia was divided into three
in 1971) asked the Zambia Board of Liturgy to consider whether this
eucharistic rite is in the right form and shape, as the answer to this
question would determine whether it should be revised, or whether some
basically different rite should supersede it. The Bishops have encouraged
the use of **Eng3** in selected parishes in order to provide a contrast, and
it is hoped this will help in answering the main question.

Rhodesia

The dioceses of Mashonaland and Matabeleland never had their own
diocesan rites, and are perhaps closer to **Afr** (even with the permitted

---

[1] Cf. **MAL**, p.55.
[2] An English translation of this, entitled 'The Northern Rhodesia Liturgy',
is printed in **LiE**, pp.145-61, in parallel columns with **Nyas**.

variations) than the Malawi and Zambian uses. Some European parishes in Mashonaland use **Eng2,** and two African areas in the same diocese use **LfA.** Otherwise there is little to note.[1]

. . . .

VARIATIONS IN **Afr**

A Schedule prepared by the Provincial Liturgical Commission at the request of the Episcopal Synod, and accepted by the Provincial Synod in 1969.

1. The celebration of the Holy Communion may be prefaced by the words 'In the Name of the Father, and of the Son, and of the Holy Ghost. **Amen**'

2. The first Lord's Prayer may be omitted.

3. The Collect for Purity of Intention may be said by priest and people together.

4. The words 'all hearts are open' may be substituted for 'all hearts be open' in the Collect for Purity and Intention.

5. The Kyries, in 3 fold or 9 fold form, in Greek or in the vulgar tongue, may be used at all celebrations of the Holy Communion. 'Upon us' may be omitted.

6. The text of the Ten Commandments from the 1964 Liturgy may be used.

7. The Gloria in excelsis may be used after the Kyries. It may be omitted on Sundays in Advent and on Sundays from Septuagesima to Palm Sunday inclusive and on weekdays not being Greater Feasts.

8. It is permissible to use one Collect *only* at each celebration of the Holy Communion notwithstanding the rubrics of the C.A.P.B.

9. An Old Testament Lesson, and a psalm or canticle, may precede the Epistle on Sundays and Greater Feasts. (The Commission recommends that the Bishop of a Diocese should authorize a series of Old Testament lessons and psalms or canticles for use on these days.)

10. The Old Testament Lesson and Epistle may be read by a lay person.

11. The phrase 'Here endeth the Epistle (or the Lesson)'[1] may be replaced by the congregational response **'Thanks be to God'.**

12. The Old Testament Lesson Epistle and Gospel may be introduced by the same formula as that laid down in the C.A.P.B. for the lessons at Morning and Evening Prayer.

13. The sermon may follow the Gospel.

14. On weekdays, not being Greater Feasts, the Creed may be omitted.

15. Alterations in the language of the 1954 Creed and Gloria in excelsis are permissible provided that such alterations fall within the limits of the 1964 Liturgy for Africa.

[1] A congregational pamphlet of the diocese of Matabeleland shows the Gloria in Excelsis still at the end, though the Intercessions of **Eng2** and **Eng3** and **LfA,** and the Acclamations of the last two, are permitted.

16. It is permissible for the offerings of bread and wine to be *brought* to the priest who shall then present them and place them on the Holy Table.

17. The Offertory Prayer 'Bless, O Lord we beseech thee, these thy gifts . . .' may be said by priest and people together.
    —Alternatively, the versicle and response provided at the Offertory in the 1964 Liturgy may be used.
    —Alternatively, the final Offertory sentence in the Authorized Liturgy may be said by the priest or priest and people together.

18. In the Prayer for the Church at the end of each paragraph, except the one beginning 'And here we do give unto Thee O Lord . . .' the people may say 'Amen'; OR ELSE at the end of each paragraph there may be said 'O Lord, hear our prayer', the people answering 'And let our cry come unto Thee'. (N.B. The Commission considers that the Archbishop should *not* be prayed for by name in the Prayer for the Church. If Suffragan Bishops are prayed for, the word 'both' should be omitted from the phrase 'that may both by their life and doctrine, etc.' (C.A.P.B. p.234)).

19. The 1954 Prayer for the Church may be replaced by the 1964 Intercession.

20. The Invitation to Communion may be omitted, except on Sundays. The 1964 form of the Invitation may be used.

21. The short Confession and Absolution may be used on any day.

22. The Comfortable Words may be omitted.

23. After the Sanctus the **'Amen'** may be omitted and the Benedictus may be said.

24. The wording of the Lord's Prayer may be changed in the following particulars:
    (*a*) 'on' earth instead of 'in' earth.
    (*b*) 'those who trespass' instead of 'them that trespass'.

25. After the Lord's Prayer the priest may break the bread.

26. After the Fraction may be said:
    V.   The peace of the Lord be always with you.
    R.   **And with thy spirit.**

27. The Agnus Dei may be said or sung as an anthem either here or at the Communion in the following form—
    ⟦The traditional form (**MAL** CF 14) of the Agnus Dei follows⟧
    At Memorials of the Departed instead of 'have mercy upon us' is said 'grant them rest' and instead of 'grant us thy peace' 'grant them rest eternal'.

28. In the rubric before the Prayer of Humble Access, the word 'kneeling' may be omitted and the whole prayer may be said by the priest and people together.

29. The words 'that our sinful bodies . . . most precious blood, and' may be omitted from the Prayer of Humble Access if desired.
    Or alternatively the 1964 Prayer of Humble Access may be used *in toto*.

30. The words of Administration of the Communion may be abbreviated to 'The Body of Christ. **Amen'** and 'The Blood of Christ. **Amen'**.

CHAPTER 13

THE CHURCH OF THE PROVINCE OF TANZANIA

The Formation of the Province

THE Synod of the Church of the Province of East Africa met for the last time on 2 June, 1970. Immediately afterwards the first meeting of the Synod of the new Province of Tanzania was held. John Sepeku, Bishop of Dar-es-Salaam, had been elected the first Archbishop and was enthroned in his Cathedral on 5 July, 1970, the date of the inauguration of the new Province.

The Provincial Constitution is not materially different from its predecessor (that of the old Province of East Africa) in its Articles on doctrine, worship and liturgy,[1] and it repeats the aim stated by the old Constitution that 'the ultimate objective of the Province must be the achievement of a common liturgy for use throughout the Province.' The Provincial Synod appointed a Theological and Liturgical Committee consisting of six members sitting under the Archbishop's chairmanship. Liturgical revision in the Province comes under the consideration of this committee.

Eucharistic Uses in 1973

The two predominant uses in 1973 were 1662 and the Zanzibar rite, or Swahili Mass (**Zan**).[2] In recent years **EAUL**[3] has been used in student services and in other services attended by Christians from various denominations; but this use has been, for the most part, occasional only, and in many areas, especially the south and west, it has never been used and is quite unknown. Since it is now out of print, this situation is likely to become permanent. Of much greater significance, however, is the fact that the largest Protestant denomination in the country, the Evangelical Lutheran Church of Tanzania, has adopted **EAUL,** with only a few minor alterations, as its own sole use and has printed it in its service books (since 1968).

---

[1] See **MAL,** p.71.
[2] The text of **Zan** is printed in **LiE,** pp.162-5. The situation prior to 1970 is described in **MAL,** pp.70-7.
[3] The text of this is printed in **MAL,** pp.77-89.

The Archbishop has ruled that Anglican ministers taking *English* services (where a great variety of nationalities and denominations are generally represented) may use their discretion as to what form of service they use, after consulting with their church councils and referring to their diocesan bishop for permission. 1662, **Eng2** and **Eng3** are all in use in this way.

The History of Liturgical Revision

On 16 August 1972, the Provincial Synod expressed its deep concern (the word 'disgrace' was frequently heard in the debate) at the continued use of two very different liturgies within the one Province, and urged the Theological and Liturgical Committee speedily to complete the work of revising **EAUL** which it had already initiated at a meeting in October 1971. Synod further resolved that in the meantime **EAUL** should be used in the Province, a resolution rendered ineffective by the fact that **EAUL** was out of print and had been for three years.

The present text (**Tan**) was produced at a meeting of the Theological and Liturgical Committee on 28-29 December 1972. It was compiled directly in Swahili, without any English translation being made. Rubrical directions were deliberately kept to a minimum, and country priests and congregations will clearly require more guidance than is supplied in this text. It is intended that the Service of the Word of God/Antecommunion should be able to stand alone as the normal worship service on days when there is no Holy Communion. **EAUL** had already set this pattern, but it is doubtful whether this intention will be readily appreciated in the many congregations where the use of the synaxis as a separate service is an unfamiliar idea.

The Archbishop, following Synod's resolution, wrote a Preface to the Liturgy (dated 21 April 1973) ordering its experimental use throughout the Province. Congregations are free to continue to use liturgies to which they are accustomed, but the use of the Provincial Liturgy is obligatory during visits from the Archbishop, and it is expected that eventually it will become the sole use throughout the Province. During the (unspecified) period of experimental use, the Committee will receive comments and criticisms, with a view to subsequent further revision. The Liturgy was first published in 1973 in an edition of 20,000 copies, selling at 50c(2½p). The Provincial Synod met 21-23 August 1974, made three amendments (specified below), and ordered a second edition of a further 20,000 copies.

The Liturgy of the Church of the Province of Tanzania (**Tan**)

Since the basis of **Tan** is **EAUL**, comment below is chiefly confined to those areas where the offspring differs from its parent.

1. *The Penitential Section.* A considerable body of opinion would like to place this immediately before the Great Thanksgiving, as the most suitable lead-in to contemplation of God's mighty acts of redemption, following the pattern of 1662, and **Eng3**. The Antecommunion would then be left without any adequate expression of penitence. One solution, already found in 1662 and **Eng2**, is to have two penitential sections— with the risk of neither being sufficiently robust. Another solution would be to have a movable penitential section, coming early when the synaxis alone is used, but before the Thanksgiving on communion days. The present text retains **EAUL**'s order. The Confession (in the first person singular, as in **EAUL**) has been enlarged by the mention of sins of omission; by expression of sorrow for sin (from **Zan**); by explicit expression of repentance (an important feature of East African spirituality and at the heart of the Revival movement); and by a reminder of the *meaning* of repentance (from **Zan,** and often forgotten in a too glib use of the word 'repent'). Apart from these additions, the aim has been to make the Confession more concise. The Absolution benefits from the addition of the name of Christ as the source of forgiveness, a repetition which can never become otiose (cf. Paul's repetition of the formula in Romans). **EAUL**'s optional prayers intruded awkwardly at this point and are omitted.

2. *The Ministry of the Word.* The modern Roman use supplies the formula 'This is the Word of the Lord' after each reading. Since some sermons may be followed appropriately by a confession of faith, and others by intercession, the relative positions of creed and sermon are at the discretion of the minister.[1] The monetary offering remains in the position prescribed by **EAUL,** but the word 'Offertory', the offertory prayers, and the rubric concerning the bringing of Bread and Wine are all dropped. This new structure allows (*a*) the catechumens to make their monetary offering at a convenient and traditional point in the service, before they depart, (*b*) the Taking to be closely associated with the other three great actions of the eucharist.[2]

3. *Intercession.* Freedom is encouraged as regards both the leader and the form he uses. A lead has been given in this respect by Roman

---

[1] Cf. *Holy Communion,* ed. R. T. Beckwith and J. E. Tiller (Marcham Manor Press 1972), p.66.
[2] Cf. **MAL,** pp.11ff.

Catholics in Dar-es-Salaam who at this point in their service invite a free contribution of prayer requests from the congregation. Such freedom, however, may be less helpful in some semi-literate rural areas, where a fixed and memorized form is desirable (see p.238 below). In the second petition, opportunity is given to pray for named ministers (not bishops only). In a Church of many congregations and few priests this is realistic, for the parish minister is absent from most services in his parish; when present he might well name *all* the catechists and church teachers who serve in his parish.

4. *The Holy Communion.* No words are prescribed at the Preparation of the Table, and each congregation is likely to follow its own tradition. The Proper Prefaces/Thanksgivings have been entirely omitted, which has brought both gain and loss. The gain is that it is no longer necessary to insert into an orderly catalogue of mighty acts a special mention of one of them in what may well be an inappropriate position (a problem which perhaps no liturgy has satisfactorily solved). But are Proper Prefaces necessary when there is a comprehensive fixed Preface? The omission of them can of course be historically justified from Hippolytus and from Eastern usage. The loss is that, since only **EAUL**'s fixed Preface is retained, Christ's death receives little emphasis at this point—although such criticism may be answered by pointing to the emphatic mention of it in the thanksgiving after the acclamations. The two Amens, which in **EAUL** interrupted the flow of the Great Thanksgiving, are omitted (though retained by the Lutherans). The removal of the Lord's Prayer from the immediate context of the Thanksgiving follows **Eng2** and **Eng3** and raises a question about the most appropriate place for it. It is *not* primarily thanksgiving, yet there is a natural reluctance to take it too far away from its traditional position. As intercession it could stand with the intercessions, or it could fittingly revert to Cranmer's position after Communion as the adopted child's confident response of Abba to his heavenly Father. In the present text, sandwiched between the optional Agnus Dei and Prayer of Humble Access, it may look rather like a devotional interruption. The words of Invitation are borrowed directly from **Eng3.** In 1973 the rubric separated the ministers' reception from that of the people, but this was recognized as unsatisfactory, and was amended in the second edition.

5. *The Post-communion.* The prayer of self-oblation and Ps. 103 have been transposed, since Ps. 103 seems the more obvious response to an invitation to give thanks, and is a suitable form of 'hallel' with which

to close the meal commemorating our redemption.[1] The prayer of self-oblation, adapted from **Eng3**, leads naturally into the Commission. The blessing is optional. A spoken blessing seems bathetic after attention has been focussed on the supreme blessing of God's own Son given for believers, but conservative tendencies are likely to demand its retention. There is in this draft no rubrical direction for consecration of further supplies of bread and wine. Psalms, lessons, and collects are not prescribed, and it is presumed that each congregation will follow the Calendar it is currently using. The 1973 Synod added a table of Old Testament lessons and Psalms.

Prospects for the Provincial Liturgy

The first hope for **Tan** must be that it will serve as an effective teaching medium. It may be debated whether liturgy should *aim* to teach, but Cranmer thought that it should, and in a semi-literate society like his—and like parts of Tanzania—its instructional value cannot be over-estimated. Very many Christians become more familiar with their liturgy than with any other written document (not excepting, unfortunately, even the New Testament).

The second hope is an ecumenical one. The use of a common Liturgy must be instrumental in further breaking down the prejudices and suspicions which have kept apart the two Anglican traditions in Tanzania, uneasy bedfellows for a hundred years. On the broader ecumenical front, **Tan** appropriately comes into use only a few weeks after the publication of the report of the conversations between Anglicans and the Lutheran World Federation, calling for closer co-operation on the local level.[2] It is on precisely this level that the two denominations have been drifting apart in recent years, and it is to be hoped that the use of a virtually common Liturgy will expose the senselessness of such division, and prompt the resumption of interdenominational conversations (see **MAL,** p.72).

Thirdly, the publication of a Tanzanian Liturgy ought to act as an incentive to further indigenization of Christian music, drama, and other cultural activities, which is essential for the continued health and even existence of the Church in a land where music is as important as it is in Wales, and cultural revolution as meaningful as it is in China.[3]

---

[1] Cf. J. Jeremias, *Eucharistic Words of Jesus* (SCM), p.55.
[2] Cf. *Anglican-Lutheran International Conversations: The Report of the Conversations* 1970-72 (London S.P.C.K. 1973), pp.22-5.
[3] Cf. J. Mbiti, *The Crisis of Mission in Africa.*

Two warnings should be given. First, in a country where radical changes are suddenly and frequently imposed by higher authority, there is danger lest diocesan bishops, in spite of the Archbishop's Preface[1], immediately impose the new Liturgy as the sole permitted use within their dioceses, thus both stifling the kind of constructive comment which is needed for the preparation of a better and more indigenous revision, and also troubling the consciences of older or semi-literate Christians who take a long time to get used to anything new. Secondly, there is one 'disgrace', far greater than that of divergent uses in one Province, which sits upon the Anglican Church throughout the Third World: that, for the great majority of Christians, Holy Communion is nothing more than an occasional service, neither regular nor frequent. Thousands of Christians are waiting for the time when the Church will take appropriate steps to set apart *in every congregation* those who are given authority to preside at the eucharist. Until this happens, eucharistic revision may well seem to most people like a game devised by the clergy for their own diversion.

THE TANZANIAN LITURGY 1973/4 (Tan)

⟦The rite was compiled entirely in Swahili, and the translation which follows is an unofficial one by the Rev. J. R. Bowen, who contributes the introduction above. A problem in translation is that whereas in Swahili the rite often follows **EAUL** (printed out in **MAL**, pp.77-89) verbatim, **EAUL** had an English version from the start, and this addressed God as 'thou'. In this translation the 'you' form is used, partly as being fairer to the mood of the Swahili, partly as being more comparable to the contemporary liturgical language in English-speaking areas. Consequently, material carried forward from **EAUL** without change in the Swahili, appears slightly altered here in the English. The two texts must be put beside each other for the full dependence to emerge. Where, as in nos. 2 and 6, an alternative is permitted but not printed (at least at this stage), congregations will use forms to which they are accustomed. The numbering here is editorial.⟧

1 *At the entry of the minister, a hymn or Psalm is sung by the people, standing.*

---

[1] See p.235 above.

2 *Minister* In the name of the Father and the Son and the Holy Spirit.
Amen.

The Minister says the following words, or the Ten Commandments
Our Lord Jesus Christ said, 'Hear O Israel, the Lord our God . . .
⟦CF 3⟧ . . . than these. On these two commandments hang all the law
and the prophets.'

first commandment] first and great commandment

3 *Minister :* Lord have mercy upon us
People :   **Christ have mercy upon us**
Minister : Lord have mercy upon us

4   Our help is in the name of the Lord
          Who made heaven and earth.
Beloved in the Lord, let us confess our sins to God:
All keep silence for a short space, kneeling :
Almighty God, heavenly Father,
I confess that I have sinned against you and against my
  neighbours,
In thought, word and deed,
And in not doing what I ought to have done.
I am very sorry,
I repent of my sins
and desire to forsake them.
For the sake of Jesus Christ forgive me
and cleanse me by your Holy Spirit,
that I may serve you in newness of life
to the glory of your name. Amen.

5 *The Minister says, standing :*
The Lord almighty and merciful grant us pardon and remission of all
our sins, through Christ our Lord. **Amen.**

6 *Then is said the Gloria or the Te Deum, the people standing.*
Glory to God . . . ⟦ICET 4⟧ . . . **God the Father. Amen.**
⟦The Te Deum (ICET 9) is not printed out here in the original.⟧

7 *Minister :* The Lord be with you;
          And with your spirit.
          Let us pray.
COLLECT OF THE DAY

8 *The people sit.*

THE OLD TESTAMENT LESSON *(if being used) is to be that prescribed in the United Liturgy for East Africa or in the Lectionary of the Church of the Province of Tanzania.*
〚1973 first edition omits everything after ' . . . used'〛

Before the lesson, the reader says :
Hear the word of God, as it is written in the book . . ., chapter . . ., beginning at . . .

At the end of the lesson he says :
This is the Word of the Lord;
Thanks be to God.

9 *A HYMN or PSALM may be sung.*

10 THE EPISTLE *(if being used)*

Before the Epistle, the reader says :
Hear the word of God as it is written in the Epistle . . ., chapter . . ., beginning at . . .
〚1973 reads 'Hear the reading of the Epistle as . . .'〛

At the end of the Epistle he says
This is the Word of the Lord;
Thanks be to God.

11 *The people stand.*
A HYMN or PSALM is sung.

12 THE GOSPEL

Before the Gospel, the reader says :
Hear the word of God as it is written in the Gospel . . ., chapter . . ., beginning at . . .
〚1973 reads 'Hear the reading of the Gospel as . . .'〛

Glory be to you, O Lord
At the end of the Gospel, he says :
This is the Word of the Lord.
Praise be to you, O Christ.

13 ANNOUNCEMENTS *(here, or after the Creed)*

14 SERMON *(here or after the Creed).*

15 *THE NICENE CREED* (*or the Apostles' Creed*)

We believe . . . ⟦ICET 3⟧ **. . . world to come. Amen.**
(**and the Son**)] OM BRACKETS

I believe . . . ⟦ICET 2⟧ **. . . the life everlasting. Amen.**

16 *ANNOUNCEMENTS* (*if not given before the Creed*).

17 *SERMON* (*if not given before the Creed*).

18 *Then follows a HYMN and the OFFERING is received.*

THE INTERCESSIONS

19 *The Intercessions may be led by a Minister or other person.*

After each petition, silence is kept for a short space, then he says:

O Lord, hear our prayer.
And let our cry come to you.

20 Almighty God, eternal Father, give to your Church in all the world
unity and peace. Where it is persecuted for your name, strengthen it;
and enable it to proclaim your Gospel to all nations.

Bless our Bishops (especially . . .), and all ministers of your Church
(especially . . .), that they with all who serve your Church may faithfully tend your flock.

Bless those who rule the nations of the world, that we may have peace;
and especially . . ., our President, the ministers of state, and all in
authority in this land, that they may lead us in justice and truth.

Direct and prosper agriculture, industry and commerce, and enable
all engaged therein to work together in justice and brotherhood.

Pour your blessings on our homes, that love and purity may flourish,
and our children and youth be reared in reverence for your holy name.
Give to all who teach, and influence the minds of men, and to all who
learn and hear, the light of your Holy Spirit.

Heal the sick (especially . . .) and help all who minister to them.
Defend the traveller, comfort the sorrowful, aid those who are in
trouble.

Bless all who are gathered here to worship you; all our absent brethren
(especially . . .) and all catechumens of your Church.

Bless all unbelievers and those separated from your Church, that their
ears and hearts may be opened, and that they may turn to you.

Rejoicing in the communion of saints, we give thanks to you for all your elect who have departed this life in your faith (especially . . .). Grant that we may rejoice with them in your eternal glory.

Grant these petitions, Father, for the sake of Jesus Christ, our Mediator and Advocate. **Amen.**

21 *Alternative forms of prayer, or extempore prayer, may be used.*

22 *If there is no Holy Communion following, the Minister and people say the LORD'S PRAYER, followed by the GRACE, or the Minister gives the BLESSING.*

23 *HYMN*

THE SERVICE OF HOLY COMMUNION

24 *The Bread and Wine are placed ready.*

25 *Minister :* The peace of the Lord be always with you.

And with your spirit.

If desired, the people may give one another the greeting of the peace.

26 *Then the Minister says :*

Lift up your hearts.
We lift them to the Lord.

Let us give thanks to the Lord our God.
It is right and our duty to do so.

It is indeed, right and our solemn duty, at all times and in all places to give thanks to you, Lord, Almighty Father, everlasting God, through Jesus Christ our Lord.

We praise you for the whole world which you have made and sustain through him, for the order of your creation, and for your many gifts of grace.

Above all we praise you for your love for us fallen men, in giving your Son Jesus Christ, to take our nature, that he might overcome sin and death and set us free to become heirs of your kingdom.

We praise you, Father, for your Holy Spirit, through whom we know that you have set your seal upon us in baptism to be your own, chosen to declare your mighty works.

Therefore with angels and prophets, apostles and martyrs, and all the company of heaven, we cry aloud with joy, evermore praising you and saying:

Holy, Holy, Holy, Lord God of Hosts,
heaven and earth are full of your glory:
Glory be to you, Lord most high.

All kneel

Glory be to you, heavenly Father, who in your tender mercy did give your only Son Jesus Christ, that all who believe in him might have eternal life. Hear us, merciful Father, we humbly beseech you, and grant that we, receiving this bread and this cup as your Son commanded, may be partakers of his Body and Blood.

In the same night in which he was betrayed, he took bread, and when he had given thanks, he broke it, and gave it to his disciples, saying: Take, eat, this is my body which is given for you. Do this in remembrance of me.

In the same way after supper he took the cup, and when he had given thanks, he gave it to them, saying: Drink of this, all of you, for this is my blood of the new covenant, which is shed for you and for many for the forgiveness of sins. Do this as often as you drink it, in remembrance of me.

His death, O Father, we proclaim:
His resurrection we confess:
His coming we await.
Glory be to you, O Lord.

Therefore, O Father, we offer you our praise and thanksgiving for the perfect sacrifice of your Son Jesus Christ, who once offered himself for our sakes upon the cross. We thank you for his mighty resurrection and ascension into heaven, where he ever makes intercession for us.

Accept us in him, we beseech you, that we may be filled with your Holy Spirit, and made one in your Church which you are gathering from all the ends of the earth; through him and in him, in the unity of the Holy Spirit, all honour and glory be to you, Father Almighty.

Blessing and thanksgiving and might
be to our God for ever and ever. Amen.

27 *Here, or at the distribution, the Minister may break the bread, saying:*
The bread which we break is a sharing of the Body of Christ. We
who are many are one Body, for we all share the one bread.

28 *The people may sing, or say:*
Lamb of God . . . [ICET 6] **. . . give us your peace**

29 *Minister:* As our Lord Jesus Christ commanded and taught us, we are
bold to say:
Our Father in heaven . . . [ICET 1] **. . . now and for ever. Amen.**

30 *And this prayer may be said:*
We do not presume . . . [CF 7] **. . . he in us. Amen.**

31 *The Minister receives the Holy Communion after saying:*
[1973 reads '*Now the Minister receives the Holy Communion, and then says:*']
Let us draw near with faith and receive the body of our Lord Jesus
Christ which he gave, and his blood which he shed, for us. Let us
remember that he died for us. Let us feed on him in our hearts by faith
with thanksgiving.

32 *When he delivers the bread, the Minister says:*
The Body of Christ keep you unto eternal life. **Amen.**
When he delivers the cup, he says:
The Blood of Christ keep you unto eternal life. **Amen.**

33 *When all have received, or at the end of the service, what remains of the
Sacrament shall be reverently disposed of. The people should remain
silent for a short space.*

34 *All stand and the Minister says:*
Let us give thanks to God.

Then Minister and people say:
Bless the Lord, O my soul,
And all that is within me, bless his holy name.
Bless the Lord, O my soul,
And forget not all his benefits.
Who forgives all your iniquity,
Who heals all your diseases,
Who redeems your life from destruction,
Who crowns you with steadfast love and mercy.
Who satisfies you with good things as long as you live,
So that your youth is renewed like the eagle's.

Bless the Lord, all his works, in all places of his dominion;
Bless the Lord, O my soul.
Glory be to the Father and to the Son and to the Holy Spirit,
As it was in the beginning, is now and ever shall be, world without end. Amen.

35 *Then the Minister and the people say*
Almighty God, we thank you . . . ⟦CF 8⟧ . . . praise and glory. Amen.

Through him we offer . . . sacrifice] In him we offer you ourselves, our souls and bodies

36 *The Minister may say:*
Jesus Christ said, As the Father sent me, even so I send you.

37 *The BLESSING may be used.*

38 *Minister:* Go forth in peace.
Thanks be to God.

39 *A HYMN may be sung as the congregation leaves.*

CHAPTER 14

THE REST OF AFRICA

In the other three Provinces of the Anglican Communion which exist wholly in Africa (as opposed to the Jerusalem Archbishopric, although it includes Egypt, Sudan and Ethiopia), there is little evidence of liturgical revision.

The Province of West Africa reports in *Partners in Mission*[1] that 'A Committee is to study the possibility of creating a liturgy for the Province', but this does not amount to anything very concrete yet. The United Liturgy in Nigeria (**NUL**)[2] never came to anything, as all plans for union were shelved under the impact of the three years of civil war. **LfA** has not been known in West Africa, though **Eng2** has been in use in the dioceses of Sierra Leone and Accra.

The Province of Uganda, Rwanda, Burundi and Boga-Zaire has seen internal disturbance more recently than Nigeria, and there also any slight stirrings towards liturgical reform have been stifled. The Province is in any case very attached to the 1662 tradition, and in Burundi at least there has still been primary translation of the 1662 Book of Common Prayer into tribal tongues taking place in the 1970s (though not of the communion rite, which was translated at an early stage of evangelization in most places). It seems safe to forecast that, in the year 2000, 1662 will be found most solidly and notably in use in this Province.

The Province of Kenya was formed in July 1970 when the previous Province of East Africa was divided into Kenya and Tanzania. A Theological and Liturgical Panel has been appointed for the Province, and an account of its first meeting is to be found in *Partners in Mission*.[3] At that meeting the Panel recommended that the use of **EAUL**[4] should be continued in the Province, but **LfA**[5] should cease. Much of what is said above about 1662 also applies, though not so strongly, to Kenya.

---

[1] *Partners in Mission,* Dublin (S.P.C.K. London 1973), p.85.
[2] Printed in **MAL,** pp.91-101.
[3] *Op cit.,* pp.80-1.
[4] Printed in **MAL,** pp.77-89.
[5] Printed in **MAL,** pp.57-69. The East Africa version of it is shown in the *apparatus* there (under **EA**), and reference should be also made to **MAL,** pp.54-5. An East African text of **LfA** was separately printed.

PART V
THE MIDDLE EAST

CHAPTER 15

THE DIOCESE OF IRAN
(JERUSALEM ARCHBISHOPRIC)[1]

THE 1967 Iran Experimental Liturgy (**Iran**)[2] was authorized without any stated period for its use being laid down. At the Synod of Clergy in February 1970 discussion of the rite was invited, and Bishop Michael Hollis, previously of South India, was present and gave considerable advice. **Iran** had of course leant heavily on **CSI,** especially in the Thanksgiving. In addition **Eng2** had been introduced for occasional use in English-language celebrations, and this too had an influence.

The changes made as a result of the discussions were as follows: Provision for Supplementary Consecration,[3] Psalm 95, and the Ten Commandments were all moved into Appendixes; the intercession was radically altered (as the reflection of Moslem custom intended in **Iran** was not a great success); the collect has been moved from the intercession to nearer its usual place in the liturgy, and the Lord's Prayer has come from the end of the Thanksgiving to the intercession; in the Thanksgiving the **CSI** epiclesis has been omitted (along with one set of acclamations), and this has left the prayer without *any* petition that the bread and wine should be for us the body and blood of Christ; Humble Access now follows the Fraction; and a new post-communion prayer, based on **Eng2**, replaces the two traditional 1662-type prayers of **Iran.** The resultant text, was then published, but the Synod of Clergy in September 1970 agreed to the use of the **Eng2** form of intercession as an alternative to that in the rite, and the rite was accordingly re-published in this form in 1971. The canon was further truncated then[4].

The Persian language version ranks as basic, and no particular attempt has been made to bring the English up to date, or to take account of the ICET texts. The English version is an accurate, but

---

[1] As in **MAL,** there is no other liturgical revision to be noted in other parts of the Archbishopric. **Eng2** and **Eng3** are found, and in St George's Cathedral, Jerusalem, the Archbishop authorised a 'Thou' form liturgy based on **Eng3** in its first published text of September 1971 (see pp.41-4 and 49 above). Note that the term 'Archbishopric' is used as the correct description of the jurisdiction for the period under review.

[2] Introduction and text printed in **MAL,** pp.247-57.

[3] This should be noted, as the editor wrongly said in **MAL,** p.18, that there was no such provision.

[4] See p.259 below.

not necessarily literary or rhythmic, translation of the Persian text into a traditional form of liturgical English.

Eng3 was introduced into the diocese in 1973 for study and trial use in English. At the end of 1974 it was made available in a Persian translation, which includes the intercession from **IranR** below as an alternative to that in the rite. Some other new material from traditional Persian sources was also included as an alternative, but this is not yet available in English. In both its English and Persian versions **Eng3** has now displaced **IranR** completely. Thus the responsive form of intercession and the inclusion of traditional poetry is the special Iranian contribution to the ongoing liturgical life of the diocese.

THE IRAN EXPERIMENTAL LITURGY 1971
(IranR)

〚The numbering here follows the numbering in the rite for the seven rubrics at the beginning of the service, but after that is editorial.〛

HOLY COMMUNION—RUBRICS

1 *The Preparation and the Ministry of the word may be read from the Prayer Desk, the Priest moving to the Table for the Ministry of the Sacrament. He may then stand behind the Table facing the people.*

2 *A layman may read the Old Testament Lesson, the Epistle and the Intercession.*

3 *In addition to the hymns included in the service, a hymn or canticle may be sung between the Epistle and Gospel and after the Creed.*

4 *In the 'Thanksgiving' the Priest shall take the paten and chalice into his hands during the words of institution, and in the 'Breaking of the Bread' he shall break the bread.*

5 *It is convenient that the Priest should clean the chalice and paten immediately after all have received Communion.*

6 *Communion of the Sick*
   When the Holy Communion is celebrated in the sickroom the service may be shortened but should always include Confession, the Gospel, and the Ministry of the Sacrament.

7 *Morning and Evening Prayer*
   The Preparation and the Ministry of the Word may be used alone as a form of Morning or Evening Prayer.

THE HOLY COMMUNION—PREPARATION

8 *Psalm* 95: 1-7 (*page* ...) *may be said or sung; or a suitable hymn may be sung.*
[Psalm 95 is printed as an Appendix after the service.]

9 *All:*   **Almighty God unto whom ...** [MAL CF 2] **... Christ our Lord. Amen.**

10 *The Collect for the Day may be read.*

11   *THE COMMANDMENTS OF GOD*

Priest (standing): Our Lord Jesus Christ said ... [CF 3] ... greater than these.

People: **Lord, have mercy upon us, and write these thy laws in our hearts.**

the only] one
You shall love] And you shall love
with all] and with all TWICE
The second is this: Love] And the second is like it, namely this; You shall love

(*The Ten Commandments* (*page* ...) *may be used in place of the above*).
[The Ten Commandments are printed as an Appendix after the service.]

12   *THE CONFESSION OF SINS*

Priest (standing): Let us, who truly and earnestly repent of our sins, and are in love and fellowship with our neighbours, and intend to lead a new life, following the commandments of God, and walking from henceforth in his holy ways, make our humble confession to Almighty God.

13 *All:*   **Almighty Father, Lord of heaven and earth,**
         we confess that we have sinned against thee
         in thought, word and deed;
         we have not loved thee with all our heart;
         we have not loved our neighbours as ourselves.
         Have mercy upon us, cleanse us from our sins,
         and help us to overcome our faults;
         through Jesus Christ our Lord. Amen.

14 *Priest (standing):* The Almighty and Merciful God grant you pardon and remission of all your sins, time for amendment of life, and the grace and comfort of the Holy Spirit; through Jesus Christ our Lord. **Amen.**

15 *ADORATION (All standing)*

Either:

Priest: O people of God, lift up your voices and glorify the living God.

People: **Holy God, Holy and Mighty, Holy and Immortal, we praise thee, we glorify thee.**

Priest: Glory be to the Father, and to the Son and to the Holy Spirit.

People: **As it was in the beginning, is now, and ever shall be, world without end. Amen.**

Or:

All: **Glory be to God on high . . .** ⟦As in **Iran** no. 20, **MAL** p.251⟧ **. . . God the Father. Amen.**

16 **THE MINISTRY OF THE WORD**

(The Old Testament Lesson or Epistle, and Psalm may be omitted.)

17 *Old Testament Lesson*

18 *Psalm*

19 *Epistle*

20 *Gospel (all standing)*

Before Gospel: **Glory be to thee, O Lord.**

After Gospel: **Praise be to thee, O Christ.**

21 *Hymn or Canticle*

22 *Sermon*

(A Short Silence may be kept)

23 *CREED (all standing)*

All: **I believe in one God . . .** ⟦As in **Iran** no. 28, **MAL** p.252⟧ **. . . world to come. Amen.**

24 *THE INTERCESSION (Either)*

Priest: Let us pray for the universal Church of Christ and for all men according to their needs.

O God, grant us thy peace.

People: **And salvation to all mankind.**

Priest: Strengthen thy Church;

People: **And increase it day by day.**

Priest: Guide all Christians in the way of unity;

People: **And grant that we may grow in thy love.**

Priest : Give thy grace to all ministers of thy Church, and especially to thy servant, . . . , our Bishop;

People : **And strengthen them in the ministry of thy Word and Sacraments.**

Priest : Bless, we pray thee, all those who work for the spread of thy Gospel in the world;

People : **And encourage the messengers of thy Word.**

Priest : Direct the minds of those who are seeking Christ;

People : **And make them strong in faith.**

Priest : Guide the world in the way of peace.

People : **And direct the leaders of the nations.**

Priest : Bring all peoples into the path of justice and harmony.

People : **And into obedience to thy commands.**

Priest : Grant the Shahanshah success and prosperity;

People : **And health to the royal family.**

Priest : Direct the officers of the government.

People : **And give them the spirit of service.**

Priest : May this city and province flourish.

People : **For the welfare and blessing of the people.**

Priest : Look with favour upon universities and schools.

People : **That knowledge may be acquired for thy glory and the benefit of mankind.**

Priest : We pray thee to heal the sick;

People : **And help all those in trouble.**

Priest : May those who are near death have the assurance of thy presence.

People : **That they may entrust themselves to thee.**

Priest : Give thy strength to those who dedicate themselves to the healing of the sick;

People : **And help them to minister to all who suffer pain.**

Priest : May the wants of the needy be supplied, and the hungry be fed.

People : **Help us to relieve their suffering.**

Priest : Grant us thy grace that we may hear thy Holy Word;

People : **And help us both to receive and fulfill it.**

Priest : We thank thee for thy servants who have died in faith;

People : **And pray that we may follow their good examples, and share with them in thy eternal kingdom. Amen.**

OR: Let us pray for the whole Church . . . [as in **Eng2**, no. 14, **MAL** pp.132-3] . . . our Saviour Jesus Christ. **Amen.**

25 *All:* **Our Father, who art . . . [MAL** CF 1] **. . . ever and ever. Amen.**

in earth] on earth
them that] those who

26 *Priest:* The grace of our Lord Jesus Christ, and the love of God, and the fellowship of the Holy Spirit, be with us all evermore. **Amen.**

27 (*Notices may be given out here and the collection taken.*)

28 *Hymn.*

THE MINISTRY OF THE SACRAMENT

29   *THE OFFERTORY* (*All standing*)

(*Bread and Wine are brought forward and placed ready for use*)

Priest: O God, who in Christ reconciled the world to thyself, we beseech thee to accept us and these gifts and use them for thy glory, for thine is the greatness and the power and the glory and the majesty.

People: **All that is in heaven and earth is thine and from thy hand we give to thee.**

(*Those who brought forward the Bread and Wine return to their places*)

30   *THE THANKSGIVING* (*All standing*)

Priest: Lift up your hearts.

People: **We lift them up unto the Lord.**

Priest: Let us give thanks unto our Lord God.

People: **It is meet and right so to do.**

Priest: It is meet, right and our bounden duty that we should at all times and in all places give thanks unto thee, O Holy Lord, Father Almighty, Everlasting God, who didst create the heavens and the earth and all that is in them, and didst make man in thine own image.

(*Proper preface*)

[The Proper Prefaces which come after the end of the service are identical to those of **Iran** in **MAL** Appendix C.]

Therefore with angels and archangels, and with all the company of heaven, we laud and magnify thy glorious name, evermore praising thee and saying:

All :   **Holy, holy, holy, Lord God of Hosts,**
heaven and earth are full of thy glory.
Glory be to thee, O Lord most High.

Priest :   All glory be to thee, Almighty God, our heavenly Father, who
of thy tender mercy didst give thy only Son Jesus Christ to take
our nature upon him and to suffer death upon the Cross, for
our redemption, who made there, by his one oblation of himself
once offered, a full perfect and sufficient sacrifice and oblation
for the sins of the whole world; and did institute and in his Holy
Gospel command us to continue, a perpetual memory of that
his precious death, until his coming again; who in the same
night that he was betrayed, took bread; and when he had given
thanks, he broke it, and gave it to his disciples saying, Take,
eat; this is my Body which is given for you: Do this in remembrance of me. Likewise after supper he took the cup; and when
he had given thanks, he gave it to them saying, Drink ye all of
this; for this is my Blood of the New Covenant, which is shed
for you and for many for the remission of sins: Do this, as oft
as ye shall drink it, in remembrance of me.

People :   **Thy death, O Lord Christ, we commemorate,**
thy resurrection we confess,
and thy second coming we await.
Glory be to thee, O Christ.

31 *THE BREAKING OF THE BREAD (All standing)*

Priest :   The cup of blessing which we bless, is it not a sharing of the
Blood of Christ? The bread we break, is it not a sharing of the
Body of Christ?

People :   **We being many are one bread, one Body, for we all**
partake of the one bread and drink of the one cup.

32   *THE COMMUNION*

Priest :   Let us pray.
         (*A short silence may be kept*)

All :   **We do not presume . . . ⟦CF 6⟧ . . . he in us. Amen.**
      your] thy THROUGHOUT
      merciful Lord] O merciful Lord
      you are] thou art

33 *Priest :* Let us draw near and receive the Communion of the Body and Blood of our Lord Jesus Christ which were given for us and feed on him in our hearts by faith with thanksgiving.

People : **We eat and drink in remembrance of thee, O Lord.**

34 *Either :*

The Priest says to each communicant :

The Body of Christ preserve you in everlasting life.
The Blood of Christ preserve you in everlasting life.

Each Communicant answers : **Amen.**

Or :

The Priest says as he gives communion :

The Body . . . [CF 7(a)] . . . thanksgiving.
The Blood . . . [CF 7(b)] . . . thankful.

The Dismissal

35 *All :* **O Lord, here we offer and present to thee ourselves, our souls and bodies,**
to be a reasonable, holy and living sacrifice to thee.
In the power of thy Spirit
send us out into the affairs of the world
so that all that we are, and all that we do
may be to thy praise and glory. Amen.

36 *Priest :* The Lord be with you.

People : **And with your spirit.**

37 (*The Priest may add one of the following :*)

The peace of God . . . [CF 9] . . . with you always. **Amen.**

Or :

Go forth into the world in peace; be of good courage; hold fast to that which is good; render to no man evil for evil; strengthen the faint-hearted; support the weak; help the afflicted; honour all men; love and serve the Lord; rejoicing in the power of the Holy Spirit: And the blessing of God Almighty, the Father, the Son and the Holy Spirit be among you and remain with you always. **Amen.**

38   *APPENDIX*

If the Bread or the Wine prove insufficient the Priest shall take more to the Table and add them to what remains, saying one of the following :

Either : We now set apart this bread/wine for the communion of his body/blood, as our Lord Jesus Christ commanded.

Or :   Holy art thou, O Father, and worthy to receive blessing and honour and glory; for that thou didst send thy Son our Saviour Jesus Christ, who on the same night that he was betrayed took (*either*) bread, and when he had given thanks, he broke it, and gave it to his disciples saying, Take, eat, this is my Body which is given for you: Do this in remembrance of me

(*or*) the cup, and when he had given thanks, he gave it to them saying, Drink ye all of this; for this is my Blood of the New Covenant, which is shed for you and for many for the remission of sins; Do this, as oft as ye shall drink it, in remembrance of me.

39   *PROPER PREFACES*

[Eight Proper prefaces are printed here. They are the same as those in **Iran,** to be found in **MAL,** Appendix C.]

40   *PSALM* 95.1-7

[Not reproduced here.]

41   *THE TEN COMMANDMENTS*

God spake these words . . . [CF 2 (Shorter form omitting portions in brackets)] . . . not covet anything that is your neighbour's.

People : **Lord, have mercy upon us, and write these thy laws in our hearts.**

Remember to keep] Remember that you keep
not commit murder] do no murder

THE END OF THE THANKSGIVING

[In 1970 the Thanksgiving continued after the Acclamations as follows:]

Priest : Wherefore, O Father, we thy servants do this in remembrance of him, as he has commanded, giving thanks to thee for the perfect redemption which thou hast wrought in him. Grant that being joined together in him, we may all attain to the unity of faith, and may grow up in all things unto him who is the Head, even Jesus Christ our Lord.

People : **By whom and with whom, in the unity of the Holy Spirit all honour and glory be unto thee, O Father Almighty, world without end. Amen.**

PART IV
ASIA

CHAPTER 16

THE CHURCH OF PAKISTAN

THE Church of Pakistan was formed on 1 November 1970[1] by a union of the dioceses of C.I.P.B.C. which were in Pakistan with the similar parts of the United Methodist Church, and Lutheran Church, and a part of the United Church of Pakistan which was mainly Scottish Presbyterian in its origins.

As in North and South India, existing liturgical uses were conserved. Thus the two C.I.P.B.C. rites (**Ind** and **IndR**) were retained alongside the non-Anglican uses. However, from the outset a unitive rite was needed for diocesan occasions and **CSI** in its Urdu version has been adopted for the moment in that role. **CSI** was in fact the basic rite used at the inaugural services for the Church, and both from the proximity of South India and the pioneering character of the rite as an ecumenical liturgy it was obviously appropriate.

The Church of Pakistan currently uses **CSI** with the following three alterations:

1. As well as the Ten Commandments and the Summary of the Law there is also 'The New Commandment' (John 13:34-35).

2. As an alternative to the Absolution, the Lutheran 'Unconditional Absolution' is used: 'By the authority of God given to me through his Church, I declare and pronounce unto you the remission of all your sins, in the name of the Father and the Son, and the Holy Spirit.'

3. The provision for supplementary consecration is the single mandatory requirement of the repetition of the words of Institution. The Plan of Union insists on this as an invariable requirement of the consecration of the elements, so it cannot be anything but mandatory.[2]

The work of liturgical revision is in the hands of Bishop William Young of Sialkot and a small committee. By 1974 they had produced a draft of the Lord's Supper in English. But it had yet to be translated into Urdu, and was not forwarded in time for this volume.

---

[1] The conflict between West and East Pakistan came only a few weeks after the Union, and with the separation of Bangla Desh from Pakistan there has come a similar division in the United Church. There is no news of liturgical developments from Bangla Desh, where there are more urgent pre-occupations.

[2] See also footnote 1 on p.277 below, where the text of the *Plan* is quoted.

CHAPTER 17

THE CHURCH OF NORTH INDIA

THE Church of North India was inaugurated on 29 November 1970, and was formed from a union of Anglicans (i.e. the dioceses of C.I.P.B.C. in that area), Baptists, Brethren, Disciples of Christ, British and Australian Methodists, and the United Church of North India (which was mainly Congregationalist and Presbyterian in its origins). As had previously happened at the South India Union in 1947, each congregation was permitted to keep its liturgical tradition intact. For the central inauguration services **CSI** itself was used, as the one text which transcended denominational differences.

When the Synod of the united Church met in April 1971, a Liturgical Commission was appointed to draw up a liturgy for the Church. At the same Synod **CSI** was authorized for use in North India. When the Commission met later that year, then **CSIR** was already available to them, **Eng3** in its report form was also published soon after, and the use of modern English and the ICET texts was accepted by them from the start.

In the event a text which was originally drafted to accord with **CSI** gradually enriched itself with material drawn from the authorized form of **Eng3**. However, neither of these points should be allowed to obscure the contribution of North Indian liturgical traditions. The actual drafting was done in the first instance by the Brotherhood in Delhi, who submitted the rite in its first draft to the Liturgical Commission in March 1973. The Commission altered it slightly, then issued it with the following note introducing it: 'Prepared by the Liturgical Commission of the Church of North India, and approved by the Executive Committee of the Synod in April 1973 for optional and experimental use where authorized by the Diocesan Bishop.'

The rite was published in this form in a printed booklet in September 1973 and was used extensively where English is spoken. Then further amendments were accepted by the Liturgical Commission in January 1974, including the moving of the acclamations to *follow* the anamnesis (as in **Aus4**), and the provision of 'General' sentences for the 'Call to Worship' and 'After Communion'. This second edition was then authorized by the Executive Committee of Synod in March 1974.

Considering the diverse liturgical background of the United Church (and indeed the diverse background of the Anglican dioceses which joined it)[1] it is noteworthy how the differences have been overcome. In the event the rite follows **Eng3** at many points, but the non-Anglican traditions can be traced in the provision that 'The Scripture Warrant', including the narrative of institution, can be read before the Peace, and when that is done the narrative may be omitted from the Thanksgiving. The wording before and after the narrative in the Thanksgiving is so drafted as to permit this running on to flow smoothly. This may take the logic of 'consecration by thanksgiving' to its natural conclusion (where the narrative is not strictly needed in the Thanksgiving), but it is unlikely that Anglicans would have ventured to this conclusion on their own.

Finally, the Liturgical Commission has been at work on an 'Outline' for a 'non-liturgical' celebration of the Lord's Supper. A first draft was published in May 1974, but at the time of writing has no further authority. It gives form to the seven 'elements' which the Plan of Union of 1970 recommended should be included in every celebration of the Lord's Supper.

THE LITURGY OF
THE CHURCH OF NORTH INDIA 1973/4 (CNI)

⟦The numbering in the text below is original to the rite. In the authorized and published text an opening page lists out 'The Structure of the Lord's Supper'. Changes from 1973 are shown in the *apparatus*. However, the 1973 text also indicated posture at nos. 8, 12, 13, 14, 17, 22, 26, and these rubrics are deleted in 1974, but *not* mentioned in the *apparatus*.⟧

AN ORDER FOR
THE LORD'S SUPPER
OR
THE HOLY EUCHARIST

THE PROCLAMATION OF THE WORD
AND THE PRAYERS

---

[1] Quite apart from extremes of churchmanship there were different texts in use—particularly **Ind** and **IndR** (both in **LiE**). See **MAL**, pp.261-3.

THE PREPARATION

1 *At the beginning of the service the minister may give a Call to Worship (see section 47)*

⟦1973 reads '*(see the foot of the page)*' and at the foot puts the title '*Suggested forms of the Call to Worship*' with the first three General Sentences now in the Appendix: Ps. 118:24, Ps. 95:6, Ps. 96:8⟧.

Or he may use one of the Seasonal Sentences (see section 47)

2 *Before or after this a hymn, a canticle or a psalm may be said or sung.*

3 *The minister greets the people, saying*

The grace of our Lord Jesus Christ and the love of God and the fellowship of the Holy Spirit be with you all. (*2 Cor.* 13.14)

All　　**And also with you.**

Or　　The Lord be with you.

All　　**And also with you.**

4 *The minister and people say together*

All　　**Almighty God, to whom . . . ⟦CF 1⟧ . . . Christ our Lord. Amen.**

5 *All sing or say*

　　　　Glory to God in the highest . . . ⟦ICET 4⟧ . . . God the Father. Amen.

Or, the Kyries

Minister　Lord, have mercy.

All　　**Lord, have mercy.**

　　　　Christ, have mercy.

All　　**Christ, have mercy.**

　　　　Lord, have mercy.

All　　**Lord, have mercy.**

Or, the Trisagion, thrice repeated

Minister　Holy God,

All　　**Holy and mighty, holy and immortal, have mercy on us.**

6 *The minister prays in his own words.*
1973: *prays] may pray*

7 *The minister may then read the Collect of the Day.*
1973: *may then read] reads*

THE MINISTRY OF THE WORD

8 *An Old Testament lesson may be read. At the end there may be said*

Reader   This is the word of the Lord.

All   **Thanks be to God.**

Silence may be kept for reflection.

9 *A Psalm may be said.*

10 *The Epistle. At the end there may be said.*

Reader   This is the word of the Lord.

All   **Thanks be to God.**

Silence may be kept for reflection.

11 *A canticle, a hymn or a psalm may be sung or said.*

12 *The Gospel. When it is announced, there may be said*

All   **Glory to you, Christ Jesus.**

At the end the reader may say

      This is the Gospel of Christ.

All   **Praise to you, Lord Jesus.**

Silence may be kept for reflection.

13 *The Sermon, beginning with a short invocation.*
1973: *beginning . . . invocation*] OM

14 *The Nicene Creed is said or sung, at least on Sundays and greater Festivals.*

All   **We believe in one God . . .** ⟦ICET 3⟧ **. . . world to come. Amen.**

      (and from the Son)] OM BRACKETS

Or, in place of the Nicene Creed, the Apostles' Creed may be used.

All   **I believe in God . . .** ⟦ICET 2⟧ **. . . life everlasting. Amen.**

Or, a suitable canticle, hymn or lyric, affirming the faith of the Church, may be sung.

15 *Brief announcements may be given, now or at any other convenient time.*

THE INTERCESSION

16 *One or other of the following forms is used; or intercession may be offered in one of the varied forms mentioned in Note 7.*

⟦1973 has the considerable verbal variation from the rubric and text of this first intercession, and it stands nearer to **CSIR**, pp.286-7⟧

A

Minister In our intercession let us join our prayer for the whole family of man with the unceasing prayer of Christ the Lord.
Let us pray to the Lord for justice and peace in the whole world, and for fullness of life for every man;
Lord, in your mercy

All **Hear our prayer.**

⟦This versicle and response follows each bidding, after the semi-colon.⟧

Minister For all who live in this place (*or*, city, town, village); for the removal of all that divides us from each other, and for true harmony in our country;

For all who work on the land and in industry, for those engaged in commerce, and for all who provide for our needs;

For teachers and students, scientists, artists and writers, and for all who influence the minds and hearts of others;

For those who are suffering, the poor and hungry, the destitute and oppressed, the sick and the dying, and for all who help them;

For all to whom authority is entrusted in this and other countries, and especially for our President, the Prime-Minister, the Governor and Chief Minister of this State, and for all others who exercise power over their fellow-men;

For the unity of all Christian people, and for the witness and service in the world;

For . . . our Moderator and . . . our bishop, and for all other ministers of your Church, that they may be faithful in their ministry;

That with all your people who have faithfully served you in this life, we may also share in the eternal joy of your kingdom;
Hasten, heavenly Father, the coming of your kingdom, and grant these petitions which we offer in the name of your Son, our Lord and Saviour Jesus Christ.

All **Amen.**

B

Or, in place of the above intercession, the following may be used.

⟦1973 adds '*It is not necessary to add special subjects for prayer in any section of the intercession.*
'*The set prayers may also follow one another as a continuous whole, with or without* "Lord, in your mercy **Hear our prayer**" '⟧

Minister Let us thank God for his goodness, and let us pray for the world and for the Church.

Almighty God, our heavenly Father, you have promised through your Son, Jesus Christ, to hear us when we pray in faith.

We give you thanks for . . .
We pray for
the nations of the world . . .
our own nation . . .
any particular need in society . . .

Silence may be kept

Give wisdom to the leaders of the nations, especially to our President, the Prime Minister, the Governor and Chief Minister of this State, and to all in authority under them; direct this nation and all nations in the ways of justice and peace; that men may honour one another and seek the common good.

1973: and Chief Minister] OM
1973: Prime Minister . . . this State] Prime Minister and the Governor of this State

Lord, in your mercy

All **Hear our prayer.**

We give you thanks for . . .
We pray for
The Church throughout the world . . .
The Church of North India and . . . our Moderator,
for this diocese and for . . . our Bishop;
the unity of all Christians . . .
any particular work or need of the Church . . .

Silence may be kept

Strengthen your Church to carry forward the work of Christ; that we and all who confess his name may unite in your truth, live together in your love, and reveal your glory in the world.

Lord, in your mercy

All **Hear our prayer.**

We give you thanks for . . .

We pray for
our neighbours . . .
those with whom we work . . .
our families and friends . . .
particular persons . . .

Silence may be kept

Give grace to us, our families and friends, our neighbours
and those with whom we work; that we may serve you in one
another, and love each other as you love us.
Lord, in your mercy.

All   **Hear our prayer.**

We pray for
the hungry and destitute . . .
the oppressed and their oppressors . . .
the sick and dying . . .
those without hope . . .

We give you thanks and pray for all those who help them . . .

Silence may be kept

Strengthen and uphold all those who suffer in body, mind or
spirit; give them courage and hope in their time of need; and
lead them to know the joy of your presence.
Lord, in your mercy

All   **Hear our prayer.**

We remember before you
your servants departed this life, especially . . .

Silence may be kept

We commend all men to your unfailing love, that in them your
will may be fulfilled; and we rejoice at the faithful witness
of your saints in every age; praying that we may share with
them in your eternal kingdom.
Hear us, heavenly Father.

All   **And accept these prayers**
        for the sake of your Son,
        our Saviour Jesus Christ. Amen.

1973: Hear us . . . **accept**] Lord, in your mercy **Accept**

THE CONFESSION OF SIN

17 *The minister may read the Summary of the Law*
>Beloved, our Lord Jesus Christ said . . . ⟦CF 3⟧ . . . greater than these.
>
>1973: *minister*] *presbyter*

18 *The minister says*
>God so loved . . . ⟦As in **Eng3,** p.54 above⟧ . . . peace with all men.
>
>1973: *minister*] *presbyter*

19 *After a short silence the presbyter and people say*
All   **Almighty God, our heavenly Father . . . ⟦As in Eng3, p.55 above⟧ . . . glory of your name. Amen.**

20 *The presbyter says*
>Almighty God, who forgives all who forgive their fellow men and truly repent of their sins, have mercy on you, pardon and deliver you from all your sins, confirm and strengthen you in all goodness, and keep you in life eternal, through Jesus Christ our Lord.

All   **Amen. Thanks be to God.**
The presbyter may say 'us' *and* 'our' *for* 'you' *and* 'your'.

THE COMMUNION

21 *Where it is the custom, the Scripture Warrant may now be read:*
Presbyter Beloved in the Lord, let us attend to the words of institution of this Holy Sacrament, as they are given by Saint Paul in the first Epistle to the Corinthians:

>I received from the Lord what I also delivered to you, that the Lord Jesus on the night when he was betrayed took bread, and when he had given thanks, he broke it, and said, 'This is my body which is for you. Do this in remembrance of me'. In the same way also the cup, after supper, saying, 'This cup is the new covenant in my blood. Do this as often as you drink it, in remembrance of me.' For as often as you eat this bread and drink the cup, you proclaim the Lord's death until he comes.   1 *Cor.* 11:23-26

1973: let us] OM
>this Holy Sacrament] the Holy Supper of our Lord Jesus Christ
>given] delivered
>in . . . Corinthians] OM
>THEREAFTER 1973 FOLLOWS THE AV TEXT OF 1 CORINTHIANS 11

THE PEACE

22 *The presbyter says*

We are the body of Christ. In the one Spirit we were all baptized into one body.

Let us pursue all that makes for peace and builds up our common life.

(1 *Cor.* 12:27, 13; *Rom.* 14:9)

The peace of the Lord be always with you.

All **And also with you.**

23 *The Peace may be given here. The manner of giving the Peace is according to local custom.*

THE TAKING OF THE BREAD AND WINE

24 *A lyric or hymn may be sung, and the offerings of the people may be collected and presented.*

25 *The bread and wine are brought forward and placed on the Table or where it is the custom, unveiled.*

1973: *or . . . unveiled*] OM

26 *The Presbyter says*

Let us present these offerings, and with them ourselves, for the service of the Divine Majesty.

1973: OMITS

27 *All* **All things come from you,**

and of your own do we give you,

Almighty God, creator of the world.

We ask you to accept these (*offerings and) gifts of bread and wine

for the glory of your name

and the good of your people;

through Jesus Christ our Lord. Amen.

〚1973 omits reference to footnote, and footnote itself, and has further rubric after this prayer '*The bearers of the offertory return to their places.*'〛

THE THANKSGIVING

28 *The presbyter says*

The Lord is here.

All **His Spirit is with us.**

★ *Omit these words if there is no offering other than bread and wine*

Lift up your hearts.

All **We lift them to the Lord.**

Let us give thanks to the Lord our God.

All **It is right to give him thanks and praise.**

29 *Presbyter* It is not only right, it is our duty and our joy, holy Father, heavenly King, almighty and eternal God, always and everywhere to offer you thanks and praise through Jesus Christ, your only Son, our Lord;

For he is your true and living Word; through him you have created all things from the beginning, and formed us in your own image;

Through him you have enlightened every man coming into the world, and from age to age have raised up prophets and wise men to point the way to you;

Through him you have freed us from the slavery of sin, giving him to be born as man, to die upon the cross, and to rise again for us;

Through him you give your holy and life-giving Spirit, to make us your children and the first-fruits of your new creation.

30 *A Proper Thanksgiving, when one is provided for the season of the Christian Year or for a special occasion, follows here (see section 47).*

[The 'Proper Thanksgivings', which come after the service, are to be found here in Appendix C (they are identical with those of **Eng3** in most cases)]

31 *All* **Therefore we join our praises to the never-ending song of saints and angels before your throne; we proclaim the glory of your name, and say: Holy, holy, holy Lord, God of power and might, heaven and earth are full of your glory. Hosanna in the highest.**

Presbyter Accept our praises, heavenly Father, through your Son, our Saviour Jesus Christ; and as we follow his example and obey his command, grant that by the power of your Spirit these gifts of bread and wine may be to us the body and blood of him who died for us and rose again;

*32 For in the same night that he was betrayed, he took bread; and after giving you thanks, he broke it, gave it to his disciples, and said: 'Take, eat; this is my body which is given for you. Do this in remembrance of me.' Again, after supper he took the cup; and having given thanks, he gave it to them, and said: 'Drink this, all of you; for this is my blood of the new Covenant, which is shed for you and for many, for the forgiveness of sins. Do this, as often as you drink it, in remembrance of me'.

33 Therefore, heavenly Father, in remembrance of him we set apart this bread and this cup; we celebrate and proclaim his perfect sacrifice made once for all upon the cross, his resurrection from the dead, and his ascension into heaven; and we look for his coming in glory.

All **Christ has died;**
Christ is risen;
Christ shall come again.

Presbyter Accept through him, our great high priest, this our sacrifice of thanks and praise; and as we eat and drink these holy gifts in the presence of your divine majesty, renew us by your Spirit, inspire us with your love, and unite us in the body of your Son, Jesus Christ our Lord.

With him, and in him, and through him, by the power of the Holy Spirit, with all who stand before you in earth and heaven, we worship you, Father almighty, in songs of everlasting praise:

All **Blessing and honour and glory and power**
be yours for ever and ever. Amen.

1973: him who died for us and rose again] Christ who loved us and gave himself for us
[1973 has the Acclamations immediately after the Narrative of Institution]

THE BREAKING OF THE BREAD

34 *The presbyter breaks the consecrated bread, saying*
We break this bread that we may share in the body of Christ.

All **We are one body, because we all share in the one bread.**
1973 ADDS **Though we are many,** BEFORE **We are**

* *When the Scripture warrant (section 21) has already been read, section 32 may be omitted.*

35 *The presbyter may take the cup into his hands in the sight of the people and*
    say

        The cup which we bless is a sharing of the blood of Christ.

All **His life is in us and we live in him.**

36 *Presbyter* As our Saviour Christ has taught us, so we pray:

        Our Father in heaven . . . ⟦ICET 1⟧ . . . and for ever.
        Amen.

        holy] hallowed
        test] time of trial

Silence

THE SHARING OF THE BREAD AND WINE

37 *The presbyter says*

        Draw near in faith. Receive the body of our Lord Jesus
        Christ which he gave for you, and his blood which he shed for
        you. Remember that he died for you, and feed on him in your
        hearts by faith with thanksgiving.

38 *The ministers and people receive the bread and wine.*

39 *The following words of administration may be used (or other words, see*
    note 12).

        The body of Christ, which was given for you.
        The blood of Christ, which was shed for you.

The communicant may reply each time,
        Amen.

40 *During this time or immediately before or after Section* 37, *one or both of*
    the following may be said or sung :

        Blessed is he . . . ⟦ICET 5(b)⟧ . . . in the highest.
        Jesus, Lamb of God . . . ⟦ICET 8⟧ . . . give us your
        peace.

        1973: *or . . . the following]* these words

41 *Any consecrated bread or wine which is not required for purposes of*
    communion is consumed at the end of the administration, or after the
    dismissal of the people.

AFTER COMMUNION

42 *A Seasonal Sentence (section* 47) *may be said by the presbyter.*
    Silence may be kept

43 *Presbyter* Having now by faith received this holy sacrament, let us give thanks to God.

44 *The Presbyter may pray in his own words. One of the following is then said by all*

Almighty God, we thank you . . . ⟦CF 8⟧ **. . . praise and glory. Amen.**
souls and bodies] ourselves

Or,

Heavenly Father,
you have fed us with the spiritual food of the most precious body and blood of your Son, our Saviour Jesus Christ.
You have assured us, in these holy Mysteries,
of your favour and goodness towards us,
and that we are living members of the body of your Son,
and heirs of your eternal kingdom.
For these great benefits we thank you.
And now, Father, send us out
to do the work you have given us to do,
to love and serve you
as faithful witnesses of Christ our Lord.
To him, to you, Father, and to the Holy Spirit,
be honour and glory, now and for ever.
Amen.
1973 ADDS *Or, the presbyter may pray in his own words* WHICH IS OMITTED FROM THE RUBRIC INTRODUCING THESE PRAYERS

45 *The presbyter gives this or the appropriate seasonal blessing (section 47).*
The peace of God, which passes all understanding, keep your hearts and minds in the knowledge and love of God and of his Son, Jesus Christ our Lord;
And the blessing of God almighty, the Father, the Son, and the Holy Spirit, be among you and remain with you always.

All **Amen.**

46 *Presbyter* Go in peace to love and serve the Lord.

All **In the name of Christ. Amen.**

The ministers and people leave and greet each other.

47 SENTENCES, THANKSGIVINGS AND BLESSINGS
⟦The Sentences and Blessings are to be found here in Appendix D, the Thanksgivings in Appendix C. In 1973 they are called 'Seasonal' in the heading, but in 1974 there are three subsections, entitled 'Seasonal', 'Special Occasions' and 'General' respectively⟧

48 CONSECRATION OF ADDITIONAL BREAD OR WINE

If either or both of the consecrated elements are likely to prove insufficient, the presbyter returns to the holy Table and adds more with these words :

> Having given thanks to you, Father, over the bread and the cup, according to the institution of your Son Jesus Christ, who said: 'Take, eat; this is my body', (*and/or,* 'Drink this; this is my blood',) we pray that this bread/wine also may be to us his body/blood, and be received in remembrance of him.

(The basic principle is that of bringing additional bread or wine into the sacramental action by associating them with the already consecrated bread or wine before the supply of the latter has been completely exhausted. For this there is good historical precedent.)[1]

NOTES

[There follow 16 Notes, concerning the conduct of the service and its adaptation to particular occasions. Some of them resemble those preceding **Eng3**. Note 12, to which reference is made in section 39 above, reads as follows:

12   *The Words of Administration (Section 39). The following alternative words are suggested for use, if desired :*

'The body of our Lord Jesus Christ, which was given for you, preserve your body and soul unto everlasting life.'

with or without these words :

'Take and eat this in remembrance that Christ died for you and feed on him in your heart by faith with thanksgiving.'

and

'The blood of our Lord Jesus Christ, which was shed for you, preserve your body and soul unto everlasting life.'

---

[1] [This footnote to the provision is a quotation from the Church of England Liturgical Commission's *A Commentary on Holy Communion Series* 3 (S.P.C.K. 1971), p.26. (This was a commentary on the original text of Series 3, not on **Eng3** as authorized). It will be noted that the Churches of North India and Pakistan include in their constitution 'In the service of Holy Communion, bread and wine shall be set apart with the unfailing use of Christ's words of institution' (*Plan of Church Union* V1.14). In Pakistan this has been interpreted strictly (see p.263 above) but the **Eng3** provision here does also include the 'words']

with or without these words :

'Drink this in remembrance that Christ's blood was shed for you, and be thankful.'

or,

'The body of Christ, the Bread of life.'
'The blood of Christ, the true Vine.'

or,

'Take, eat: this is the body of Christ which is broken for you: this do in remembrance of him'.
'This cup is the new covenant in the blood of Christ, which is shed for many unto remission of sins: drink, all of you, of it.']

CHAPTER 18

THE CHURCH OF SOUTH INDIA

THE CSI *Book of Common Worship* borrowed much material, only slightly changed, from Anglican, Presbyterian, Methodist, and other forms of worship generally in use at the time of union in 1947. Such entirely new composition as it contains was drafted in the Cranmerian style still almost universal in the uniting churches of that period. This was partly because the CSI Liturgy Committee did not then trust itself to compose liturgical formulae radically new in modern English, when other churches had not yet dared to adopt such novelty; partly because fears of innovation on the part of conservative Christians in South India and elsewhere had to be allayed, and it was rightly judged that a Cranmerian 'language of worship' would be more acceptable to them.

This Committee had been set up by the first meeting of the CSI Synod in 1948, and it wrote a eucharistic liturgy in draft and presented it to the 1950 Synod, which authorized it.[1] Slight amendments were made in 1954,[2] and in the third edition in 1962 a whole series of Proper Prefaces were added,[3] and the service was then incorporated into the *Book of Common Worship* published in 1963. The service has been translated into the four languages of South India, Tamil, Telugu, Malayalam, and Canarese, and in a more or less contemporary form of these languages. But in its English original, from which the translations are made, it remained in the Cranmerian style in which it began.

This has not only led to **CSI** feeling slightly dated in some English-language congregations in South India. It has also meant that the liturgy which was hailed for so long as a pioneering pacesetter on the international scene has come, as others have updated their language, to appear as a somewhat archaic pioneer.

Of course in South India itself, even now the demand for forms of worship in modern English is only liable to be voiced by the small minority who have become acquainted with **Eng2** or **Eng3,** the new

---

[1] Cf. T. S. Garrett, *Worship in the Church of South India* (Lutterworth London 1958), pp.19-42.

[2] It is the 1954 text which is reprinted in **LiE** (as **CSI**).

[3] The additional Proper Prefaces were noted and listed in Appendix C of **MAL.**

Roman Catholic Mass, and other similar ventures. Of the very small number of congregations in South India who worship in English the great majority are content with the old style, or may even still be wedded to 1662. The translations into the Indian languages used by more than 90% of our congregations are not much affected by the style of the English original.

The minority, however, who thought CSI ought to be more modern in its worship was sufficiently articulate to persuade the Synod of 1968 to authorize the Liturgy Committee to prepare a draft of the Lord's Supper in modern English. Earlier than that there had been repeated demands in several quarters for a shorter and simpler liturgy for use in village congregations. The 'Short Order for the Lord's Supper', printed at the end of BCW, only gives permission for the shortening of the ante communion and was by many thought not to have gone far enough in this direction. In 1968 the diocese of Madras therefore ventured on the experiment of a simple eucharistic service in Tamil for use chiefly in village congregations. The English draft of this was in modern English and was not only translated into Tamil but adopted in Mysore and translated into Canarese.

The English typescript from which translations were made attracted the attention of staff and students of the United Theological College, Bangalore, South India's premier institution for the training of ministers. They liked it and recommended it as the basis for the projected revision. Though a number of modifications of this experimental rite were made by the CSI Liturgy Committee in the years 1969-71, it still remained basically the prototype of the new service. Thus two demands combined to produce what we have here: the demand for modern English and the demand for simplification and abbreviation. Even if it was the expression of the former which actually set the revision in motion, the latter was more insistent in the Church at large.

The revised rite was authorized for use by the Synod Executive Committee in September 1971 and first celebrated publicly at the meeting of that Committee. Its general release took place at the Jubilee Synod of January 1972.

The new rite follows the old fairly closely in general pattern, order, and content. This has the merit of making transition from one to the other easy. Congregations which have become used to the old rite should still feel at home in the new. This is particularly so in the Indian languages. Though effort has been made to improve and simplify the style of translation into these, much more remains the same than it does in English.

The most significant points of revision are:

1. The ecumenically agreed ICET texts in modern English of the Lord's Prayer, the Creeds, the Gloria in Excelsis, the Sanctus and Agnus Dei have been taken from *Prayers We Have in Common.*

2. The intercessions for the Church and the world have been radically revised with the intention of making them (*a*) more elastic and variable, (*b*) less inward-looking and 'church centred' and more relevant to the needs of the world at large.

3. Greater variability is provided at the offertory by the addition of special sentences for Christmas, Easter, and Pentecost.

4. Further variability and wider choice will shortly be available, whatever the form of Sunday worship, in the provisions of an alternative selection of collects and lections throughout the year.

THE MODERN ENGLISH
SOUTH INDIA LITURGY 1972 (CSIR)

〖The numbering here is editorial.〗

1   **THE LORD'S SUPPER**
                OR THE HOLY EUCHARIST
                    (*A Revised Version*)

2   *THE PREPARATION*
As the ministers come to the Lord's Table, the people stand. The presbyter, or one of those with him, carries in both hands the Bible from which the lessons are to be read, and places it on the Table or on a lectern. The presbyter may stand behind the Table, facing the people.

3 *The presbyter says, the people standing :*
                    Let us pray
ALMIGHTY God, you know our thoughts and our desires, and no secret is hidden from you. By your Holy Spirit prepare us now, so that we may love and worship you as we ought, through Jesus Christ our Lord. **Amen.**

Where there is a processional hymn the above prayer of preparation may be said at the door before the procession begins.

4 *A hymn or lyric is sung.*

5 *Or all sing or say:*

Glory to . . . ⟦ICET 4⟧ . . . Father. Amen.

6 *Or this ancient hymn thrice repeated:*

Holy God:

Holy and mighty, holy and immortal, have mercy on us.

7 *Or this litany, the deacon leading the responses:*

WORTHY is the Lamb that was slain, to receive all power and wealth, wisdom and might, honour and glory and praise.   *Rev.* 5:12.

To the Lamb be glory!

Praise and honour, glory and might, to him who sits on the throne and to the Lamb, for ever and ever.   *Rev.* 5:13b.

To the Lamb be glory!

You are worthy, because you were slain, and with your blood bought for God men of every tribe, and language, people and nation.
Rev. 5:9

To the Lamb be glory! Victory to our God who sits on the throne, and to the Lamb. Praise and glory and wisdom, thanksgiving and honour, power and might be to our God for ever and ever. Amen.   *Rev.* 7:10, 12

8 *Then the presbyter says:*

WE have come together to hear God's word, to praise Him, and to share in the Lord's Feast. Let us call to mind our sins and our need of His grace.

All kneel.   After a short silence the presbyter says:
          Let us confess our sins to God.

9 *The deacon leading, all say together:*

HEAVENLY Father, we confess that we have sinned against you and our neighbour. We have lived often in darkness rather than in light; we profess to believe in Christ, but continue to do evil. For the sake of Jesus Christ, have mercy on us and forgive us our sins. Grant us by your Holy Spirit to discern good from evil and to do only what is right. Enable us to forgive others, that with new life we may serve you and all men. Amen.

Or the presbyter may use certain other forms.

10 *Then the presbyter stands and says:*
   This is God's word in Christ to all who turn to Him:
   One of more of the following sentences shall be said, or the presbyter may use any other appropriate verses of Scripture.

   Come to me, all whose work is hard, whose load is heavy; and I will give you relief.   *Matt.* 11:28

   God loved the world so much that he gave his only Son, that everyone who has faith in him may not die but have eternal life.   *John* 3:16

   Christ Jesus came into the world to save sinners.   1 *Tim.* 1:15b

   Should anyone commit a sin, we have one to plead our cause with the Father, Jesus Christ, and he is just. He is himself the remedy for the defilement of our sins, not our sins only, but the sins of all the world.
                                                         1 *John* 2:1b, 2

11 *After a short silence the presbyter says:*
   ALMIGHTY God our heavenly Father has promised to forgive all those who forgive their brothers and return to him in faith. May he have mercy on us, pardon our sins, and set us free from them, make us strong to do good, and give us eternal life in Jesus Christ our Lord.

12 *Or he says:*
   ALMIGHTY God have mercy on you, pardon and deliver you from all your sins, confirm and strengthen you in all goodness, and keep you in life eternal, through Jesus Christ our Lord.
   Amen. Thanks be to God.

13   *THE MINISTRY OF THE WORD OF GOD*
   The Lord be with you:
   And also with you.

14   Let us pray
   The Collect of the Day, or another short prayer is said.

15 *The people may stand for the reading of the Scripture, or at least for the reading of the Gospel. Before each lesson the reader says:* Hear the Word of God: the Book of . . . the . . . chapter, beginning at the . . . verse; *and after it he says:* Here ends the lesson.

16 *The lesson from the Old Testament is read, and after it the people say:*
   Thanks be to you, O God.

17 *A Psalm or hymn or lyric may be sung.*

18 *The Epistle is read, and the people say:*
   Thanks be to you, O God.

19　*The Gospel is read and the people say :*
　　Praise be to you, O Christ.

20　*The Sermon is preached, the people sitting.*

21　*The Apostles' Creed is said or sung by all, standing.*
　　I believe . . . ⟦ICET 2⟧ **. . . everlasting. Amen.**

22　*Or the Nicene Creed is said or sung by all, standing.*
　　We believe . . . ⟦ICET 3⟧ **. . . come. Amen.**
　　(and the Son)] OM BRACKETS

23　*Or a suitable hymn or lyric, affirming the faith of the Church, is sung.*

24　*Announcements may be made here, and the collection may be taken.*

25　*A hymn or lyric may also be sung.*

26　*One of these litanies is said or sung, the deacon leading : or the minister offers intercession in his own words for the Church and the world.*

27　　　　　　　　　　　　　Let us pray

We pray for your Church in all the world, that it may be obedient to your will and strong in your Spirit to show your love and glory to all men.

Here the minister prays briefly in his own words, mentioning special needs of the local church, the diocese, or the Church in its wider fellowship. This and the following petitions will end with the words :

Lord in your mercy:
Hear our prayer.

We pray for our country, and for all countries, that men may live at peace with justice and honour (*special needs, national and international, are mentioned*).

We pray for the poor and helpless, the sick, the bereaved, and all the victims of greed or persecution, that you may rescue them (*any such people known to the congregation may be named*).

We remember with gratitude the lives of those who have died in faith and pray that we too may be given strength and courage to follow in your way to the end (*when names of individuals are mentioned the minister says :* 'especially we remember . . .').

28 *The second litany:*

Biddings for prayer may be made:

For peace and justice in the whole world, and for the fullness of life in Christ for all men:

Lord, in your mercy hear our prayer (*and so after each bidding*).

For our country, its President, Ministers, and those who serve in its Government:

For all who work in fields and factories, in workshops and mines, and all who labour with their hands to provide for our needs:

For teachers and students, scientists, artists and craftsmen, and those engaged in the work of healing:

For those who are suffering: the poor and hungry, the destitute and oppressed, the sick and the dying:

For the unity of all God's people and for their work and witness in the world:

For bishops and all other ministers, especially . . . our Moderator, and . . . our Bishop, that they may be faithful in their ministry:

For ourselves that we may make known the goodness and power of him who called us out of darkness into his light:

That with all his people who have faithfully served him here and have died, we may also come to eternal joy in his presence:

29 *After either Litany the presbyter says:*

Let us pray

Lord, you know what we and all men need. We do not rightly know. Answer our prayers according to your wisdom, and teach us to know and do your will, for Jesus' sake. **Amen.**

30 *The presbyter then gives the first benediction:*

The grace of the Lord Jesus Christ, the love of God and the fellowship of the Holy Spirit be with you all. **Amen.**

31 *Those who leave shall leave now.*

32 ### THE BREAKING OF THE BREAD

All stand, and the presbyter says:

How good and joyful it is when brothers live in unity. (*Ps.* 133:1)

We who are many are one body, for we all share the one bread. (1 *Cor.* 10:17)

I will offer the sacrifice of thanksgiving and call on the name of the Lord in the presence of all his people.

⟦The seasonal sentences which follow here are to be found with the Offertory Sentences in Appendix B⟧

33 *The Peace may be given here. The manner of giving the Peace is according to the local custom.*

34 *A lyric or hymn is sung and the offerings of the people including the bread and the wine are brought forward and placed on the Table.*

35 *All standing, the presbyter says:*

HOLY Father, you have opened a new living way for us to come to you through the self-offering of Jesus. We are not worthy to offer gifts to you, but through him we ask you to accept and use us and our gifts for your glory. **Amen.**

The bearers of the offertory return to their places.

36 *The presbyter and the people say together:*

BE present, be present, O Jesus, our good High Priest, as you were with your disciples, and make yourself known to us in the breaking of the bread. Amen.

37 *The presbyter says:*

The Lord be with you:
And also with you.

Lift up your hearts:
We lift them up to the Lord.

Let us give thanks to the Lord, our God.
It is right to give him thanks and praise.

It is good and right, always and everywhere to give you thanks, O Lord, Holy Father, Almighty and everliving God;

[1]Through Jesus Christ, your Son, our Lord, for through him, you created all things from the beginning, and made us men in your own image; through him you redeemed us from the slavery of sin; through him you have sent out your Holy Spirit to make us your own people, the first-fruits of your new creation.

And so we join the angels and the saints in proclaiming your glory as we sing [say]:

Holy, Holy, Holy Lord, God of power and might, heaven and earth are full of your glory. Hosanna in the highest.

---

[1] *Instead of the words,* 'through Jesus Christ . . . your new creation', *another Preface proper to the season of the Christian year or to the occasion may be said* [The Proper Prefaces, which are printed after the service, are to be found in Appendix C.]

The presbyter remains standing, the people may kneel.
The presbyter says:

Truly holy are you, our Father. In your love for us you gave your Son Jesus Christ to be one of us and to die on the cross for us. By that one perfect sacrifice he took away the sins of the whole world, and commanded us to remember his death until he comes again. So, on the night he was betrayed, he took bread, gave thanks to you, broke it and gave it to his disciples, saying: Take, eat; this is my body given for you; do this in remembrance of me. So also after supper he took the cup, gave thanks to you, gave it to them and said: Drink it, all you, for this is my blood of the new covenant, shed for you and for all men, to forgive sin. Do this, whenever you drink it, in remembrance of me.

Amen. Your death, O Lord, we remember, your resurrection we proclaim, your final coming we await. Christ, to you be glory.

And so Father, remembering that Jesus, your Son and our Lord, was born and lived among us, suffered and died, rose again and ascended, we, your people, are doing this to remember him as he commanded until he comes again, and we thank you for reconciling and restoring us to you in him.

O Lord, our God, we give you thanks, we praise you for your glory.

And we humbly ask you Father, to take us and this bread and wine, that we offer to you, and make them your own by your Holy Spirit, so that our breaking of the bread will be a sharing in Christ's body and the cup we bless a sharing in his blood. Join us all together in him. Make us one in faith. Help us to grow up as one body, with Jesus as our head. And let us all together, in the Holy Spirit, bring glory to you, our Father. **Amen.**

38   Let us pray with confidence to the Father in the words our Saviour gave us:
Our Father . . . ⟦ICET 1⟧ . . . for ever. Amen.

39 *Silence is kept for a space.*

40 *The presbyter breaks the bread, saying:*
When we break the bread, is it not a sharing in the body of Christ?

41 *The ministers and the people receive the bread and the wine.*
The following words of administration may be used:
The body of our Lord Jesus Christ, the Bread of life.
The blood of our Lord Jesus Christ, the true Vine.
Or certain other words may be used.

42 *During this time these words may be said or sung:*
Jesus, Lamb of God . . . ⟦ICET 8⟧ . . . **give us your peace.**

43 *When all have partaken the presbyter says:*
ALMIGHTY God, heavenly Father, you have accepted us as your children in your Son Jesus Christ. You have fed us with his body and blood. We thank you Lord. Direct our minds, so that we do what you want and not what the world wants us to do. Help us to obey you on earth and to rejoice with all your saints in heaven, through Jesus Christ our Lord, who lives and reigns with you and the Spirit, one God, for ever.

Amen. Praise and glory and wisdom and thanksgiving and honour, power and might, be to our God for ever and ever. Amen. *Rev.* 7:12

44 *The presbyter gives the second benediction:*
GO out into the world as witnesses and servants of Christ, and the blessing of God Almighty, the Father, the Son and the Holy Spirit be with you always. **Amen.**

45 *After the benediction the ministers go out carrying with them the Bible, the gifts of the people, and the vessels used for the communion. Any bread or wine set apart in the service, which remains over, is carried out to the vestry and there is reverently consumed.*

46 *If the bread and wine set apart be insufficient, the presbyter, taking more, may say:*
Obeying the command of our Lord Jesus Christ, we take this bread, (wine) to be set apart for this holy use, in the name of the Father, and of the Son and of the Holy Spirit. **Amen.**
Or the words of the Institution may be repeated.

CHAPTER 19

THE ANGLICAN CHURCH OF CEYLON (SRI LANKA)

THE two dioceses of Ceylon became extra-provincial dioceses of the Canterbury jurisdiction in November 1970, when C.I.P.B.C. ceased to exist on the inauguration of the united Churches of North India and Pakistan and the Province of Burma. The path to union in Ceylon has been a chequered one and the outcome is still uncertain. In liturgical terms also the two dioceses are in an interim position. At the last General Synod of the C.I.P.B.C. in January 1970, at the request of the Liturgical Commission of the (Anglican) Church of Ceylon, variations were permitted from the text of **IndR** and **Cey**[1] as follows:

1 **The Ministry of the Word (Synaxis),** may take the form of a Bible Study with meditation or dialogue.
The Ministry of the Sacrament may then commence with the Offertory, and the Intercession and Penitential section may be omitted if they have been included in the first part of the Service.
2 **The Creed.** The Creed may be omitted on working Sundays, except when they are Festivals.
3 **Penitential Section for Working Sundays.** The shorter Confession and Absolution in the opening Devotion may be substituted for the Invitation, Confession, Absolution, Comfortable Words.
4 **The Intercession.** Instead of the Intercession as set, short litanies, or prayers, or extempore biddings may be used instead.
As alternatives to the Intercession in the Order, the Intercessions of the Church of England Series II Services [**Eng2**[2]] or of the East Africa United Liturgy [**EAUL**[3]] may be used instead.
5 **Prayer of Humble Access** may be revised as in most recent Anglican revisions, the word 'property' being changed to 'nature', and the words 'our sinful bodies' to 'blood and' may be omitted.
6 **Post Communion Section.** The following simpler alternatives for the Prayer of Thanksgiving may be used:
Then shall the Priest say,

Let us Pray.

[The two alternative prayers from **Eng2** (**MAL** p.138) follow]

[1] These are printed in **LiE** on pp.114-26 and pp.82-93 respectively.
[2] See **MAL**, pp.132-3.
[3] See **MAL**, pp.82-4.

7 **The Gloria in Excelsis.** As alternatives to the Gloria the following may be used: the Te Deum, the Magnificat or the Benedictus.

The Gloria in Excelsis shall be sung or said on all Sundays and other festivals, except the Sundays in Advent, Pre-Lent and Lent. The Gloria *may* also be omitted on Sundays after Epiphany I and after Trinity.

8 **Dismissal.** 'A simple sending out, without a blessing' on lines similar to the following:

V. The Lord be with you

R. **And with thy spirit**

V. Go forth into the world in peace

R. **Thanks be to God**

V. Let us serve the Lord

R. **In the person of His brethren.**

9 **The Ceylon Liturgy [Cey].** In using this Order it shall be permissible to adopt any of the following prescribed in the Provincial Order of 1960 [**IndR**]:

The Confession and Absolution
The Old Testament Lesson
The Offertory Prayer
Either form of the Intercession
The collect at the end of the Intercession with response and any of the Proper Prefaces.

10 It shall also be permissible

(*a*) to omit the Agnus Dei
(*b*) for the Sermon to precede the Creed, and
(*c*) the Intercession to precede the Kiss of Peace and the Offertory.

[There then follow in full the two alternative forms of intercession: first, that from **Eng2** (**MAL** pp.132-3), second the right-hand column of the intercession in **EAUL**[1] (**MAL** pp.82-3)]

These variations are all designed to accommodate the liturgy to 'Working Sundays', which have been a strong though not an invariable feature of the Buddhist Calendar followed in Ceylon. In *Partners in Mission* the Liturgical Commission is said to be considering the desirability of an alternative eucharistic canon, but there is no sign yet of any draft.

[1] Is this an example of cross-fertilization due to **MAL**?

CHAPTER 20

THE CHURCH OF THE PROVINCE OF THE INDIAN OCEAN

THE scattered pieces of the Anglican Communion in the Indian Ocean were brought together in 1973 in the Province of the Indian Ocean. The diocese of Madagascar, the liturgy of which (**Mad**) was printed in English for the first time in **MAL**[1], was divided into three separate dioceses in 1969, and the use of this Malagasy rite continues in those dioceses. In Mauritius, the Bishop (now Archbishop) convened a small group and produced a bilingual rite for the one diocese. In 1973 this diocese divided into Mauritius and Seychelles, and both use the rite.

As stated in **MAL**, the traditional Mauritius use is the 'Interim Rite' (somewhat comparable to the variants from 1662 in **Eng1**). French is in use as a living language of worship, as well as English,[2] but this new compilation is the first time the two languages have been set out side by side in a single booklet. The English language version is traditional in its language, and reads like the 'Interim Rite'. The Gloria in Excelsis comes at the beginning, the Intercession is the 1662 Church Militant prayer virtually unamended ('Christian Kings, Princes and Governors' are now 'the leaders of the nations of the world'[3]), the 'Offertory' comes after the Comfortable Words, the longer form of the **Eng1** canon is used, and then come the Lord's Prayer, the Fraction, Peace, Prayer of Humble Access, Agnus Dei, and Communion.

The Archbishop expresses a hope that in time the Province will move to a common use, perhaps through the medium of a Provincial Liturgical Committee. In fact, although the *languages* differ enormously, the Mauritius Interim Rite is little different from **Mad**.

---

[1] See **MAL**, pp.103-10.

[2] French has been used since 1662 in the Channel Islands, though it has now been virtually wholly replaced by English, and in French-speaking parts of Canada and Melanesia. But it is unusual as a medium for Anglican worship.

[3] The last paragraph of the prayer is still in 1662 form, so that, although 'Militant here on earth' has been dropped from the bidding, it might well appear that this rite has no petitions for the departed. This is true up to a point—but there *is* provision for 'Grant them rest' and 'Grant them rest eternal' to be used with the Agnus Dei at commemorations of the faithful departed.

CHAPTER 21

THE COUNCIL OF THE CHURCH OF SOUTH-EAST ASIA

THE various dioceses of South-East Asia are bound together by the Councils of Bishops, which exercises metropolitical functions for the area. The dioceses of Taiwan and the Philippines belong to the PECUSA jurisdiction (and sphere of liturgical influence). The two dioceses of Korea are the subject of the succeeding chapter. Apart from these two areas the situation is as follows.

In Burma a separate Province was formed in 1970, when the C.I.P.B.C. split up, and most of the dioceses were involved in forming the new united Churches of North India and Pakistan. The use of **IndR** continues and its translation into the various tribal tongues is being completed. No other liturgical initiatives are being taken. The dioceses of Hong Kong and Sabah have their own rites,[1] reported in **MAL,** and there has been no further revision of these uses. The dioceses of Singapore and West Malaysia do not have their own uses, but allow rites from elsewhere to be tried. **Eng2** in particular has been used in English-speaking congregations.

The diocese of Kuching had its own 'Interim Rite', as reported in **MAL.** However, the Kuching Liturgical Commission went on in 1973 to produce a new modern English rite (as a basis for translation into five different languages), and this was used experimentally in English-speaking parishes, then amended and approved for a two year experimental period from 1 September 1973 at the Diocesan Council in August 1973. The intercession is taken from **Eng2,** and the Thanksgiving shows the influence of **LfA.** The Liturgical Commission, whilst introducing 'you' forms, has also drawn upon the ICET texts, but has handled the Lord's Prayer with some freedom (partly following **Eng3**), and has retained 'I' in the creed.

---

[1] **HK1** and **HK2** are printed in **MAL,** pp.271-83. The Sabah rite is a simple variant on 1662 described in **MAL,** p.264.

THE KUCHING EXPERIMENTAL
LITURGY 1973 (Kuch)

[The numbering is editorial. Because this is a diocesan rite, with a short-term expectancy of life, some details are omitted. The rite has no title except 'Proposed Revision of the Liturgy Amended'.]

1   *RUBRICS*

[A series of brief opening notes and rubrics is set out here.]

THE PREPARATION

2 *The people stand at the entry of the choir and ministers who go to their stalls.*

3 *A psalm or hymn.*

4 *Kneel*

    Priest: Almighty God, to whom . . . [CF 1] . . . Christ our Lord.
    Amen.

        hid] hidden
        the thoughts of our hearts] our thoughts
        the inspiration of] OM
        that] so that
        perfectly] truly
        magnify] praise

5 *Priest:* Let us confess our sins to Almighty God.

    People: **Almighty God** . . . [As **Eng2** no. 18, **MAL** p.134, with 'you' 'your'] . . . **of your name. Amen.**

6 *Priest:* Almighty God have mercy . . . [CF 5] . . . our Lord.
    Amen.

        confirm and] OM

7 *The Kyries*

    [A ninefold 'Lord, have mercy' 'Christ have mercy' etc. is set out.]

8 *Gloria in Excelsis*

Glory to God . . . [ICET 4] . . . **God the Father. Amen.**

THE LITURGY OF THE WORD

9 *Priest:* The Lord be with you

   People: **And also with you**

   Kneel

        Let us pray
        Collect of the Day

10 *Sit*

The reader announces the Epistle:

A reading from the Epistle (*or* Book) of . . . Here ends the reading.

11 *Stand*

Hymn

12 *The Gospel is announced*

A reading from the Gospel of Saint . . .

People: **Glory to Christ our Saviour**

After the Gospel the People say:

Praise to Christ our Lord.

13 *Sermon*

14 *Stand*

The Nicene Creed

I believe . . . ⟦ICET 4⟧ . . . **world to come. Amen.**
(and the Son))] OM BRACKETS

15 *Banns, notices and collection*

16 *Hymn*

17   *THE INTERCESSION*

Kneel

Let us pray for the whole Church of God in Christ Jesus, and for all men according to their needs.

Almighty God, you have promised . . . ⟦As **Eng2** no. 14, **MAL** pp.132-3, with 'you' 'your' throughout⟧ . . . our Saviour Jesus Christ. **Amen.**

and Elizabeth our Queen] the Agong and all our rulers

18 *OR*

Almighty God, creator and preserver . . . ⟦This is a modernised version of 'All Sorts and Conditions' with the versicle and response from no. 17 above after the paragraphs (cf. **Eng2** Appendix 2)⟧ . . . Grant these our prayers, merciful Father, for the sake of your Son, our Saviour Jesus Christ. **Amen.**

19 *Hymn*

20 *The ministers vest and go to the altar.*

     THE LITURGY OF THE SACRAMENT

21 *Priest:* We are the body of Christ, for by one Spirit we were all baptized into one Body.

People: **Let us keep the unity of the Spirit in the bond of peace.**

22   THE OFFERTORY

Bread and wine shall be placed upon the altar in silence.

23   THE EUCHARISTIC PRAYER

Priest : The Lord be with you;

People : **And also with you.**

Priest : Lift up your hearts;

People : **We lift them up to the Lord.**

Priest : Let us give thanks to the Lord our God;

People : **It is right to give him thanks and praise.**

Priest : It is right and our duty that we should at all times and in all places, give thanks to you Father, holy, almighty, everlasting God, through Jesus Christ, your only Son our Lord, because through him you have created the heavens and the earth, redeemed us, and given to us your Holy Spirit;

⟦The Proper Prefaces which come after the end of the service are to be found in Appendix C.⟧

Therefore with angels, the whole company of heaven and with the faithful who rest in him, we joyfully praise you and say:

People : **Holy, Holy, Holy, Lord God of all; heaven and earth are full of your glory: Glory to you Lord God most high.**

Priest : ALL GLORY to you Holy Father who gave your only Son Jesus Christ to be the one perfect sacrifice for the sin of the world: Hear us, Father, and send your Holy Spirit on this bread and wine that these gifts may become to us His Body and His Blood.

For on the night that he was betrayed, he took bread and when he had given thanks he broke it and gave it to his disciples, saying: Take, eat, this is my body given for you. Do this in remembrance of me. In the same way, after supper, he took the cup, and when he had given thanks he gave it to them saying: Drink this, all of you, for this is my blood of the new covenant which is shed for you and for many for the forgiveness of sins. Do this as often as you drink it, in remembrance of me. Wherefore, Father, we do this as your Son commanded,

People : **His death we show forth,**
         His resurrection we proclaim,
         In his ascension we rejoice,
         His coming we await.

Priest : And we offer to you, with this holy bread and cup, our praise and thanksgiving for his sacrifice once offered upon the Cross. Accept us in him, and grant that all we who receive this holy communion may be filled with the Holy Spirit, and made one in your holy Church, the Body of your Son Jesus Christ our Lord, through whom and in whom, in the unity of the Holy Spirit, all honour and glory be to you, Almighty Father, for ever and ever. **Amen.**

24 As our Saviour Christ has taught us, we say:
Our Father in heaven . . . 〚ICET 1〛 . . . from evil. Amen.
holy] hallowed
do not bring us to the test] lead us not into temptation

25   THE BREAKING OF THE BREAD
Priest : The peace of the Lord be always with you.
People : **And also with you.**

26   *Agnus Dei*
People : **Lamb of God, you take away the sin of the world, have**
          mercy on us.
          Lamb of God, you take away the sin of the world, have
          mercy on us.
          Lamb of God, you take away the sin of the world, grant
          us your peace.
〚There follows provision for a 'Requiem' where the endings change to
'grant them rest' (twice) and **'grant them rest everlasting'.**〛

27   THE COMMUNION
Priest : Draw near and receive the Body and Blood of our Lord Jesus Christ in remembrance that Christ died for you, and feed on him in your hearts by faith with thanksgiving.
    (*He who delivers the sacrament shall say to each one who receives,*)
The Body and Blood of Christ.[1]
    (*and he who receives shall reply,*)
    Amen.

28 *Hymn*

29   Let us pray
Priest and People :
Kneel **Almighty God, we thank . . . 〚CF 8〛 . . . praise and**
          glory. Amen.
          Send us out] Send us out into the world

    [1] 〚This provision seems to imply a regular practice of intinction.〛

THE DISMISSAL

30 *Priest:* The Lord be with you.

People: **And also with you.**

Priest: Go forth in peace.

People: **We go in the name of Christ.**

[Provision is made '*At a Requiem*' for the salutation to be followed by 'May they rest in Peace'. **'Amen'.**]

31 *At his discretion the Priest may use this form of dismissal:*

Priest: The Lord be with you.

People: **And also with you.**

Priest: Go in peace. Love and serve the Lord. Be full of joy in the power of the Holy Spirit. And the blessing of God Almighty, the Father, the Son and the Holy Spirit, be with you and stay with you always.

People: **Amen.**

32 [An Appendix contains the Proper Prefaces, to be found here in Appendix C.]

CHAPTER 22

THE ANGLICAN CHURCH
IN KOREA

Background

THE Anglican Church in Korea is a small body with a uniformly catholic tradition. During the 1920s its eucharistic practice followed anglo-catholic developments in England, and in 1939 a liturgy was authorized which was based on 1549 with important elements from 1928 and the Tridentine rite. This is the service in the present Korean BCP (**Kor**).[1]

After the Korean war of 1950-53 there was an increasing demand for revision, at first because the literary language used (corresponding in style to seventeenth-century English) was outmoded, and the vocabulary used by Anglicans differed in some details from that of both Roman Catholics and Protestants, and therefore from the words of the only available translation of the Bible into Korean. By 1960 the influence of the worldwide liturgical movement began to be felt, and interest in changing the structure of the service was aroused.

In 1965 the Korean Church, till then a single diocese, was divided into two dioceses, and a conservatively revised BCP was issued. The Tridentine devotions in the eucharistic liturgy were made optional and important but minimal vocabulary changes were made. Some conservative clergy ignored the new provisions, but most Anglicans welcomed them. In many churches, especially in the provinces, ceremonial tended to be simplified, and all possible opportunities were taken to extend lay participation.[2] (This has become most moving where the 'prayer for the Church' is used as an interpolated litany led by members of the congregation at random.)

The Compilation of the 1973 rite (**Kor1**)

In Taejon diocese widespread experimentation with the order of the service was permitted, and restricted experiment with a 'Hippolytan' type of canon in modern language. The National Synod of 1968

---

[1] The text of **Kor** is in **LiE** (2nd edn 1964) pp.166-77. The text in the first edition of **LiE** is incorrect at many points.
[2] These changes were recorded in **MAL**, pp.292-3.

established a Liturgical Commission which submitted a draft experimental eucharistic rite to the Synod of 1972. This draft revised the order of the service and slightly modified the language, without radically changing the style. The synod criticized the draft, chiefly on the grounds that the language needed further revision, and returned it to the Commission, asking for it to be revised further in the light of the synodical discussion, and presented to the bishops as soon as possible so that they could authorize it for experimental use until the National Synod of 1976.

The Commission now consisted of an English bishop, five Korean priests, a Korean layman, and a Korean nun. The bishop, one of the priests, and the layman had more than average experience as writers of Korean. Only two of the members of the Commission had not visited either England or the USA and were unable to read liturgical texts in English. They completed their work on the eucharist in the new year of 1973, and it was authorized by the bishops, as requested by the synod, on 29 June 1973.

General Principles

Linguistic style was the principal problem facing the Commission. It was finally decided to borrow common parts of the service from the Roman Catholic Korean mass, so as to avoid further multiplication of translations. (In fact a few minor modifications were found necessary.) The Roman authorities agreed to consult with the Anglican Church in further revision of these parts. All scripture passages, including the Lord's Prayer and the Words of Institution, were taken from the 1971 joint R.C./Anglican/Protestant translation of the NT, which was also used as a primary standard for vocabulary.

The rest was written in Korean. Nothing was translated from any other language, though previous Korean texts (Anglican and R.C.) and other Anglican liturgies were much referred to. So it is original.

Korean uses third person address, avoids pronouns, has no articles, and rarely expresses plurality ('the Word of God' can be distinguished from 'God's words' only by circumlocution). The drafters deliberately eschewed ornamental expression, but the text they produced is not so jejune as the plain translation may appear to be. They were often careful to reflect biblical phrases and metaphors, but did not shrink from traditional Korean images where they came naturally.

(E.g. the Oriental use of 'mirror' in preface 18[1]). The result may fairly be said to be a better use of the native resources of Korean, aesthetically and pastorally more satisfying than the present BCP.[2] **Kor1** therefore, unlike **Kor,** presents the translator with all the problems of translating any original Korean text into English. It is no longer possible to find the phrases of 1549 and 1928 that were represented by the Korean text. The ambiguities, verbal redundancies, and grammatical imprecisions of the Korean language cannot be resolved by reference back to the English prayer books.

Specific problems

One word proves particularly intractable: *chesa* (etymologically the same as the Chinese *chi-she*). This widely used Korean word is usually translated 'sacrifice', but in this translation it is sometimes rendered as 'oblation' or 'offering' or even as 'service'. It is an ancient term, used for religious rites as variable as shamans' sacrifices of animals, the elaborate uncooked food offerings of Confucians, grain and fruit offerings of Buddhists and the wine and food offerings of folk religion. It is etymologically related to the word for a secular 'festival'. In the bible it is the normal word for all kinds of sacrifice in both testaments. An invaluable contribution to Asian theology could be made by anyone who would study the use of *chesa* by Korean Christians. The concept of sacrifice involved is materially different from the concept rejected by evangelicals, and it is only the influence of western apologetics too literally translated that has led Protestant Koreans to avoid using the word. (Westernized theology has often read western meanings into Chinese terms selected by western missionaries to express basic Christian concepts, and thereby created subtle theological confusions in Korean minds.) If the caveat is borne in mind, it should be possible, whilst acknowledging the catholic tradition that has formed Korean Anglican usage, to understand the theology of this liturgy in a manner less offensive to evangelicals than this English translation may at first sight appear.

---

[1] [This is the Proper Preface for 'Any Saint' in Appendix C—Editor.]

[2] The English translation of **Kor1** which follows aims only at showing the content of the text to those who cannot read Korean. No attempt has been made to produce an English version suitable for public liturgical use. Such things as the frequently occurring Korean causative verb expressed by the pragmatic English 'to make (someone do)' are stiff; but literal renderings of this kind avoid ambiguities which are not in the Korean, and faithfully transmit the sense.

The liturgy of the departed requires a similar understanding. Deeply ingrained devotion to the departed is typical of Korean culture, and gives great importance to memorial services in all denominations. The essence of this devotion is affection for the dead, and it is a mistake to interpret it in terms of European Reformation categories. The distinctive feature of Korean prayers for the dead is hope of the Resurrection. Like the restrained but treasured devotion of Korean Anglicans to the Blessed Virgin, these prayers have for the laity a character which sets them outside English experience. Again, as Koreans express themselves in their own language, it becomes increasingly difficult, but also increasingly illuminating, to evaluate their theology in English terms.

Comparison with **Kor**

The most noticeable difference between **Kor** and **Kor1** (apart from the modernized language) is the increased weight apportioned to the liturgy of the Word. A revision of Morning and Evening Prayer is envisaged which will make possible a neater dovetailing of either of those services with the eucharist than the field-surgery implied in the opening instructions. (There is, for instance, the possibility of putting the collect at the beginning of the office.)

The notices, however, belong not to the service of the word, but to the activity of the congregation, so they have been detached from the sermon, and placed after the communion. This not only removes their distracting insertion between the reading and the exposition of scripture, but takes account of the almost universal Korean practice of lengthy notices by the churchwardens after the dismissal and the exit of the celebrant. Bringing parochial matters into close relation with the communion, and before the dismissal, puts the whole life of the assembly—including preparations for parish picnics and evangelistic visiting—into the context of the sacral assembly and the fellowship of the eucharistic meal.

The three canons are (1) Hippolytus meditated and then written in Korean; (2) a vigorous remodelling of the 1939 prayer (of the 1549 type, but with reversal of the former order of ideas in the last two sentences, and the interchanging of 'bread and wine' with 'bread of life and cup of salvation' in a manner felt by the Korean drafters to be a great improvement on the present text); and (3) a fresh Korean product with echoes from Byzantine liturgies, expressing a different form of eschatological devotion.

Seasonal varations are limited to collects, post-communion prayers, and proper prefaces. Hymns and readings are judged the most important variable parts of the service. These, like much else previously covered by explicit rubrics, including the choice of proper preface, have been intentionally left to the discretion of the celebrant.

A musical setting of the new texts to familiar melody-types has been prepared, and put in the leaflets for the people's use. These leaflets do not, however, contain the texts of collects, proper prefaces, canons or postcommunions, because it is hoped to wean the congregation from 'following the book'. For many people 'following the book' proves a distraction from listening to the prayers and readings and responding to or taking part in them.

The following details merit further comment.

1. The optional Greek form of the Kyrie is retained chiefly for the sake of familiar and well-loved musical settings.

2. Revised collects are in preparation. They retain the traditional collect form, but all are addressed to the Father. They are brief, emphasizing the function of the collect as a prayer for opening the assembly.

3. In the early years of the Korean Mission the sacrament was received in the hands by the faithful. This practice was discontinued here, as in some other regions, after the proliferation of accidents in crowded congregations with a low educational level. There are signs of a desire to restore the more typically Anglican practice.

4. The National Synod has approved a canon on the eucharist which provides for the bishop to license layfolk to assist in the distribution of Holy Communion.

THE KOREAN EXPERIMENTAL LITURGY 1973 (Kor1)

⟦This Liturgy was compiled in Korean, and an English cyclostyled version was prepared by the Liturgical Commission for the purposes of information. The text below is substantially that of the cyclostyled version, but it has been worked over by Bishop Richard Rutt, who contributes the introduction above, and he alone takes responsibility for this translation. The intention has been to render the meaning of the Korean text accurately. The numbering is original to the rite⟧

GENERAL INSTRUCTIONS ON CELEBRATION

⟦There follow 19 'General Instructions' under four headings: The Celebrants (1-6), Other Rites in Conjunction with the Eucharist (7-9), Ceremonial (10-15) and Holy Communion (16-19). The Instructions printed out below are nos. 6, 16, 17, 18 and 19⟧

When no priest is present a deacon may lead the service as far as the end of the Prayer of the Faithful, and then place the reserved sacrament on the altar before performing the rest of the rite from the Lord's Prayer to the end, except the breaking of the bread.

The faithful may receive holy communion either standing or kneeling.

It is permitted to receive the host in the hands if the circumstances are favourable.

Communion may be given by intinction if the diocesan bishop approves.

It is the solemn duty of the celebrant to see that sufficient bread and wine are consecrated. If there are many communicants additional wine may be consecrated in suitable flasks and used to replenish the chalice at the time of communion. If, however, additional consecration is necessary, the part of the eucharistic prayer from the memorial of the last supper to the end of the anamnesis in the first form of the canon should be said over the additional elements.

THE ORDER OF THE EUCHARIST

1 *OPENING PRAYERS*

1 *An ENTRANCE SONG may be sung.*

2 *At the discretion of the celebrant the KYRIES may be said or sung, (sixfold), in Korean or Greek; or they may be omitted.*

3 *The GLORIA IN EXCELSIS is said on all Sundays out of Lent, and on Christmas day. At other times it may be omitted.*
Glory to God . . . ⟦ICET 4⟧ . . . God the Father. Amen.

4 *THE SERVICE MAY START FROM THIS POINT*
The celebrating priest greets the people:
Priest The Lord be with you.
People **And with you.**

5 *After the greeting the priest may explain briefly the special intention of the service or the significance of the occasion.*

6 *Priest* Let us pray
He then recites a COLLECT. On weekdays the collect of the previous Sunday is said, but the priest may choose some other collect if he wishes. Only one collect is to be said.
The conclusion of the collect is: Through Jesus Christ our Lord, who is one God with the Father and the Holy Spirit.
People **Amen.**

2 *SERVICE OF THE WORD*

7 *A lesson from the OLD TESTAMENT may be read. The reader first says:*
The lesson from the Old Testament begins from . . . chapter . . . verse . . . and ends at verse . . .
At the end he says: This is the lesson from the Old Testament.
People **Thanks be to God.**
Silence may be kept for a while.

8 *A psalm or hymn may be said or sung.*

9 *The EPISTLE, or other scripture lesson in its place, is read. The reader first says:* The epistle begins from . . . chapter . . . verse . . . and ends at verse . . .
At the end he says: This is the lesson from the epistles (*or* scripture).
People **Thanks be to God.**
Silence may be kept for a while.

10 *A psalm or hymn may be sung.*

11 *A priest or deacon reads the GOSPEL. First he says:* Let us hear the Lord's words. *The people stand up. Then he says:* The gospel begins from . . . verse . . . chapter . . . and ends at verse . . .
People **Glory to God!**
At the end of the gospel the reader says: These are the Lord's words.
People **Praise be to Christ!**
Silence may be kept for a while.

12 *The SERMON is preached.*

13 *The CREED. The Nicene Creed is said on all Sundays and the great feast days. The Apostles' Creed may be said instead, except on Christmas day, Easter day, Whitsunday and Trinity Sunday.*
We believe in one God . . . ⟦ICET 3⟧ . . . **world to come. Amen. (and the Son)]** OM BRACKETS

I believe in God . . . ⟦ICET 2⟧ . . . **life everlasting. Amen.**

14 *THE PRAYER OF THE FAITHFUL*

Priest: Let us pray

The prayer is led by the priest or by one of the faithful. Any other form of prayer authorized by the diocesan bishop may be used instead of that provided here. At wedding and requiem masses and in services where the litany is used, the prayer of the faithful may be omitted.

a Let us pray for the Church of Christ

(*Specific intentions may be mentioned. The bishop of the diocese is always to be prayed for by name.*)

Lord, inspire your Church always with the grace of truth and unity, so that the faithful may live in love and peace with one another and show your glory to the world.

People **Lord, hear our prayer.**

b Let us pray for justice and peace throughout the world.

(*Specific intentions may be mentioned, including the Korean state, international affairs, social matters etc.*)

Lord, give peace to the world, put an end to wickedness and evil practices, keep us in truth and justice.

People **Lord, hear our prayer.**

c Let us pray for the poor and the sick and for all who are in trouble. (*Specific intentions may be mentioned.*)

Lord, comfort and save all who are worried and troubled in this ever-changing world.

People **Lord, hear our prayer.**

d (*Next any specific intention not included under the other headings may be mentioned.*)

Lord, search our wills, and grant that everything may be according to your will, not ours.

People **Lord, hear our prayer.**

e Let us pray for the dead. (*Individuals may be remembered by name.*)

Lord, grant mercy, light and peace to all the faithful dead who now await the resurrection.

People **Lord, hear our prayer.**

f Almighty Father, we pray with earnestness in the name of Jesus Christ our Lord.

People **Amen.**

3 *THE OBLATION*

15 *PREPARATION FOR THE OBLATION.* (*This may be omitted at the discretion of the priest.*)

Priest : Brothers and sisters, so that we may more worthily present a holy oblation, let us be at peace with one another and reflect upon our sinfulness.

Silence is kept for a while ; then the priest leads the people in saying :

I confess to Almighty God,

and to my brothers and sisters here,

that I have often sinned

in thought, word, and deed,

and often failed to fulfil my duties.

(*They strike the breast three times*)

It is my fault,

my own fault,

my own most grievous fault.

So I earnestly beg

that Mary Mother of God,

all the holy ones,

and my brothers and sisters here

will pray God for me.

Priest May Almighty God have mercy on us, forgive our sins, and bring us to eternal life.

16 *THE KISS OF PEACE.* (*This may be omitted at the discretion of the priest.*)

Priest The Lord's peace be with you.

People **And with you.**

Priest Let us share the blessing of peace.

Each person bows to those standing near him.

17 ## THE OFFERTORY

During the offertory a hymn or psalm may be sung. Representatives of the congregation bring bread, wine, money and other gifts to the altar. A priest or deacon prepares the bread and wine upon the altar. A little water is poured into the wine. When everything is ready the priest washes his hands.

18 ## THE EUCHARISTIC PRAYER

(*The priest chooses one of three forms provided.*)

Priest The Lord be with you.

People **And with you.**

Priest With hearts uplifted

People **to the Lord,**

Priest let us give thanks to God, our Lord.

People **It is right and proper.**

Priest. Almighty God, our Father, it is truly our proper duty to give you thanks through Jesus Christ our Lord, everywhere and always.

(*Here a proper preface is said.*)
⟦The Proper Prefaces, which are set out after the end of the service, are to be found here in Appendix C.⟧

Therefore with all heaven's angels and saints we praise your name with unceasing hymns:

Holy, holy, holy (*The congregation sings SANCTUS and BENEDICTUS*)

The celebrating priest chooses one of the three forms for the eucharistic prayer, and alone recites it.

(Form I)

Holy Father, listen to our prayers, accept our sacrifice of thanksgiving through Jesus Christ, and send your Holy Spirit so that this bread and wine become for us the body and blood of Christ.

(Form II)

Almighty Father, we thank you that you loved mankind so much that you sent your only son Jesus Christ into the world, to offer himself upon the cross as a perfect victim according to your will, to do away with all the sins of men.

He established this service in memory of his sacrifice and ordered us to observe it. Therefore, until he comes again, we offer this oblation of a sacred banquet as he commanded.

Merciful Father, bless this bread and wine by your Holy Spirit, so that they become for us, as Jesus promised, the body and blood of Christ.

(Form III)

Holy you are, Father, Almighty God! Holy you are, Only begotten Son of God, Jesus Christ! Holy you are, Holy Spirit of God! Man was made in God's image by you, O Father, so that he might be holy too, but he fell into sin. Yet of your great love you caused your only begotten Son Jesus Christ to be born of the virgin Mary to save us, and make us holy again by the Holy Spirit of glory.

(All three forms)

On the night before he suffered in joyful obedience to your will Christ took bread, offered a prayer of thanks, then broke the bread and distributed it to his disciples, saying, 'Take this and eat it. It is my body that is given for you. Do this ceremony in memory of me.' Then after the meal he took a cup, offered a prayer of thanks, and gave it to them saying: 'All of you, take this cup and drink from it. It is my blood of covenant, that I shed so that your sins and the sins of many may be forgiven.'

Therefore, we offer this bread and wine in memory of Jesus Christ's sufferings and resurrection, looking forward to the coming of his kingdom. Father, accept this oblation, and grant that all the faithful who partake in this holy act may become one with Christ through the power of the Holy Spirit.

Therefore we unworthy servants offer this bread and wine to you in memory of the sufferings, resurrection and ascension into heaven of Jesus Christ. Although our sins are so many that we have no right to offer you any sacrifice at all, do not reckon our merits, but accept the sacrifice of our obedience. Through the merits of Christ forgive our sins and the sins of all who receive this bread of life and cup of salvation, wherever they may be; clothe them with heavenly grace, make them one body with Jesus, and by the power of the Holy Spirit make us worthy to offer our souls and bodies as sacrifices to you.

Therefore till the Saviour comes again we unworthy servants offer this oblation of bread and wine as Christ commanded, in memory of his sufferings, resurrection and ascension. Praying in union with Mary, the mother of God, all the angels and all the saints of heaven and earth, we thank you for all the graces you have given us. Father, you who are love, accept our offering; send the Holy Spirit on this bread and wine to make them become the body and blood of Jesus Christ. Make all the faithful who eat this bread and drink this cup holy in body and soul; make them one in the mystical body of Christ; make them live holy lives to show your glory in this world, and enjoy the glory of participation in your godhead.

The prayer in all three forms then continues with the doxology on the next page, unless one of the special insertions is used.]

(One or more of the following three insertions may be used in any of the three forms at this point)

When there has been baptism or confirmation
Look especially upon those who have been born again and had their sins washed away by water and the Holy Spirit, and fulfil your grace in them through this holy communion.

at weddings
Look especially on *A.* and *B.* who have now become man and wife by exchanging marriage vows. Make them love one another as Christ loves his Church, and bring them to your eternal kingdom.

for the dead
Remember especially *A.* whom you have called from this world. Like Christ he (she) has died; like Christ make him (her) rise again from death.

(all three forms)
Almighty Father, all praise and glory is yours through Christ, with Christ, and in Christ, together with the Holy Spirit.

People **Amen.**

4 *COMMUNION*

19 *Priest* Let us pray as Christ taught us:
Our Father in heaven . . . ⟦ICET 1⟧ . . . deliver us from evil.
Priest Deliver us from all evil, Lord; save us from wickedness as we look forward to the return of our Saviour Jesus Christ, and keep us in peace, free from anxiety.
People **For the kingdom, the power and the glory are yours for ever. Amen.**

20 *The BREAD IS NOW BROKEN, during which time the AGNUS DEI is said or sung.*

21 *The priest holds the bread and cup aloft, facing the people, and says :*
The Lamb who takes away the sins of the world is here; happy they who are invited to this holy meal.
People **Lord I am not worthy to bear you within me. Speak only one word, and my soul will be healed.**

The celebrant receives the body and blood saying :
The holy body of Christ. Amen.
The precious blood of Christ. Amen.

The body and blood are distributed to the people. The priest or deacon who administers communion says to each communicant The holy body of Christ *or* The precious blood of Christ *and the communicant answers* **Amen.**

A psalm or hymn may be sung during the communion. When the communion is finished silence may be kept for a while. If nothing has been sung during the communion a song may be sung now.

When all have communicated the priests and deacons consume all that remains of the body and blood. The chalice is to be rinsed with water, but this may be done in the sacristy after the service.

22 *Priest* Let us pray
One of the prayers after communion is then said (see separate schedule[1])

5 *CLOSING CEREMONY*

23 *NOTICES are now given by the priest or churchwardens.*

24 *Priest* The Lord be with you
People **And with you.**
Priest May almighty God, Father, Son, and Holy Spirit, bless you.
People **Amen.**

Deacon or priest Let us go out and work for the Lord.
People **In the name of Christ. Amen.**

From the paschal vigil till Pentecost the final Amen is omitted and Alleluia, alleluia *is added to the last versicle and to its response.*

25 *A final hymn may be sung.*

[1] ⟦An appendix to the rite includes 25 different *PRAYERS AFTER COMMUNION*, all of which are brief and twelve of which are suited for use at the major seasons of the Church year, on festivals, or on special occasions such as weddings and funerals. The remaining thirteen are general prayers. Choice of prayer is at the celebrant's discretion. Virtually all have reference to the sacramental feeding just concluded—e.g. 5 (*Easter*) 'God, we have received the sacraments of the paschal mystery. Fill us with the Holy Spirit of love, and make us of one mind in that love.' 15 (*General*) 'God, we have received the bread of life and cup of salvation. What we have received with our mouths may we honour with pure hearts.'⟧

CHAPTER 23

THE HOLY CATHOLIC CHURCH OF JAPAN (NIPPON SEI KO KAI)

THE current eucharistic rite of the Anglican Church in Japan is the 1959 liturgy (**Jap**), which is printed in **LiE** pp.127-35 and is introduced and summarized in **MAL** pp.286-91. This rite remains the only legal usage of the Japanese Church. It is in classical Japanese (Bungotai), except for the rubrics, which are in modern language.

The rite has never been officially translated into English. The text in **LiE** was an unofficial one for which Bishop Viall was mainly responsible. However, in 1971 there was published by the Rev. C. L. Webber, Rector of St Alban's Church Tokyo, a booklet containing two English versions of **Jap**. The first is that in **LiE,** virtually *verbatim*. The second is a modern English rite, including the ICET texts (though not for the Agnus Dei, where the translation is more traditional). The translation of the Great Thanksgiving ('The Consecration') shows some freedom, at least when compared with the traditional language rite. The booklet remains a private production.

Also in 1971 the General Synod asked for a revision of the Prayer Book into a colloquial Japanese. The Committee on the Prayer Book then began work on the Daily Offices, and was not due to begin on the eucharist until after the Synod of May 1974.

PART VII
AUSTRALASIA

CHAPTER 24

THE CHURCH OF ENGLAND
IN AUSTRALIA

The Constitutional Position

THE Liturgical Commission of the Church of England in Australia, which had been set up by resolution of the General Synod in September 1966[1] with the tasks, *inter alia*, of 'carrying on the work of draft revision of the Book of Common Prayer' and of 'bringing to General Synod recommendations concerning Prayer Book revision and other liturgical matters', was reconstituted by canon of General Synod in September 1969 with the additional function of 'undertaking the preparation and printing of draft forms of service for use in accordance with Section 4 of the Constitution'.

The constitutional context within which liturgical change may take place in Australia has not itself altered since the present Constitution came into effect in January 1962. The 1662 Prayer Book is still, with the 39 Articles, 'the authorised standard of doctrine and worship in this Church', and no forms of worship authorised under the Constitution, or alterations in such forms, may contravene 'any principle of doctrine or worship laid down in such standard'. The General Synod has not yet, however, taken any steps to order forms of worship by canon. The continued use of the 1662 Book depends on Section 71 of the Constitution, under which the law of the Church as it was before 1962 remains in force until varied under the Constitution. A proviso of Section 4, however, gives a diocesan bishop power to permit deviations from 'the existing order of service' under certain conditions, and it is in terms of this proviso that all trial use of services and other deviations since 1962 have taken place. There was not at first universal agreement that a whole new service, like *A Modern Liturgy* (**Aus2**) or **Eng2**, could properly be regarded as a 'deviation from the existing order of service', but the General Synod's canon, authorising the Commission to produce draft forms of service 'for use in accordance with Section 4', endorsed

---

[1] [This is not the 'Prayer Book Commission' which produced **Aus1** and **Aus2** (printed out in **MAL**, pp.305-20). That Commission was appointed in 1962 and superseded in 1966 by the 'Liturgical Commission' (see p.316 below). The contributor, Bishop Robinson, was on both Commissions.—Editor.]

the view that such new services could be regarded as 'deviations' within the terms of the Constitution.[1]

In reviewing its task, and to set itself clear objectives in relation to the ultimate purpose of liturgical revision, the Commission at its meeting in May 1971 decided to 'make it its main aim to prepare a Book of Common Prayer for presentation to General Synod in 1977 for enactment (if deemed expedient) by canon as 'an order of service' of the Church of England in Australia'. The Commission's view was that the Church, having taken to itself in its Constitution 'plenary authority to order its forms of worship', should be encouraged to proceed to do so in the proper canonical manner as soon as it was reasonably sure of its mind, and should not let the period of provisional deviations drift on indefinitely. It was not the Commission's aim to bring the process of revision to an end by means of an enacted Prayer Book, but to put the further process on to a more responsible and controllable basis, related to a definite set of forms of worship which could be said to be 'an order of service' of the Church in terms of the Constitution.

It was envisaged that the book would contain revised forms of all the main Prayer Book services, with more radical alternative services in some cases. In particular, it was envisaged that the 1662 Communion service would appear in a revised version, together with a new alternative 'Service of Holy Communion for Australia, 1977'. This stated aim was basically in line with the recommendations of the original Prayer Book Commission (1962-6) that revision should proceed along both 'conservative' and 'radical' lines, and the work produced by the Liturgical Commission since 1966 has in fact exemplified the aim. On the one hand it has produced a further minor recension of the 1662 Communion service (1971), followed by a more thoroughgoing modernization (**Aus1A**) as part of *Sunday Services Revised* published in December 1972. On the other hand it has produced *A Service of Holy Communion for Australia,* 1969 (**Aus3**) and *A Service of Holy Communion for Australia* 1973 (**Aus4**), which are, so to speak, counterparts of **Eng2** and **Eng3**.

The diocesan bishop's power under Section 4 of the Constitution to permit 'such deviations from the existing order of service, not contravening any principle of doctrine or worship as aforesaid, as shall be submitted to him by the incumbent and churchwardens of a parish' is limited by the words 'until other order be taken by canon made in

---

[1] For fuller background information see **MAL,** pp.298-9.

accordance with this Constitution'. It was widely understood that this 'taking other order' had reference to the ordering of forms of worship for the Church (as envisaged in the main clause of this Section 4, to which reference has been made above) by revision or replacement of 'the existing order of service'. On this understanding, the deviations proviso was in its nature a temporary expedient which the canonical ordering of forms of service would automatically bring to an end. Indeed, it was precisely this expectation which influenced some in the first General Synod of 1962 to propose the cautious terms of reference of the Prayer Book Commission, namely 'to explore the possibilities of revision of the Book of Common Prayer, and to report to the next session of Synod'. Some expressed the fear that *any* canonical enactment relating to liturgy, even the change of name of a member of the royal family, or provision for lay assistance at the communion, would, being 'other order taken by canon' in the area covered by Section 4, automatically bring the deviations proviso to an end, and with it all opportunity for further experiment, unless otherwise specifically provided for.

Uncertainty as to the limitation of the proviso was having an unsettling effect on the Commission as it planned its work, so during 1972 it sponsored the reference of certain questions to the Appellate Tribunal, which has power to determine questions of interpretation of the Constitution. The Tribunal, in its ruling of 18 September 1972, gave the words, 'until other order be taken by canon,' an interpretation different from that usually canvassed, for it disconnected them from the context of 'order of service' and gave them the meaning, 'until a canon be made expressly terminating the bishop's power to permit deviations'. The effect of this ruling is that the deviations proviso will remain in force notwithstanding any canon which might authorise new services or even a complete new Prayer Book.

It is hard to say what may prove to be the effect of the Tribunal's ruling on the course of revision. To bring in new services by canon would still have the advantage of allowing their use in any parish without it needing to apply for them as a deviation. But procedures for passing canons in matters like liturgy are extraordinarily difficult in Australia, and such canons only operate, when passed, in such dioceses as accept them. It is possible, therefore, that the present situation will continue indefinitely, with all changes—at least all legal changes!—being made, parish by parish, under the proviso of Section 4. Only if new services, whether conservative or radical, establish themselves nearly universally

by their excellence *in actual usage* can it be expected that the Church
will exercise its authority to order its form of worship by means of a
canon.

Conservative Revision (**Aus1A**)

When the Commission decided in May 1971 to prepare two forms of
Holy Communion for inclusion in a Prayer Book by 1977, it was
considered that at least one further type of each should be published as
soon as possible, to allow maximum use and comment. The preparation
of a draft of a revised 1662 order was thereupon committed to Brother
Gilbert Sinden, s.s.m., of St. Michael's House, South Australia, and
Canon Donald Robinson of Moore College, Sydney, as a first step to
what a viable, up-to-date 1662 service might look like. The object was
to keep 'the authorised standard', with its doctrinal and structural
strengths, in acceptable use. There was reason to believe that a great
many parishes would not want anything beyond 1662 in a more or less
modern dress. The modern translation of Evening Prayer put out by
the Church Pastoral-Aid Society had proved acceptable in many
parishes, and Sinden and Robinson had before them the Latimer
Monograph on *The Service of Holy Communion and its Revision*[1] which
argued cogently for 'bringing 1662 into the twentieth century'. Already
in 1971 the Commission had published a form of 1662 which made a
few more verbal adjustments to **Aus1** (see **MAL**, pp.305-10). Examples
of the changes are *them that/those who, unto/to, hid/hidden, in the same
night that/on the night, vouchsafe to/graciously.* 'O' was omitted,
except where rhythm seemed to demand it. An additional rubric
allowed for suitable psalms and hymns at various points, and for a
hymn instead of the Gloria in excelsis. The only change of substance was
the substitution of 'gifts' for 'creatures' in the Prayer of Consecration.
This recension was not widely used, or even noticed, though the exercise proved useful to the Commission. It was realised almost as soon as
the order was published that the tide had turned in favour of 'you' in
address to God, and it was also recognised that, once this change was
agreed on, a more extensive recension would be necessary. Such was
put in hand at once, in accordance with the decision mentioned above,
and *Sunday Services Revised,* containing **Aus1A** along with Morning
and Evening Prayer and the Litany, appeared in December 1972. It

---

[1] Ed. R. T. Beckwith and J. E. Tiller (Marcham Manor Press 1972).

was published for the Commission by the General Board of Religious Education in a well-designed octavo booklet of 52 pages.

The style of **Aus1A,** though often reproducing 1662, is markedly less heavy and honorific, and the frequency of words like 'holy' is reduced. Many phrases are retained intact ('not weighing our merits, but pardoning our offences'), though others are translated ('satisfied through your favour and heavenly blessing') or streamlined ('oblation and satisfaction' disappears). 'Mystical body' remains through sheer inability to agree on the right modern expression, and 'this our sacrifice' testifies to the unwillingness of the one party to drop 'this', or the other party to drop 'our'! Some flexibility is allowed in regard to omissions and transpositions, notably at the introduction to The Lord's Supper, but the rationale of 1662 remains paramount in the main text. There is no ghost of the 'Interim Rite'. The 1662 structure is emphasised by making a clear break between the Intercession and the Exhortation, with the latter (greatly reduced in length) restored to its logical role of setting the direction for the second part of the service. There are two main headings, 'The Word and the Prayers' and 'The Lord's Supper', but individual items are mostly given a name in the margin. Apart from the added provision for an Old Testament lesson, and a psalm, hymn, or canticle between readings, the main departure from the structure of 1662 is that the priest places the bread and wine on the table before the Exhortation rather than before the Intercession (though a note allows the original order if desired), in accordance with the 'break' between the two parts of the order. Another change is the addition of the words 'takes the bread and wine' in the rubric before the Prayer of Consecration, which, with the new opening formula, 'All glory to you, our heavenly Father', provides a 'taking' and a 'thanksgiving' by the priest in addition to the imitative gestures of the manual acts at the recitation of the institution narrative. 'Creatures' and 'gifts' are combined in the phrase 'these gifts of your creation, this bread and wine'.

To judge by its sales, **Aus1A** has been an initial success, especially in areas where the 1662 service has always held its own (and where Morning and Evening Prayer are still congregational Sunday services). The feeling among members of the Commission is that **Aus1A** may well, with only slight further modification, prove to be the form in which the 1662 order will take its place in a 1977 Prayer Book.

Radical Revision (**Aus3** *and* **Aus4**)

A Modern Liturgy (**Aus2**), published in 1966, proved a useful catalyst in the Australian Church. It was used experimentally in most dioceses and was much commented on. Some of its features, notably the position of the Lord's Prayer at the end of the Intercession and the separate thanksgivings for the bread and wine, have held their place in both its successors, not to mention some of its language. At first the Commission intended to make specific amendments to it, but the 'draftmaster' for the revision now became the Reverend Philip Grundy, and a new start was made using as a basis a service which had itself been influenced by **Aus2,** the St Philip's Liturgy, devised in the parish of St Philip in Canberra.

Aus3 was in many ways less radical than **Aus2.** The Collect for Purity, the Decalogue, Humble Access, and a more conventional canon were restored. The text of the Gloria, Creed, and Lord's Prayer was that of ICET (as at April 1969). But the order was shorter and more manageable, and the language simpler and more direct. An (optional) Exhortation was retained from **Aus2,** which evoked strong reactions, favourable and unfavourable. **Aus2**'s separate thanksgivings for bread and cup were incorporated into **Aus3**'s main prayer, which was given the flavour of a 'grace' for 'food for the needs of men' by the deliberate adoption of an introductory rubric modelled on that of the *Apostolic Tradition* of Hippolytus, 'The Priest shall take the bread and wine, and shall say this Thanksgiving'. The Commission was aware that this prayer contained some duplication of ideas, but considered it important not to delay the publication of its thinking thus far. In this it was particularly encouraged by two distinguished observers who attended its 1969 meeting, the Roman Catholic Archbishop of Hobart, Dr. Guilford Young, and the Congregationalist scholar Dr. Harold Leatherland.

Aus3 was published for the Commission by the General Board of Religious Education in a small edition about the size of **Eng2.** The rubrics were printed in green and the people's part was in bold type. The service was widely used and proved generally acceptable. There was some evangelical objection to the (optional) words in the Intercession, 'we leave in your keeping N.', as being tantamount to a prayer for the repose of the departed, although this inference was denied by others; and the Archbishop of Sydney would not permit the operation of the rubric—borrowed from **Eng2**—which had been interpreted in

England as allowing reservation of the sacrament. The Bishop of Adelaide, for his part, would not allow the use of the Prayer of Humble Access in which the adverb 'so' had been transferred to what the Commission considered to be the correct grammatical position in modern idiomatic English. And there were other queries. Two modifications were in fact made in printings of **Aus3** from 1971 onwards. In the words of distribution 'strengthen you' was bracketed for optional omission; and, for an additional consecration, the words of institution could be used along with the adding of other bread and wine to what remained, the latter on its own being considered a possible contravention of a principle of the Prayer Book (and certainly of Canon 21 of 1603).

Philip Grundy left the Commission in 1971, and his place was taken by Dr. Evan Burge of Canberra, who was given the role of 'draftmaster' for the next stage of revision. His work in collating reports on **Aus3** and in preparing, and securing comments from consultants on, drafts for **Aus4,** was prodigious. There was also, at this stage, the use in Australia of **Eng2** to be evaluated. It enjoyed fairly wide popularity, some 'catholic' parishes in particular preferring it to **Aus3**; but only one or two parishes in the largely evangelical diocese of Sydney used it, the Archbishop having permitted it only with half a dozen specific modifications. When the report containing the proposed Series 3 service appeared in 1971, the Commission reckoned that certain of its features were likely to commend themselves. Therefore, in pursuing its own task of producing a service for Australia, the Commission took particular account of the English services, including the final form of **Eng3**, which became available by January 1973. Where **Eng3** and **Aus4** invite comparison but do not concur,[1] it can almost always be assumed that the Australian Commission has after careful deliberation and consultation preferred its own view or style.

Like **Aus3**, **Aus4** was meant to be an improved version of its predecessor, but turned out to be a fresh composition, although the continuity of thinking can easily be perceived. Once more there are trends in a conservative direction. The Collect for Purity, and Humble Access, are more traditional in language (allowing in the latter the restoration of 'so to eat . . .' without conceding the contention that the more modern wording in **Aus3** had implied a change of meaning); the penitential section is restored to the preparation for communion;

---

[1] Some comparison of **Aus4** with **Eng3** (in both original and final forms) can be made by use of the table of eucharistic prayers in Appendix F.

proper prefaces are restored, **Aus2** and **Aus3** having preferred an invariable preface; the 1662 words of distribution are primary, which has the effect of determining the sense in which the shorter alternative form is to be understood; the Lord's Prayer is restored (alternatively) to its 1662 position after communion; and the 1662 blessing is restored. Some will think that too much provision for alternative positions is allowed. The reasons for it lies in the variety of strongly expressed preferences of which the Commission was made aware during the process of consultation. It is hoped that trial use may reduce these alternatives by 1977, and at least it has been possible, with an octavo page and good design, to make the items accessible to the eye without turning a page, when taken in an alternative position.

A supplement of 'Canticles and Hymns' includes Te Deum, Benedictus, and Venite, to encourage their use in the first part of the service. The Intercession retains 'through Jesus Christ our Lord' (from **Aus2** and **Aus3**) as the people's response, and the Lord's Prayer as its conclusion, but with an alternative conclusion. The reference to the departed conforms in structure to the prayer in the 1662 burial office, with some wording from a petition suggested by the English Archbishops' Commission on Christian Doctrine (*Prayer and the Departed,* S.P.C.K. 1971, p.51), which 'asks for such things as we are scripturally persuaded are in accordance with God's will and have not already been granted'. The Exhortation has gone, under strong pressure from those who dislike being exhorted, but the disciplinary note is retained among the sentences which begin the Preparation for the Lord's Supper. In the Thanksgiving the seasonal prefaces are inserted at different places according to their appropriateness, and to avoid confusion the whole of the opening section of the prayer is set out afresh for each group, but not on the main page. The Thanksgiving retains from **Aus2** and **Aus3** the separate 'blessings' for the bread and the cup, but with the appropriate words of institution attached to each. There was some misgiving on the Commission at the length of the section which intervenes between these 'blessings' and the distribution, but a note allows that 'the consecrated elements may be distributed separately after the appropriate words of institution'. The sacramental idiom keeps fairly closely to that of 1662, and the sacrificial terminology in regard both to praise and to the worshippers themselves follows the communion. The notion of 'consecration by contagion', when more bread and wine is called for, with which **Aus3** toyed, has been abandoned, and the appropriate 'blessing', with words of institution, as in

Aus2, is used. The **Aus3** reference to consecrated bread and wine 'which is not required for the purposes of communion' has been dropped.

Aus4 was published on 1 September 1973, the first production of the Commission to appear under its own imprimatur as publisher. It is handsomely printed by the Lutheran Publishing House, Adelaide. Rubrics are red, and the people's part is in bold type. The octavo page allows greater clarity in layout of the main sections of the service. The first printing of 50,000 was more ambitious than anything yet attempted, but it was mostly sold within the first month.

THE AUSTRALIAN 1662 RECENSION MODERNIZED 1972 (Aus1A)

[The numbering here is original to the rite. The asterisk before some numbers indicates that the section is optional, following a convention in the published rite].

THE ORDER FOR THE HOLY COMMUNION THE WORD AND THE PRAYERS

1 *The people kneeling, this prayer of PREPARATION is said by the priest, or the priest and people together.*

Almighty God . . . [CF 1] . . . Lord. **Amen.**
hid] hidden

2 *The priest recounts the COMMANDMENTS (or the alternative following) ; and the people ask God's forgiveness for their past transgressions, and the grace to keep God's laws in the future.*

God spoke these words, and said:

I am the LORD your God. You shall have no other gods but me.

This response is made by the people after each commandment except the last. **Lord, have mercy upon us: and strengthen our will to keep this law.**

You shall not make a carved image for yourself nor the likeness of anything in the heavens above, or on

The commandments may also be read as a continuous whole without the responses except that which follows the tenth commandment.

the earth below, or in the waters under the earth. You shall not bow down to them or worship them.
[For I, the LORD your God, am a jealous God. I punish the children for the sins of their fathers to the third and fourth generations of those who hate me. But I keep faith with thousands, with those who love me and keep my commandments.]

You shall not make wrong use of the name of the LORD your God.
[The LORD will not leave unpunished the man who misuses his name.]

Remember to keep the sabbath day holy.
[You have six days to labour and do all your work. But the seventh day is a sabbath of the LORD your God; that day you shall not do any work, you, your son or daughter, your slave or your slave-girl, your cattle or the alien within your gates; for in six days the LORD made heaven and earth, the sea, and all that is in them, and the on seventh day he rested. Therefore the LORD blessed the sabbath day and declared it holy.]

Honour your father and your mother
[that you may live long in the land which the LORD your God is giving you].

You shall not commit murder.

You shall not commit adultery.

You shall not steal.

You shall not give false evidence against your neighbour.

You shall not covet your neighbour's house; you shall not covet your neighbour's wife, [his slave, his slave-girl, his ox, his ass,] or anything that belongs to him.

Lord, have mercy upon us; and write your law on our hearts by your Spirit.

OR   Our Lord Jesus Christ said:
                       Love the Lord your God with all your heart and
                       with all your soul and with all your mind. This is the
                       great and first commandment. And the second is this:
                       love your neighbour as yourself.
                       **Lord, have mercy upon us; and write your law
                       on our hearts by your Spirit.**
OR on weekdays   Lord, have mercy upon us.
                       Christ, have mercy upon us.
                       Lord, have mercy upon us.

3 *The priest says* Let us pray.
                       The COLLECT of the day.

*4 *The people sit; a lesson from the OLD TESTAMENT may be read.*

*5 *A psalm, hymn, or canticle may be sung between the readings.*

6 *The EPISTLE, or lesson from the New Testament, is read.*

7 *The people stand for the GOSPEL, which may be introduced:*
                       The holy gospel is written in the . . . chapter of the
                       Gospel according to Saint . . ., beginning at the
                       . . . verse.
                       [Glory to you, Lord Christ.
After the   This is the gospel of the Lord.
gospel   **Praise to you, Lord Christ.]**

*8 *The SERMON may be preached here, or after the creed.*

*9 *The NICENE CREED is said or sung, all standing. It may be omitted
on weekdays.*

[1]We believe . . . [[MAL CF 6 with variants]] . . . world to come. Amen.
I]We THROUGHOUT
**God of . . . very God] God from God, light from light, true God from
    true God
By whom]through whom
Ghost] Spirit TWICE
And was crucified] he was crucified
And the third] on the third
And ascended] he ascended
sitteth on] is seated at
with glory] in glory
quick] living
Whose kingdom shall] and his kingdom will
proceedeth] proceeds
believe one] believe in one**

---

[1] The plural 'we believe' is original to the Nicene Creed, which was a
corporate expression of faith; while the singular is appropriate in the Apostles'
Creed, which is the act of personal commitment at baptism. In this service,
however, the Nicene Creed may be said in the singular.

10 *The SERMON is preached here if it has not been preached earlier.*

11 *The OFFERTORY SENTENCE*

The priest reads one or more of these, or other appointed verses from the Bible. If there is a collection, this is brought to the priest, who places it on the holy table.

[The Offertory Sentences which follow are to be found in Appendix B.]

12 *The priest may bid special prayers and thanksgivings, and then says*
The INTERCESSION, the people kneeling

Let us pray for all people and for the church throughout the world.

Almighty and everliving God, we are taught by your holy word to offer intercessions and thanksgivings for all men; we ask you in your mercy to receive our prayers [and to accept our gifts].[1]

We pray that you will lead all nations in the way of righteousness, and guide their rulers to wise decisions and just actions for the welfare and peace of all. Bless especially your servant Elizabeth our Queen, and her ministers and parliaments, that by them we may be godly and quietly governed in this land. Grant that the judges and magistrates may impartially administer justice, restraining wickedness and vice, and maintaining goodness and your true religion.

Fill your church throughout the world with the spirit of truth, unity, and peace, and grant that all who confess your name may agree in the truth of your word and live in unity and godly love.

Give grace, heavenly Father, to all bishops and other ministers [especially N. our bishop], that by their life and teaching they may declare your true, life-giving word, and rightly administer your holy sacraments. And to all your people give your heavenly grace, especially to this congregation, that they may receive your word with reverent and obedient hearts, and serve you in holiness and righteousness all the days of their life.

And we pray you, of your goodness, Lord, to comfort and sustain all who are in trouble, sorrow, need, sickness, or any other adversity. And we also bless your holy name for all your servants who have died in the faith of Christ. Give us grace to follow their good examples, that with them we may share in your eternal kingdom.

[1] [The following note appears in the margin of the original text: *If there is no collection of gifts, the words in brackets are omitted.*]

Grant this, Father, for Jesus Christ's sake, our only mediator and advocate, who lives and reigns with you in the unity of the Holy Spirit, one God, now and for ever.

Amen.

A hymn may be sung here

If there is no communion, the service concludes here with the Lord's Prayer, other authorised prayers at the discretion of the minister, and the grace or the blessing.

NOTE. *Instead of proceeding with §13-19, The Lord's Supper, in the order of sections as printed, the following order of sections may be used :*

§16 'Hear the words of assurance . . .'

§13 (final paragraph) 'Draw near to him by faith . . .'

§14 **'Almighty God, Father of our Lord Jesus Christ . . .'**

§15 'Almighty God our heavenly Father . . .'

*§18 'We do not presume . . .'
[The peace of the Lord be always with you.
And also with you.]

§17 [The Lord be with you.
And also with you.]
'Lift up your hearts . . .'

§19 'All glory to you . . .'

THE LORD'S SUPPER

13 *The priest places on the holy table the bread and wine for the communion and reads this EXHORTATION*

Brothers and sisters in Christ, [we who come to receive the holy communion of the body and blood of our Saviour Christ can come only because of his great love for us. For, although we are completely undeserving of his love, yet in order to raise us from the darkness of death to everlasting life as God's sons and daughters, our Saviour Christ humbled himself to share our life and to die for us on the cross. In remembrance of his death, and as a pledge of his love, he has instituted this holy sacrament which we are now to share.]

Those who would eat the bread and drink the cup of the Lord must examine themselves, and truly and earnestly repent of their sins. They must love their neighbours, and intend to lead a new life, following the commandments of God, and walking in his holy ways. Above all they must give him thanks for his love towards us in Christ Jesus.

Draw near to him by faith, therefore, and take this holy sacrament to strengthen you; but first, examine yourselves and make a humble confession of your sins to almighty God.

14 *Silence may be kept.*

All then say this GENERAL CONFESSION, kneeling

Almighty God, Father of our Lord Jesus Christ,
maker of all things, judge of all men,
we acknowledge the many sins we have committed against you.
The guilt is ours and we deserve your judgment.
We are heartily sorry for all our misdoings;
the remembrance of them grieves us;
and the burden of them is intolerable.
Have mercy upon us, most merciful Father.
For your Son our Lord Jesus Christ's sake
forgive us all that is past,
and grant that we may serve and please you,
living a new life to your glory;
through Jesus Christ our Lord. Amen.

15 *The priest or, if he is present, the bishop stands and pronounces this ABSOLUTION facing the people*

Almighty God our heavenly Father, who has promised forgiveness to all who confess their sins and turn to him in faith: have mercy on you; pardon and deliver you from all your sins; confirm and strengthen you in all goodness; and keep you in eternal life; through Jesus Christ our Lord.

Amen.

16 *THE WORDS OF ASSURANCE*

The priest says one or more of these sentences

Hear the words of assurance for those who truly turn to Christ:

Jesus said: Come . . . [CF 4] . . . he is the perfect offering for our

sins, and not for ours only but also for the sins of the whole world.
1 *John* 2:1, 2

Hear what . . . says] OM TWICE
anyone does sin] anyone sins

17 *The priest begins the THANKSGIVING AND COMMUNION*

Lift up your hearts.
We lift them to the Lord.

Let us give thanks to the Lord our God.
It is right to give him thanks.

It is our duty and our joy that we should at all times and in all places give thanks to you, Lord, holy Father, mighty Creator, and eternal God.

On certain days, a special preface (see pages . . . [i.e. after no. 24]) is said here.
[The Proper Prefaces which come after the service are to be found in Appendix C.]

The priest, or the priest and the people together, say

Therefore with angels and archangels, and with the whole company of heaven, we proclaim your great and glorious name, for ever praising you and saying:

Holy, holy, holy Lord of hosts,
heaven and earth are full of your glory.
Glory to you, Lord God most high.

18 *The priest, or the priest and people together, say*

We do not presume . . . [CF 6] . . . he in us. **Amen.**
this your table] OM this

19 *The priest takes the bread and wine and says this PRAYER OF CONSECRATION*

> All glory to you, our heavenly Father, for in your tender mercy you gave your only Son Jesus Christ to suffer death on the cross for our redemption. By offering himself there once for all, he made a full, perfect, and sufficient sacrifice for the sins of the whole world; and he instituted, and in his holy gospel commanded us to continue, a perpetual memory of his precious death until his coming again.
> Hear us, merciful Father, and grant that we who receive these gifts of your creation, this bread and

wine, according to your Son our Saviour Jesus Christ's holy institution, in remembrance of his death and passion, may be partakers of his most blessed body and blood;

1 *here the priest takes the bread in his hands*

For on the night he was betrayed he took bread[1], and when he had given you thanks, he broke it[2]; he gave it to his disciples saying[3], 'Take, eat; this is my body which is given for you; do this in remembrance of me'.

2 *he breaks the bread*

3 *he lays his hand on the bread*

4 *he takes the cup or cups in his hands*

Likewise after supper he took the cup[4], and when he had given you thanks, he gave it to them saying[5], 'Drink from this, all of you; for this is my blood of the new covenant, which is poured out for you and for many for the remission of sins; do this, as often as you drink it, in remembrance of me'.

5 *he lays his hand on the cup or cups*

All answer   **Amen.**

20 *THE COMMUNION*

After receiving the sacrament in both kinds himself, the priest distributes it similarly to the other communicants: first to any bishops, priests, and deacons, who are present; and then to the other communicants; into their hands.

When he gives the bread he says

The body . . . ⟦CF 7(a)⟧ . . . thanksgiving.

When he gives the cup he says

The blood . . . ⟦CF 7(b)⟧ . . . thankful.

21 *When all have communicated, a silence may be kept.*

Then the priest says Let us pray.

Our Father . . . ⟦ICET 1⟧ . . . **now and for ever. Amen.**

holy] hallowed
Do not . . . test] Lead us not into temptation

22 *The priest continues with this PRAYER OF SELF-OFFERING.*

Lord and heavenly Father, we your servants entirely desire that, of your fatherly goodness, you would accept this our sacrifice of praise and thanksgiving. Grant that, by the merits and death of your Son Jesus Christ, and through faith in his blood, we and your whole church may receive forgiveness for our sins, and all other benefits of his passion.

And here we offer ourselves to you, as a reasonable, holy, and living sacrifice, praying that all we who share in this holy communion may be satisfied through your favour and heavenly blessing.

And although we are unworthy, through our many sins, to offer you any sacrifice, yet be pleased to accept this, the duty and service we owe, not weighing our merits, but pardoning our offences; through Jesus Christ our Lord, by whom and with whom, in the unity of the Holy Spirit, all honour and glory are yours, Father of all, now and for ever. **Amen.**

AND/OR this prayer

Eternal Father, we who have received these holy mysteries, according to our Saviour's word, heartily thank you for feeding us with the spiritual food of his precious body and blood. We thank you for assuring us in this way of your favour and goodness towards us; that we are true members of the mystical body of your Son, united in the blessed company of all faithful people; and that we are also heirs, through hope, of your eternal kingdom, by the merits of the suffering and death of your dear Son.

And, Father, we pray that by your grace we may continue in that holy fellowship and do all such good works as you have prepared for us to walk in; through Jesus Christ our Lord, to whom with you and the Holy Spirit be all honour and glory, now and for ever. **Amen.**

23 *This HYMN OF PRAISE (Gloria in excelsis).*
   Glory to God . . . [ICET 4] **. . . the Father. Amen.**

24 *The Priest lets the people depart with this BLESSING*
   The peace . . . [CF 9] . . . always. **Amen.**
   among] amongst

SPECIAL PREFACES TO THE THANKSGIVING

[Eight proper prefaces which are printed here are to be found in Appendix C.]

ADDITIONAL NOTES AND DIRECTIONS

[There are three notes here relating to Holy Communion. The first permits the priest to begin the service at the prayer desk; the second directs consumption of the remains, as in **Aus1** no. 36; the third permits the use of the exhortations from the Book of Common Prayer.]

PERMITTED VARIATIONS AT THE HOLY COMMUNION

1 *Suitable psalms or hymns may be sung at the beginning of The Holy Communion; between the readings; during the collection; when the bread and wine are brought to the holy table; during The Communion; and at the end of the service.*

2 *The Old Testament lesson and the epistle are announced,* 'A/The lesson from... chapter... beginning at verse...'. *The reader may conclude either* 'Here ends the lesson' *or* 'This is the word of the Lord'. *If the latter is said, the congregation may respond,* **'Thanks be to God'.**

3 *The reader may preface the announcement of the gospel with the salutation,* 'The Lord be with you', *to which the people respond,* **'And also with you'.**

4 *The sermon may be omitted on weekdays.*

5 *The priest may place the bread and wine for the communion on the Lord's table after §11 instead of at §13.*

6 *Formal notices may be given before the sermon, or after the Nicene Creed, or after the intercession.*

7 *At the Communion,*
in giving the bread, the priest may say,
'The body of Christ keep you in eternal life'
or, 'Take and eat: the body of Christ strengthen you';
in giving the cup, the priest may say,
'The blood of Christ keep you in eternal life',
or, 'Drink from this: the blood of Christ strengthen you';
and the communicants may answer, **'Amen'.**
If the priest uses these short forms,
either he must, before receiving the sacrament himself, say to the congregation,
'Come, let us take this holy sacrament of the body and blood of Christ in remembrance that he died for us, and feed on him in our hearts by faith with thanksgiving';
or, before he distributes the communion, he must read the forms in §20 to the congregation.

General Note: Except where indicated in these Notes, in the forms of service in this book, or in accordance with deviations permitted in particular parishes by authority under The Constitution of The Church of England in Australia, the rubrics set out in The Book of Common Prayer of 1662 (including the declaration on kneeling) apply in the conduct of these services.

THE AUSTRALIAN EXPERIMENTAL
LITURGY 1969 (Aus3)

[The numbering here is original to the rite. *P.* Denotes words to be said by the presiding priest or bishop. *M.* Denotes words which may be said by another minister or ministers. ★ Denotes a section that may be omitted. It is understood that postures are optional—hence brackets here].

A SERVICE OF HOLY COMMUNION

At the entry of the ministers the people stand.

★1 Psalm or hymn.

 2 *P.* The God of peace be with you;
The grace of Christ be with us all.
[*Kneel*]

 3 *P.* Let us pray.
Almighty God, to whom the secrets of our hearts are known; purify our thoughts by your Holy Spirit, so that we may truly love you and worthily praise your holy name; through Christ our Lord. Amen.

★4 either

P. God spoke all these words . . .
[CF 2 slightly altered] . . .
neighbour's.
After each commandment, the people may respond:
Lord, have mercy on us, and incline our hearts to keep this law.
and after the last commandment they shall say:
Lord, have mercy on us, and write all these laws in our hearts, we beseech you.

or

P. Lord Jesus, who came to call sinners to repentance,
have mercy on us.
P. Lord Jesus, sent to heal those who are burdened in soul,
have mercy on us.
P. Lord Jesus, now seated at the Father's right hand to intercede for us,
have mercy on us.

 5 *P.* In repentance and faith, let us confess our sins.
**Most merciful God, our heavenly Father,
we confess that we have sinned against you,
through our own fault,
in thought, word and deed,
and in what we have left undone;
we have not loved you with our whole heart;**

we have not loved our neighbours as ourselves;
for your Son our Lord Jesus Christ's sake,
forgive us all that is past,
and strengthen us to love and obey you
in newness of life,
for the glory of your name. Amen.

The Priest, or Bishop if present, shall say:

P. Almighty God, who has promised forgiveness to all who truly repent, of his great mercy grant you pardon and release from all your sins, the assurance of his love, and strength to do his will; through Jesus Christ our Lord.

Amen.

6 *P.* Let us pray.

The collect(s) appointed for the day.

[*Stand*]

*7 *This hymn, or another hymn of praise:*

Glory to God . . . ⟦ICET 4⟧ . . . **the Father. Amen.**

⟦This follows the '1969' variants in the *apparatus* to ICET 4⟧

THE MINISTRY OF GOD'S WORD

[*Sit*]

*8 *The lesson from the Old Testament. The reading may conclude with the words:*

M. This is the word of the Lord.

Thanks be to God.

 * *An appointed psalm.*

10 *The Epistle or Lesson which may conclude:*

M. This is the word of the Lord.

Thanks be to God.

[*Stand*]

*11 *A psalm, hymn or canticle.*

12 *The Gospel, which may be introduced thus:*

M. The Gospel of our Lord Jesus Christ, according to N., [*chapter . . . , verse . . .].

Glory to you, Lord Christ.

After the Gospel:

M. This is the word of the Lord.

Praise to you, Lord Christ.

[*Sit*]

★13 *The Sermon.*

[Stand]

★14 *On Sundays and holy days there shall be said or sung :*

We believe . . . ⟦ICET 3⟧ . . . to come. Amen.

⟦This follows the '1969' variants in the *apparatus* to ICET 3. It also omits the brackets from **'and the Son'.**⟧

THE INTERCESSION

15 *Any necessary notices may be given here or before the final hymn. Notice may also be given of any requests for the special prayers of the people.*

16 *M.* Let us pray.

[Kneel]

Almighty God, whose Son Jesus Christ has promised that you will hear the prayers of those who ask in faith, receive the prayers we offer. Unite us in truth with all your people throughout the world, so that we may live together in love and proclaim your peace among the nations.

Father, hear our prayer
through Jesus Christ our Lord.

Give grace to all the clergy, especially N. our bishop, that they may commend the word of life by their example and teaching, and rightly administer your holy sacraments. Give strength to all who serve you, especially the people of this *parish*. Grant that we may recognise your will for us, and do it without fear.

Father, hear our prayer
through Jesus Christ our Lord.

Guide with your loving wisdom all governments and their leaders, so that men may share with justice the resources of the earth, and live together in peace and trust. Especially we pray for Elizabeth our Queen, for this Commonwealth of Australia, for those who make and administer our laws, and for all who have responsibility among us.

Father, hear our prayer
through Jesus Christ our Lord.

Protect and comfort, merciful Lord, all who are in any kind of trouble, sickness or want. Give them patience and a firm trust in your goodness, and relieve them according to their needs.

Father, hear our prayer
through Jesus Christ our Lord.

We praise you, Lord God, for all your faithful servants in every generation in whose lives Christ has been honoured [*and in faith and trust we leave in your keeping N.]. Encourage us by their examples to run the race that is set before us, looking to Jesus the source and perfecter of our faith, in whose name we are confident to say:

Our Father in heaven . . . [ICET 1] . . . and for ever. Amen.
[This follows the '1969' variants in the *apparatus* to ICET 1.]

THE LORD'S SUPPER

[*Sit*]

*17 *The Priest may read this exhortation :*

P. The apostle Paul tells us that when we meet as the Church of God for the Lord's Supper, it is essential that we have a right regard for one another. To the Corinthians he says, 'Let a man examine himself and so eat the bread and drink of the cup; for anyone who eats and drinks without discerning the body eats and drinks judgment on himself.' Therefore, if you do not come to God by him, or if you do not love your brother from your heart, you ought not to be sharers of this holy table.

18 *The following prayer may be said, the Priest first saying :*

P. If anyone sins, we have an advocate with the Father, Jesus Christ the righteous.

Let us pray.

[*Kneel*]

**We do not presume to come to your table, Lord,
trusting in our own righteousness,
but in your great mercy.
We are not worthy even to gather up
the crumbs under your table.
But you are the Father, and your mercy never fails.
We pray therefore that we may eat the body
and drink the blood of your dear Son,
so that we, being cleansed in body and soul,
may live in him, and he in us. Amen.**

[*Stand*]

19 *P.* We are the body of Christ;
by one Spirit we were all baptised into one body.
Let us keep the unity of the Spirit
in the bond of peace.
The peace of the Lord be always with you;
and also with you.

20 *A hymn may be sung while the gifts of the people are collected and brought to the Lord's table, which is then set for the Communion. The Priest shall take the bread and wine for the Communion and shall say this Thanksgiving :*

P. Lift up your hearts;
we lift them to the Lord.
Let us give thanks to the Lord our God;
he is worthy of all praise.

You, Lord God, are worthy to receive glory and honour, and we are bound to give thanks to you, holy Father, almighty, everlasting God; for you have created the heavens and the earth, and you provide food for the needs of men.

But chiefly we praise you for our saviour Christ, your eternal Word, and clear image of your glory; for he, through whom all things were made, was born in the likeness of men; he took the form of a servant and died our common death.

Yet he is the true passover lamb, who was offered for us and has taken away the sin of the world. By his death he destroyed death, and by his rising to life again he has restored to us everlasting life. He ascended up on high and has poured out on us your promised Holy Spirit.

Therefore, with angels and all created things, with the patriarchs and apostles and the whole Church in heaven and earth, we honour your glorious name, and sing with never-ending praise:
Holy, holy, holy, sovereign Lord of all,
Heaven and earth are full of your glory;
yours is the victory, Lord God most high.

Great is your victory, almighty God, for you have reconciled us to yourself in Christ your Son, our great high priest, who by his death on the cross offered once and for all the true sacrifice for sin, and intercedes for us at your right hand on high.

And now, Father, we thank you for this bread that we will break and eat in remembrance of Christ, the true and living bread who comes down from heaven and gives life to the world.

We thank you for this cup in remembrance of our saviour Christ, the true vine, who commanded us to love one another as he has loved us; by whose blood you have bound us to be your people in a new and lasting covenant.

For on the night he was betrayed he took bread, and when he had given thanks he broke it, and gave it to his disciples, saying 'Take, eat, this is my body given for you. Do this in remembrance of me'. In the same way, after supper, he took the cup, and when he had given thanks he gave it to them, saying, 'Drink of it, all of you, for this cup is the new covenant in my blood. Do this as often as you drink it, in remembrance of me'.

Therefore, Father, with thankfulness for the perfect redemption he has won for us, we do as he commanded, as we wait for his coming again. Give us life by your Holy Spirit that we may be partakers of the body and blood of your Son, and share the feast in your eternal kingdom.

Accept our praise and thanksgiving, through Jesus Christ our Lord, to whom with you and the Holy Spirit be glory and honour, now and for ever. Amen.

21 *After breaking the bread in the sight of all, the Priest shall say:*
[*Kneel*]
P. Come and take this holy sacrament of the body and blood of Christ in remembrance that he died for you, and feed on him in your heart by faith, with thanksgiving.

22 *After receiving the sacrament himself the Priest shall distribute it to the other communicants. And when he gives the bread he shall say to each communicant:*
The body of Christ strengthen you

and when the cup is given:
The blood of Christ strengthen you.

And in each case the communicant may answer:
Amen.

OR
The Priest may omit the invitation after breaking the bread, and in this case he shall say as he gives the bread:
The body . . . ⟦CF 7(a)⟧ . . . thanksgiving.

and when the cup is given:
The blood . . . ⟦CF 7(b)⟧ . . . thankful.

THE DISMISSAL

23 *M.* Let us pray.

[*Kneel*]

**Almighty God, we offer ourselves to you
as a living sacrifice.
Send us out in the power of your Holy Spirit,
to live and work as faithful witnesses
of our Lord Jesus Christ.
Grant that at his coming,
we may be ready to meet him
so that, with all your saints,
we may worship you for ever. Amen.**

[*Stand*]

★24 A hymn of thanksgiving, which may be the Gloria in Excelsis if it has not been used in §7.

25 *P.* God has given us his blessing;
thanks be to God.

Go on your way rejoicing;
The God of peace is with us.

NOTES

1 *It is recommended that the psalm at § 1 be normally Psalm 95 (or vv. 1 to 7). Other alternatives might be: during Advent and pre-Lent Psalm 42 vv. 1 to 5; during Lent Psalm 51 vv. 1 to 12, or Psalm 43; during Eastertide the Easter Anthem, viz. 1 Corinthians 5:7, Romans 6:9, 1 Corinthians 15:20.*

2 *At § 20 the bread and wine to be used for the Communion are to be taken by the Priest and so placed on the Lord's table that he may give thanks over them.*
It is suggested that the Priest hold the bread in his hand, or place his hand on it, at the words we thank you for this bread; *and similarly with the cup at the words* we thank you for this cup.

3 *In § 20, it might be considered desirable, at the discretion of the local congregation, for the people to kneel from the words* Great is your victory.

4 *If the bread or the cup, or both, prove insufficient for the Communion, the Priest shall take more to the holy table and add them to what remains, saying :*

P. We now set apart this bread★ for the communion of his body★★, as our Lord Jesus Christ commanded us.

★*or* 'wine' *or* 'bread and wine'.
★★*or* 'blood' *or* 'body and blood'.

5 *What remains of the consecrated bread and wine which is not required for the purposes of communion shall be reverently consumed after all have communicated, either by the Priest or by the other ministers, or it shall be left on the holy table until the end of the service and then consumed.*

6 *A pause should be allowed after § 4 before proceeding to the general confession.*

7 *In the Intercession, § 16, a brief pause should be allowed after each prayer before the minister says* Father, hear our prayer.

8 ⟦Provision for when there is no communion⟧.

THE AUSTRALIAN EXPERIMENTAL LITURGY 1973 (Aus4)

⟦The numbering is original to the rite. Before the Preface in the booklet some printing conventions are noted. The following are relevant here: *Sections marked ★ are optional. P—Presiding Minister. D.—Deacon or assisting priest. M—Other ministers or authorised assistant. The words* 'Stand', 'Sit', 'Kneel' *are suggestions only. Where parts of the service are sung to musical settings, the words for which these settings were composed may be used.*⟧

A SERVICE OF HOLY COMMUNION

THE WORD AND THE PRAYERS

[*Stand*]

★1 *A PSALM, HYMN, or ANTHEM may be sung when the ministers enter or after the sentence of scripture (no. 3).*

2 *THE GREETING*

P. The Lord be with you.

And also with you.

[*During the Easter Season may be added:*

Christ is risen.

He is risen indeed.]

*3 *A SENTENCE of scripture appropriate to the day may be read.*

[*Kneel*]

4 *A PRAYER OF PREPARATION*

Let us pray.

Almighty God . . . [CF 1] . . . Christ our Lord. Amen.
    hid] hidden

5 *The TEN COMMANDMENTS, the TWO GREAT COMMAND-*
MENTS, or one of the other forms on the opposite page is used.

[The Decalogue, Summary, Kyries and Trisagion are printed out opposite this
rubric in the original. Their form is as in **Aus1A** on pp.323-25 above, with the
parts in square brackets omitted, except 'You have six days to labour and do all
your work. But the seventh day is a sabbath of the Lord your God'—which is
included. Other changes in the Decalogue are :
Introduction: 'Hear the Commandments which God gave to his people Israel:'
No. 1   ADD who brought you out of the land of slavery.
No. 2   in the heavens] that is in the heaven
          on the earth] that is on the earth
          waters] water
No. 10 that belongs to him] that is his
The Summary is unchanged, the Kyries are sixfold, and the Trisagion single.]

*6 *Then may follow the CONFESSION and ABSOLUTION.*

[These are printed out at no. 17 below, but in the original are also printed out
on the opposite page as with the Commandments at no. 5 above.]

*7 *This HYMN OF PRAISE (Gloria in Excelsis) may be sung or said, all*
standing.

Glory to God . . . [ICET 4] . . . God the Father. Amen.

8 *P.* Let us pray.

         THE COLLECT OF THE DAY
[*Sit*]

9 *The reading from the OLD TESTAMENT*
and/or
The reading from the NEW TESTAMENT (other than the Gospels).
At the end of each reading may be said :

Here ends the reading.

OR

This is the word of the Lord.

Thanks be to God.

★10 *A PSALM or HYMN may be sung or said between any of the readings.*

[*Stand*]

11 *The GOSPEL*

D. The gospel of our Lord Jesus Christ according to . . . , chapter . . . , beginning at verse . . . .

Glory to you, Lord Christ.

After the gospel

This is the gospel of the Lord.

Praise to you, Lord Christ.

12 *The SERMON is preached here, or after the Creed.*

[*Stand*]

13 *The NICENE CREED is said or sung. It may be omitted on weekdays.*

We believe . . . ⟦ICET 3⟧ **. . . come. Amen.**

(and the Son)] OM BRACKETS

THE INTERCESSION

14 *The PRAYERS may be offered as a single intercession as set out below (with or without the versicle and response) or with the addition of some of the petitions and thanksgivings suggested. Pauses may be allowed for silent prayer and thanksgiving.*

P. Let us pray for all people and for the church throughout the world.

[*Kneel*]

M. Almighty God, whose Son Jesus Christ has promised that you will hear us when we ask in faith, receive the prayers we offer. Unite all your people in the truth so that we may live together in love and proclaim your peace.

We pray for/we give thanks for the church in other countries; the church in Australia; this diocese.

Silence may be kept.

Strengthen your people for their witness and work in all the world, and empower your ministers faithfully to proclaim the gospel and to administer the sacraments. Especially we pray [for ———,] for N. our bishop, and for the people of this *parish,* that we may seek your will and do it without fear.

Father, hear our prayer
through Jesus Christ our Lord.

We pray for/we give thanks for the peoples of the world and their leaders; Elizabeth our Queen; all men and women in their daily work.

Silence may be kept.

Give wisdom to those in authority in every land, and guide all peoples in the way of righteousness and peace, so that we may share with justice the resources of the earth and live together in trust and goodwill. Especially we pray for this Commonwealth of Australia, for those who make and administer our laws, [for ———,] and for all who have responsibility among us.

Father, hear our prayer
through Jesus Christ our Lord.

We pray for/we give thanks for our community; people known to us [especially ———].

Silence may be kept.

We commend to your keeping, Father, our families, our neighbours, and our friends. Enable us by your Spirit to live together in love for you and for one another.

Father, hear our prayer
through Jesus Christ our Lord.

We pray for those who suffer; the lonely; the outcast; the persecuted; those who mourn; those who care for them.

Silence may be kept.

Comfort and heal, merciful Lord, all who are in sorrow, need, sickness, or any kind of trouble. Give them a firm trust in your goodness; help us to minister to them; and bring us all into the joy of your salvation.

Father, hear our prayer
through Jesus Christ our Lord.

We give thanks for the life and work of ———

Silence may be kept.

We praise you, Lord God, for your faithful servants in every age, and we pray that we, with all who have died in the faith of Christ, may be brought to a joyful resurrection and the fulfilment of your eternal kingdom.

Either

Accept our prayers through Jesus Christ our Lord, in whose name we say:

Our Father in heaven . . . ⟦ICET 1⟧ . . . and for ever. Amen.
holy] hallowed
Do . . . test] Lead us not into temptation

Or

Hear us, Father,
through Jesus Christ our Lord,
who lives and reigns with you
in the unity of the Holy Spirit,
one God, now and for ever.
Amen.

*15 *A HYMN may be sung.*
When there is no Communion the service ends with the section on page . . .
⟦i.e. Appendix 4⟧.

PREPARATION FOR THE LORD'S SUPPER

One or more of these (or other suitable passages of Scripture, e.g. 1 Cor. 12:31b-13:7; Hebrews 4:12-13; Hebrews 4:14-16) may be read.

M. Jesus said: 'Come to me all who labour and are heavy laden, and I will give you rest. Take my yoke upon you and learn of me; for I am gentle and lowly of heart, and you will find rest for your souls. For my yoke is easy, and my burden is light'. *Matt.* 11:28-30

Jesus said: 'I am the bread of life; he who comes to me shall not hunger, and he who believes in me shall never thirst'. *John* 6:35

Jesus said: 'If you are offering your gift at the altar, and there remember that your brother has something against you, leave your gift there before the altar and go; first be reconciled to your brother, and then come and offer your gift'. *Matt.* 5:23-24

God so loved the world that he gave his only Son,
that whoever believes in him should not perish but
have eternal life.   *John* 3:16

Saint Paul said: 'As often as you eat the bread and
drink the cup of the Lord, you proclaim the Lord's
death until he comes. Whoever, therefore, eats the
bread or drinks the cup in an unworthy manner
will be guilty of profaning the body and blood of
the Lord. Let a man examine himself, and so eat
of the bread and drink of the cup.' 1 *Cor.* 11:26-28

17   *D.* Let us confess our sins to Almighty God.

[*Kneel*]

This
CONFESSION   **Merciful God,**
is said unless it has   **our maker and our judge,**
been used at no. 6   **we have sinned against you:**
                          we have not loved you with our whole heart;
                          we have not loved our neighbours as
                          ourselves.
                          Father, forgive us.
                          Strengthen us to love and obey you
                          in newness of life;
                          through Jesus Christ our Lord. Amen.

and the   *P.* Almighty God,
ABSOLUTION   who has promised forgiveness to all who turn to
is pronounced by   him,
priest, or by the   pardon you
bishop if present. and set you free from all your sins,
                      strengthen you to do his will,
                      and keep you in eternal life;
                      through Jesus Christ our Lord.

                      Amen.

*18 *This PRAYER OF APPROACH may be said, all kneeling.*

                      We do not . . . [[CF 6]] **. . . us. Amen.**
                      this your] OM **this**

[*Stand*]

19 *The greeting of PEACE is given.*

> *P.* We are the body of Christ.
> **His Spirit is with us.**
>
> Peace be with you.
> **And also with you.**

20 *The OFFERTORY.*

A HYMN may be sung. The gifts of the people are brought to the Lord's table.

THE THANKSGIVING

21 *The priest takes the bread and wine for the Communion and says this THANKSGIVING.*

> *P.* Lift up your hearts.
> **We lift them to the Lord.**
>
> Let us give thanks to the Lord our God.
> **It is right to give him thanks and praise.**

On certain days, the special additions on pages . . . [i.e. Appendix 3] are used here.

All glory and honour, thanksgiving and praise
be yours at all times and in all places,
Lord, holy Father, true and living God.
Through your eternal Word
you created the heavens and the earth
and made man in your own image.

Though we turned away from you,
in your great love you gave your Son
to be born a man and to share our common life.
In obedience to your will
he gave himself up to death on the cross;
through him you freed us from the slavery
    of sin
and reconciled us to yourself,
our God and Father.

You raised him from death
and exalted him to your right hand on high;
and through him you have sent upon us
your holy and life-giving Spirit.

Therefore, Father, we praise you,
joining with angels and all created things,
with the patriarchs and apostles
and the whole church in heaven and earth:

Holy, holy, holy Lord,
God of power and might.
Heaven and earth are full of your glory:
Hosanna in the highest.

The priest
continues

And now, Father,
we thank you for this bread
which we break and eat as Christ our Lord
   commanded.
For on the night he was betrayed
he took bread and gave you thanks;
he broke it and gave it to his disciples, saying:
Take, eat. This is my body given for you.
Do this in remembrance of me.

We thank you for this cup
which we drink in obedience to our Saviour Christ,
by whose blood you have bound us to be
   your people
in a new and lasting covenant.
For after supper, he took the cup
and again giving you thanks
he gave it to his disciples, saying:
Drink from this, all of you.
This is my blood of the new covenant,
which is shed for you and for many
for the remission of sins.
Do this, whenever you drink it, in remembrance
   of me.

Therefore, Father, with this bread and this cup
we proclaim his perfect sacrifice
made once for all upon the cross;
we celebrate the redemption he has won for us;
and we look for his coming
to fulfil all things according to your will.

Christ has died:
Christ is risen:
Christ will come again.

Grant that we who eat and drink these holy things
may be filled with your life and goodness for ever.
Renew us by your holy Spirit,
that we may be united in the body of your Son
and be brought with all your people
into the joy of your eternal kingdom;
through Jesus Christ our Lord,
with whom and in whom,
by the power of the Holy Spirit,
we worship you, Father Almighty,
in never-ending praise:

Blessing and honour and glory and power
are yours for ever and ever. Amen.

THE COMMUNION

If the Lord's Prayer (no. 24) has not already been said, it is said here or after the Communion.

22 *The priest breaks the bread.*

[*He may do so in silence or he may say:*

P. We who are many are one body in Christ.
for we all share in the one bread.]

23 *The priest and the other communicants receive the holy communion.*
When the minister gives the bread he says

The body . . . ⟦CF 7(a)⟧ . . . thanksgiving.

or The body of Christ keep you in eternal life.

The communicant may answer **Amen.**

When the minister gives the cup he says

The blood . . . ⟦CF 7(b)⟧ . . . thankful.

or The blood of Christ keep you in eternal life.

The communicant may answer **Amen.**

During the Communion hymns or anthems (including those on page . . .
⟦*i.e. in Appendix 1*⟧*) may be sung.*

AFTER COMMUNION

When all have received the holy communion, the priest continues:
[*Kneel*]

*24 *P.* As our Saviour Christ has taught us, we pray:
Our Father in heaven . . . ⟦ICET 1 with amendments in no. 14
above⟧ . . . **and for ever. Amen.**

25 *A PRAYER OF THANKSGIVING AND DEDICATION*
P. [Let us pray.]
Father, we thank you
for feeding us with the spiritual food
of the body and blood of your Son Jesus Christ.
We thank you for this assurance
of your goodness and love.
Accept our sacrifice of praise and thanksgiving,
and grant that, united with all your people,
we may live as true members of the body of your Son
and worship you with all your saints for ever.
[*Stand*]
Father, we offer ourselves to you
in Jesus Christ our Lord.
Send us out in the power of your Spirit
to live and work to your praise and glory.
Amen.

*26 *A HYMN* may be sung, which may be Te Deum Laudamus, or Gloria in
Excelsis if it has not been used at no. 7.

27   *THE DISMISSAL*
P. The peace . . . ⟦CF 9⟧ . . . always. **Amen.**
    among] amongst
D. Go in peace to love and serve the Lord.
Amen. The God of peace is with us.

APPENDIX 1
CANTICLES AND ANTHEMS

⟦The following are printed here: (1) Gloria in excelsis. (2) Te Deum
Laudamus. (3) Psalm 95 (Venite). (4) The Song of Zechariah (Benedictus). (5) A Hymn of the Risen Christ. (Easter Anthems). (6) Benedictus qui venit. (7) Agnus Dei.
The text of the items 1, 6, and 7 are ICET texts and that of item 4 is
substantially the ICET text.⟧

APPENDIX 2
SEASONAL SENTENCES

for use at no. 3 on certain days.
[Ten sentences follow. They are to be found in Appendix D below]

APPENDIX 3
SPECIAL ADDITIONS TO THE THANKSGIVING

[Provision is made for special additions for Christmas, Epiphany, Lent, Easter, Ascension, Whitsun, Trinity, Saints' Days, Dedication Festivals and 'when appropriate'. These are 'Proper Prefaces' and are to be found in Appendix C. However, the whole of the Preface down to the Sanctus is reprinted as the context for the Prefaces (which fit at different places in it as in **Eng2** or **NZR**).]

APPENDIX 4

[Provision for when there is no Communion.]

ADDITIONAL NOTES AND DIRECTIONS

1 *The service is set out for three different ministers (see introductory Note 3 on page ...), but their parts may be assigned differently to suit circumstances. The parts of the service assigned to 'M.' may be read by one or more assisting priests or authorized laymen; OR the parts assigned to 'P.' and 'D.' may be read by the priest; OR all three parts may be read by the priest. When there is no Communion, all three parts may be read by authorized laymen (but see page ...).*

2 *The optional sentence of scripture read at no. 3 may be sung as an anthem by the choir at no. 3, or before the opening greeting; or it may be read immediately before the Collect.*

3 *Gloria in excelsis may be used wherever a hymn is permitted (instead of at no. 7). During Advent and Lent and on weekdays it may be omitted.*

4 *When Baptism or Confirmation is administered during this service an appropriate sentence and collect, together with appropriate readings, may be used instead of any or all of those set for the day.*

5 *A pause for reflection may be observed at any of the following: before the Collect, after any of the readings, before the Confession, or after all have received the holy communion.*

6 *Although the recommended position for the sermon is after the Gospel, it may be after the Creed, or before or after any of the readings. A sermon should normally be preached at this service.*

7 *The plural* 'we believe' *is original to the Nicene Creed, which was a corporate declaration of faith; while the singular is appropriate to the Apostles' Creed which is an act of personal commitment at baptism. Nevertheless, in this service the Nicene Creed may be said in the singular.*

8 *In the prayers (no. 14) the minister need not use all the detailed suggestions on each occasion, nor need he use the precise forms* 'we thank you' *and* 'we pray for'. *Any other forms used should be clearly addressed to God (rather than biddings to the congregation).*

9 *The Litany published on pages 27ff of Sunday Services Revised or* 'A prayer for all people' *on page 24 of the same book may be used on occasion in place of the prayers (no. 14). The Litany may begin with no. 4* 'Receive now our prayers, Lord God' *and end with the Lord's Prayer, or with the final petition* 'Hear us, good Lord' *followed by the prayer of St. Chrysostom.*

10 *The priest exchanges the greeting, the Peace, with the congregation by using the versicle and response. When circumstances permit, all may then exchange the greeting, accompanying it with a handclasp or other similar action.*

11 *This prayer may be said at the presentation of the gifts (no. 20):*
Accept these offerings, Father, and of your goodness
use them and us in the service of your kingdom;
through Jesus Christ our Lord. **Amen.**

12 *The greeting* 'The Lord be with you/**And also with you**' *may be used at the beginning of no. 21 when a hymn has been sung at no. 20.*

13 *It is appropriate for all to remain standing throughout the Thanksgiving (no. 21) and the Breaking of the Bread (no. 22). However, it may be considered desirable, at the discretion of the local congregation, for the people to kneel.*

14 *At no. 21 the bread and wine to be used for the Communion are to be taken by the priest and so placed on the Lord's table that he may give thanks over them. At the words* 'we thank you for this bread (cup)' *the priest should indicate by taking it into his hands, or placing his hands over it, the bread (wine) for the Communion.*

15 *The consecrated elements may be distributed separately after the appropriate words of institution. In this case, the bread is to be broken at the words* 'he broke it'; 'Therefore, Father, . . . ' *is said after Communion; and no. 22 is omitted.*

16 *When the shorter forms of words are used at the administration of the Communion (no. 23) the priest may, before receiving the sacrament himself, say to the congregation:*

> Come, let us take this holy sacrament of the body and
> blood of Christ in remembrance that he died for us, and
> feed on him in our hearts by faith with thanksgiving.

17 *If the consecrated bread and/or wine are likely to prove insufficient for the communion, the priest is to take more bread and/or wine saying the appropriate portions of no. 21, beginning* 'We thank you, Father, for this bread (or cup)' *and ending* 'in remembrance of me'.

18 *The consecrated bread and wine which remains after all have received the holy communion is to be reverently consumed before, or immediately after, the end of the service.*

19 *Notices may be given before the hymn at no. 15 or at no. 26 or, when appropriate, before the intercession.*

20 *In the selection of hymns, careful attention should be given both to the appropriateness of the words to the theme of the service and also to the relation of the hymn chosen to its position within the service.*

CHAPTER 25

THE DIOCESE OF
PAPUA NEW GUINEA

THE Diocese of Papua New Guinea is a missionary diocese of the Church of England in Australia, with a monochrome Anglo-Catholic tradition. The Liturgical Commission of the Church of England in Australia in the late 1960's gave permission to the Diocese to produce its own rite, and the canonical position in Australia[1] then allows a Diocesan Bishop to permit any uses he chooses for experimental purposes. The Diocesan Liturgical Commission worked at a 'you' form liturgy largely by modernising **Eng2**. The text (**NG**[2]) was approved by the Bishop and printed for use in 1970.

The style of English used was consciously based on the TEV (*Good News for Modern Man*), both in order to afford simplicity in English-language services and in order to provide a good simple rite for translation into vernacular tongues. The text stands on its own in this respect, as the Liturgical Commission does not seem to have seen the **MLT** text, which governed the modernizing of **Eng2** in South Africa, nor the ICET forms, which first became available only shortly before the booklets were printed. At the time of going to press it is learned that a new edition incorporating the ICET forms will shortly be available.

The points at which the text departs from **Eng2** should be noted.[3] The structure has brought the penitential section to the beginning (except for Humble Access which has moved on to its 1549 position immediately before communion). The Lord's Prayer has been moved, perhaps by the older 'Western' instinct of the diocese, to follow the end of the canon. The intercessions have the versicle and response of **Eng2**, but the text and ethos owe much more to **NZ** (the New Zealand 1966 rite). Finally the distinctive Papua New Guinea rubric should be mentioned—a '*Bell, Drum or Rattle*' occurs at three points.[4]

---

[1] See **MAL** pages 298-300, and also pages 316-17 above.
[2] The code '**NG**' is used rather than 'PNG' (which is the usual abbreviation for the diocese). This is because the rite has as its own printed title 'Niugini Liturgy', for which '**NG**' is the obvious code.
[3] The actual verbal variants in the canon can be seen at a glance in the comparative table of eucharistic prayers in appendix F.
[4] See page 25 above.

THE NEW GUINEA
EXPERIMENTAL LITURGY 1970 (NG)

[The numbering in this rite is editorial].

NIUGINI LITURGY
(*Approved by the Bishop*)

THE PEOPLE MAKE THEMSELVES READY
(THE PREPARATION)

(*May be sung separately when the Liturgy is to be sung.*)

1 *Kneel*

We have a great High Priest Who has passed into heaven, Jesus the Son of God; so let us draw near with a true heart and a sure faith, and make our confession to our heavenly Father.

(*Short silence*)

2 *The Priest and People will then make this confession:*

Almighty God, our heavenly Father, we have sinned against You, through our own fault, in thought, and word, and deed, and in the good things we have not done. For the sake of Your Son our Lord Jesus Christ, forgive us all that is past, and help us to serve you in the new life, to the glory of Your name. Amen.

3 *The Priest will then say:*

Almighty God have mercy on you, forgive you and save you from all your sins, make you strong in all goodness and keep you in eternal life, through Jesus Christ Our Lord. **Amen.**

THE FIRST PART OF THE SERVICE
(THE INTRODUCTION)

4 (*When the Ministers come in, a psalm, or part of a psalm, or a hymn, may be sung.*)

5 *Then this prayer shall be said by the Priest and People together:*

Almighty God, to Whom all hearts are open, all wants known, and from Whom no secrets are hidden, clean the thoughts of our hearts by the work of Your Holy Spirit, that we may truly love You, and worthily praise Your holy name, through Jesus Christ Our Lord. Amen.

    Lord have mercy (*three times*)
    Christ have mercy (*three times*)
    Lord have mercy (*three times*)

7 *Then the Priest and People will sing or say :*
Glory be to God on high, and on earth peace, goodwill towards
men. We praise You, we bless You, we worship You, we glorify
You, we give thanks to You for Your great glory, O Lord God,
heavenly King, God the Father almighty. O Lord, the only
begotten Son, Jesus Christ: O Lord God, Lamb of God, Son of
the Father, You Who take away the sins of the world, have mercy
on us; You Who take away the sins of the world, receive our
prayer. You Who sit at the right hand of God the Father, have
mercy on us. For You only are holy, You only are the Lord, You
only O Christ, with the Holy Spirit, are the Most high in the glory
of the Father. Amen.

8 *Priest*   The Lord be with you.
People   **And with you.**
Priest   Let us pray.
The Collect shall be said.

THE READINGS AND THE PREACHING
(THE MINISTRY OF THE WORD)
Sit

9 *(On Sundays, a Lesson from the Old Testament should be read, and then
a canticle can be sung or said.)*

10 *Then a Lesson from the New Testament shall be read. (After this Lesson
a psalm, or a canticle, or a hymn may be sung.)*
V.   The Lord be with you.
R.   **And with you.**
Stand

11 *Then a Lesson from the Gospels shall be read.*
Before the Gospel the people say :
Glory be to You, O Lord.
After the Gospel the people say :
Praise be to You, O Christ.

12 *Then the Sermon shall be preached, on Sundays and on other occasions.*

13 *On Sundays and other holy days the Creed shall then be sung or said.*
**I believe in one God . . . [MAL CF 6 with variants] . . . world
to come. Amen.**

Ghost] **Spirit** TWICE
sitteth] **sits**
quick] **living**
proceedeth] **proceeds**

THE PRAYERS OF THE CHURCH
(THE INTERCESSION)

14 *The Priest or one or more of the people shall offer the prayers of the Church.*
Kneel

After each petition, or group of petitions, the reader shall say: 'Lord in your mercy *and the people shall answer* **Hear our prayer.**[1]

Reader: Let us pray.

Almighty God, You have promised to hear the prayers of those who ask in faith, we pray for Your whole Church in Jesus Christ, and for the needs of all men: For the peace that comes from above, and for the salvation of our souls.

. . . .

For the peace of the world;
For our country, for this place (town or village) and for all who live here:
For all leaders and governors, especially for our Queen, Elizabeth:
For all in authority in this country, especially those in this district (or town).

. . . .

For the unity of your Church:
For all Christian people throughout the world;
For this diocese, and for the bishops and clergy of Christ's Church (especially for N. . . our bishop(s)).
For all evangelists, for the brothers and sisters of religious communities, and other servants of the Church:
For unbelievers, that they may come to know the truth in Christ:
For the spread of the Gospel in this and every land:

. . . .

For teachers and those who lead others by their words:
For our homes and all parents and children:
For all men and women in their daily work:
For our food and crops, that they may grow well:
For all who travel by land, sea, and air.

. . . .

---

[1] [The versicle and response are printed out each time they come in the prayer, but are here represented by a dotted line at the relevant places.]

For the sick and the suffering in mind and body, and for those who serve them:

For those who have died:

For ourselves, that we may follow the blessed saints and martyrs in being good soldiers and servants of Christ, and that we may have a holy and happy death, rest in Paradise, and a share in your glory.

. . . .

Grant these prayers of ours, O merciful Father, for the sake of your Son Our Saviour Jesus Christ. **Amen.**

Stand

15 *Then the Priest and People shall say:*

We are the Body of Christ. By one Spirit we were all baptised into one Body.

Priest: Try to keep the unity of the Spirit and to hold together in the way of peace.

The peace of the Lord be with you always.

People: **And with you.**

16 THE OFFERING

(THE PREPARATION OF THE BREAD AND WINE)

The bread and wine shall then be placed on the altar and the gifts of the people may be given at the same time.

Priest: Lord, to You, belong the Greatness, and the Power, and the Glory, and the Victory, and the Majesty.

People: **All that is in the heavens and on the earth is Yours, and of Your own we give back to You.**

(A hymn may be sung).

17 THE THANKSGIVING

Stand

Priest: The Lord be with you.

People: **And with you.**

Priest: Lift up your hearts.

People: **We lift them up to the Lord.**

Priest: Let us give thanks to the Lord our God.

People: **It is good and right to do so.**

Priest : It is good and right that we should at all times and in all places give thanks to You, O Lord, holy Father, almighty, everlasting God, through Jesus Christ Your only Son, Our Lord: Because through Him you made all things from the beginning and made us in Your own likeness:

Through Him You saved us from being slaves to sin, giving Him to be born as man, to die on the cross and to rise again for us:†

> †(*During Christmas time there is also said :*[1]
> For by the work of the Holy Spirit He was made man of the Virgin Mary his mother, and without any sin, to make us clean from all sin.)

> †(*During Passion time there is also said :*[1]
> For He became man, humbled Himself, and walked the path of obedience to death—His death on the cross. For this reason You raised Him to the highest place above, and gave Him the Name that is greater than any other name.)

> †(*During Easter time there is also said :*[1]
> For He is the true Lamb of sacrifice which was offered for us and Who has taken away the sin of the world; Who by His death has destroyed death and by His rising to life again has given everlasting life back to us.)

Through Him You made us a people for Yourself, lifting Him to Your right hand on high, and sending out through Him Your holy and life-giving Spirit.††

> ††(*From Ascension Day to the Saturday after Pentecost there is also said :*[1]
> For by the gift of the Spirit you have given Your people power to preach the Good News among the nations and to serve You well as the King's Priests.)

So through Him, with angels and archangels and all the company of heaven, we praise You with joy and say:

People : **Holy, Holy, Holy, Lord God of all,**
Heaven and earth are full of Your glory.
Glory be to You, O Lord most high.
Blessed is He Who comes in the Name of the Lord,
Hosanna in the Highest.

(*Bell, Drum or Rattle*)

Kneel

---

1 [The Proper Prefaces are printed here only, and are not set out again in Appendix C. The indenting and smaller type are editorial.]

Priest: Hear us, O Father, through Christ Your Son, our Lord. Through Him receive our sacrifice of praise and thanksgiving, and make these gifts of bread and wine to be to us His Body and Blood; In the same night that He was betrayed, He took bread; and, when He had given thanks to You, He broke it, and gave it to His disciples saying, 'Take eat, this is My Body which is given for you. Do this in remembrance of Me.' Then after supper He took the cup; and, when He had given thanks to You, He gave it to them saying, 'Drink this, all of you, for this is My Blood of the new covenant which is shed for you and for many for the forgiveness of sins; Do this, as often as you drink it, in remembrance of Me.' And so, O Lord, with this bread and this cup we make the memorial of His saving passion, His resurrection from the dead and His glorious ascension into heaven, and we look for the coming of His Kingdom. We ask You to receive this duty and service of ours, and to let us eat and drink these Holy Things that we may be filled with Your grace and heavenly blessing. Through the same Christ our Lord, by Whom and with Whom, and in Whom, in the unity of the Holy Spirit, all honour and glory be given to you, O Father Almighty, from the whole company of heaven and earth, throughout all ages, world without end.

People: **Amen.**

(*Bell, Drum or Rattle*)

18 *Then shall the Priest and the People together say the Lord's Prayer. The Priest first will say:*

Let us pray.

As our Saviour Christ has commanded and taught us, we are bold to say,

Our Father in heaven; Hallowed be Your name; Your Kingdom come; Your will be done; on earth as it is in heaven. Give us this day our daily bread. And forgive us our trespasses, as we forgive those who trespass against us. And lead us not into temptation; but deliver us from evil. For Yours is the Kingdom, and the power, and the glory, for ever and ever. Amen.

19 THE BREAKING OF THE BREAD

Then the Priest shall break the bread which has been blessed.

Priest : The Cup which we bless,

People : **Is it not a sharing in the Blood of Christ?**

Priest : The Bread which we break,

People : **Is it not a sharing in the Body of Christ?**

Priest : Because there is one Bread, we who are many are one body,

People : **For we all share in the one Bread.**

20 *Priest and People :*

O Lamb of God, You take away the sin of the world, have mercy on us.

O Lamb of God, You take away the sin of the world, have mercy on us.

O Lamb of God, You take away the sin of the world, grant us your peace.

21 THE SHARING OF THE SACRAMENT

The Priest invites the people to share the Holy Sacrament saying :

Come with faith; take the Body of Our Lord Jesus Christ which was given for You and His Blood which was shed for you, and feed on Him in your heart by faith and thanksgiving.

22 *The Priest and People say together :*

We do not trust in our own goodness, O Lord, when we come to Your table, but in Your many and great mercies. We are not good enough even to pick up the crumbs under Your table. But because You always have mercy, help us, O Lord, to eat the Flesh of Your dear Son Jesus Christ, and to drink His Blood, that we may always live in Him, and He in us. Amen.

(Bell or Drum or Rattle)

23 *Then the Priest and other Ministers receive the Blessed Sacrament, and shall then give It to the People, saying to each one who receives :*

The Body of Christ, *and,* The Blood of Christ.

(Hymns may be sung while the People are receiving the Sacrament.)

THE ENDING
(THANKSGIVING)

24 *Priest :* The Lord be with you.

People : **And with you.**

25 *Priest :* Let us pray.

Almighty and everliving God, we thank You for feeding us in this Holy Sacrament with the Body and Blood of Your Son our Saviour Jesus Christ, and for keeping us in the Body of Your Son, which is the blessed company of all faithful people; and we pray that we may continue to be living members of that holy fellowship, and do all those good works You have made ready for us.

Priest and People :

And here we offer You ourselves, our souls and bodies, to be a living sacrifice through Jesus Christ our Lord. Send us out into the world in the power of Your Spirit, to live and work to Your praise and glory. Amen.

26 *Priest :* Go in peace; love and serve the Lord; be full of joy in the power of the Holy Spirit; And the blessing of God Almighty, the Father, the Son, and the Holy Spirit, be with you and stay with you forever. Amen.

27 *The Ministers shall then go out*

(A hymn may be sung before all the People go out.)

28 *Blessed bread and wine which are not wanted for communion shall be eaten and drunk by the Priest immediately after the communion of the People, by one of the other Ministers while the Priest continues the service, or it shall be left on the altar until the end of the service and then it will be eaten and drunk or reserved in the tabernacle.*

CHAPTER 26

THE CHURCH OF THE PROVINCE
OF NEW ZEALAND

The 1966 *Liturgy* (NZ)

IN April 1966 the General Synod of the Church of the Province of
New Zealand authorized the experimental use of the 1966 Liturgy
(NZ),[1] the first fruit of two years work of the Provincial Commission on
Prayer Book Revision. Six months later, after receiving the assent of a
majority of the diocesan synods, this service came into wide use in
New Zealand. It was soon evident that there were certain deficiencies in
the revision, and in June 1967 a comprehensive popular evaluation of
the service was undertaken. A questionnaire was handed to every church
attender throughout the country on a set Sunday in that month. This
was followed later that same year by a more detailed opportunity for
comment by clergy on the strengths and weaknesses of the service.

The results of these two surveys were clear. The service generally was
appreciated. But further revision would be necessary. Criticisms of
NZ centred on:

the omission of the Ten Commandments (and even the Summary of
the Law)

the language style of the Collects and certain other parts of the
service

the form of remembrance of the departed in the Intercessions

the substance and wording of the Canon

the absence of a spoken blessing at the end

the form of the supplementary consecration.

But the general structure and balance of the service met with widespread
approval.

The 1970 *Liturgy* (NZR)—*Characteristics*

In the light of these criticisms the Commission set itself the major task
of a comprehensive rewriting of the service to bring before the 1970
session of General Synod. The outcome of this work was the *New
Zealand Liturgy,* 1970 (NZR).

---

[1] The text is printed in **MAL**, pp.329-39.

NZR is a clear derivative of **NZ**, but it has continued away from resemblance to 1662. Even more than **NZ**, its language conveys the terseness of much modern speech. Rubrics in the text have been reduced to a minimum, and they allow even greater freedom of choice on the part of the minister.

These are the principal changes from **NZ** to **NZR**:

(1) As a contribution to the service from our Maori heritage the initial greeting has been highlighted, and a Maori alternative provided. This is not a translation but a cultural equivalent. A change has been made to the response in English which is now 'The Lord bless you'. This style has been followed through the service.

(2) The agreed texts of the International Consultation on English Texts have been adopted for Gloria in excelsis, the Nicene Creed, the Lord's Prayer, and the Sanctus. Of these, the version of the Lord's Prayer has been the least well received, particularly the phrase, 'Do not bring us to the test.'

(3) Provision has been made for reading the Ten Commandments (in an abbreviated form), the Summary of the Law, or the New Commandment.

(4) The confession has been partly rewritten to make the personal acknowledgement of sin more positive and more meaningful.

(5) Most of the Collects have been amended or rewritten.

(6) A complete alternative set of lections has been provided. With this, certain Sundays and Holy Days have been renamed. For example, Sundays after Trinity now become Sundays after Pentecost. General Synod in April 1972 approved a Revised Calendar containing commemorations of names notable in the history of the Church in New Zealand. This Calendar includes a collection of Propers (themes, set psalms, sentences of the day, collects, lections) for use with the Liturgy on the days appointed.

(7) Certain changes have been made in the three alternative Intercessions. These include: (*a*) a prayer 'for those whose conscience leads them into conflict with authority', reflecting the age of protest in which this revision was done; (*b*) more acceptable references to the departed, dropping the 1928 petition for rest eternal and light perpetual, and emphasizing the note of thanksgiving; (*c*) the corporate saying of the Lord's Prayer as an optional conclusion to the Intercession.

(8) Considerable revision took place in the Eucharistic Prayer. The main changes were as follows: (*a*) A more evident note of joy and thanksgiving has been woven into this part of the service compared with **NZ**. (*b*) In response to a request from the 1968 General Synod, a set of Proper Prefaces, entitled 'Additions to the Eucharistic Prayer', was provided with **NZR**. These are inserted at various points of the set preface, according to their significance. These additions provide not only for major Christian festivals, but also, under a heading 'Of Thanksgiving', for a variety of special circumstances for which appropriate recognition and praise to God might be desired in the course of a celebration of Holy Communion. (*c*) The anamnesis in **NZR** has been given a much tighter style of writing and bears markedly fewer overtones of 1662 than did **NZ**. (*d*) The manual acts in 1966 closely followed the traditional pattern of 1662. In **NZR** they are reduced to a bare minimum to avoid suggestion of a 'moment of consecration' and to emphasize the whole fourfold action of taking, thanksgiving, breaking bread, and distributing as the essential eucharistic movement. (*e*) The acclamations of the people immediately following the narrative of institution, derived from the old Syrian liturgy via **CSI** and **LfA,** have been made an address to Christ instead of to the Father.

(9) Also in response to a request from the 1968 General Synod, the option of a blessing given before the Dismissal is provided in **NZR**.

(10) That same General Synod also faced up to the widespread dissatisfaction with the Form of Supplementary Consecration which had been provided in 1966. Rather than wait for the major revision of the whole service, the Synod withdrew authorization for the original form and substituted another. The 1966 form had provided for additional consecration by declaration of intent with manual acts. This new form provided for further consecration by simple prayer[1] but *without* requirement of manual acts. As an alternative, authority was also given for the words of institution from **NZ** to be used, presumably *with* manual acts as required by the rubrics at that part of the service.

NZR resolved this dilemma and took matters a stage further by deleting all reference to 'supplementary consecration' (which became

---

[1] The wording was: 'Obeying the command of our Lord Jesus Christ, we take this *bread* and pray that *it* also be set apart for this holy use, so that *it* may be to us the *Body* of our Lord Jesus Christ. Amen.' [This change, as it actually applied to **NZ,** and still does where that rite is in use, supersedes the text shown in **MAL,** p.339. It is one of the very few points where **MAL** was out of date at the point of publication—Editor].

now simply provision for setting apart more bread and/or wine), by making the wording more clearly a prayer to God the Father, and by not authorizing the use of the words of institution as an alternative. Behind this lay the conviction that should there be need for further bread or wine, the context of eucharist is still present—it only requires taking what is needed and by prayer to the Father bringing it within that context.

NZR—*Use and Status*

NZR has now been in use for five years in New Zealand. The extent of its use and the warmth of its reception increases year by year and no sign of demand for further revision has yet appeared. The congregational edition (without the Propers) is now into its sixth printing. Over 45,000 copies have been sold of this edition alone. Extensive sales have been made of an identical edition containing also the collects, lections etc. An altar edition with a lay-flat vinyl cover with spirex binding is sold out. Musical settings of the service are multiplying and a Children's Edition is under consideration. The Christian Education Departments in several dioceses are producing resource packs for clergy, offering material for more imaginative use of the service both in worship and in preaching.

A Maori translation of **NZR** was completed in 1973. An academic controversy accompanied this work, debating whether a translation of this sort from a dominantly European-shaped service should be the goal, or the new writing of a truly Maori service. Once the decision was taken to translate rather than to rewrite, a further question arose: Should traditional or modern Maori language be used? The decision was to retain largely the terms the Maori had always associated with worship, while introducing some modern terms at certain points.

The 1662 Holy Communion continues to be used in some parts of the Church in New Zealand, sometimes with the lections and Collects of **NZR**. It is probable that authorization for use of **NZ** will not be renewed at the General Synod which meets in March 1974. Meanwhile **NZR** stands in the Church of the Province of New Zealand on a par with the 1662 Holy Communion and with those portions of the 1928 Prayer Book authorized in 1958. No longer an experimental service, **NZR** is well on the way to becoming the universally used eucharistic service for the Anglican Church in this country.

THE NEW ZEALAND LITURGY 1970 (NZR)

⟦The numbering in this rite is original.⟧

THE NEW ZEALAND LITURGY 1970
GENERAL DIRECTIONS

No change in Eucharistic doctrine from that implied by the Book of Common Prayer is intended by the changes in structure or language of this rite.

Those who come to receive Holy Communion should prepare themselves in penitence and forgiveness.

The ancient discipline of fasting is a preparation for Holy Communion which may, or may not, be used according to each man's custom and conscience.

This ORDER is intended for the use of the People led by the Priest who shall speak throughout in a clear and audible voice. Neither private nor individual devotions must interfere with its course.

The ORDER as printed is the normal Sunday form; the PEOPLE'S PART is printed in HEAVIER TYPE. The Sections of the Order are numbered and the first part (Nos. 1-21), with the Lord's Prayer and the Grace or a Blessing may be used as a complete service.

Any section marked with a * may be omitted at the discretion of the Minister.

On weekdays the following may be omitted: the Gloria (No. 4), except on Holy Days and during Eastertide; the Sermon (No. 15); and the Creed (No. 16), except on Holy Days.

On special occasions the Priest may add certain words to the Eucharistic Prayer; these are set out on Page . . . ⟦i.e. Appendix e⟧.

ORDER OF SERVICE

THE PREPARATION

*1 *Minister :* The Lord be with you [*OR* Kia ora ano tatou.]

People : **The Lord bless you** [*OR* **Kia ora ano koe.**]

Minister : This is the day which the Lord has made:

People : **Let us rejoice and be glad in it.**

*2 *The Minister may read the Sentence of the Day.*

3 *Minister or Minister and People :*
Almighty God, to whom . . . ⟦CF 1⟧ . . . Christ our Lord. **Amen.**

hid] hidden
the thoughts of our hearts] our thoughts
the inspiration of] OM
perfectly] truly
magnify] praise
⟦This is the **NZ** form of the Collect for Purity.⟧

4 **Glory to** . . . ⟦ICET 4⟧ . . . **Father. Amen.**

Kneel

*5 *The Minister may use one of the following :*
The Ten Commandments.
Our Lord's Summary of the Law.
The New Commandment.
The Kyries in English or Greek.
(The text for these is in the Appendix, Page . . .).

*6 *Minister :* Hear God's word to all who turn to him through Jesus Christ:
Come to me . . . ⟦CF 4⟧ . . . save sinners.
If we confess our sins, he is faithful and just, and will forgive
our sins and cleanse us from all unrighteousness.

Hear what St. Paul says] OM
saying is true] saying is sure
⟦This is the **NZ** form of the Comfortable Words⟧

7 *Minister :* Let us (then) draw near with true penitence in full assurance
of faith, and make our confession to our heavenly Father.

8 *Minister and People :*
**Almighty Father, Judge of all men, we have sinned
against you in what we have thought, and said, and
done. We have sinned in ignorance; we have sinned in
weakness; we have sinned through our own deliberate
fault. Forgive us for our Saviour Christ's sake, and
help us to serve you in newness of life, to the glory of
your name. Amen.**

9 *Priest :* Almighty God, our merciful Father, who has promised
forgiveness of sins to all who truly repent, turn to him in
faith, and are themselves forgiving; have mercy on you,
pardon and deliver you from all your sins, strengthen you in
all goodness, and keep you in life eternal; through Jesus
Christ our Lord. Amen.

If a priest is not present the following prayer may be said:

> Almighty God, have mercy on us, forgive us all our sins and deliver us from all evil, strengthen us in all goodness, and keep us in life eternal, through Jesus Christ our Lord. Amen.

THE MINISTRY OF THE WORD

*10 *Minister:* The Lord be with you.

People: **The Lord bless you.**

*11 *The Theme of the Day may be announced.*

The Sentence of the Day shall be said. Then shall follow the Collect or Collects appointed, the Minister saying:

12 *Minister:* Let us pray. . . .

The people concluding:

People: **Amen.**

Sit

13 *OLD TESTAMENT LESSON.*

EPISTLE.

Stand

When the GOSPEL is announced the People shall answer:

14 *People:* **Glory to you, Lord God.**

After the GOSPEL they shall answer:

People: **Praise to you, Lord Christ.**

15 *The SERMON.*

Stand

16   THE NICENE CREED

**We believe . . . ⟦ICET 3⟧ . . . world to come. Amen.
(and the Son)⟧** OM BRACKETS

Notices concerning the life and worship of the Church may be given here.

THE INTERCESSION[1]

17 *Minister :* Let us pray for the whole Church of Christ and for all men according to their needs.

Kneel

After each petition or group of petitions the Minister shall say :

18 *Minister :* Let us pray to the Lord.

         And the people answer :

People :   **Lord, hear our prayer.**

Minister : For the union of all Christians in one holy Church,
For Bishops, Priests, Deacons, and other ministers (especially . . .),
For other servants of the Church (especially . . .),
For this parish (especially . . .),

For all men that they may hear and receive his Word,
For the peace of the whole world,
For the rulers of all nations and for just government in accordance with his holy will,
For our own country, and for Elizabeth our Queen,
For those who exercise authority among us (especially . . .),
For those whose conscience leads them into conflict with authority,

For our homes, and for parents and children everywhere,
For places of healing, teaching, study or research (especially . . .),
For travellers (especially . . .),
For all men and women in their daily life and work (especially . . .),

For the poor and the hungry, the homeless and the unemployed,
For the persecuted and the oppressed,
For those in prison,
For the lonely and the sorrowful,

---

[1] [No indication is given that the forms of intercession are alternatives.]

For the sick and suffering in mind and body (especially ...),
For the dying,
For those who have died (especially ...), that we may share with them in his eternal glory.

Let us pray in silence for our own needs.

Minister : Hear us Lord.

People : **Lord, hear our prayer.**

19 *Minister :* Almighty God, we have been taught by your holy Word to pray for all men.

We ask you to receive our prayers for the Universal Church, that it may be filled with the spirit of truth, unity and concord, and that all who confess your holy name may agree in the truth of your holy Word, and live in unity and love.

We pray for the rulers of the nations, and especially for your servant Elizabeth, our Queen, and for all who have authority and responsibility among us, that they may wisely and justly govern, and promote peace and welfare among all peoples.

We pray for ministers of your Word and Sacraments, especially for your servant N., our Bishop, that both by their life and teaching they may show forth your glory and draw all men to you.

Guide and prosper, we pray, those who are labouring for the spread of your Gospel among the nations, and enlighten with your Spirit all places of work, learning and healing.

To all your people in their many callings give your heavenly grace, and especially to this congregation, that they may hear your holy Word with reverent and obedient hearts, and serve you truly all the days of their life.

We ask you, Father, that your love and compassion may strengthen and uphold, comfort and help all who are in trouble, sorrow, need or sickness.

We remember before you with thanksgiving all your servants who have died in the faith of Christ; praying that we may enter with them into the fulness of your unending joy.

Grant this, holy Father, for Jesus Christ's sake. **Amen.**

20 *Minister :* Father, you have taught us in Holy Scripture to pray for all men. Hear us when we pray for your Holy Catholic Church;

People : **That we may all be one, so that the world may believe.**

Minister : Grant that every member of the Church may truly and humbly serve you;

People : **That your name may be glorified by all people.**

Minister : We pray for all Ministers of your Word and Sacraments, and especially for (. . . and) N., our Bishop,

People : **That they may be faithful in your service.**

Minister : Inspire and lead all who govern and hold authority in the nations of the world;

People : **That there may be peace and justice among all men.**

Minister : Help us to do your will in all that we undertake;

People : **That the life of Christ may be revealed in us.**

Minister : Have compassion on those who suffer from any sickness, grief or trouble;

People : **That they may be delivered from their distress.**

Minister : We remember those who have died;

People : **Father, into your hands we commend them.**

Minister : We praise you for all your saints (especially . . .), who have entered your eternal glory;

People : **May we also come to share your heavenly kingdom.**

Minister : Let us pray in silence for our own needs: . . .
Hear us Lord.

People : **Lord, hear our prayer.**

After the INTERCESSION the LORD'S PRAYER may follow, the Minister first saying :

★21   As our Lord has taught us, we pray:

People : **Our Father . . . [ICET 1] . . . and for ever. Amen.**

THE OFFERTORY

Stand

The Priest, facing the people, shall say :

22 *Priest :* Brethren, we are the Body of Christ.

People : **By one Spirit we were baptised into one Body.**

Priest : Keep the unity of the Spirit in the bond of peace.

People : **Amen.**

Priest : The peace of the Lord be always with you.

People : **And with you also.**

Then shall bread and wine be placed in order upon the holy table or altar, and the gifts of the people may be presented at the same time.

*23 *Priest:* To you, Lord, belongs the greatness, and the power, and the glory, and the victory and the majesty.

People: **All that is in the heavens and in the earth is yours, and of your own we give you.**

*24 *Priest:* Come, Holy Spirit, Sanctifier, everliving God, and bless us and these gifts prepared for your use.

THE EUCHARISTIC PRAYER

*25 *Priest:* The Lord be with you.

People: **The Lord bless you.**

26 *Priest:* Lift up your hearts.

People: **We lift them to the Lord.**

Priest: Let us give thanks to the Lord, our God.

People: **It is right to give him thanks.**

Priest: It is right indeed, it is our joy and salvation, holy Lord, almighty Father, everlasting God, at all times and in all places to give thanks to you through Jesus Christ your only Son;

For through him you have created all things from the beginning and made man in your own image;

Through him in the fulness of time you redeemed us, when we had fallen into sin, giving him to be born as man, to die on the Cross, and to rise again for us, setting him in glory at your right hand;

Through him you have made us a holy people by sending forth your holy and lifegiving Spirit;

Through him therefore with the faithful who rest in him and all the glorious company of heaven, joyfully we praise you and say:

People: **Holy, holy, holy Lord, God of power and might, heaven and earth are full of your glory.**

Hosanna in the highest.

*27 **Blessed is he who comes in the name of the Lord.**

Hosanna in the highest.

Kneel

28 *Priest :*   All glory and thanksgiving to you, Holy Father,
because you gave your only son Jesus Christ,
to be the one perfect sacrifice
for the sin of the world,
that all who believe in him
might have eternal life.

     The night before he died on the cross

The Priest takes the bread into his hands he took bread;
and when he had given thanks,
he broke it, gave it to his disciples
and said;

Take, eat, this is my body
which is given for you;
do this to remember me.

The Priest takes the cup into his hands After supper he took the cup
and when he had given thanks,
he gave it to them and said;

Drink this, all of you,
for this is my blood of the new covenant
which is shed for you and for many
for the forgiveness of sins;
do this as often as you drink it,
to remember me.

People :   **Glory to you, Lord Christ:**
your death we show forth:
your resurrection we proclaim:
your coming we await:
Amen; Come Lord Jesus.

Priest :   Therefore, Father, looking for the coming of your kingdom,
We now celebrate the memorial of our redemption
with this bread of life and this cup of salvation;
Accept us, unworthy though we are;
accept us in him we pray,
with this our sacrifice of praise and thanksgiving.
Grant that this bread and wine which we receive
may be to us the body and blood of Christ;

Fill us with your Holy Spirit
and by his grace and power
make us one in the body of Christ
with all who share these holy things:

People :   **All glory and honour to you**
almighty Father,
here and everywhere,
now and forever.
Amen.

★29 Priest :   As our Lord has taught us, we pray:

People :   **Our Father . . . [ICET 1] . . . ever. Amen.**

THE BREAKING OF THE BREAD

Then shall the priest break the bread, saying :

30 *Priest :*   The bread we break is a sharing in the Body of Christ.

People :   **We who are many are one body, for we all partake of**
the one bread.

THE COMMUNION

★31 Priest or Priest and People :

We do not . . . [CF 6] . . . he in us. **Amen.**

this your table] your holy table
manifold and great mercies] great mercy
so much as] even
gather up] OM up
under] from under
flesh] body

Here, or during the Communion, may be said or sung :

★32 People :   **Lamb of God, you take away the sin of the world, have**
mercy on us.
Lamb of God you take away the sin of the world, have
mercy on us.
Lamb of God, you take away the sin of the world,
grant us your peace.

33 *Priest :*   Draw near and receive the Body and Blood of our Lord
Jesus Christ in remembrance that Christ died for you, and
feed on him in your hearts by faith with thanksgiving.

The Priest shall receive the Holy Communion himself and it shall next be administered to the Ministers who assist the Priest and then to the rest of the People. He who delivers the consecrated bread and wine shall say to each one who receives:

34   The Body of our Lord Jesus Christ given for you.

[*OR:* Ko te Tinana o to tatou Ariki, o Ihu Karaiti, i tukua nei mou.]

(*The recipient may say:* **Amen.**)

The Blood of our Lord Jesus Christ shed for you.

[*OR:* Ko nga Toto o to tatou Ariki, o Ihu Karaiti, i whakahekea nei mou.]

(*The recipient may say:* **Amen.**)

THANKSGIVING AND DISMISSAL

★35   *The LORD'S PRAYER (which is to be used at least ONCE in this service) may be said here if it has not been said at 29.*

36   *Priest:*   Almighty and everliving God, we thank you with all our hearts for feeding us with the spiritual food of the most precious Body and Blood of your Son our Saviour, Jesus Christ. We thank you for your love and care in assuring us of your gift of eternal life and uniting us with the blessed company of all faithful people.

People: **Therefore, heavenly Father, keep us steadfast in your holy fellowship, And now we offer ourselves, soul and body, to serve you faithfully in the world, through Jesus Christ our Lord, to whom with you and the Holy Spirit be all honour and glory, world without end. Amen.**

★37   *A blessing may be given (for a suggested form see the Appendix).*

38   *Priest:*   Go forth into the world in peace.

People: **We go in the name of Christ.**

APPENDIX

a. *THE TEN COMMANDMENTS*

The Minister shall say:

Minister: Hear the commandments which God gave to the people of Israel by his servant Moses.

After each commandment, or after the Fourth and the Tenth, the People shall reply :

People :   **Amen. Lord, have mercy.**

Minister :   You shall have no other Gods . . . [CF 2, omitting portions in brackets] . . . not covet anything which belongs to your neighbour.

> for yourself any graven image] make yourself idols.
> bow down to them, nor worship] worship them or serve
> to keep holy the Sabbath day] the sabbath day and keep it holy
> commit murder] murder

b. *THE SUMMARY OF THE LAW*

Minister :   Hear these words of Jesus Christ:

> You shall love . . . [CF 3] . . . you shall love your neighbour as yourself.

People :   **Amen. Lord, have mercy.**

> with all] INSERT and BEFORE EACH EXCEPT FIRST
> first] first and greatest
> The second] and a second

c. *THE NEW COMMANDMENTS*

Minister :   Our Lord Jesus Christ says: A new commandment I give to you, that you love one another as I have loved you.

d. *THE KYRIES*

Minister :   Lord, have mercy.   Kyrie eleison.

People :   **Christ, have mercy.** *OR* **Christe eleison.**

Minister :   Lord, have mercy.   Kyrie eleison.

Repeating each three times if desired.

e. *ADDITIONS TO THE EUCHARISTIC PRAYER*

[The 'Proper Prefaces' which are printed out here are to be found in Appendix C. The Preface itself is printed out with six different sets of key words in capitals with a code number beside each. The 'Proper Prefaces' themselves then start with the various key words in capitals, and also have the code number to ensure that they are fitted in the right place. The key words in capitals are repeated in Appendix C.]

f. COMMUNION

If insufficient bread and wine has been set apart for the Communion, the Priest shall take in his hands as much as is needed and say :

Priest :   Heavenly Father, obeying the command of our Lord Jesus Christ we take this bread† and pray that it also be set apart for this holy use, so that it may be to us the Body†† of our Lord Jesus Christ. Amen.

† *or* wine, *or* bread and wine.

†† *or* Blood, *or* Body and Blood.

g. A SUITABLE BLESSING

Priest :   The peace of God . . . [CF 9] . . . be with you now and forever. **Amen.**

the knowledge and love of God, and of his Son] OM
Jesus Christ our Lord] Christ Jesus

NOTES

[There follow twelve general notes on announcing of lessons, dress of ministers, and use of options, etc.]

CHAPTER 27

THE CHURCH OF THE PROVINCE
OF MELANESIA

UNTIL January, 1975, when it became an independent Province[1], Melanesia was a missionary Diocese of the Church of the Province of New Zealand. It was made famous in Anglican history by the labours and martyrdom of its first Bishop, John Coleridge Patteson, who was Bishop from 1861 to 1871. The Province of Melanesia consists of the British Solomon Islands, the New Hebrides (including the Banks and Torres Groups), and the French territory of New Caledonia. The New Hebrides is unique in being a Franco-British Condominium.[2]

The 1662 rite has been translated over the last century into certain Melanesian languages. Later the English 1928 rite slightly amended was used as a basic 'Melanesian rite', but was not translated into all the vernacular languages, thus leaving a proportion of the diocese still using 1662. Later still the New Zealand rite of 1966 (**NZ**)[3] was authorized for the diocese, but shortly after that, when it became clear that **NZ** was unacceptable in Melanesia[4] the General Synod gave permission for the missionary dioceses to establish their own rites. Thus the Bishop, the Rt. Rev. J. W. Chisholm, started the move towards a Melanesian rite soon after his appointment as diocesan in 1967. He drafted a rite which was tried out at the cathedral and in the theological college and elsewhere, and was then redrafted in the light of comment received. His main idea was to compile a rite in modern English with no alternatives, in order to make it as easy as possible to use and translate.

---

[1] See *Partners in Mission*, pp.32-33, where this was recommended.

[2] This can be picked out in the liturgy by the paragraph in the intercessions which names Queen Elizabeth and adds '(and the President of France)'. This is different from, say, the Church of Ireland, where prayer is made for *either* the Queen *or* the President of the Republic. Here, in the appropriate territory, as nowhere else on earth, the Queen and the President of a Republic are joined together in the prayers.

[3] For the text see **MAL**, pp.329-39. For mention of its authorization for Melanesia and Polynesia see **MAL**, p.326.

[4] Polynesia in fact accepted **NZ**, and translated it into Fijian, Hindi, and Tongan. Since then the seasonal propers of 1970 (**NZR**, see pp.368-79 above) have been adopted, as have the **NZR** provisions for supplementary consecration and the blessing. 1662 is used only at Suva Cathedral, and there on Sundays only once a month.

The Bishop then set up in 1968 a Liturgical Committee, chaired by the Ven. D. A. Rawcliffe, Archdeacon of Southern Melanesia, and this Committee revised the drafts and produced a definitive 'Liturgy for Melanesia', which was approved by the Diocesan Conference (for optional use) in 1969. Since then the Liturgical Committee has been producing a complete 'Modern English Prayer Book'. In the light of experience, the eucharistic rite was amended slightly at the point of incorporation into this Prayer Book. The Prayer Book itself is intended to replace all previous books (in whatever language), and thus the Melanesian rite will, as it is translated and printed in all languages[1], soon replace other existing uses. It is the rite from the Modern English Prayer Book which is set out here as **Mel.** The debt of the rite to 1928, **Eng2,** and **NZ** will be easy to discern. Its distinctive features are: there is no Old Testament reading (unlike virtually every other new Anglican rite since 1960); there is a local modern English rendering of the Lord's Prayer (obviously simplified to help further translation); and the theological Gordian Knot of *eis ten emen anamnesin* is briskly cut with the words 'Do this in remembrance of me and know that I am with you'. It may be that this helps those translating into vernacular tongues—but it is doubtful if it would translate back into Greek in such a way as to look like the Pauline text without remainder.

THE MELANESIAN LITURGY 1973 (Mel)

[In the text below the numbering is editorial. The ICET and other Common Forms have not been cited, as the modern English is not related to these forms, but is a local updating of traditional forms.]

A LITURGY FOR MELANESIA

PRIVATE PREPARATION

[Some guidance on preparation is printed here, followed by a version of the Prayer of Humble Access.]

THE LITURGY

(THE HOLY COMMUNION)

1 *Stand*

In the name of the Father, and of the Son and of the Holy Spirit. **Amen.**

---

[1] The 'Modern English Prayer Book', in its 1973 edition became called 'The Melanesian Prayer Book'.

2 *All say :*

Almighty God, all hearts are open, and all desires known to you, and no secrets are hidden from you; cleanse our thoughts by the breath of your Holy Spirit, so that we may truly love you, and worthily praise your holy name; through Jesus Christ, our Lord. Amen.

		OR
Lord have mercy	[Repeat twice more]	**Kyrie eleison**
Christ have mercy	[Repeat twice more]	**Christe eleison**
Lord have mercy	[Repeat twice more]	**Kyrie eleison**

3
GLORIA

Glory be to God on high, and on earth peace to men of goodwill. We praise you, we bless you, we worship you, we glorify you, we thank you for your great glory, O Lord God, heavenly King, God the Father Almighty.

O Lord, the only-begotten Son, Jesus Christ; O Lord God, Lamb of God, Son of the Father, you take away the sin of the world, have mercy on us. O Lord, you take away the sin of the world, receive our prayer. O Lord, you sit at the right hand of God the Father, have mercy on us.

You only are the Holy One, you alone are Lord, you alone, Jesus Christ, with the Holy Spirit, are most high in the glory of God the Father. Amen.

4 Let us pray.

THE COLLECT (Pages 19-44 *Modern English Prayer Book)*

5 *THE EPISTLE* Sit

6 *THE GOSPEL* Stand

V. The Lord be with you,

R. **And with you.**

Before the Gospel :

Glory be to you, O Lord.

After the Gospel :

Praise be to you, O Christ.

7 *SERMON*

8 THE CREED

We believe in one God, the Father Almighty, Maker of heaven and earth, and of all things seen and unseen.

And in one Lord Jesus Christ, the only-begotten Son of God, eternally begotten from the Father; God from God; Light from Light; true God from true God; begotten not made; being of one substance with the Father; through whom all things were made; who for us men and for our salvation came down from heaven, and was made flesh, by the Holy Spirit, of the Virgin Mary, and became man; and was crucified also for us under Pontius Pilate; he suffered and was buried; and the third day he rose again according to the Scriptures; and ascended into heaven and sits at the right hand of the Father; and he shall come again, with glory, to judge both the living and the dead; his rule shall have no end.

And we believe in the Holy Spirit, the Lord, the giver of life, who comes from the Father and the Son; who with the Father and the Son together is worshipped and glorified; who spoke by the Prophets.

And we believe one holy Catholic and Apostolic Church; we believe one baptism for the forgiveness of sins; and we look for the resurrection of the dead and the life of the world to come. Amen.

9   THE INTERCESSION

Kneel

Let us pray for the whole Church of Christ and for all men according to their needs:

Almighty God, as we have been taught by your holy Word to give thanks and to pray for all men, so now we give thanks for all your blessings . . .

V. Let us bless the Lord.

R. **Thanks be to God.**

We ask you to receive our prayers for the whole Church of Christ, that it may be filled with the spirit of goodness and peace, and that all who believe in your holy Name may agree in the truth of your holy Word and live as a family in unity and love.

V. Lord in your mercy

R. **Hear our prayer.**

Fill with grace all ministers of your Word and Sacraments, especially your servants . . . our bishops, and all the priests and deacons of this diocese . . . , that by their life and teaching they may show your glory and draw all men to you.

V. Lord in your mercy

R. **Hear our prayer.**

We pray for the rulers of the nations, and especially for your servants Queen Elizabeth (and the President of France), and all who have authority and rule . . . , that they may wisely and justly govern, and give peace and care to all peoples.

V. Lord in your mercy

R. **Hear our prayer.**

Guide and help, we pray, those who are working for the spread of your good news in every place . . . , and bring the light of your Spirit to all places of work, learning and healing . . .

V. Lord in your mercy

R. **Hear our prayer.**

To all your people in their many callings give your heavenly grace, and especially (. . . and) to us your servants, that we may all hear your holy Word with good and willing hearts, and serve you truly all the days of our life.

V. Lord in your mercy

R. **Hear our prayer.**

We ask you, Father, that your great love and kindness may comfort and help all who are in trouble, sorrow, need or sickness . . .

V. Lord in your mercy

R. **Hear our prayer.**

We pray for all your servants departed this life in your faith and fear . . . , and we praise you for all your saints . . . , for whose goodness we give you thanks and whose good ways we pray that we may follow, and enter with them into your endless joy.

Grant these our prayers, O holy Father, if they are according to your will, through your Son Jesus Christ our Lord. **Amen.**

ALTERNATIVE INTERCESSION

(*It is not necessary to use all these petitions. They may be left out, joined together, or added to, as the person conducting them wishes.*)

(*The response after* 'We thank you' *or* 'We pray to you' *is :* **'Lord, hear our prayer.'**)

For . . . , we thank you;

For the union of all Christians in one holy Church, we pray to you;

For all bishops, priests and deacons, and all other servants of the Church (especially . . .), we pray to you;

For all men that they may hear and receive your Word (especially . . .), we pray to you;

For all the heathen of our islands (especially . . .) and all who work among them, we pray to you;

For the peace of the whole world (especially . . .), we pray to you;

For the rulers of all nations that they may govern according to your holy will, we pray to you;

For our own country and for Queen Elizabeth (and the President of France) and for all our leaders (especially . . .), we pray to you;

For all men and women in their daily life and work (especially . . .), we pray to you;

For all who work in towns and on plantations and ships, we pray to you;

For our relations and friends, and for parents and children everywhere, we pray to you;

For all who teach or learn in our schools and colleges (especially . . .), we pray to you;

For all who travel by land, sea and air (especially . . .), we pray to you;

For the poor and hungry and those without homes, we pray to you;

For those in need of work, we pray to you;

For the lonely and those who are badly treated by others (especially . . .), we pray to you;

For our enemies and those we have hurt, we pray to you;

For the sick and suffering in mind and body (especially . . .), we pray to you;

For the dying and those who have departed this life (especially . . .), we pray to you;

Let us pray in silence for our own needs.

SILENCE

V. Lord in your mercy

R. **Hear our prayer.**

Grant these our prayers, O Holy Father, if they are according to your will, through your Son Jesus Christ our Lord. **Amen.**

11 *THE INVITATION*

Now let us come with sorrow and true faith and make our confession to our heavenly Father.

SILENCE

12 *CONFESSION*

Almighty Father, Judge of all men, we have sinned against you in what we have thought, said and done. We have not loved you with all our hearts; we have not loved your people as ourselves. Forgive us for the sake of your Son our Saviour Jesus Christ, and help us to serve you in the new life, to the glory of your Name. Amen.

13 *ABSOLUTION*

Almighty God, our merciful Father, who has promised forgiveness of sins to all who are truly sorry, turn to him in faith and are ready to forgive others; have mercy on you, pardon and save you from all your sins, make you strong in all goodness, and keep you in life eternal; through Jesus Christ our Lord. **Amen.**

14 *OFFERTORY*

Stand

V. The Peace of the Lord be always with you,

R. **And with you.**

V. We are the body of Christ,

R. **By one Spirit we were baptised into one Body.**

V. Try hard to keep the unity of the Spirit,

R. **In the bond of peace.**

15 *Bread and wine are offered and the following is said:*

V. To you Lord belong the greatness, and the power and the glory, and the victory and the majesty.

R. **All that is in the heavens and in the earth is yours, and of your own we give you.**

16   *THE GREAT THANKSGIVING*

V. Lift up your hearts,

R. **We lift them up to the Lord.**

V. Let us give thanks to the Lord our God.

R. **It is good and right to do so.**

It is good and right that we give all praise, glory and thanksgiving to you heavenly Father, through Jesus Christ your Son our Lord, because through him you have created all things from the beginning and made us in your likeness; through him in the fullness of time you redeemed us, when we had fallen into sin, giving him to be born as man, to die on the Cross and to rise again for us; setting him in glory at your right hand. To us you gave your Holy Spirit to make us a holy people, to fill us with new life and to give us hope for the coming of your Rule.

And so with angels and archangels and all the glorious company of heaven, joyfully we praise you and say:

Holy, Holy, Holy, Lord God of hosts, Heaven and earth are full of your glory. Glory to you, O Lord most high.

Blessed is he who comes in the Name of the Lord.

Hosanna in the Highest.

Kneel

ALL GLORY TO YOU, heavenly Father who in your loving mercy gave your only Son Jesus Christ that all who believe in him might have eternal life.

Hear us Father, through your Son Jesus Christ our Lord; through him accept our offering of praise, and grant that by the power of your Holy Spirit these gifts of bread and wine may be for us his body and blood.

On the night before he suffered on the Cross, he took bread, and when he had given thanks to you he broke it, and gave it to his disciples, and said, 'Take, eat, THIS IS MY BODY WHICH IS GIVEN FOR YOU; DO THIS IN REMEMBRANCE OF ME AND KNOW THAT I AM WITH YOU'. In the same way after supper he took the cup, and when he had given thanks to you, he gave it to them, and said, 'DRINK THIS, ALL OF YOU, FOR THIS IS MY BLOOD OF THE NEW COVENANT WHICH IS SHED FOR YOU AND FOR MANY FOR THE FORGIVENESS OF SINS; DO THIS AS OFTEN AS YOU DRINK IT, IN RE-MEMBRANCE OF ME AND KNOW THAT I AM WITH YOU.'

All say :

His death Father we show forth, his resurrection we proclaim, his coming we await, Glory to you, Lord most high.

Priest :

And so Father we do this as your Son commanded, and we offer to you the bread of life and the cup of salvation as our sacrifice of praise and thanksgiving, showing forth his death on the Cross for the sin of the world, his mighty resurrection and glorious ascension.

Accept us in him our Saviour, who offered the one perfect Sacrifice, and grant that all we who receive this holy Communion may be made one in your holy Church, the body of your Son Jesus Christ, our Lord; through whom in the unity of the Holy Spirit all honour and glory be to you, Almighty Father, for ever and ever. **Amen.**

17   *SILENCE*

18 As our Lord has taught us we say:

Our Father in heaven, holy be your Name, your rule come, your will be done, in the world as it is in heaven. Give us this day our food for today. Forgive us what we do wrong as we forgive those who do wrong to us. Bring us not into trouble to try us, but save us from evil. For yours is the rule and the power and the glory for ever. Amen.

19   *THE BREAKING OF THE BREAD*

V. The bread we break, it is a sharing in the body of Christ.

R. **There is one bread, and we who are many are one body, for we all share in the one bread.**

O Lamb of God, you take away the sin of the world, have mercy on us.

O Lamb of God, you take away the sin of the world, have mercy on us.

O Lamb of God, you take away the sin of the world, give us your peace.

20 Draw near with faith—receive the Body of our Lord Jesus Christ which was given for you, and his Blood which was shed for you, and feed on him in your hearts by faith with thanksgiving.

In giving the Holy Food the Priest says :

V. THE BODY of our Lord Jesus Christ.

R. **Amen.**

V. THE BLOOD of our Lord Jesus Christ.

R. **Amen.**

21 *After the ablutions the Priest says:*
Let us pray.

Almighty and everliving God, we thank you with all our hearts for feeding us with the holy food of the body and blood of your Son, our Saviour Jesus Christ. We also thank you for your love and care for us in making us members of his living body which is the family of all your people, and for giving us a share in eternal life.

All say:

And so Father keep us in your grace, that we may do the good work that you have made ready for us. And here we give ourselves, our souls and bodies to you, to be a holy and living sacrifice, through Jesus Christ our Lord, to whom with you and the Holy Spirit be all honour and glory for ever and ever. Amen.

22   *THE BLESSING*

Go in peace; love and serve the Lord, be full of joy in the power of the Holy Spirit.

And the Blessing of God Almighty, the Father, the Son and the Holy Spirit, be with you and stay with you for ever. **Amen.**

If more bread or wine are needed the Priest will say:

23 Let us pray

Hear us Father, through your Son Jesus Christ; through him accept our offering of praise and grant that by the power of your Holy Spirit this gift of bread (or wine) may be for us his Body (or Blood).

On the night before he suffered on the Cross

(for bread)

He took bread, and when he had given thanks to you, he broke it and gave it to his disciples and said—'Take eat, this is my Body which is given for you; do this in remembrance of me and know that I am with you.'

(for wine)

He took the cup, and when he had given thanks to you, he gave it to them and said—'Drink this all of you, for this is my blood of the New Covenant which is shed for you and for many for the forgiveness of sins. Do this as often as you drink it, in remembrance of me and know that I am with you'

24   *AFTER COMMUNION*

[There follow suggestions for private meditations and prayers.]

APPENDIXES

COMMON FORMS

THESE forms are printed here once for all, following the principle employed in **LiE** and **MAL**. They are, however, different forms from the 1662 ones which, with a few extras, comprised those in the previous books. The change to the 'you' form of address to God, along with other modernization, has led to a whole new set of 'Common Forms'.

The texts are divided into two. The first set (with the code lettering of 'ICET') comes from the International Consultation on English Texts,[1] and these are translated texts of material common to all Christians. An *apparatus* to these texts gives the 1970 form where it differed from the definitive 1971 form, and also, where relevant, the 1969 draft forms, and forms from *Modern Liturgical Texts* (1968)[2] or from the Roman Catholic International Committee for English in the Liturgy (as they were used in **SAfr1** in 1969[3]). It also includes the 1974 further revisions, which were agreed in early 1974, but only released whilst the volume was at the press. These were adopted in **Can1**, but it is the 1971 texts which are standard for most rites in this book.

An almost complete set of ICET texts is here given,[4] though no citing of ICET 'Common Forms' is done in the various liturgies for parts which come within the Great Thanksgiving. Thus, even where the Sanctus from ICET is followed *verbatim* in a rite, it will still be printed out. The ICET forms are printed here in such cases purely for the sake of comparison. The second set ('CF') is mainly drawn from **Eng3**, and it provides the texts for specifically Anglican material. The two exceptions are the Words of Administration, where the **Eng2** form of the 1662 words is given, and the Decalogue, where **Eng3** has a different text from the traditional versions. In the latter case, a 'consensus' translation is here offered, which does not appear *verbatim* in any rite, but provides a useful point of departure for indicating variants.

Because of the division of the Common Form material into two separate sets, and because of its linguistic discontinuity with the past,

---

[1] Details of the Consultation are to be found on pp.10-12 above.

[2] For details of this see p.4 above. The variants below are labelled 'MLT' rather than '**MLT**', as they come from the body of the booklet, rather than from the updated version of **Eng2** at the end of it.

[3] These are labelled 'ICEL'. They are *not* the same as recent ICEL ones.

[4] The omissions are Benedictus, Nunc Dimittis and Magnificat.

any comparison with Common Forms in **LiE** and **MAL** is unnecessary and probably misleading. The titles given are those of ICET in the first set, and are standard editorial ones in the second. The various forms are referred to in the text of the rites thus: [ICET 4], [CF 6]. Where a liturgy uses a Common Form with variants, then the changes are shown in the notes in the text. Where the changes are substantial, then at intervals editorial discretion has decreed that it is preferable to present the entire text without reference to the Common Forms.

The cue words at the beginning and end of each citation of a Common Form in the texts are important. Changes from the Common Form are not recorded in the notes if they occur in these cue words, and on occasion the cue words have been extended to a whole sentence or more in order to convey such changes. Omissions can also be inferred in the same way.

Differences of punctuation, spelling, use of capitals, and lining out have been ignored in the citations. Whether or not the Common Form, or any part of it, is to be said or sung congregationally cannot be indicated in this Appendix (where no texts are printed in bold type), but is shown from the rubrics and the bold type in the actual texts.

A. ICET Forms

ICET 1. THE LORD'S PRAYER

Our Father in heaven,
  holy be your Name,
  your kingdom come,
  your will be done,
    on earth as in heaven.
Give us today our daily bread.
Forgive us our sins
  as we forgive those who sin against us.
Do not bring us to the test
  but deliver us from evil.

For the kingdom, the power, and the glory are yours
  now and for ever.

MLT: COMPLETELY DIFFERENT
1969: holy be] glorify
      Do not bring us to the test but] Save us from the time of trial and
1974: holy] hallowed
      Do not bring us to the test but] Save us from the time of trial and

ICET 2. THE APOSTLES' CREED

I believe in God, the Father almighty,
  creator of heaven and earth.
I believe in Jesus Christ, his only Son, our Lord.
  He was conceived by the power of the Holy Spirit
    and born of the Virgin Mary.
  He suffered under Pontius Pilate,
    was crucified, died, and was buried.
  He descended to the dead.
  On the third day he rose again.
  He ascended into heaven,
    and is seated at the right hand of the Father.
  He will come again to judge the living and the dead.
I believe in the Holy Spirit,
  the holy catholic Church,
  the communion of saints,
  the forgiveness of sins,
  the resurrection of the body,
  and the life everlasting.

MLT: God, the Father almighty] God the Father, the Almighty TWICE
  was crucified . . . to the dead] he was crucified, and died;
                                     he was buried, and went down to the dead
  everlasting] eternal

ICEL: God, the Father almighty] God, the Father, the Almighty
  was crucified] he was crucified
  descended] went down
  hand of the Father] hand of God the almighty Father.
  life everlasting] everlasting life

ICET 3. THE NICENE CREED

We believe in one God,
  the Father, the Almighty,
  maker of heaven and earth,
  of all that is seen and unseen.

We believe in one Lord, Jesus Christ,
  the only Son of God,
  eternally begotten of the Father,
  God from God, Light from Light,
  true God from true God,
  begotten, not made, one in Being with the Father.

Through him all things were made.
For us men and for our salvation
  he came down from heaven:
by the power of the Holy Spirit
  he was born of the Virgin Mary, and became man.
For our sake he was crucified under Pontius Pilate;
  he suffered, died, and was buried.
    On the third day he rose again
      in fulfilment of the Scriptures;
    he ascended into heaven
      and is seated at the right hand of the Father.
He will come again in glory to judge the living and the dead,
  and his kingdom will have no end.

We believe in the Holy Spirit, the Lord, the giver of life,
  who proceeds from the Father (and the Son).
With the Father and the Son he is worshipped and glorified.
He has spoken through the Prophets.
We believe in one holy catholic and apostolic Church.
We acknowledge one baptism for the forgiveness of sins.
We look for the resurrection of the dead,
  and the life of the world to come. Amen.

MLT: DIFFERENT

ICEL: that is seen and unseen] things visible and invisible
      in one Lord] in the one Lord
      only] only-begotten
      eternally begotten of the Father] Son of the Father from all eternity
      one in Being] one in Godhead[1]
      On the third day he rose again] He arose on the third day
      who proceeds] he proceeds
      (and the Son)] OMIT BRACKETS
      With the Father] Together with the Father

1969: IDENTICAL

1974: is seen] is, seen
      one in Being] of one Being
      was born of] became incarnate from
      became man] was made man [but **Can1** reads 'became man']
      suffered, died] suffered death
      in fulfilment of] in accordance with

[1] ['One in Godhead' takes its origin from MLT.]

ICET 4. GLORIA IN EXCELSIS

Glory to God in the highest,
  and peace to his people on earth.
Lord God, heavenly King,
almighty God and Father,
  we worship you, we give you thanks,
  we praise you for your glory.
Lord Jesus Christ, only Son of the Father,
Lord God, Lamb of God,
you take away the sin of the world:
  have mercy on us;
you are seated at the right hand of the Father:
  receive our prayer.
For you alone are the Holy One,
you alone are the Lord,
you alone are the Most High,
  Jesus Christ,
  with the Holy Spirit,
  in the glory of God the Father. Amen.

MLT: DIFFERENT, CLOSER TO ORIGINAL

ICEL: the highest] heaven
     and peace] Peace and grace
     LINES 3-6 COME IN THE ORDER 6, 5, 3, 4
     for your glory] for your great glory
     Lord Jesus . . . Lamb of God] Lord Jesus Christ, Lamb of God
                                     Lord God, only Son of the Father,
     are seated] sit
     receive] hear
     For you alone] You alone
     God the Father] the Father

1969: the highest] heaven
     sin] sins

1970: mercy on] mercy upon

ICET 5(a). SANCTUS

Holy, holy, holy Lord, God of power and might,
heaven and earth are full of your glory.
  Hosanna in the highest.

ICET 5(b). BENEDICTUS

Blessed is he who comes in the name of the Lord.
  Hosanna in the highest.

ICET 6. GLORIA PATRI

Glory to the Father, and to the Son, and to the Holy Spirit:
  as in the beginning, so now, and for ever. Amen.

ICET 7. SURSUM CORDA

The Lord be with you.
And also with you.
Lift up your hearts.
We lift them up to the Lord.
Let us give thanks to the Lord Our God.
It is right to give him thanks and praise.

1970: The Lord be] The Spirit of the Lord be[1]
1970, 1974: Our] our

ICET 8. AGNUS DEI

Jesus, Lamb of God:
  have mercy on us.
Jesus, bearer of our sins:
  have mercy on us.
Jesus, redeemer of the world:
  give us your peace.[2]

ICET 9. TE DEUM

You are God: we praise you;
You are the Lord: we acclaim you:
You are the eternal Father:
All creation worships you.
To you all angels, all the powers of heaven,
Cherubim and Seraphim, sing in endless praise:
  Holy, holy, holy Lord, God of power and might.
  heaven and earth are full of your glory.
The glorious company of apostles praise you.
The noble fellowship of prophets praise you.
The white-robed army of martyrs praise you.
Throughout the world the holy Church acclaims you:
  Father, of majesty unbounded,
  your true and only Son, worthy of all worship,
  and the Holy Spirit, advocate and guide.

---

[1] [This translation derives from MLT, where an argument for it is given on pp.31-2. **Eng3**, however, has gone on to another rendering still.]

[2] [This text is taken *verbatim* from the **MLT** modernized version of **Eng2** (see pp. 4 and 39 above). It is presented in the liturgical texts in three lines, not six.]

You, Christ, are the king of glory,
eternal Son of the Father.
When you became man to set us free
you did not shrink from the Virgin's womb.
You overcame the sting of death.
and opened the kingdom of heaven to all believers.
You are seated at God's right hand in glory.
We believe that you will come, and be our judge.

    Come then, Lord, to the help of your people,
    bought with the price of your own blood,
    and bring us with your saints
    to everlasting glory.

[1]Save your people, Lord, and bless your inheritance.
Govern and uphold them now and always.
Day by day we bless you.
We praise your name for ever.
Today, Lord, keep us from all sin.
Have mercy on us, Lord, have mercy.
Lord, show us your love and mercy;
for we put our trust in you.
In you, Lord, is our hope:
May we never be confounded.

1970: acclaim] hail
       sing in endless praise] continually sing
       Throughout the world the holy Church] The holy Church throughout
         the world
       advocate] counsel
       are the king] are king
       eternal Son of the Father] the Father's everlasting Son
       set us free] deliver us
       shrink from] spurn
       overcame] removed
       the kingdom of OMIT
       at God's right hand in glory] in glory at God's right hand
       Lord, to the help of your people] deliver your people
       everlasting glory] glory everlasting
       Save your people . . . be confounded OMIT
1974: we acclaim] [and] we acclaim
       eternal Son] the eternal Son
       shrink from] spurn
       to the help] and help
       everlasting glory] glory everlasting
       may we never be confounded] and we shall never hope in vain

[1] [The last ten lines are *capitella* which were not part of the original canticle. They are omitted in MLT (which at other points lies behind the text above) and in 1970. In 1971 and 1974 they are set out as '*Versicles and responses after the Te Deum*'.]

B. Other Common Forms

CF 1. THE COLLECT FOR PURITY (**Eng3**)

Almighty God,
to whom all hearts are open,
all desires known,
and from whom no secrets are hid:
cleanse the thoughts of our hearts
by the inspiration of your Holy Spirit,
that we may perfectly love you,
and worthily magnify your holy Name;
through Christ our Lord. Amen.

CF 2. THE DECALOGUE (A 'consensus' text).

God spoke these words and said:

I am the Lord your God; you shall have no other gods but me.

You shall not make for yourself any graven image, [nor the likeness of anything that is in heaven above, or in the earth beneath or in the water under the earth]. You shall not bow down to them, nor worship them.

You shall not take the Name of the Lord your God in vain.

Remember to keep holy the sabbath day. [Six days you shall labour, and do all that you have to do; but the seventh day is the Sabbath of the Lord your God.]

Honour your father and your mother.

You shall not commit murder.

You shall not commit adultery.

You shall not steal.

You shall not bear false witness [against your neighbour].

You shall not covet.

CF 3. THE SUMMARY OF THE LAW (**Eng3**)

Our Lord Jesus Christ said: The Lord our God is the only Lord. You shall love the Lord your God with all your heart, with all your soul, with all your mind, and with all your strength. This is the first commandment. The second is this: Love your neighbour as yourself. There is no other commandment greater than these.

CF 4. THE COMFORTABLE WORDS **(Eng3)**

Hear the words of comfort our Saviour Christ says to all who truly turn to him.

Come to me, all who labour and are heavy-laden, and I will give you rest.

God so loved the world that he gave his only Son, that whoever believes in him should not perish but have eternal life.

Hear what St Paul says.

This saying is true and worthy of full acceptance, that Christ Jesus came into the world to save sinners.

Hear what St John says.

If anyone does sin, we have an advocate with the Father, Jesus Christ the righteous; and he is the expiation of our sins.

CF 5. THE ABSOLUTION **(Eng3)**

Almighty God, who forgives all who truly repent, have mercy upon you, pardon and deliver you from all your sins, confirm and strengthen you in all goodness, and keep you in life eternal; through Jesus Christ our Lord. Amen.

CF 6. THE PRAYER OF HUMBLE ACCESS **(Eng3)**

We do not presume
to come to this your table, merciful Lord,
trusting in our own righteousness,
but in your manifold and great mercies.
We are not worthy
so much as to gather up the crumbs under your table.
But you are the same Lord
whose nature is always to have mercy.
Grant us therefore, gracious Lord,
so to eat the flesh of your dear Son Jesus Christ,
and to drink his blood,
that we may evermore dwell in him,
and he in us. Amen.

CF 7(a). THE WORDS OF ADMINISTRATION FOR THE BREAD (Eng2—longer form)

The Body of our Lord Jesus Christ, which was given for you, preserve your body and soul to everlasting life. Take and eat this in remembrance that Christ died for you, and feed on him in your heart by faith with thanksgiving.

CF 7(b). THE WORDS OF ADMINISTRATION FOR THE CUP (Eng2—longer form)

The Blood of our Lord Jesus Christ, which was shed for you, preserve your body and soul to everlasting life. Drink this in remembrance that Christ's Blood was shed for you, and be thankful.

CF 8. POST-COMMUNION PRAYER OF THANKSGIVING AND SELF-OFFERING (Eng3)

Almighty God,
we thank you for feeding us
with the body and blood of your Son Jesus Christ.
Through him we offer you our souls and bodies
to be a living sacrifice.
Send us out
in the power of your Spirit
to live and work
to your praise and glory. Amen.

CF 9. THE BLESSING (Eng3)

The peace of God, which passes all understanding, keep your hearts and minds in the knowledge and love of God, and of his Son Jesus Christ our Lord;
And the blessing of God Almighty, the Father, the Son, and the Holy Spirit, be among you, and remain with you always. Amen.

OFFERTORY SENTENCES

THIS Appendix does not reproduce all the material in **MAL** in the way that **MAL** reproduced **LiE**'s. The use of 'Offertory' Sentences has diminished very considerably in the new texts, and they barely warrant the use of a separate Appendix at all. The following points should be noted:

1 The sentences for general use come from **Amer1-3**[1], **Aus1A**, **ChilR**, and **Ire1** only. **CSIR** and **Ire1** contribute the only seasonal ones.

2 The sentences for general use are numbered from 1 to 20 consecutively, with the **LiE/MAL** corresponding numbers shown in brackets beside them. A similar procedure is used for the **Ire1** seasonal sentences.

3 No notice has been taken of sentences used at the presentation of elements or offerings at the Table. These are always set out in the text of the rites. The sentences here precede any such presentation. It is solely their position in the rite which qualifies them for inclusion here.

4 No distinctions have been made between Bible versions. The forms shown here are copied from **LiE/MAL** as far as possible but most rites now use a more modern version. It should be noted however that the **Amer1-3** selection includes both 'thou' and 'you' forms of 1 Chron. 29:11 and Rev. 4:11, as it has to serve both 'thou' and 'you' form rites (**Amer1** being 'thou' and the others 'you'). Thus the forms here do not indicate which version is prescribed in the original rites. **ChilR** of course was drafted in Spanish. The listing here tells *which* sentences of Scripture are employed, but not their form.

---

[1] This coding is used because the sentences appear in an Appendix to the three services **Amer1**, **Amer2** and **Amer3**, and are provided for use with any of them.

TABLE I

SENTENCES FOR GENERAL USE

1(1) Let your light . . . is in heaven (Matt. 5:16) **Aus1A**

2(2) Lay not up . . . break through and steal (Matt. 6:19) **ChilR**

3(4) Not everyone that saith . . . is in heaven (Matt. 7:21) **Ire1**

4(9) He that soweth . . . cheerful giver (2 Cor. 9:6f.) **ChilR**

5(10) Let him that is taught . . . he reap (Gal. 6:6) **Aus1A**

6(11) While we have time . . . household of faith (Gal. 6:10) **Aus1A, ChilR**

7(15) To do good . . . is pleased (Heb. 13:16) **Aus1A, Ire1**

8(16)[1] Whoso hath this world's . . . God in him? (1 John 3:17) **ChilR**

9(21) Remember the words . . . than to receive (Acts 20:35) **ChilR, Ire1**

10(24) Offer unto . . . most Highest (Ps. 50:14) **Aus1A, Ire1**

11(32) Thine, O Lord . . . head above all (1 Chron. 29:11) **Amer1-3**

12(33) Walk in love . . . sweet-smelling savour (Eph. 5:2) **Amer1-3**

13(34) I beseech you therefore . . . reasonable service (Rom. 12:1) **Amer1-3**

14(36) Give the Lord the glory . . . his courts (Ps. 96:8) **Amer1-2,[2] Ire1**

15(37) Therefore . . . thy gift (Matt. 5:23-24) **Amer1-3**

16(38) Call upon . . . glorify me (Ps. 50:15) **Aus1A**

17(39) He who . . . honours me (Ps. 50:23) **Aus1A**

18(40) Through Jesus . . . his name (Heb. 13.15) **Aus1A**

19(45) Bring . . . blessing (Mal. 3:10) **ChilR**

20(new) Worthy art thou . . . and were created (Rev. 4:11) **Amer1-3**

Non-biblical 'Bidding': **Amer1-3** follows its selection of sentences in this appendix to the three services with this:

Or this Bidding

Let us with gladness present the offerings and oblations of our life and labour unto the Lord.

---

[1] The same sentence appears as no. 46 also in **MAL**, and this is an error noted in Appendix G on p.422 below.

[2] This sentence is printed out in the *text* of **Amer1** and **Amer2**, and not in the Appendix containing the others. It is thus not in **Amer3** as this has no text.

TABLE II

SEASONAL SENTENCES

Ire1 alone has a standard set of Seasonal Sentences. These are set out here in the order they come in the Appendix to the rite. In most cases they repeat the sentences in **IreR** shown in **MAL**, but there have been a few changes.

1. ADVENT (1(a)) Rejoice greatly, O daughter . . . unto thee (Zech. 9:9)

2. CHRISTMAS (2(a)) Ye know the grace . . . might be rich (2 Cor. 8:9)

3. EPIPHANY (3(c)) Let your light . . . in heaven (Matt. 5:16)

4. LENT (4(b)) I beseech you, brethren . . . reasonable service (Rom. 12:1)

5. PASSIONTIDE (5(c)) Walk in love . . . sacrifice to God (Eph. 5:2)

6. EASTER (7(a)) Christ our passover . . . the feast (1 Cor. 5:7)

7. ROGATION (9(b)) He who sows . . . cheerful giver (2 Cor. 6:7)

8. ASCENSION (New) We see Jesus . . . with glory and honour (Heb. 2:9)

9. PENTECOST (10(a)) God hath sealed us . . . our hearts (2 Cor. 1:22)

10. TRINITY (11(a)) Now unto the King . . . for ever and ever (1 Tim. 1:17)

11. SAINTS' DAYS (18(a)) All thy works praise . . . unto thee (Ps. 145:19)

12 HARVEST (New and 23(b)) Rejoice in all the good which the Lord your God has given to you and to your house. Honour him with your wealth. (Deut. 26:11, Prov. 3:9)

13. EMBERTIDE AND MISSIONARY OFFERINGS
    (a) (ss(b)) How are men to call . . . are sent? (Rom. 10:14)
    (b) (22(c)) The harvest is rich . . . into his harvest (Luke 10:2)[1]

14. CHARITABLE OFFERINGS
    (a) (25(a)) Truly I say . . . to me (Matt. 25:40)
    (b) (25(c)) As we have . . . of faith (Gal. 6:10)
    (c) (25(d)) If anyone . . . in him? (1 John 3:17)

---

[1] This sentence is shown in **MAL** as beginning 'Jesus said', but in **Ire1** it begins as shown above.

CSIR has a distinctive provision, which is more probably related to the Peace than to the Offertory, but comes in a position which may well include the latter even without excluding the former.

The general provision is set out at no. 32 in **CSIR** in the main text of the book. The rite then continues as follows:

Or at Christmas

The people who walked in darkness have seen a great light (*Is.* 9:2a)
To us a child is born, to us a son is given (*Is.* 9:6a)
When the time had fully come, God sent forth his Son, born of woman, born under the law. (*Gal.* 4:4)
To redeem those who were under the law so that we might receive the adoption as sons. (*Gal.* 4:5)

Or at Easter

We know that Christ being raised from the dead will never die again; death no longer has dominion over him. (*Rom.* 6:10)
The death he died, he died to sin once for all; but the life he lives, he lives to God. (*Rom.* 6:10)
So you also must consider yourselves dead to sin and alive to God in Jesus Christ. (*Rom.* 6:11)

Or at Pentecost

This is what was spoken by the prophet Joel; and in the last days it shall be, God declares, that I will pour out my spirit upon all flesh.
(*Acts* 2:16, 17a)
God's love has been poured into our hearts through the Holy Spirit which has been given to us. (*Rom.* 5:5b)
The fruit of the Spirit is love, joy, peace, patience, kindness, goodness, faithfulness, gentleness, self-control; against such there is no law.
(*Gal.* 5:22f.)
If we live by the Spirit, let us also walk by the Spirit. (*Gal.* 5:25)

PROPER PREFACES

In this Appendix a new form of presentation of Proper Prefaces[1] is employed. The pull-out table has the seasons down the left-hand side, in the order followed in **LiE/MAL**: *temporale, sanctorale*, commons, votives. There are ten columns of materials from thirteen different rites—four of them (**ChilR, CNI, Eng3** and **SAfr2**) having a common source in **Eng3**, and usually a common text, which enables them to form one column only, with variants shown where necessary (but not of punctuation and capitals). A clean break is observable in the sphere of language: no Proper Preface exhibited in **MAL** followed a 'you' form of address to God,[2] whilst none shown here has a 'thou' form.

The following points should be noted:

1 **Aus3, Mel, Tan** have an invariable preface, and therefore are not represented here.

2 **IranR** keeps the forms shown in **MAL** (i.e. nos. 5, 12, 29, 30, 32, 36, 40, 63), and these are not repeated here. They are of course in a 'thou' form.

3 **BrazR** also retains the forms shown in **MAL**, which are of course in Portuguese in their original form, and there seemed no point in now translating them into 'you' form English. In no. 9 'his Mother' is omitted and 'sons of God' is changed to 'your sons'. Nos. 12, 18, 30, 32, 36, 43, 70 and 81 remain identical. 94 and 98 are omitted.

4 **Eng1-2A** has two eucharistic prayers, with two separate provisions for Proper Prefaces. The second is covered in the next paragraph. The first prayer derives from **Eng1**, and includes the **Eng1** provision from **MAL** (i.e. nos. 5, 12, 29, 30, 32, 37, 40, 63, 71, 91).[3]

---

[1] In several texts these are called 'Proper Thanksgivings', 'Seasonal Thanksgivings', 'Seasonal Additions' etc. The use of traditional terminology here (for the sake of clarity) does not indicate the terms used in particular texts.

[2] The 'you' form liturgies in **MAL**—**Aus2, Chil**, **NZ**—all had invariable Prefaces.

[3] In nos. 5 and 40 read 'Spirit' for 'Ghost'; no. 5 is in the '*out of Christmastide*' form; no. 30 has 'true' for 'very', and 'has' for 'hath' (thrice); no. 37 has 'after' for 'after that'; no. 71 has 'example' for 'ensample' and is for '*Saints' Days*'.

5 **Amer1-3**[1] has Prefaces in both 'Traditional' and 'Contemporary' wording. The former follow the uses of **AmerR** (in **MAL**) closely, whilst the latter only involve a change from 'thou' to 'you' (and 'art' to 'are' etc.). The latter are printed in the Table, and the former may be inferred by reversing the process. A similar process has been followed in the Prefaces for the second eucharistic prayer of **Eng1-2A**, where the **Eng3** forms must be translated in reverse to produce the 'thou' form.

6 **NG** and **SAfr1** follow **Eng2** closely, and the four short Proper Prefaces are shown in the main text (as with **Eng2** in **MAL**), but not here (unlike **MAL**).

7 The Table itself uses the following conventions:

(a) Cue words. **NZR** has followed **Eng2** in having insertions at different points. In the original and here the cue words are shown by the use of capitals. In **Aus4** the Proper Preface often makes part of the standard Preface redundant, so cue words are also printed at the end to show where the standard Preface is rejoined.[2]

(b) Seasons for use. The left-hand margin usually gives sufficient information, but italicised instructions are sometimes added above the actual Preface (not always *verbatim*). Rules for precedence have been omitted. 'Whitsuntide' includes 'Pentecost'. The limits of seasons have usually been ignored.[3]

(c) Optional use. Asterisks indicate that the included portion is explicitly optional. Probably many others are implicitly so.

(d) **ChilR** and **Kor1** are unofficial translations only. **ChilR**, however, reflects **Eng3** so consistently that the Spanish has been easily rendered back into **Eng3** terminology.

---

[1] See footnote on p.403 above.

[2] In the rite this is done in an appendix by setting out the whole Preface *in extenso* for the various seasons in such a way that on each occasion it can be read virtually straight through. The use of capitals here avoids the printing out *in extenso*.

[3] Thus if in the Church of England the Advent season were extended to nine Sundays before Christmas, it would be logical to expect the use of the 'Proper Thanksgiving' to be extended *ipso facto*.

every case with 'And the blessing of God Almighty . . .' etc. Differences of punctuation have not been noted. No limits to the seasons are mentioned in any of the texts. All the material is optional, as far as can be discerned. The lesser table comes first as it only needs one page.

TABLE I

THE PROPERS UNIQUE TO **CNI**

IN Table II on the next six pages, the only Propers which are shown are for those occasions for which **Eng3** makes provision. **CNI**, however, in its successive texts of 1973 and 1974, has made further provision as follows:

OCCASION	CALL TO WORSHIP	SENTENCES AFTER COMMUNION
APOSTLES AND EVANGELISTS *[From list (1) 'Seasonal'— 1974 only]*	You are no more strangers and sojourners, but you are fellow citizens with the saints and members of the household of God, built upon the foundation of the apostles and prophets. (*Eph.* 2:19-20)	Jesus said: 'Peace be with you. As the Father has sent me, even so I send you.' (*John* 20:21)
NEW YEAR OR ANY ANNIVERSARY *[This and the next three are from 1973 and list (2) 'Special Occasions' in 1974, except as shown under 'Commemoration of the Departed']*	They that wait upon the Lord shall renew their strength; they shall mount up with wings as eagles; they shall run, and not be weary; they shall walk, and not faint. (*Is.* 40:31)	
IN TIME OF TROUBLE	God is our hope and strength, a very present help in trouble. (*Ps.* 46:1)	
NATIONAL DAYS	O let the nations rejoice and be glad; for you will judge the folk righteously, and govern the nations upon earth. (*Ps.* 67:4)	
COMMEMORATION OF THE DEPARTED *[1973 has no 'Sentence after Communion']*	Blessed are the dead who die in the Lord, for they rest from their labours. (*Rev.* 14:13)	Jesus said: 'I am the resurrection and the life; he who believes in me, though he die, yet shall he live, and whoever lives and believes in me shall never die.' (*Jn.* 11:25-6)
GENERAL *[These are list (3) of 1974 (1973 has the first 3 'Call to Worship' texts as a footnote in the rite)]*	*Ps.* 118:24, *Ps.* 95:6, *Ps.* 96:8, 1 *Cor.* 5:7, *John* 4:24, *Ps.* 96:6, *Ps.* 43:3-4, *Ps.* 50:5, *Ps.* 50:14, *Hab.* 2:2, *Is.* 6:3, *Gn.* 28:16-17.	*John* 1:12, *John* 12:26, *Matt.* 6:20-1, *Matt.* 7:21, *John* 15:4, *John* 15:5, *John* 10:9, *John* 10:27-8, *Matt.* 20:26-7, *John* 14:21

TABLE II PROPERS FOR SEASONS

SEASON   SEASONAL SENTENCES
(**CNI**: CALL TO WORSHIP)
Eng3, Aus4, CNI

ADVENT

The glory of the Lord shall be revealed, and all mankind shall see it.   (*Is.* 40:5)
Aus4: see it] see it together

CHRISTMAS

I bring you news of great joy, a joy to be shared by the whole people. Today in the town of David a saviour has been born to you; he is Christ the Lord.
Aus4, CNI: Behold I bring you good news of a great joy which will come to all the people; for to you is born this day in the city of David a Saviour, who is Christ the Lord.   (*Luke* 2:10-11)
CNI: of a great] of great

EPIPHANY

The grace of God has dawned upon the world with healing for all mankind.   (*Titus* 2:11)
Aus4: The Lord will arise upon you, and his glory will be seen upon you.   (*Is.* 60:2)

LENT

Compassion and forgiveness belong to the Lord our God, though we have rebelled against him.
                          (*Daniel* 9:9)
Aus4: Humble yourselves therefore under the mighty hand of God, that in due time he may exalt you.
                          (1 *Peter* 5:6)

PASSIONTIDE

Christ himself bore our sins in his body on the tree, that we might die to sin and live to righteousness. By his wounds you have been healed.   (1 *Peter* 2:24)
Aus4: By his . . . healed] OM
CNI: For our sake Christ humbled himself and in obedience accepted even death—death on a cross.
                          (*Phil.* 2:8)

SENTENCES AFTER COMMUNION
Eng3, CNI

Our Lord says, 'Surely I come quickly.' Even so: come, Lord Jesus!   (*Rev.* 22:20)

The bread of God is he who comes down from heaven and gives life to the world. (*John* 6:33)

Jesus said, 'You are those who have continued with me in my trials; you shall eat and drink at my table in my kingdom.'
          (*Luke* 22:28, 30)

As we eat this bread and drink this cup, we proclaim the death of the Lord until he comes.
          (1 *Cor.* 11:26)
CNI: death of the Lord] Lord's death

SEASONAL BLESSINGS
Eng3, CNI, Ire1

The Sun of righteousness shine upon you and scatter the darkness from before your path;
Ire1: upon you] ADD gladden your hearts
your path] you

Christ the Son of God gladden your hearts with the good news of his kingdom;
Ire1: Christ, who by his incarnation gathered into one all things earthly and heavenly, fill you with his joy and peace.

Ire1: *As Christmas*

Christ give you grace to grow in holiness, to deny yourselves, take up your cross, and follow him;
CNI: to deny] by denying
take] taking
follow] following
Ire1: to grow in holiness] OM
take] and to take

Christ the Saviour draw you to himself, so that you find in him crucified a sure ground for faith, a firm support for hope, and the assurance of sins forgiven;
CNI: you find in him crucified] in him crucified you find
Ire1: the Saviour] OM
draw you] draw you near
so that] and grant that
him crucified] his cross
the assurance] assurance

SEASON

SEASONAL SENTENCES
(**CNI**: CALL TO WORSHIP)
Eng3, Aus4, CNI

EASTER

It is true: the Lord has risen: alleluia!
CNI: Christ is risen! He is risen indeed. Alleluia.
Aus4: Thanks be to God who gives us the victory through our Lord Jesus Christ.　　(1*Corinthians* 15:57)

ASCENSION

Christ has gone up on high: alleluia!
Aus4: God has highly exalted him and bestowed on him the name which is above every other name, that at the name of Jesus every knee should bow, in heaven and on earth and under the earth, and every tongue confess that Jesus Christ is Lord, to the glory of God the Father.
(*Phil.* 2:9-11)
CNI: Since we have a great high priest who has passed through the heavens, Jesus the Son of God, let us boldly draw near to the throne of grace, that we may receive mercy and find grace to help in the time of need.
(*Heb.* 4:14, 16)

WHITSUNTIDE

God's love has been shed abroad in our hearts through the Holy Spirit he has given us.　　(*Rom.* 5:5)
Aus4, CNI: shed abroad in] poured into
Aus4: he has] who has been
Aus4: us] to us

SENTENCES AFTER COMMUNION
Eng3, CNI

Jesus said, 'He who eats my flesh and drinks my blood has eternal life, and I will raise him up at the last day.' (*John* 6:54)

God has highly exalted his Son, and given him a name which is above all other names, that at the name of Jesus every knee shall bow. (*Phil.* 2:9-10)

God who raised Christ Jesus from the dead will also give life to your mortal bodies through his Spirit who dwells in you.
CNI: The Spirit you have received is not a spirit of slavery leading you back into a life of fear, but a Spirit that makes us sons, enabling us to cry 'Abba Father!' (*Rom.* 8:15)

SEASONAL BLESSINGS
Eng3, CNI, Irel

The God of peace, who brought again from the dead our Lord Jesus, that great Shepherd of the sheep, through the blood of the everlasting covenant, make you perfect in every good work to do his will, working in you that which is well-pleasing in his sight;
Irel: God raise you up from the death of sin that you may walk with Christ in the newness of his risen life.

Christ our king make you faithful and patient to do his will, that you may reign with him in glory;
CNI: patient] strong
Irel: our king] OM

The Spirit of truth lead you into all truth, give you grace to confess that Jesus Christ is Lord, and to proclaim the word and works of God:
CNI: lead you into all truth]OM
Christ] OM
word and works] mighty acts
Irel: give] giving
word and] wonderful

SEASON   SEASONAL SENTENCES
                  (**CNI**: CALL TO WORSHIP)
                  Eng3, Aus4, CNI

TRINITY   By day and by night around the throne they sing: Holy,
                  holy, holy is God the sovereign Lord of all; he was, he
                  is, and he is to come.   (*Rev.* 4:8)
                  CNI: he was, he is, and he] who was, and is, and

                  Aus4: God is love, and he who abides in love abides
                  in God, and God abides in him.   (1 *Jn.* 4:16)

ALL SAINTS   Since we are surrounded by so great a cloud of witnesses,
                  let us lay aside every weight, and sin which clings so
                  closely, and let us run with perseverance the race that is
                  set before us.   (*Heb.* 12:1)
                  CNI: *Saints' Days* [as in **Eng3** in 1971]
                          ADD AT END looking unto Jesus.

SAINTS' DAYS   The righteous will be remembered for ever: the memory
                  of the righteous is a blessing.
                  Aus4: OMIT
                  CNI: AS *All Saints*

HARVEST   The earth is the Lord's and all that is in it. (*Ps.* 24:1)
                  Aus4: OMIT

DEDICATION   Truly the Lord is in this place; this is no other than the
                  house of God; this is the gate of heaven. (*Gen.* 28:16-17)
                  Aus4: OMIT

UNITY   How good and pleasant it is when brothers live together
                  in unity!   (*Ps.* 134:1)
                  Aus4: OMIT
                  CNI: brothers] brethren

SENTENCES AFTER COMMUNION
Eng3, CNI

We were chosen of old in the purpose of the Father, hallowed to his service in the Spirit, and consecrated with the blood of Jesus Christ.

CNI: Jesus said: 'If you love me, you will keep my commandments. And I will pray the Father, and he will give you another Counsellor, to be with you for ever, even the Spirit of truth.'   (*John* 14:15-16)

[No provision except for '*Saints' Days'*]

You have come to Mount Zion, to God the judge of all, to the spirits of just men made perfect, and to Jesus the mediator of the new covenant.   (*Heb.* 12:22-24)

The heaven of heavens cannot contain our God; how much less this house that we have built!
     (1 *Kings* 8:27)

Through Christ Jesus we all have access to the Father in the one Spirit.   (*Eph.* 2:18)
CNI: Jesus] OM

SEASONAL BLESSINGS
Eng3, CNI, Ire1

God the Holy Trinity make you strong in faith and love, defend you on every side, and guide you in truth and peace;
CNI: on every side] at all times
Ire1: OMIT

[No provision except for '*Saints' Days'*]

God give you grace to follow his saints in faith and hope and love;
Ire1: OMIT

Christ the good shepherd bring you and all who hear his voice to be one flock, gathered into one fold;
Ire1: OMIT

THE **CSI-LfA** 'FAMILY' OF RITES

A FEATURE of **MAL** was that its texts were historically bounded at one end by Lambeth 1958, and at the other by the authorization and publication of **Eng2**. As this volume now shows (e.g. in Appendix F following this), **Eng2** has given rise to a new 'family' of rites, and this has taken much of the attention from the most influential family of the period from 1958 to 1967, that of **CSI-LfA**. A discussion of the further influence of this 'family' is contained in chapter 1, on p.15 above. However, it is possible here to set out diagrammatically the traceable dependence relationships in the 'family'. For fuller details about the 1958-67 period, recourse should be had to **MAL**.

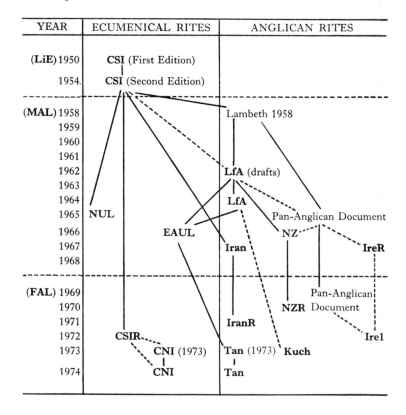

APPENDIX F

THE Eng2-Eng3 'FAMILY' OF EUCHARISTIC PRAYERS

THE Table overleaf sets out nine eucharistic prayers which belong (directly or indirectly) to the same 'family'. There is a known dependence of some upon others, and this is set out diagrammatically in the chart on the next page. The prayers are not arranged chronologically but rather according to the 'family' relationships. The first prayer in the Table is **Eng2**, which is also printed in **MAL** pages 135-6, but not elsewhere in this volume.[1] The third one, **MLT**, is not printed elsewhere in either volume, and the sixth one, **Eng3** in its originally published form, is also only printed here. The other prayers all belong to rites in their final and authoritative form, and are all also printed under their particular countries in this volume.

For the purpose of standard presentation the prayers have here been stripped of their rubrics. Thus **Eng2** in fact has two manual acts in the narrative of institution, **NG** prescribes *'Bell, drum or rattle'* after the Sanctus and Benedictus and again after the Amen, and **CNI** makes the narrative of institution optional.[2] The first four rites prescribe Proper Prefaces for Christmas, Passiontide and Ascension after the 'INCARNATION, ATONEMENT, RESURRECTION' paragraph, and a single one for Ascension and Whitsuntide after the next paragraph.[3] The next four have a full set of Proper Prefaces in this latter place, whilst **Aus4** in the last column has Proper Prefaces which come at different places in the prayer.[4]

The paragraphing is standard throughout, and the spelling, punctuation, and use of capitals of the original are kept. Where the Table gives a standard paragraph, but the particular prayer does not have a paragraph, then the continuation of the prayer is indented to show that it

[1] This prayer is the *last* of the 'thou' prayers in the family, but the *first* prayer of the Table. Its own period of gestation from December 1965 to July 1967 must be learned from **MAL** pp.118-22, and from the Table of Draft Texts on **MAL** p.142.

[2] The earlier rubrics only allow this where it is already the custom, and the narrative of institution has been read earlier as a 'Warrant'. See pp.271, 274 above.

[3] The text of these Prefaces is printed out where the rite comes in the two volumes. For **Eng2** it is on **MAL** p.135, for **NG** on p.358 above, and for **SAfr1** on p.208 above.

[4] The text of these Proper Prefaces is printed out in Appendix C above.

runs on. Because of the structure of the prayers of **Aus4** and **CNI**[1], the standard paragraphing has here been abandoned for part of the text, and new headings inserted instead.

The relationships can be set out diagrammatically as follows, but for a full account reference must be made to the particular chapters. In the diagram strong dependence is expressed by unbroken lines, more allusive dependence by broken ones. There is a timescale which can be gleaned from the diagram, but reference elsewhere must be made for more exact details.

DIAGRAM OF RELATIONSHIPS

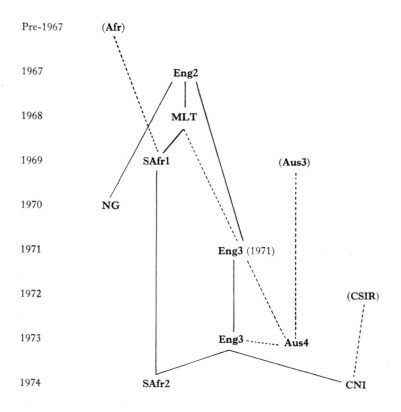

---

[1] The only **CNI** text given is that of 1974 (cf. the diagram above). The 1973 text was more akin to **Eng3** in its structure (see p.274 above).